The *Angelic* ORIGINS of the SOUL

"*The Angelic Origins of the Soul* is a comprehensive, traditional, and creative exploration regarding the angelic orders, our Souls, and incarnations. McCannon shows how humanity's perception of the Soul's evolution, mastering qualities such as love and power, happens over many incarnations and planets. The reader will gain a broad understanding for discovering their own Soul themes and life purpose as members of a celestial community on Earth."

BOB HIERONIMUS, PH.D., AND ZOHARA HIERONIMUS, D.H.L., AUTHORS, BROADCASTERS, AND ARTISTS

"*The Angelic Origins of the Soul* is an encyclopedia of myths and traditions woven together by their universal truths to form one magical tapestry. After your first read, you will continue to refer to it over and over again, and every time you pick it up you will marvel at the new wisdom you discover."

MAUREEN J. ST. GERMAIN, AUTHOR OF *WAKING UP IN 5D*

"On the frontiers of consciousness Tricia McCannon does it again! She bridges the dimensions between the human soul and the heavenly state of being. She gives us the landscape of eternity that we are destined to embrace. Beautifully illustrated and divinely inspired, we now have a map for the journey of life to follow the path of the heart, which is our birthright."

ALAN STEINFELD, FOUNDER OF NEW REALITIES

"In *The Angelic Origins of the Soul* Tricia McCannon reminds us that we are not just machines made of matter that emerged by chance in an accidental universe. We are eternal sparks of God, and we are in a world that offers us the chance to revive our divine consciousness. This is a message the modern world very much needs to hear."

MICHAEL A. CREMO, AUTHOR OF *HUMAN DEVOLUTION: A VEDIC ALTERNATIVE TO DARWIN'S THEORY*

The *Angelic* ORIGINS of the SOUL

Discovering Your Divine Purpose

Tricia McCannon

Bear & Company
Rochester, Vermont • Toronto, Canada

Bear & Company
One Park Street
Rochester, Vermont 05767
www.BearandCompanyBooks.com

Text stock is SFI certified

Bear & Company is a division of Inner Traditions International

Library of Congress Cataloging-in-Publication Data

Names: McCannon, Tricia, author.
Title: The angelic origins of the soul : discovering your divine purpose /
    Tricia McCannon.
Description: Rochester, Vermont : Bear & Company, 2017. |
    Includes bibliographical references and index.
    Identifiers: LCCN 2017005084 (print) | LCCN 2017036693 (e-book) |
    ISBN 9781591432715 (pbk.) | ISBN 9781591432722 (e-book)
Subjects: LCSH: Soul. | Heaven. | Angels. | Spiritualism. | Incarnation.
Classification: LCC BF1999 (e-book) | LCC BF1999 .M2187 2017 (print) |
    DDC 133.901/3—dc23
LC record available at https://lccn.loc.gov/2017005084

Printed and bound in the United States by Lake Book Manufacturing, Inc.
The text stock is SFI certified. The Sustainable Forestry Initiative® program
promotes sustainable forest management.

10 9 8 7 6 5 4 3 2 1

Text design and layout by Priscilla Baker
This book was typeset in Garamond Premier Pro, with Gill Sans and Kepler used
as display typefaces

To send correspondence to the author of this book, mail a first-class letter to the
author c/o Inner Traditions • Bear & Company, One Park Street, Rochester, VT
05767, and we will forward the communication, or contact the author directly at
triciamccannonspeaks.com.

This book is dedicated to all those
Who have had the courage to come into this world
To bring more healing and light in this time of spiritual awakening.

It is also dedicated to my wonderful friends
Who have passed to the Otherside:
Sylvia Laurens, my beloved fairy friend and illustrator;
Ron Yanda, my fellow Egyptian initiate and Druid priest;
James Parsons Cameron, my British shaman beloved;
Dolores Cannon, a dear friend and explorer of consciousness;
Jim Marrs, a brave and ardent writer, researcher, and seeker of truth;
Lori Marcus, whose heart was as big as the California sky;
My father, John McCannon, who persevered through
hell and high water;
My beloved cat Sabrina, who passed during the writing of this book;
And my mother, Carolyn, who has always been a wisdom elder,
Even when she didn't know it.

Contents

PART 1

THE COSMOLOGY OF THE SOUL

PART 2

THE LANDSCAPES OF HEAVEN

PART 3

OUR GENESIS MATRIX

PART 4

THE COURSE CURRICULUM OF THE SOUL

A Short Note to Welcome You to Planet Earth

. . . That You Forgot to Read Before You Came to Earth

Welcome to Planet Earth!

You have arrived on a complex planet that is not for the faint of heart. You now have a physical body. Take care of it. It is the only one you will receive this time around, so if you abuse it, you will pay the price. But remember, this body is *not who you really are*. You are a spark in the body of God, and you will live forever.

That's the good news. The bad news is that since you are now mortal, your body will eventually perish. Whatever choices you make with your mind, body, and spirit will not only affect your present life, they will also affect how you move forward on the long road of your many successive lifetimes, for this is but one chapter in your Soul's journey. In each life you can either embrace the path of mastery or you can stand still. Each life contributes or detracts from your overall evolution. Your thoughts, actions, words, and intentions will all affect where you will go when you die, as well as the next set of choices in future lifetimes. So be wise. Take your time. Be patient with yourself and others, and try not to burn any bridges. The person that you help today may be the very person who is there to help you tomorrow. That's how it works. Our deeds come back to us, and there is no escaping this cosmic law. So remember to be kind.

This book is to remind you that you came to Earth for a reason. Your existence is not random; it was planned. Now you must figure out what that reason is, because even though you once knew it—in fact, you chose it—you have forgotten. That's one of the most difficult things about coming to planet Earth—the amnesia. There are planets where this veil is not in place—a veil meant to allow you to start fresh in each new life. But Earth is not one of these places, so you'll have to get your memories back for yourself. But don't worry, there will be clues along the way, the first being the circumstances of your birth. Whatever pain, suffering, and hardship you may have experienced, this may actually be a clue as to your life's true purpose. So if you landed in one of those many dysfunctional families here on Earth, you may have actually come to this planet to better understand the problems of humanity from the inside out, and to change them for the better. This is good, not only for you, but for all of humanity.

One bit of advice: Every life has two interconnected missions: an outer task and an inner task; and these are usually linked. Each one of us has an inner challenge, a hardship designed to test our character at the core of our being. This is for the learning of the Soul. Someone dies; there is not enough money; you are in the middle of a bitter divorce; you lose your home or your country; or the environment that you grow up in is difficult, to say the least—these kinds of scenarios are the setup, the challenge that you signed up for that will set you on your unique path.

The second task involves what you do with these challenges, which if met, will bring you to a point of resolution and wisdom that will point you toward your greater mission. This is the reason you were born. And if you manage to succeed in overcoming your difficulties, you will gain the strength and power needed to triumph in your assignment. So treat each challenge as an opportunity, not a problem. If you do, then it will inspire you to turn your deficits into strengths, bringing you right to the heart of your purpose.

One word of wisdom: There is no escaping this Course Curriculum, and suicide is not an option because you'll only have to come back and face the same problems all over again. Life does not work by running away or anesthetizing yourself with any of the many substances and obsessions that human beings use to keep themselves medicated and out of touch with their true essence. Getting hooked on alcohol or drugs is a sure way to waste the precious time that you are allotted. You're on the clock, so get to work and figure it out!

Life works by asking yourself why you incarnated into your particular family in the first place. Why did you choose *those* parents, *this* race, *that* gender, or *that* set of economic conditions? Once you can figure this out, then you can use this as a foundation to reach higher ground. Hidden in your seeming travail is the heart of the lessons you came to learn, and it is learning these lessons that will bring you to greatness. In fact, this may be the very wisdom that you came to teach. When you have decoded this equation, then you will have figured out the direction of your life. After all, you planned it.

Yes, we know that this Course Curriculum is not easy, but that's all a part of the game. What would be the fun of it if you could figure it out in a minute? And while your amnesia is really a bummer, it has been put in place to help you and some of your fellow human beings begin again, because if you were to remember your past choices, you might be so filled with regret that you would never be able to start anew. And it's true, there are easier planets you could have chosen. Some planets only have physical challenges like weather, food, or survival. Others have mental challenges. But Earth has it all—mental, physical, emotional, and spiritual. So it's a very advanced Curriculum, and if you succeed, you will be light-years ahead of those who never tried.

Just remember, no one forced you to come here, and we wouldn't have let you if you weren't ready. So be brave. Believe in yourself. Take time to breathe. Remember to help people, animals, and the planet. Above all, listen to your heart and remember to love. Tune in to nature and you'll start to hear the whispers of your true Self. It is always within you, and you are never alone. And remember, we believe in you.

Good luck, and see you on the Otherside.

YOUR COUNCIL OF LIGHT

Introduction to Our Angelic Origins

Mankind is a weaver who, from the wrong side, works upon the carpet of time. One day he will see the right side of the carpet and will understand the splendor of the pattern that he has woven with his own hands through the centuries, whilst seeing naught but a tangle of string.

ALPHONSE DE LAMARTINE

This book is a journey, a journey into the immortal nature of the Soul and the purpose behind our life. It is a voyage into the discovery of our own angelic origins, the landscapes of Heaven, and our ultimate return to those worlds. During the course of this expedition we shall discover much about what mystics and near-death experiencers have told us about the eternal nature of the Soul and the celestial realms from which we source. We will explore the questions that lie at the very heart of human life, such as: What is the nature of the Soul, and what does it mean to be truly human? Is there a divine destiny for each of us, and how is it possible that we have somehow forgotten it? How do we fit into the puzzle of the cosmos, and are there specific spiritual laws that govern the cycles of Soul evolution? Are there young Souls, old Souls, and Souls that are in-between? What are the lessons we must master if we are to achieve enlightenment?

Throughout human history many great philosophers, statesmen, saints, and healers have asked these same perennial questions, and every religion in the world has its own take on the answers. Most traditions assert that the Soul exists long before we are ever born, and that it departs when we die, only to continue on another plane of existence. The Soul, this eternal part of us, is born from the nature of God, lives in the worlds of God, and returns to the bosom of God. Like its maker, it is intelligent, curious, loving, explorative, and creative. Furthermore, this part of us longs to love and to be loved, to know itself and to be known by others. Since life itself is built on the vibrational principle of love, the Soul, which is created from love, longs to return to this place of nurturance. While this divine light expresses itself uniquely in each and every one of us, in truth we are all a part of the same eternal intelligence that animates the universe.

In the pages of this book you will learn about the Soul's angelic origins and its journey to claim its innate divine inheritance. You will travel the journey that each Soul makes as it descends from the highest Heavens to arrive in the worlds of form, taking first one expression, and then another. During our expedition you will also learn about the great Course Curriculum that each Soul must master, and how time and experience are the prime movers that assist us in moving through these many phases of development. You will discover the six stages of the Soul's evolution that we must all experience to reclaim our place as angelic beings. Along the way we will discover the mechanisms of *Adi-karma,* a Sanskrit term meaning "first karma," referring to the mechanisms by which we come to believe the illusion that we are separate from God or Source, a mechanism that allows the Soul to become dense enough to descend into the world of duality, thereby resulting in the existence of the Shadow.[1] This Shadow, or Great Adversary, causes us to move away from the light of our own eternal nature. When the Shadow is projected outward, as it so often is, it becomes a belief in evil, which wraps us in fear, darkness, ignorance, and suffering, causing us to project our greatest fears onto those around us. Our job in this and every lifetime is to find a way to remember our own essence and dispel these false beliefs that keep our planet trapped in war, conflict, and struggle. When we finally dispel the Shadow, the path opens, and we can begin to figure out what we have come here to do, why we have chosen this incarnation. This reframing of our essential nature and the events around us is the first step in a transformative journey that leads to self-empowerment and embracing the love and joy that resides eternally at the core of our being.

In these pages we will also explore the vast territories of light that lie on the Otherside, realms that have been called "the Far Country." We will hear from modern and ancient travelers who have crossed over to the Otherside and returned, giving us incredible accounts of our true home. We will also discover our own origins among the nine angelic orders of these heavenly realms, and how, by knowing about them, we can live more fulfilling lives in alignment with our dharma, or life's mission. William Wordsworth, the nineteenth-century transcendentalist and poet, expresses the idea of our divine origins beautifully in his *Ode: Intimations of Immortality from Recollections of Early Childhood*:

> *Our birth is but a sleep and a forgetting:*
> *The Soul that rises with us, our life's Star,*
> *Hath had elsewhere its setting,*
> *And cometh from afar:*
> *Not in entire forgetfulness,*
> *And not in utter nakedness,*
> *But trailing clouds of glory do we come*
> *From God, who is our home:*
> *Heaven lies about us in our infancy!*
> *Shades of the prison-house begin to close*
> *Upon the growing Boy . . .*
> *The youth, who daily farther from the east*
> *Must travel, still is Nature's Priest,*
> *And by the vision splendid,*
> *Is on his way attended;*
> *At length the Man perceives it die away,*
> *And fade into the light of common day. . . .*
> *Of the eternal Silence: truths that wake,*
> *To perish never. . . .*

Though inland far we be,
Our Souls have sight of that immortal sea
Which brought us hither . . .[2]

Here Wordsworth speaks about the celestial realms from which we all emerge, realms that have been known by many names throughout time: Paradise, the Summerland, the Isles of the Blessed, Heaven, Asgard, and Nirvana, just to name a few. These are the high-vibrating realms of light where the deepest part of ourself resides, and it is where we shall return to when the arc of our voyage is over. Yet how did we arrive on Earth, and what is our true purpose in being here? How can we make the most of this life, and is there some reason why we can't remember our higher mission?

We All Come from Heaven

In my work as a clairvoyant who has read for over six thousand people around the world over the past thirty years, I am constantly in touch with the world of Spirit. In my readings I have learned to look past the conditions of a client's present life to see just who she really is at the deeper level of the Soul. I have learned how to travel back to the genesis matrix, the angelic place of origin that each of us comes from, to discover the experiences that layer a person's Soul in order to ferret out the Soul's major themes. I have learned how to locate the source of our unhealed wounds and look for the greater reasons behind why a person has come into this world. I have learned how to discover a person's spiritual gifts and untangle the web of karmic relationships that is often the source of our greatest wounding and the resulting patterns that arise. Along the way I have learned a great deal about the nature of the Soul, and it is my intention to share some of what I have learned with you in this book.

As a clairvoyant I have seen that all of us originate in the higher realms, and that on our journey here we come through a series of dimensional planes, picking up various matrixes of experience along the way. These matrixes shape us, providing fertile ground for the sculpting of our individuation and allowing for the exercise of free will, a major part of our human experience. Yet the greater part of us, the Soul itself, resides safely in the realms of light, hidden from our conscious awareness, even while another, more limited part of us takes birth in the worlds of form. This means that even while our human, egoic self evolves in each lifetime, our true, higher Self remains safe in Heaven. This higher Self is always full of light, even if our human life is filled with pain, darkness, and despair. And at the end of each life, this human part reconnects with its higher Self to evaluate how we have done with our life on Earth.

Nowhere do I see this connection with the angelic wisdom of the Soul more strongly than in the magic of children. Oftentimes when I encounter young children I can see them looking at my aura, watching the colors of my energy field radiating out its golden and blue rays. Toddlers still have the ability to perceive the sea of spiritual energies that moves all around us, and thus they know instinctively who to trust and who brings discordant energies. We arrive as infants still carrying the joy and wonder of these celestial realms with us. Have you ever noticed how children have an innate capacity to tune in to nature or to feel a natural, inborn love of animals? They experience the presence of magic because their hearts are open; they are still in touch with the worlds of celestial light behind our own, the mystical dimensions that sages have told us inform this visible world. For many, these hidden realms are only perceived when our inner senses are developed. Yet there are many young children with invisible friends, children who speak with beings and spirit guides on the Otherside. In time, however, our access to the world of Spirit begins to dim, so that usually by the age of six or seven we are no longer able to tap into that larger field of knowing. Past-life memories fade, and the child who once spoke of spirit friends enters her first years at school and begins the process of conforming.

The Remembrance of Things Forgotten

I remember years ago one of my students, a single mother with a charming three-year-old daughter. Whenever she brought the child to class the little girl would climb onto her mother's lap and touch her face. Then she would say, "Remember, Mommy, long ago, when I was *your* mommy and you were *my* child?" Or "Remember, Mommy, that life when I drowned in the river? Oh, don't cry, Mommy, don't cry, it didn't hurt at all!" The child's mother would shake her head in amazement and hug her daughter, but she never invalidated her child's memories. She realized that something miraculous was happening, and she embraced it wholeheartedly. Sometimes the little girl would stare at other class members and talk about the pretty pink and yellow lights around them, auric colors that have to do with love and learning. These spiritual abilities continued for two or three more years in the child, but by the time she was six her memories began to fade. Then, like all of us, she was off on the adventure of a new Earth life.

Such connection with the past is not uncommon for newly arrived Souls. If you listen, children will tell you astonishing things. I once read a story about a little boy who asked his parents if he could spend some time alone with his two-year-old sister. The parents, curious to know why, listened to the baby's monitor while their son was in his sister's room. After a moment they heard their six-year-old son saying to his little sister, "Okay, now tell me about God again. I'm starting to forget."[3]

My Own Intimations of Other Lives

From a very young age I knew that I was an ancient one, but I had only fragments of my Soul's history. By some terrible twist of fate those memories had been taken from me. Looking up at the heavens, I knew, as surely as I knew my name, that I had come from those realms and that I would return there when I died. I had incarnated on Earth for a mission, something about helping planet Earth, but I could not remember what it was. Lying beneath the majesty of those whispering, singing stars, my spirit leapt up into the sky. *How could anyone doubt there is a God when they behold the splendor of that firmament?*

Like many others, I was later to discover, I had glimpses of my former lives, and yet I could not understand why people did not speak openly of reincarnation. This was the mechanism that Spirit uses to perfect our inner natures, allowing us chance after chance to learn our spiritual lessons and awaken to who we truly are. I knew that we each have many lives, yet I could only remember broken fragments of my own lives—in Britain, Persia, Ireland, and Egypt, as well as a life in which I died in a concentration camp during World War II. But why could I not remember the rest? Later, my parents told me that as a toddler I had said, "Aye, madam," instead of "Yes, madam" when they were trying to teach me how to use my words. I also spoke in a strange, complex language in my sleep, a tongue that no one seemed to understand. In the many years that have passed since then, others have also heard me speak this strange language and called it the "language of light," a language spoken by the Angels—yet another clue in a long line of breadcrumbs as I set about trying to discover my own ancient origins.

Many of us have experienced this deeper sense of knowing, this knowledge that we belong to something greater than ourself. This may come from flashes of déjà vu or moments of Soul recognition when we meet someone from a past life. Some people know intuitively where to turn down a village road or city block, even though they have never visited that place before. These are echoes from past lives, breadcrumb droppings along the trail that prompt us to reflect on the eternal Self that lives within us all.

Today, millions of people can recall fragments of their past lives, which is evidence that when the physical body perishes, the Soul does not die. Some people relate stories of taking journeys to the heavenly realms through out-of-body travel, near-death experiences, and deep, somnambulistic states of hypnosis. Plato writes that being born is actually "a sleep and a forgetting," since the Soul moves from a state of greater spiritual awareness to a more limited human consciousness. And when all the clues of past lives and near-death experiences are gathered, we get a sense of the immensity of a far greater journey than our human culture generally acknowledges. In truth, death is but a doorway into the magnificent realms of light, where we unite with the deeper aspect of ourself that is the Soul.

Among the greatest explorers in the field of past-life memory is the late, great Ian Stevenson, a professor of psychiatry at the University of Virginia School of Medicine. For over four decades Dr. Stevenson investigated thousands of cases of people who remembered their former lives. He traveled from Sri Lanka to India, from Brazil to Turkey, and from Lebanon to Alaska in his pursuit of those who believe that reincarnation is real. Using stringent guidelines, Dr. Stevenson and his team investigated over three thousand cases of people who recall, in intimate detail, their former lives. He even discovered children who could speak fluently in languages they had never heard, an ability he called *xenoglossy*. Many of these people had detailed memories of people, places, and events that were otherwise impossible to explain. In some cases there were talents carried over from past lives, or birthmarks on a person's body where they had perished as a result of gunshot wounds in a previous life.

Echoes from a Past Life

Take the case of Katsugoro, a boy born in the village of Nakanomura, Japan. Katsugoro claimed that in his previous life he had been called Tozo and was the son of a farmer named Kyubei and his wife, Shidzu, who had lived in the village of Hodokubo. Katsugoro explained to his new parents that he had died of smallpox at the age of six, only a year after his former father's death. Katsugoro then went on to describe his own burial, the appearance of his parents, and even the house where they had all lived. Eventually his new parents took Katsugoro to his former village. The boy led the way through the village to his mother's home, pointing out a newly built shop and a tree that had not been there before in his previous life. When he was reunited with his previous mother, she rejoiced at seeing him again.[4]

Over a period of more than thirty years Dr. Stevenson's team gathered evidence for the continuation of the Soul through time. He went on to write some three hundred papers and fourteen books, as well as a 2,268-page two-volume set published in 1997 called *Reincarnation and Biology: A Contribution to the Etiology of*

Birthmarks and Birth Defects. What Dr. Stevenson had discovered was a critical body of evidence for the mechanism of reincarnation, the instrument through which the Soul continues to learn on the great Wheel of Time.

The great philosophers and religious thinkers of the past believed that we are each immortal beings and that our life does not end when our body perishes. They taught that each one of us is just visiting this world in order to learn and grow in the realms of form. Each new life is an opportunity to move forward in self-awareness and to learn intrinsic lessons that the Soul must master over the course of its evolution. How well we do with the Course Curriculum presented to us in each lifetime in "Earth school" has a direct bearing on where we will go when we die. Our success or failure in these spiritual lessons also has a direct bearing on the choices that we will make in future lifetimes, for whatever we do not master in one life will be presented to us again in the next.

These various parts of ourselves, developed throughout time, live within us as subpersonalities. While they contain affinities, talents, and acquired or developed abilities, they also contain certain emotional and mental patterns that we are challenged to overcome. These various aspects may speak to us in dreams or visions and often seep into our taste in furniture, clothes, makeup, jewelry, art, or even our choices in food. They may nudge us in various directions, explaining our fascination with various cultures, making one person choose rich brocades while another is attracted to Japanese simplicity, or French tapestries, or inlaid Italian furniture, or Native American flute music, or Celtic bagpipes. They may influence our attraction to politics, religion, athletics, science, or military service. These subtle voices from our past may urge us to visit the sacred sites of Egypt, the steppes of Peru, or the moors of the Scottish Highlands, or they may direct us toward certain professions or gift us with the musical genius of a Beethoven.

These many aspects that live on within us as subconscious personalities can either help or hinder our current life plans. For example, if you have been a nun, a monk, or a priest in many previous lifetimes, you may find it harder to access your sexuality, no matter how much you wish to have a passionate, fulfilling love life. Someone who has been a Puritan, a Quaker, or Amish might lean toward a life of simplicity, nature, or religious fundamentalism, carrying with him or her the inclinations from the past. A Soul that has excelled in military leadership may naturally be the best football player on the team or dream of joining the Marines. Someone who has been an artist may be the odd man out if born into a family of lawyers, and may have to embark on a direction that his or her family simply doesn't understand. Many times we identify our current success in life with the same field of interest in which we formerly excelled, as feelings from the subconscious mind can seep through unless the Soul has finished with those patterns and decided to begin a brand new chapter of learning.

My Own Quest

Prompted by the suffering I saw in my own family, I first began asking important questions about the nature of God and reality while still a child. I experienced this suffering in the form of the angry wounds created by my father's painful drinking bouts, my mother's pleading desire to heal him of his addiction, and the reactions of my two lovely sisters, both of whom developed their own coping mechanisms while living as children of a brilliant, but abusive, attorney father. I again saw suffering in the cruel pranks of teenagers who bullied one another at school, and in the viciousness of the cheerleaders, who beat up anyone who got in their way—the "mean girls" depicted in movies. I saw it in the suffering of hundreds of handicapped people at the Sunland center in Florida where I worked during the summers between my junior and senior years in college. And I saw it every night on the news, in the political posturing of dishonest politicians who were sending young men to their deaths in the Vietnam War. Most of these politicians would never know the wounds of battle themselves, yet they had no problem letting other men die for their financial and political objectives. I also saw this same kind of cruelty reflected in the mores of a society that taught that animals do not have souls, and that it's okay to kill, maim, and torture them for sport or commercial gain. I saw it in the fear-based dogma of our Christian and Jewish religions that taught judgment and hellfire and damnation alongside a God of unconditional love. I also saw it in the oppression of women and children, the silent suffering of domestic abuse, and the growing sex trade that enslaves women, girls, and boys in pursuit of animalistic, carnal greed.

Amid this sea of suffering I often found myself asking how could a loving God permit the afflictions of war, rape, torture, and injustice? Why didn't people treat one another with kindness, honesty, and respect? Why was evil allowed to flourish or even be rewarded in the name of wealth, religion, leadership, and personal ambition? How could others be so caught up in their own selfish agendas that they did not seemingly feel the pain of those they oppressed? Why were the meek exploited and the deceitful rewarded? None of this made any sense to me, and most of all it seemed horribly unfair.

So these were the questions that drove me for many years, until finally, when I was nineteen years old, all of this began to change. This was when I first encountered the great Vairagi masters—those who are no longer bound to material existence—who initiated me into the Mysteries.[5] I first met these spiritual teachers at the end of my sophomore year in college at Florida State University. These wise disincarnate masters had spent centuries trying to answer the very same kinds of questions I had, and had found answers as a result of having mastered the ancient art of Soul travel. This is the ability to travel into the higher realms while still remaining in a physical body—an ability that each of us has, if only we bother to learn it. In these higher realms one can study the hidden history of the universe and learn about the laws that govern the evolution of the Soul. One can visit temples of Golden Wisdom, attend discourses with spiritual masters, and discover why one person incarnates into one set of circumstances, while another chooses a completely different kind of life.

This was my kind of path—the seeker who has learned how to rise above the human drama to understand why life unfolds the way it does. These sages had a roadmap to the inner planes. By cultivating my higher abilities, I soon came to realize that I might learn to see the cosmos from the point of view of God. If I could learn to Soul travel, then I might finally understand what we are all doing in this crazy, mixed-up, extraordinary experience we call life. Eventually, through many years of challenges and initiations, I discovered the answers to these profound questions, and this is, in part, the reason why I have written this book.

In those first years of study I often reflected on the Great Chain of Being that the forest Angel had told me about as a child. He had explained that consciousness exists in everything and everyone to a greater or lesser degree, and that the Soul descends from the higher realms to take on life in its many forms—as a plant, an animal, a human, and eventually as a sage, slowly climbing the ladder of spiritual evolution to finally reclaim the knowledge of our true angelic origins. Renowned mystic and founder of the Philosophical Research Society (dedicated to "Truth Seekers of All Time") Manly P. Hall (1901–1990) writes about this process:

> A stone, a flower, a man, and a god are all in the differentiation of one life. A vegetable is in the process of becoming an animal; and an animal is a stage in the unfoldment of a planet; while an electron is a god in the process of becoming. All things are stages in the expression of one connected life, which at the present time is engaged in the task of liberating itself from the dense crystals of physical substance.[6]

This was not what I had been taught in Sunday School! I had been told that human beings are the pinnacle of God's creation; that we are superior to all beings (except God). This is what gave us the right to kill, maim, and pillage the Earth. I had also been taught that men were superior to women, and that humans and Angels were completely different species. But was any of this true? All of life seemed sacred to me, and if the Soul was eternal, then it could have a life as either a male or a female, making the philosophy of superiority, as taught by the patriarchy, only a reflection of our vast ignorance of these cosmic laws.

My information about the Angels was more limited. I knew intuitively that the forest Angel I had met so long ago had never had a life as a human being before. He had come from elsewhere, having evolved from the elemental kingdom over many long ages to become a highly sentient guardian. He was not really of this world, although he was in service to it. As he continued in his spiritual evolution, I knew he would eventually become the protector of larger and larger territories, such as entire cities and sacred sites. This was the path of *his* spiritual evolution, at least until such time that he decided to enter the human world and begin his long journey of evolution that each of us is treading now.

While it was clear to me that the forest Angel was far more connected to the harmony of the universe than I was, I could still tell that there were levels of complexity he did not have. These are levels of density that human beings have enfolded into themselves to experience a broader plateau of feeling. For example, he did not have an ego like ours, although he clearly had his own individuality. He did not have an emotional body like ours, although he was kind and well-intentioned. And he did not have a busy mind that jumped from place to place like our minds do. He was serene and one-pointed in his purpose and far more omniscient than I was. He was connected to Spirit in a way that I was not, but he was also far less complex than I was in many ways.

Later I was to realize that this was because he had not acquired the other subtle-energy bodies that humans have—complexities that are part of what makes up the human personality. Yes, he had individuation, but he did not have the same kind of free will that we humans have. He was completely aligned with Spirit, and his only desire was to serve the greater plan. He was in harmony with the universe, the Logos or the Word, content to fulfill his mission until someone else took up that charge. He might choose to remain as the overlighting Angel of that forest for hundreds of years. Then, one day, perhaps a thousand, or ten thousand years from now, that Angel would take birth as a human being. Then he would begin a completely different type of journey, taking on the same complex challenges that we have today.

So I wondered if this meant that we were all Angels long ago, in service to the greater plan? Had we all once been beings of light somewhere in the universe before we began our earthly journeys? And if this was true, would we become Angels once again when we graduated from Earth school? Or was the next rung up the ladder to become a sage, a master, or a demigod? What were the stages of Soul evolution? Are there young Souls, old Souls, and those in-between? Is the spiritual maturity of a Soul the major reason why some people are generous and good while others are selfish and cruel? Are the inconsistencies in human behavior merely the result of a person being at a different stage of spiritual evolution? Is there a Course Curriculum that we must master in order to graduate from Earth school? And if so, what are the lessons and the stages of the journey?

Over the next few years these became the questions that drove me as I embarked on a series of powerful spiritual initiations with the disincarnate masters who presented themselves to me. Slowly, over decades, I learned how to travel in the inner realms, attuning to the light and sound of God. Years later I read the words of the great Theosophists about the journey that each Soul makes as it travels from the higher realms into the lower ones, and then back again:

A heavy task lies before us, and beginning on the physical plane we shall climb slowly upwards: but a bird's eye view of the great sweep of evolution and of its purpose may help us. . . As we watch we see strata appearing of successive densities, till seven vast regions are apparent. . . . Narrowing down our view still further to our own globe and its surroundings, we watch human evolution, and see man developing self-consciousness by a series of many life periods . . . each life period adding to his experience, each life period lifting him higher in purity, in devotion, in intellect, in power of usefulness, until at the last he stands where They [the great masters] stand who are now the Teachers, fit to pay to his younger brothers the debts he owes to Them.[7]

Eventually, as I moved forward, meeting spiritual masters, cosmic divinities, gods, goddesses, and profound beings of light along the way, I gained the ability to consciously study the Soul records of those who came to me for help. Through the reading of each person's individual Soul records I learned more and more about the nature of the Soul, our connection with the spirit worlds, and the hidden history of our planet. Each reading was like a piece of a vast jigsaw puzzle spanning multiple dimensions. Time and again I sought to pull back the veil to the higher realms of light, discovering the true nature, purpose, and journey of the Soul through eons of time, and it is this sacred knowledge that I am sharing in this book.

How to Use This Book

This book is designed to give you insight into the nature and mission of your Soul and to address the Course Curriculum that every Soul must follow during the unfolding of its evolution. In these pages you will learn about the various stages of Soul evolution, the challenges that the Soul must face, and the deeper reasons behind why we came to Earth in the first place. This book is a powerful reference for discovering more about the vast landscapes of Heaven, the nature of your Soul, and your own link to the angelic kingdoms. It also serves as an evaluation tool to help you gain insight into where you are at in your own spiritual journey, to discover what your life lessons might be and what you have already mastered along the way. Finally, it is intended to help you to discover where you may be stuck along the way.

This book is organized into four interconnected sections:

- In part 1 we take a look at the beliefs of our ancestors, discovering what some of the greatest minds on this planet have had to say about the nature and history of the Soul. This includes insights from many great spiritual and philosophic traditions: Egyptian,

Tibetan, Greek, Jewish, Druid, Buddhist, Taoist, Hindu, and Christian.

- Part 2 takes you on a journey into the Afterlife to discover the vast landscapes of Heaven, the traps of the lower astral plane, and the many dimensional levels that lie between these two extremes. This section includes many stories from those who have returned from the Far Country and beheld incredible Crystal Cities of Light, giving us a powerful glimpse into the celestial realms, where the highest part of us resides.

- In part 3 we embark on the discovery of our genesis matrix and our angelic place of origin. We learn about the nine orders of Angels, the six stages of Soul evolution, and the mechanism of Adi-karma that causes us to forget our true Self. We also explore the concept of the Angelic Twin—our counterpart in the celestial realms who awaits the day when our human self will awaken and unite with it.

- In part 4 we take a look at the great Course Curriculum of the Soul and the many life lessons we each must master to complete our mission here on Earth. We address the primary wounds resulting from Adi-karma, which causes us to fall into the illusion of separation from Source. This is related to our belief in evil. This duality pulls us toward our baser natures, and thus the ancients called it "the Great Adversary." This Shadow aspect lives within each of us and is linked to all of our negative actions, thoughts, and beliefs that take us away from the light of our essential nature. This Shadow is connected to fear and ignorance, engendering anger, greed, vanity, falsehood, sorrow, and all manner of human suffering. It is the reason why human beings struggle so much on Earth.

  Part 4 also addresses the four primary defense mechanisms we humans use to keep ourselves in denial, and the four ways that people may try to steal each others' power. It covers the negative dynamics of the Persecutor-Victim-Rescuer triangle, a game that many people in the world are playing. No doubt you will recognize many aspects of yourself and your loved ones in these pages, giving you a divine blue-print to assist you in remembering the incredible being that you truly are.

So now, let us begin to discover what the great masters have to say about the eternal nature of our being.

PART 1

THE COSMOLOGY
OF THE SOUL

*The spiritual journey does not consist of
arriving at a new destination where a person
gains what he did not have, or becomes what
he is not. It consists in the dissipation of one's
own ignorance concerning oneself and life,
and the gradual growth of that
understanding which begins
the spiritual awakening.*

ALDOUS HUXLEY

1

The Eternal Flame

*I did not begin when I was born, nor when I was conceived.
I have been growing, developing, through incalculable
myriads of millenniums. All my previous selves have their
voices, echoes, promptings in me. Oh, incalculable times
again shall I be born.*

JACK LONDON

Our earliest ancestors had an innate understanding of the universe and the nature of the Soul. As keen observers of the natural world, they marked the waxing and waning cycles of the sun and the moon, the yearly rotation of the seasons, and the birth, death, and rebirth of their crops each year. They saw the sun rise at dawn, disappear on the horizon each night, only to be reborn the next day, repeating the sacred circle of life. They saw generations of humans and animals living and dying and being reborn, and they realized that all of life is a circle. Today, with the advent of the modern telescope and electron microscopes, we now know that this great circle of life repeats in the rotation of the planets, the whirl of the galaxies, and the spin of electrons around the nucleus of every atom, echoing Creation's continual renewal as an endlessly revolving wheel.

The ancients also realized that these same universal principles hold true for Souls. Mummified bodies found in Europe, Egypt, and the Americas all attest to a belief in a world beyond our own and the existence of an Afterlife. Buried in caves, caverns, pyramids, stone cairns, and earthworks, mummies are often found in the fetal position, as if curled into the womb, awaiting the joy of rebirth in the celestial realms. Romanian professor Mircea Eliade, a historian at the University of Chicago, writes about this eternal circle in *The Myth of the Eternal Return:*

> The death of the individual and the death of humanity are alike necessary for their regeneration. Any form whatever, by the mere fact that it exists as such and endures, necessarily loses vigor and becomes worn: to recover vigor, it must be reabsorbed into the formless, if only for an instant: it must be restored to the primordial unity from which it issued. . . . What predominates in all of these cosmico-mythological lunar conceptions is the cyclical recurrence of what has been before, in a word, the eternal return . . . projected upon all planes—cosmic, biological, historical, human.[1]

Thus our ancestors embraced the belief in reincarnation, the mechanism through which the Soul leaves this world and then returns to it again, learning its lessons over vast cycles of time. This cycle of living, dying, and being reborn is just as essential to the Soul as sleep is to the body each night. Just as we travel into these inner worlds to dream at night, so too does the Soul return to its celestial home at the end of every lifetime to assess its progress and renew its reconnection with Source of who it is. Thus every life is but a day of unfolding in the progress of our Soul's evolution. All of us come to Earth, face challenges, live out our dreams, and then return to the heavenly realms from which we came to integrate what we have learned. Once there, the Soul has access to a far more expanded awareness of itself and the Oneness that connects us all. As we shall see, there are many levels to these heavenly realms, and we are each drawn to the vibrational level that is most appropriate to our current level of evolution. In just this way, each Soul progresses from lifetime to lifetime with those of similar spiritual maturity, moving through the many stages of growth, including beginner, young, intermediate, advanced, and finally master, where we finally become a fully realized human being. And just as we are given various examinations in the different grade levels of school, so too does the Soul face certain tests appropriate to its level of evolution. All this leads to the eventual knowledge of our eternal Self.

The Breath of God

Many wisdom traditions have different symbols to represent the essence of the Soul. For some, the Soul or life force of Spirit is associated with the power of the breath. In fact, the English verb *to animate*, which means "to move or bring to life," is derived from the Latin word *animus*, from the Greek *anemos*, meaning "wind."[2] Similarly, in Greece, the word for *spirit* derives from the verb *psuchein*, a word that means "to breathe." In Hebrew the word for *spirit* is *ruah*, meaning "wind," as in "the Spirit of God that moved upon the Waters." "The Waters" refers to the premanifest space known in Greek as *Okeanos*, the "Mother substance" or *Prima materia*. In Sanskrit, "the Mover upon Spirit upon the Waters of the Great Deep" is *Narayana*,[3] just as in Christianity the Holy Spirit is the "breath of God," the carrier wave on which Spirit of life travels.

Chinese sages taught this same powerful connection with the word *chi*. Chi is the animating life force of God, equivalent to the Indian word *prana* and the Japanese *qi*. This life force has two complementary expressions, a yang and a yin polarity, equating with the masculine or expanding currents, and the feminine or contracting currents.

Thus to stay alive we must all breathe in and out each day, reenacting the endless circle of life with every breath. When a person stops breathing, she dies, since it is the breath that animates her physical body. Thus the breath is the living spirit of divine energy that animates the cosmos. It was this energy that descended over the Apostles as the Holy Spirit, giving them the power to transmit healing energy to others. This is also why the breath has always been so important in meditation

*Figure 1.1. The ancient Taoist symbol
for unity that encompasses yin and yang*

practices. When we breathe in a deeper, more deliberate way, we shift
our consciousness into higher and higher levels of awareness, reuniting
the spirit of the Divine with our personal selves.

Symbols of the Soul

Some philosophers and mystics have conceived of the Soul as a single
drop of water in the vastness of a great Cosmic Ocean—each drop
unique, yet each a part of the same essential Source. This Source is
the plenum of infinite intelligence that is sometimes referred to as
the Waters of Life, the Divine Mother, the Sacred Womb, the Cosmic
Ocean, or the unknowable *Ain* of Hebrew wisdom. This is the eternal
Ocean of Love and Mercy from which all things are born, and from
which we, as shining drops of consciousness, are released into the many
dimensions or worlds of form.

Sages have also taught that the Soul is a living flame, a spark born
from the Great Central Sun. Just as our visible sun is the source of illumination in our world, so the Great Central Sun is the light of divine
consciousness that is hidden behind the visible universe.

This is the pure white fire of our true being, our Angelic Self that
lies hidden behind everything else that we appear to be. Egyptian scriptures teach that it is this flaming presence that lives in every star, giving light to the universe. Hence the Soul is an individual spark that
becomes a flame and is eventually reunited with the supreme fire of the

Figure 1.2. The flame as a symbol for the illumination of the Soul

Creator itself. In the Hebrew alphabet, each of the twenty-two letters is composed of tiny flames joined together in various combinations, with the number of flames ranging from one to four with each letter. The Kabbalah, which teaches the esoteric path of Hebrew wisdom, says that these tiny flames are the foundations of the universe itself.[4]

The *Emerald Tablet,* believed to have been written between the sixth and eighth centuries and attributed to the Egyptian god Thoth, says: "The soul of man is a divine fire, a flame cast forth from the great fire, yet still bound by the ether coalesced around, yet ever it flames until at last it is free. Lift up your flame from out of the darkness, fly from the night and ye shall be free."[5] This pure white fire is fueled by the energy of the trifold flame of the heart, a flame that consist of the blue energies of the Divine Father, the rose energies of the Divine Mother, and the merging of the two, which produces the violet or gold flame of our own being.

In a two-thousand-year-old Christian work called *The Celestial Hierarchy* (*De Coelesti Hierarchia*), attributed to the theologian Pseudo-Dionysius the Areopagite, a disciple of the Apostle Paul, we also read about the link between the symbolism of the flame and the illuminating presence of God. "Sometimes," the author writes, "they celebrate Deity itself with lofty symbolism as the Sun of Justice, as the Morning Star rising mystically in the mind, or as Light shining forth unclouded and intelligibly; and sometimes they use images of things on earth, such as fire flashing forth from harmless flame, or water affording abundance of life symbolically flowing into a belly and gushing out in perpetually overflowing rivers and streams."[6] Thus through time, the Soul has been seen as an everlasting aspect of the universal light. The author goes on to say, Spirit molds "and perfects its participants in the holy image of God like bright and spotless mirrors which receive the Ray of the Supreme Deity . . . and being mystically filled with the Gift of Light, it pours it forth again abundantly, according to the Divine Law upon those below itself."[7]

Love, Light, and Sound

In truth, the symbolism of light has always been linked to both the Creator and to the enduring power of the Soul or flame within each one of us. Many esoteric traditions have taught that God, the Divine One, manifests through the twin powers of light and sound, bringing all things into being through the power of the Logos, or Holy Word. Inherent in the Logos, the controlling principle of the universe, are three eternal principles: love, sound, and light. These three aspects are also reflected in all nine orders of Angels, for Angels can appear as moving waveforms of color, light, and sacred geometry, and they are often accompanied by the sounds of celestial melodies. Ancient sages in both the ancient Egyptian and Eastern spiritual traditions taught that it is through these three principles that the entire universe came into being. Today, through quantum physics, we know that it is sound that creates and sustains the visible world. Science calls these packets of sound *phonons,* which are then converted into photons, or visible units of light, eventually becoming the foundation for all physical matter.

In the Gospel of John (1:1) we read, "In the Beginning was the Word." The Word is the sacred sound that sets everything in motion, a waveform that emerged from the eternal presence of the Divine One. This Divine One has been known by a thousand names in a hundred different religions: to the Native Americans it is the Great Spirit; to the Jews it is Yahweh; the Egyptians call it Atum; Moslems refer to Allah; and Christians call it the living Christ. It is the Supreme Creator, pure consciousness, divine intelligence, and the Lord of the

Universe. In Hindu theology this Source is known as Saguna Brahman, the "Unknowable One" or "Supreme Brahman," or "the Absolute with qualities." This is the source from which the Soul emerges. "Beyond the universe, Brahman, the supreme, the great, hidden in all beings according to their bodies, the one Breath of the whole universe, the Lord, whom knowing (men) become immortal. I know that mighty Spirit, the shining sun beyond the darkness. . . . I know Him, the unfading, the ancient, the Soul of all, omnipresent by His nature, whom the Brahman knowers call unborn, whom they call eternal."[8]

Saguna Brahman contains all three functions of creation, preservation, and destruction, thus encompassing the Trimurti or Trinity of Hinduism: Brahman the Creator, Vishnu the Preserver, and Shiva the Destroyer. Yet only Brahman is the supreme source of consciousness that gives birth to the Golden Egg of Creation. This Golden Egg is called *Hiranvagarbha,* or "golden womb." In Vedic philosophy this Cosmic Egg is thought to be the source of the manifested cosmos and is found in the creation myths of many ancient cultures. It is said that the first primordial aspect of the Divine was birthed from it, marking the beginning of the universe. In Egypt this first created being was called Ra, the Lord of Light. In Hinduism it is Brahma, the creator god. In Theosophy it is the Adam Kadmon or universal being that represents the fullness of our human godlike potential. Vedic cosmology believes that each multitudinous universe is created by one of these great Cosmic Eggs floating on the cosmic waters of space. This is a great description of the millions of galaxies we have discovered with our telescopes, each a universe unto itself in the vastness of space. Saguna Brahman however, is the One who resides in the many, the spark of the Soul itself, "That Universal Being, that contains all, and which is all, put into motion the Soul and the World, all that nature comprises . . ."[9] Below Saguna Brahman there are other great Souls who have been put in charge of a galaxy, a universe, or even an entire dimension, yet each of these powers is but a more limited expression of the great eternal One. In the Hindu tradition these universal guardians are called *Brahmandas,* or "those who oversee material manifestation." They are the overseeing consciousnesses that help to regulate the immensity of creation in every universe.

While far more immense than human beings, they are nevertheless living sparks in the body of God.

Eastern wisdom teaches that a spark of Brahman lies buried deep within each of us. This is the indwelling Soul of the Creator called the Atman, which slumbers like a cosmic seed waiting to be awakened. Like the Greek word *atmos,* meaning "air," this is the living life force or Spirit that animates our Soul. If Brahman is the Soul of All That Is, then Atman is the Cosmic Soul that has been scattered throughout the universe in us, the One whose living fire indwells and sustains all living beings.

The Lotus Flower and the Rose

The Buddha likened the idea of our rising consciousness to a lotus flower rising from the muck and mire. In one of his most famous sermons he didn't speak at all, but merely held up a lotus flower. Both Hindu and Egyptian cultures chose the lotus to symbolize the eternal journey of the Soul that, like the lotus, rises from the muddy depths, representing all the pain and ignorance that we seem to endure on our path to enlightenment.

As the lotus pushes up toward the light, it blossoms into the thousand-petal lotus, a symbol of the crown chakra, which allows us to connect with our divine Self as we awaken into the light of our own being.

Many spiritual paths have conceived of the Soul as a feminine

Figure 1.3. The lotus, flower of enlightenment

expression of the Great Mother sojourning in the worlds below. In fact, there are elements in the natural world that support the idea that the Soul is feminine in nature. In the past sixty years science has discovered that all mammals are created biologically female first; the male is formed only by the release of an additional androgen,[10] which is, of course, contrary to the teachings of the patriarchal religions that would have us believe that it is the male who is created first. Since the microcosmic world is a reflection of the macrocosmic realms ("As above, so below"), then the Creator has long been believed to be a feminine presence. After all, it is only women who give birth, so who could have birthed the cosmos but the Divine Mother of us all? She is the hidden principle of the plenum, the dark matter; she is the Black Madonna, the Virgin of the World who gives birth to the universe before anything else existed. In Persian culture she is called Armaiti, the goddess of wisdom who created the universe. Some call her the Earth Mother or goddess of the Underworld, for she regulates all cycles of life, death, and rebirth.[11] We emerge from her cosmic womb to be reborn to a human mother. We live on Gaia, or Mother Earth. At night we gaze up at the Milky Way, the Mother's "milk" of stars. We drink from her springs each day and eat from her fields. She is constantly giving birth to a million myriad forms of life. From the womb to the tomb, we are children of the sacred feminine, and we carry her divine spark within us.

It is important to note that some near-death experiencers who have traveled to the Otherside and returned reveal that they have also encountered this divine presence, as in the following: "My situation was, strangely enough, something akin to that of a fetus in a womb. In this case, the 'mother' was God, the Creator, the Source who is responsible for making the universe and all in it. This Being was so close that there seemed to be no distance at all between God and myself. Yet at the same time, I could sense the infinite vastness of the Creator, could see how completely minuscule I was by comparison."[12]

In *The Divine Comedy,* Dante relates that when he reached the Empyrean of the highest heaven what appeared to him was an image of the Queen of Heaven, embodied first in Dante's spiritual guide, Beatrice, and then in her higher manifestation as the Mother of All.

Her symbol, he writes, is the white rose, layered like the Soul itself, with the many petals that comprise our subtle-energy bodies.

The Cosmic Seed and the Tree of Life

In Plato's time, the various mystery schools compared the Soul to a cosmic seed that has fallen from the Tree of Life, and certainly this oval form is the shape of our auric body.

The ancients believed that the Soul, like a seed, is imbued with a blueprint of the entire cosmos, yet it knows it not. Instead it is layered with various energy bodies—physical, astral, mental, emotional, and causal—and these are both helpful in its growth and development, as well as limiting in the Soul's ability to be in touch with its own eternal nature. The seed can only grow into awareness over time, by meeting the various lessons and challenges of lifetimes; it does so best when it is nourished by love.

The Tree of Life is the Soul's parent, a force that is rooted in the Absolute. The Katha Upanishad describes this as the eternal Aswatha tree, which spreads its shoots downward, thus creating billions of worlds

Figure 1.4. The Celtic Tree of Life

beneath it that are spread out in all dimensions. This mystical tree is the energetic bridge between the realms of Heaven and the Earth, providing a roadmap so that the Soul can find its way back home. One day, ancient wisdom teaches, each Soul will become one with the Tree of Life, having attained mastery over many countless eons of time. The tree is the rainbow bridge that binds Heaven and Earth together. Therefore, it is not surprising that many of the great world saviors have been linked to this Tree, including Jesus, Osiris, Krishna, Odin, Thoth, and Quetzalcoatl. As fully realized God-men, their job was to act as mediators, or bridges, between the heavenly realms and the dimension of form that is the Earth, reminding each Soul that the divine spark lives inside of us.

In sacred geometry this seed of life is drawn with six perfect circles around a central circle, representing the six movements of Creation spoken of in the Bible. These movements were honored as the six days of Creation around a seventh day of rest, represented by the holy day of the Sabbath.

This six-sided mandala also symbolizes the six *lokas,* "worlds" or dimensional planes written about in the Bardo Thodol, better known in the West as the Tibetan Book of the Dead. These six dimensions

Figure 1.5. The six-petal seed of life around a central circle symbolizes the six moments of Creation around the unifying principle of One

all rotate around a seventh celestial kingdom, where it is said our true Self resides. These seven lokas, or dimensions, were also taught in the Mystery Schools as corresponding to the seven chakras and the seven subtle-energy bodies that comprise the matrix of who we are. This six-sided geometry (six around a seventh central circle) is embedded in many places in creation, forming the hexagonal basis for the entire mineral kingdom.

Mystical teachings reveal that it is from this Tree of Life that the Flower of Life emerges. The flower is a template for how the growth of one kingdom becomes the foundation for the next. This is not only true in the building blocks of matter, but also in the interdependence of all the various kingdoms, from mineral to plant, animal to human, each kingdom building on the last. This Flower of Life design was taught in the temples of ancient Egypt and can still be found today in the ruins

Figure 1.6. The multidimensional Flower of Life that grows from the seed

of the Temple of Abydos, lasered onto one of the granite stones. The Abydos temple was once the Temple of Osiris, the Lord of Resurrection who taught the principle of spiritual rebirth. We will return to this subject later when we discuss the great Mystery Schools of Egypt.

Knowledge of these principles was then passed from the Egyptians to the Hebrews through the teacher Moses, who was both a priest and an initiate in the Egyptian city of Heliopolis, at the Temple of Ra-Atum. This temple was dedicated to both the visible and invisible forces behind Creation, honoring Ra, the visible light of the Sun, and Atum, the invisible and imperishable One behind the manifest worlds. Moses brought the knowledge of the Tree of Life, the Flower of Life, and the Seed of Life with him out of Egypt, and from there it made its way into the temples of Persia and Greece. Finally, this teaching came to the Essenes, from whom it was disseminated throughout the world. That is why we find indications of this sacred geometry in the temples, mosaics, and artwork of ancient Sumeria, Babylon, Greece, Persia, and Rome (although by the time of the Roman Empire much of the esoteric meaning behind these symbols had been lost). Later, a derivative of this six-pointed design would become known as the Star of David, a symbol representing the balance of the yin and yang forces in Creation—the Mother and Father of the All. While the Seed of Life and the Flower of Life were eventually lost to the Hebrews, the Star of David remains as one of their most enduring icons.

At an even deeper esoteric level, this six-sided figure is the shape of

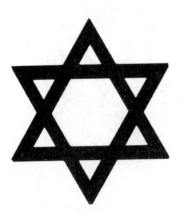

Figure 1.7. The six-pointed Star of David that encompasses the yin and yang polarities

Figure 1.8. A woman within the Merkaba as she activates her subtle-energy bodies for spiritual travel (illustration by Tricia McCannon)

one of our seven subtle-energy bodies. When fully activated it becomes the Merkaba field, the energetic vehicle used by the Soul to travel into the inner planes that is developed through meditation practice. In Enochian literature the Merkaba was known as the "chariot," an indication of its ability to transport our consciousness between the human and celestial realms of light.

Persephone, the Eternal Soul

The concept of the Soul as the cosmic seed that has fallen from the Tree of Life was woven into the deepest initiation rites of the Eleusinian Mysteries over three thousand years ago, told in the story of the Greek goddesses Demeter and Persephone, the Divine Mother and Daughter. This is similar to the concepts of the Divine Father and

Son in Christianity. In this story, told as an initiatory tale, Persephone is the innocent, unevolved Soul, the cosmic seed who has fallen from the Tree of Life. She is the innocent maiden who has fallen away from her connection with the Divine Parent to become lost in the worlds of matter. In this tale, Persephone is out picking flowers in a meadow one day when suddenly the ground beneath her opens up and Hades, the god-king of the Underworld, arrives in his chariot. He scoops her up and carries her off to the realm of lost spirits, Souls in the Underworld that have become lost to themselves, having forgotten their connection to the divine spark within. After her abduction, Persephone's mother, Demeter, looks for her daughter in vain. Because Demeter is the Earth Mother of Life, her grief causes the earth to begin to dry up so that even the other gods become alarmed. Eventually Hermes, the Greek god of wisdom,* reveals to Demeter that Persephone has been kidnapped and now resides in the realm of shadows. Demeter goes to the council of gods and goddesses and demands the return of her daughter. Not wanting to anger Hades, they nevertheless reluctantly consent. But once they discover that Persephone has eaten six red pomegranate seeds during her stay in the Underworld, they decree that she must now spend six months of every year trapped in the lower worlds with Hades, and the rest of the time she can return to the world of light to be reunited with her mother.

Symbolically, this is the story of each one of us. We are each the innocent seed that has fallen into the lower worlds, separated from the great Tree of Life. We are thus Souls who have forgotten our connection to the Source and are lost in the Underworld. Two of Persephone's magical names give us great insight into the deeper meaning of this initiatory story: Kernel and Koré (i.e., the small *kernel* of wheat that has fallen from the Tree of Life), which is the very *core* of who we really are. Like Persephone, we each spend a portion of time lost in the shadow world, returning to the heavenly realms between lifetimes. The Underworld is the land of spiritual amnesia, the dimension where we

---

*Hermes Trismegistus, or Thrice Great Hermes, is another name for the Egyptian god Thoth, the lord of wisdom, travel, communication, healing, and writing.

*Figure 1.9. Demeter and Persephone
(illustration by Tricia McCannon)*

have forgotten our divine origins. In these shadowy realms the forces of light and darkness are juxtaposed, pulling us first one way and then another. This creates an opportunity for the Soul to make myriad choices in its lifetime; it can choose the path of love or fear, of sharing or selfishness, of hope or despair. Every day we make decisions about giving or taking, anger or forgiveness, kindness or cruelty. Thus each lifetime is a classroom of learning; and our free will determines the outcome. And then, when we die, we rise back into the realms of light and are reunited with our Divine Mother.

The Deathless One Who Lives Within

All of these analogies are merely metaphors for the Soul: the drop of water, the eternal flame, the cosmic seed—all are symbols of the eternal, deathless One who lives within. Like a great traveler moving through time, the Soul possesses the spark of the Creator, but it is largely unaware of its own light. In the higher realms it knows some of who or what it is, but as it descends lower and lower through the dimensional planes into material form the Soul goes from knowing to not knowing, from remembrance to amnesia, and finally, through its own efforts over countless lifetimes, it returns to knowing once again. During the course of its long journey it travels into the various kingdoms of God, experiencing all manner of forms, spending time in the mineral, plant, and animal kingdoms until it finally incarnates into the human world, where it can begin to awaken to its divine potential. Eventually, as we graduate from this plane of existence, we become sages, masters, gods, and Angels, taking our rightful place in the pattern of Creation.

The Persian poet Rumi (1207–1273) writes:

Like grass I have grown over and over again. I passed out of mineral form and lived as a plant. From plant I was lifted up to be an animal. Then I put away the animal form and took on a human shape. Why should I fear that if I died I shall be lost? For passing human form, I shall attain the flowing locks and shining wings of angels. And then I shall become what no mind has ever conceived. O let me cease to exist! For non-existence only means that I shall return to Him.[13]

Manly P. Hall says this about the evolutionary journey of the Soul:

Man is an integral part of the whole plan of life, and the realization of this fact strengthens him for the accomplishment of his spiritual labor. A noble destiny awaits humanity, a way planned by a God of Wisdom, ordained by a God of Justice, perpetuated by a God of Life, and rendered secure by a God of Love. For our well-being, it is essential that we understand more of this Royal Road to Truth.

This universe—with its loves and hates, its hopes and fears—is really what it seems to be, and more. The planets march in endless obeisance to their sovereign liege, the sun. Plants and animals—yes, even stones, are really pulsating, living, thinking things. Within the all is the latent power to achieve, and this indwelling divinity has decreed that sometime they shall come to know the purpose for their own existence, and with joyous concord move together toward that end. *It is the destiny of all that they shall accomplish all.*[14]

This journey that the Soul takes through all of its multiple sojourns in Earth school is part of learning the Course Curriculum for the Soul. While the ancient teachings tell us that the eternal part of us remains in Heaven, another part boldly chooses to come into the worlds of form to experience the wonders, sorrows, and transformation of the worlds of duality. So in truth, as a divine spark of God, the Soul has voluntarily chosen to fall into amnesia so that it may experience all things anew. This is how it grows and evolves. Yet because the Soul is intrinsically a pure spark of God-consciousness, it cannot participate in the material realm without acquiring the energetic bodies needed to be in a physical form. These are the life force, emotional, mental, astral, causal, etheric, and Soul bodies, which are acquired on each of the planes above the physical world. Each of these subtle-energy bodies equates with one of the seven dimensional planes, allowing the Soul to experience life in that dimension, just as our physical body allows us to participate in

Earth school. When the physical body perishes, the Soul continues to live on in the other dimensional planes. While the Atman, or Soul Self, remembers this, the physical, astral, and mental bodies have forgotten their origin. Yet each time we take birth, some part of us has deliberately chosen the conditions of that lifetime in order to learn a certain set of lessons, and how we respond to these lessons, once we arrive on Earth, is a matter of personal choice and free will. The results can be seen in how we are living our life today.

Let us step back for just a moment and look at this plan. A journey of this magnitude is profoundly courageous, and the Soul who undertakes it does so in order to learn, or to help its fellow citizens. Yet at the higher levels, the Soul knows itself to be immortal. In these higher realms, the Angelic Self remembers who it is; however when we are born on Earth we seem to fall into a largely amnesic state, completely identifying with our five physical senses, believing in the world of illusion and the "movie" that we are making for ourselves here. Throughout the thousands of years of the Soul's experiences it embraces the emotions of love, joy, beauty, and communion, but it also knows pain, separation, illness, suffering, fear, and illusion. It is through these various states of contrast, that it is able to learn how to make wise choices. Until finally, of its own free will, the Soul will align with the light of its own being and begin the return journey back home.

The Power of Love

What awakens us from this stupor of forgetfulness? It is the power of love. This is why the heart has always been the key to our spiritual growth. Love can awaken us to a new way of seeing the world, allowing us to open to the miracle of life and perceive the magical unseen realms that lie beyond the physical world. Awakening the heart arouses our spiritual senses and creates a longing to connect with the infinitude of the Creator. Love begins the yearning of the Soul to connect with something beyond the world of matter. Then, as the Soul becomes more aware of its own essence, it has the opportunity to become a spiritual guide for others. This is the path of the initiate who becomes the teacher, the sage, and finally the master in service to other Souls who are still trapped in the dualistic world of form. Thus in time the Soul may become a spirit guide for others still struggling in the physical world. And eventually, after it graduates from Earth school, its capacity to transmit light grows so strong that it may even became a teacher on the Otherside, an archivist in the Hall of Records or a member of the Council of Light (or Council of Elders), helping other Souls still trapped in the worlds of matter to move forward in their evolution. Eventually, the Soul reclaims its own angelic nature in the Great Chain of Being, a term that refers to the mystical concept of the descent of Spirit into the worlds of form and back again. Upon its return to its angelic origins it may then become involved in the creation of entire planets, planetary systems, galaxies, or universes. This is a larger view of the Course Curriculum of the Soul.

We Have Always Existed

In the Hindu scripture the Bhagavad Gita, Lord Krishna, the great avatar, refers to the Soul's immortal nature. In this passage Krishna addresses his student Prince Arjuna as they both stand astride a chariot on the frontline of an enormous battle. Arrayed around them on the battlefield are thousands of friends and foes; in this scene Arjuna's heart has grown faint as he considers having to fight against relatives who have chosen a path of injustice. Seeing his student's hesitation, Lord Krishna says,

> Never have I not existed, nor you, nor these kings; and never in the future shall we cease to exist. Just as the embodied self enters childhood, youth, and old age, so does it enter another body . . . Nothing of non-being comes to be, nor does being cease to exist. The boundary between these two is seen by men who see reality. Indestructible is the presence that pervades all this; no one can destroy this unchanging reality. Our bodies are known to end, but the embodied self is enduring, indestructible, and immeasurable. Therefore, Arjuna, fight the battle!

He who thinks the self a killer, and he who thinks it killed, both fail to understand; it does not kill, nor is it killed. It is not born, it does not die; having been, it will never not be; unborn, enduring, constant and primordial, it is not killed when the body is killed . . . As a man discards worn out clothes to put on new and different ones, so the embodied self discards its worn-out bodies to take on other new ones. Weapons do not cut it, fire does not burn it, waters do not wet it, wind does not wither it . . . it is enduring, all pervasive, fixed, immoveable and timeless.[15]

This is a teaching about reincarnation, also known as the *transmigration of the Soul*. As the Soul discards one body, it puts on another in an endless cycle of experiences designed to help us discover our true nature. Though our body may be destroyed, our Soul never dies. We are ever-enduring, timeless, and immortal.

Vedic Wisdom

Vedic philosophy embraces the idea that the Soul existed long before the body came into being, and at death it returns to the realms from whence it came. The Upanishads state that the Atman is uncreated and unchanging, residing beyond the physical realms. It is both infinite and finite, eternal yet temporal, for within this Soul lies Saguna Brahman, the Creator, the seed of all things, hidden as pure consciousness within everything. Saguna Brahman, expressing itself as the Atman, our Witness Self, the divine presence that watches everything. As the Atman, the spirit within us allows the Soul to be free of all human qualities. It has no anger, lust, greed, vanity, fear, or undue attachment. It is the Inner Master that lies within. The Upanishads say: "Two birds, inseparable companions, perch on the same tree. One eats the fruit, the other looks on. The first bird is our individual self, feeling all the pleasures and pains of this world; the other is the Universal Self, silently witnessing all."[16]

Vedantists also recognize this abiding presence as the divine Purusha, the universal cosmic male, the manifested Brahman or creative consciousness that sets in motion the entire creative process. Purusha has two forms—perishable and imperishable. In his human form he is the subject, as well as the object, of sacrificial ceremonies, whose self-sacrifice results in the manifestation of life and worlds. This is the universal savior god whose self-sacrifice grants spiritual liberation into the higher realms. Yet in his imperishable form he is the Witness Self that dwells within us all, the selfless Self that permeates the Universe. Divine Purusha is one of two aspects of Saguna Brahman that bring the universe into being.

The other aspect is Prakriti, the universal Mother. She also has a perishable and imperishable aspect. Her eternal aspect is the life giving energy by which all living beings are upheld. In Christianity she is called the Holy Spirit. The perishable aspect consists of the elements that comprise the material world. These are the eight-fold aspects of nature: air, earth, fire, water, ether, mind, reason, and the ego. Together Prakriti and the Purusha are the male and female aspects of Saguna Brahman, the Creator, that bring all things into being.[17]

So the divine Purusha is the indwelling Christ, the eternal witness who lives within our Souls. In his age, Gautama Buddha was considered the Maha Purusha or "Great Purusha" of his time because of his unity with this eternal presence, just as Issa (Jesus) is considered the Maha Purusha of our age. Frances Vaughan, a psychologist and the author of *Shadows of the Sacred,* writes: "Although the aim of self-transcendence as understood in classical yoga is often criticized for being oriented to escape from the world . . . it can instead, provide a view of reality in which the apparent dichotomy between Spirit and matter, Soul and body, is itself perceived as a play of illusion. The awakened Soul recognizes all things as projections of the imperishable Brahman."[18]

Hebrew Wisdom

The Talmud teaches that the Soul is a mystical being created by God that protests its descent to Earth at the time of physical birth and then protests again when the body is about to die. After death it travels back into the higher realms to be rejoined with the Creator. Hebrew wisdom views the body as a prison from which the Soul escapes at death. In sleep, the Soul ascends to Heaven during dreamtime, only to return at dawn renewed. If it is not allowed to do this then the body becomes depleted. This is why people who are deprived of theta and delta sleep become emotionally unbalanced. We need to dream because we must recharge our Souls as long as we are in this world of form. According to the Kabbalah, the mystical teachings of the Tree of Life, human beings are entrusted with the task of reintegrating that which has become flawed in the material world. Our job as human beings is therefore to "redeem" this world, to enlighten it, and it is through each one of us that the imbalance of the universe can be corrected.[19]

The Kabbalah teaches that the purpose of the Soul entering this body is to display its powers and actions in this world, for it needs an instrument. By descending to this world, the Soul increases the flow of its power to guide the human being through the world, thereby perfecting itself above and below, attaining a higher state of fulfillment in all dimensions. If the Soul is not fulfilled both above and below, it is not complete. Before descending to this physical world, the Soul is emanated from the Great Mystery at the highest level. While in this world it is completed and fulfilled by this lower world. Departing this world, it is filled with the fullness of all the worlds, the world above and the world below.[20]

Native American Wisdom

Native American elders tell us that there is only one great Soul behind it all. This means that all are members of the same universal family. This includes plants, trees, rocks, and stars—all are our brothers and sisters. The Lakota phrase *O Mitakuye Oyasin* means "All My Relations." Thus when we consider that we are all part of this one Great Being, this Oneness, we should treat everyone with kindness. This is why Jesus admonished us to "love our neighbors as ourselves," since each and every being is a part of who we are. Through us the Creator is engaged in the unceasing dance of experience. Through us, God suffers and loves, learns and feels, knows the celebration of victory and the pain of defeat. Never far, ever-present, God knows the frailty and uncertainty of mortality, at the same time existing as an eternal, imperishable being. So, through our dance the Great Spirit is constantly forgetting and remembering its own essence, while simultaneously observing the cosmic dance in every realm.

2

Mysteries of the Hidden Wisdom

The soul of man is like to water; from Heaven it cometh, to Heaven it riseth. . . . And then returning to earth, forever alternating.

JOHANN WOLFGANG VON GOETHE

Let us now take a look at some of the earliest teachings we have about the nature of the Soul and its journey between our world and the higher realms. These teachings come from the ancient cultures of Egypt, India, Persia, Gaul, and Greece. Most of these civilizations embraced the concept of an Afterlife, much as the later Abrahamic religious traditions do today. It is for this reason that the ancients called these teachings the Mysteries, for they knew about the hidden realms of light behind our own world. These sages understood the mechanisms of Soul evolution and thus they set up great centers of learning and initiation known as Mystery Schools so that those who sought the deeper truths could discover them for themselves. These schools existed some four thousand years before the birth of Christ and some four hundred years after Jesus's death. Today they are the templates for our present universities, yet unlike modern colleges and universities these schools were not focused only on the sciences and the humanities, but also on discovering the deeper reasons behind our very existence.

The Teachings of the Greek Mystery Schools

For many, the bedrock of Western civilization is considered to be the Greek culture, and for many excellent reasons. Certainly the Greeks were the first nation to choose democracy instead of the "divine right" of kings to rule, and they combined logic, science, and mysticism in a way that has resonated throughout human history. The Greeks distilled their wisdom from a variety of ancient sources, including Persia and Chaldea, but Egypt was the main source for the Greek Mysteries. Pythagoras studied for many years in the Mystery Schools of ancient Egypt, as did Socrates, Plato, and other Greek sages. Herodotus, the fifth-century Greek historian, writes in his ten-volume work *The Histories* that "everything of any importance, the Greeks got from Egypt."[1] However, Greek philosophers were also brilliant in and of themselves, investigating not only the outer world of the sciences, but the inner nature of the Soul. Not merely content with exploring the realms of statesmanship, law, mathematics, logic, physics, and healing, the Greeks also sought answers to the fundamental questions about the hidden principles of the universe.

The Greek Mystery Schools not only taught astronomy, physics, mathematics, music, and all of the sciences known at that time, they also brought an experiential aspect to the curriculum that was designed to propel initiates into an awareness of their true Soul identity. This was facilitated through meditation, ritual, yoga, sacred plant journeys, out-of-body travel, deliberately induced near-death experiences, and other initiation processes that tested the student to the limit of his or her faculties. Neurosurgeon and best-selling author Eben Alexander says:

> In the mystery religions, as in most ancient initiations, the person being initiated died as the earthly person he or she had been, and was reborn as a new, spiritual one. Not in some vague, theoretical

way, but for real. The central concept of the mysteries, as of most ancient initiatory practices, was that as humans we have a dual heritage: an earthly one and a heavenly one. To know only one's earthly heritage is to know only half of oneself. The mystery initiations allowed people to recover a direct knowledge of what we could call their heavenly lineage. In a sense, the initiate wasn't turned into anything new, so much as he or she was reminded, in a powerful and immediate way, of who and what he or she had started out as before coming to earth, of what he or she really had been all along.[2]

Thus those who graduated from these initiations became known as the "twice-born," signifying they had been "born again" through a near-death experience. These schools also taught many practical processes to aid in this spiritual awakening. These included setting an intention at the start of each new day, daily meditation, taking an evening inventory of your conscience to see what you could have done better, and envisioning your future so that you learned to create from positive intentions rather than negative programming or fears. These processes also included dream journaling, governing your inner dialogue, philosophical life reflection, and working with positive affirmations, called *maxims*. While there were literally hundreds of these maxims that a student could commit to memory, here are a few that I find to be quite insightful:

> As within, so without. As without, so within.
> Try to bring back the God in you, to the divine in the All.
> The just man is the freest of anyone from anxiety, but the unjust man is perpetually haunted by it.
> The long way to happiness is through words, but the short way is through the daily practice of deeds.
> According to the Rules of Order, little things must precede the greater, if we would make the ascent.
> If this way of practicing philosophy is unpleasant, it is a shortcut.
> It leads to happiness even though we have to walk through fire.

Students were also encouraged to contemplate making death a

friend as one of their spiritual practices. The philosopher Epicurus taught that "the exercise of living well and the exercise of dying well are one and the same thing."[3] In Plato's *Phaedo*, known to ancient readers as *On the Soul*, he asks Socrates about the link between the study of the Soul and the Afterlife. "Is not philosophy the practice of death?" So the practice of death became a measurement of how a Soul has lived based on the understanding that, since we are immortal, when we face death we are simultaneously asking ourselves what value our lives have had. How have we used the time that has been given to us?[4]

In many ways the Mystery Schools provided deep therapy in the midst of human savagery, political intrigue, war, violence, ambition, and treachery, not to mention the day-to-day conflicts and suffering that seem to accompany human life. But like all cures administered to someone who is sick or out of balance, philosophy had to be practiced in stages, beginning with whatever one's current life conditions were. Then the initiate could slowly progress through successive phases until the cure became successful, resulting in a balanced, wise, and happy life.

Socrates believed that people are only bad as a result of blind ignorance; if they really understood the spiritual laws of the universe and their place within it, all people would want to do good. So in this way the Mystery Schools were imminently practical, for they were about ridding oneself of ignorance and changing one's life for the better. Plato asserted, "No soul is willingly deprived of truth. And it is the same with justice, moderation, loving kindness, and all the like. It is essential to keep this ever in mind, for it will make you gentler toward all."[5]

In Greece there were three different branches of the Mystery Schools—the Orphic Mysteries, the Eleusinian Mysteries, and the Mysteries of Dionysus—each with its own ceremonies and centers. Yet even though these three branches emphasized different gods, such as Dionysus, Orpheus, Serapis, Mithras, Demeter, Persephone, and Isis,*

---

*Isis is a name that has been corrupted by political terrorists and media sound bites. The Islamic terrorist group that is active in the world today is not actually called Isis, but Isil. For some reason the patriarchy and the institutions that serve it are bent on corrupting the name of the Divine Mother, polluting this association in the subconscious minds of people around the world.

they all understood that there was but one intelligence behind them all, and that these divinities were merely different faces or expressions of the one transcendent Creator.[6]

The Three Levels of Initiation

The Mystery Schools were organized into three levels of initiation. This is where we get our template for the three levels of education today: elementary, middle, and high school. This is also the template for our bachelors, masters, and Ph.D. degrees. In Greece these degrees were called *purification, illumination,* and *revelation,* and in the final degree the initiate was said to have direct experience of the gods.

The first level of initiation taught the importance of living a virtuous life—fundamentally the same concepts taught in the Ten Commandments. In other words, don't lie, cheat, steal, kill, or covet your neighbor's wife—all excellent principles for creating a just and moral society. This first level also taught the universal laws of karma and reincarnation, describing in detail the consequences of a person's actions in the hereafter and in subsequent lives based on the choices we make in this one. The first level also emphasized the importance of spiritual service to others, for it is through giving that we ultimately grow, learn, and receive the blessings of love. First-level initiates were also taught herbalism, healing, botany, and the development of their spiritual energy bodies, in some cases resulting in what we would call "miracle healing" today. This curriculum took at least seven years to complete and throughout the centuries produced thousands of proficient healers, who then passed their knowledge on to others.

The second level of the Mysteries was dedicated to the disciplines of science and the unseen forces behind the visible world. This included the study of mathematics, sacred geometry, astronomy, astrology, music, engineering, and *physis,* the Greek word for "nature" that is the inspiration for the word *physics* today. This second level also included philosophy, theology, cosmology, psychology, logic, science, and ethics. The goal in all of these studies was to learn right thinking using knowledge obtained from logic, philosophy, and direct mystical experience to understand *who* we really are, and *how* we should live in harmony with the universe, inspiring us to practice *right action* in our daily lives.[7]

The Inner Initiations

While there is still much that we do not know about the highest level of initiation in the Mysteries (since initiates were sworn to secrecy), we do know that these teachings have been held in the highest regard by some of the greatest minds of any age, enduring for thousands of years before the Abrahamic religions took hold. We also know that purity of heart was one of the requirements for entry into the higher levels of the Mysteries, because travel into the higher dimensions cannot be accomplished by someone whose intention is not pure. In fact, these higher spiritual regions can only be reached by people who are spiritually attuned to them. Without the proper vibration, a person is simply locked out. So one must harmonize one's own frequency to the higher dimensions or else they remain closed to you forever.

The ancient sages understood that the physics of Heaven are different from the laws that govern Earth. Each dimensional plane has its own set of bindings or laws (a subject we will explore in greater detail in part 2 of this book). What is important to realize at this point is that each Soul is only allowed entrance into these celestial realms when it has reached a state of consciousness that allows the person to resonate with these realms. And while knowledge is golden in the Kingdom of Heaven, ultimately the true key to this inner door is governed by the purity and love that emanates from a person's heart.

In essence, the Mysteries were designed to allow each student to discover and experience his or her own immortal nature, for it is only by traveling into the higher registers of the astral or mental planes that a student could hope to realize the spiritual reality that lies behind our physical world. Therefore, students were encouraged to travel out-of-body and to have near-death experiences so that they could have their own internal *gnosis,* discovering firsthand that we have each existed beyond the mere physicality of the body. Ultimately such a realization helps us to realize that what we do in each lifetime has a direct bearing on the quality of our next incarnation, as well as on our destination in the Afterlife. As millions of near-death experiencers have realized, this understanding has the power to fundamentally change a person's priorities in life. When we stand at the doorway of these vast realms of light and meet the beings who oversee these celestial worlds, then we can begin to view life from an entirely different perspective, at which point we want to turn away from a life of selfishness and materialism and build a life based on more enduring principles.

In time, initiates came to realize that each lifetime is a series of spiritual trials. How well we do with these tests determines how fast we will progress as a Soul. What matters most in each and every lifetime is not the acquisition of money, fame, or power, but the depth of one's character. Initiates discovered that at the close of every life we are drawn back into that realm that resonates with our current level of consciousness. The lower our consciousness while we are alive in the mortal realms, then the lower the realm of arrival in the Afterlife, while the higher our vibration at the end of each lifetime, the more lofty our destination on the Otherside.

Orpheus, the Divine Musician

The Orphic Mysteries were perhaps the oldest school of wisdom in ancient Greece. They were based on the teachings of Orpheus, the half-human, half-divine son of the god Apollo. Orpheus was deeply revered by all the Greeks as the greatest of poets and musicians. The fifth-century BC poet Pindar called him "the father of songs." Orpheus's music, it was said, could charm the wild beasts, coax the trees into dancing, divert the course of rivers, and had power to move even the hearts of the gods. His shrines became oracular centers of wisdom in Greece, and he is credited with writing the Orphic Hymns, some of which still survive today.

Orpheus was the son of Calliope, chief of the Seven Muses and the mother of ecstatic song. His father was believed to be Horus/Apollo, the god of music, healing, and the arts. These associations may help to explain some of the profound wisdom that Orpheus transferred to human culture about the nature of music, the inner realms, and healing. While some scholars suppose that Orpheus was really the son of the Thracian King Oeagrus, history reports that Orpheus met Apollo at King Oeagrus's palace. There Apollo gave him a golden lyre and taught him to play, while his mother, Calliope, instructed him in musical verse. Together they trained Orpheus in what would become his divinely inspired gifts.

As a young man Orpheus traveled widely and studied for many years in Egypt. He returned to Greece as both a seer and a magician, bringing back the knowledge of medicine, writing, agriculture, and astrology, which he then imparted to the Greeks. He set up the Orphic Mystery Schools as well as centers dedicated to Apollo and Dionysus, the Greek names for the Egyptian gods Horus and Osiris. Orpheus also brought the worship of Demeter Chthonia to Greece. Demeter is the Greek name for Isis, and Persephone (or Artemis) was the savior maiden Kores Soteiras. Thus Demeter, the goddess of grain, was the wife of Dionysus, the god of wine. This is the Egyptian Isis and Osiris, who were the parents of the Egyptian Horus or Greek Apollo. Isis, Osiris, and Horus were three teachers of incomparable wisdom who helped Thoth, the Egyptian god of wisdom, establish chapters of the Mystery Schools across the world. As we now know, Persephone came to represent the innocence of the Soul itself that has descended into the world of form.

Much like the Christian sacrament of Communion, Orphic rites taught a sacrament of wine and bread too, but the real intoxication that initiates sought was union with the Divine. Like indigenous shamanic practices the world over, Orphic mystics believed that they could acquire knowledge of the inner worlds by developing altered states of consciousness. They did this through meditation and out-of-body travel. Orphism taught that the Soul and the body were separate and that reincarnation is the means by which the Soul evolves. The Orphics also taught specific spiritual practices to ensure a blessed Afterlife. These teachings described the landscapes of the heavenly realms as places filled with celestial gardens, luminous groves, and flowing streams of water. Orphic wisdom taught that deep within each human being there resides a godly particle, much like the way a body is encased within a tomb at death. The Mysteries sought to release this God particle through mystical rites and righteous living. Gold-leaf tablets found in the tombs of fourth-century BCE Orphic followers give instructions for how the Soul could find its way through the Underworld after death. Here are just a few of the instructions the initiate was supposed to recite before Persephone, Queen of the Underworld:

"I also avow me that I am of your blessed race. . . . I have flown out of the sorrowful weary Wheel. I have passed with eager feet to the Circle desired." They hoped the goddess would respond, saying, "Happy and Blessed One, thou shalt be God, instead of mortal."[8] Another such tablet states: "Hail Thou, who suffereth the suffering . . . thou art become God from man."[9] From such statements it is clear that one of the goals of the Mysteries was to help the Soul attain a godlike level of consciousness throughout eternity.

The Story of Orpheus

The most famous story about Orpheus concerns the day that he was to be married. Eurydice, his beloved, was walking along the riverbank and was set upon by a satyr. In her effort to escape she fell into a nest of vipers and suffered a fatal bite on her heel. When Orpheus discovered her limp body he was so overcome with grief, that he played such a mournful dirge that even the gods wept. Grief-stricken, he decided that he would enter Hades to get her back. The only problem was that this was Acheron, the Land of the Dead. A Bulgarian tradition says that Orpheus entered the Underworld via a cave called the Devil's Throat (Dyavolsko Gurlo), which was close to Trigrad, in the Rhodope mountains of southern Bulgaria.

When at last he stood before Hades, king of the Underworld, Orpheus begged for Eurydice's release. Then he played his lyre. His music was so beautiful that it was said that Hades wept, granting his beloved safe passage out of Acheron on one condition: Orpheus was not to look at her face until they reached the upper world. Together the two set off, walking single file through the darkened caverns of

*Figure 2.1. Orpheus the musician and his beloved Eurydice
(illustration by Tricia McCannon)*

the Underworld. But as the hours wore on, Eurydice began to plead with him to turn and look at her. Finally, just as Orpheus reached the upper world and emerged from the cave, he turned to see her face. But Eurydice had not yet emerged from the cave. The spell was broken, and Eurydice was forced to return to the Land of the Dead, now completely beyond Orpheus's powers to save her.

Orphic Teachings

Orphic wisdom teaches that all Souls are immortal, and that human beings are made of the substances of both Heaven and Earth. Since there is an eternal spark within us all, it is our nature to aspire to freedom. Yet humankind is held in fetters by the passions of this world until we can liberate ourselves from their hold on us. When we die, our contract with this world ends, freeing us to ascend once more into the celestial realms. However, in each new life we enter into a new contract, and thus we are imprisoned on the Cosmic Wheel once again until we can spiritually awaken.

This concept of an ever-rotating wheel is familiar to both Eastern and Western theological traditions. This is the wheel of life, death, and rebirth, or the Wheel of Awagawan, the road that all beings must travel on their way to enlightenment. At one moment we are on top of the world—full of money, fame, beauty, and success. The next moment we are at the bottom—poor, struggling, and unknown. In the Vedic tradition that was adopted by the Buddhist teachings this is called *samsara,* the Wheel of Becoming, referring to the endless cycle of birth, death, and rebirth. *Becoming what?* you might ask. Becoming one with the Divine. This is why the Orphics taught that if you had lived a pure life, you could attain salvation. Purity was achieved through wholesomeness of intention, thought, and action, which in the Orphic system included being a vegetarian and only eating meat on special occasions so as to avoid causing suffering to animals.

The Orphics also embraced reincarnation, which was called *transmigration* or *metempsychosis* in the ancient world. They believed that the purpose of each lifetime was to learn compassion, patience, humility, wisdom, and love, and to build on this greater knowledge until we reached mastery. The late-nineteenth-century German philosopher and theologian Eduard Zeller, celebrated for his writings on ancient Greek philosophy, writes about these beliefs:

> The doctrine of metempsychosis seems really to have passed from the theology of the mysteries into philosophy . . . in the Orphic theology . . . transmigration is clearly to be found. . . . We have every reason to believe that it was taught in the Orphic mysteries prior to the date of Pythagoras. According to Herodotus, the Orphics obtained . . . [this doctrine] from Egypt. But it is also conceivable that this belief . . . may have originally emigrated from the East with the Greeks themselves, and had been at first confined to a narrow circle, becoming afterwards more important and more widely diffused.[10]

Manly P. Hall also speaks about the universal logic of this ancient belief:

> The doctrine of reincarnation declares that we can neither suffer from the sins of another nor be bound by any shackles other than those of our own forging. All the powers we possess today are the sum of past achievements; likewise the miseries from which we suffer are the fruitage of our own past abuses . . . Reincarnation explains that slow but inevitable process by which both sage and savior have lifted themselves above the mediocrity of the masses and thus demonstrated the presence of the potential God in every creature.
>
> The Creator, furthermore, is discovered to be an *evolving* rather than a creating Deity, the inconceivable interval of cosmic space between God and the atom being filled with innumerable orders of unfolding lives. Reincarnation places man upon his own merits and measures, his future status by his daily work. It is not a doctrine of excuses, evasions or vague references to the disposition of an outrageous Providence. Man thus becomes, in truth, the master of his destiny and the captain of his soul.[11]

The Eleusinian Mysteries

While the Orphic Mysteries were the first Mysteries to be taught in ancient Greece, the Eleusinian Mysteries are probably the most famous. They were seeded by the priestesses of Isis around 700 BCE and went on to inspire philosophers, statesmen, and thinkers around the world. These beliefs would later influence Jewish and Christian theologies and the intellects of countless men and women, and became the bedrock of the teachings of Pythagoras, Socrates, and Plato.[12] The center of the Eleusinian Mysteries lay only a few miles west of Athens, and their greatest rites took place inside of caves. Doing ceremonies in caves, or living in a cave, is one way to connect with sacred energies of the Earth, and this practice can be found in many religious traditions including the Essenes, Buddhists, Hindus, Druids, Jews, Christians, Maya, Native Americans, and the Inca.

Like the Orphics, the Eleusinian Mysteries taught that humans are spiritual beings whose true home lies in Heaven, which is free from the bondage of our limiting earthly concepts. On Earth the Soul is trapped in a false and impermanent body that is like a tomb, and this is the source of our greatest suffering. Manly P. Hall writes, "To the Eleusinian philosophers, birth into the physical world was death in the fullest sense of the word, and the only true birth was that of the spiritual soul of man rising out of the womb of his own fleshly nature."[13] In his poem "A Psalm of Life," the nineteenth-century American poet Henry Wadsworth Longfellow writes, "The soul is dead that slumbers," speaking of how unawake most of us are during the course of our physical lives on Earth.

Eleusinian teachers also taught that all things are connected in the cosmos, and that by following the laws of nature we can stay in balance. Epicurus noted, "Insofar as you forget nature, you will find yourself in trouble and create for yourself endless fears and desires."[14] They knew that the entire universe is an expression of the One Divine Mind, of which our Souls are a part.

Always think of the cosmos as one living being,
having one substance and one Soul,

and how all things trace back to a single sentience,
and how it does all things with a single intention,
and how all things are the causes of all that exists,
and how intertwined is the fabric
and how closely woven the web.[15]

Like the other branches of the Greek Mystery Schools, the Eleusinians had the Lesser and Greater Mysteries. The Lesser Mysteries taught the precepts of morality and law and helped initiates focus on making the best use of their time on Earth. This first level also revealed the horrors that would await the candidate on the Otherside if they lived a life of violence, hate, and selfishness. This refers to the lower levels of the astral plane, a topic we will address in greater depth in part 2 of this book. The pitfalls of Hades were vividly depicted in a series of complicated subterranean mazes fraught with dangers that initiates had to pass through. If successful, they were awarded the title *Mystes,* or "one who sees through a clouded veil." This veil had to be torn away when initiates passed through the higher degrees.[16] This is the source of the word *mystic,* meaning "one who is able to pull aside the veil of illusion" and follow one's heart to the Source, which is unseen in the physical world.

In the Eleusinian Mysteries, the Greater Mysteries were dedicated to Demeter, the Great Mother, who was often depicted carrying two torches, one of reason and one of intuition. Demeter's name, *De-meter,* can easily be decoded as "the measure of all things," just as Isis, *Is-is,* is the I AM principle of life itself. These names immediately mark these sacred rites as cosmological in nature. Persephone, daughter of the Great Mother, Demeter, is the human Soul who must constantly travel back and forth between the realms of Heaven and Earth in order to discover her true identity, until she finally frees herself of the seeds of karma she has sown in the worlds below.

The Eleusinian Mysteries also stressed the importance of not committing suicide, warning that a great sorrow comes to those who do.[17] This is because when we take our own life we break the many Soul contracts that we have made with other people at the start of each new incarnation. This brings grief and chaos to everyone, leaving a void in the lives of those left behind. Then the Soul, once freed from the body, is steeped in regret, for it quickly realizes what it has done. It also realizes that it must return to Earth and retake its lessons, but now under a heavier karmic burden than before. Great effort is put into the choice of each of our lifetimes by the Lords of Karma, who excel in helping with our life plans. If the Soul had persevered instead, who knows what it might have accomplished or learned? The one exception to this rule against suicide applies to those who are elderly, in great pain, or terminally ill. In the case of Souls who have basically completed their missions here, grace is given, even in the case of suicide.

A Global Legacy

Those who graduated from these Greek Mystery Schools reads like a Who's Who of ancient philosophers, thinkers, and scientists. The list includes Pythagoras, Socrates, Plato, Aristotle, Pindar, Herodotus, Heraclitus, Zeno, Anaxagoras, Democritus, Plotinus, Porphyry, Iamblichus, Hypatia, and many others—each representing a milestone in Western thought. Greek archaeologist George E. Mylonas (1898–1988) writes of the profundity of the teachings of these great schools:

> When we read . . . statements written by the great, or nearly great, of the ancient world . . . we cannot help but believe that the Mysteries of Eleusis were not an empty, childish affair devised by shrewd priests to fool the peasant and ignorant, but a philosophy of life that possessed substance and meaning and imparted a modicum of truth to the yearning human soul. That belief is strengthened when we read in Cicero that Athens has given nothing to the world more excellent or divine than the Eleusinian Mysteries.[18]

So now let us take a deeper look at the wisdom of Pythagoras, Socrates, and Plato and see what they have to say about the eternal nature of the Soul and the realms of the Afterlife.

3

Reincarnation and the Circle of Life

I am confident that there truly is such a thing as living again, that the living spring from the dead, and that the souls of the dead are in existence.

SOCRATES

*P*ythagoras (507–582 BCE) was perhaps the most brilliant of the Greek philosophers, a student of many ancient streams of knowledge, including the Orphic and Eleusinian Mystery Schools. He also studied with the sages of Phoenicia, Judea, Chaldea, Egypt, Persia, and India.[1] His birth was prophesied by the Oracle at Delphi, who foretold that he would surpass all other men in beauty and wisdom and bring great good into the world.[2] Because of this, his father was instructed to have no sexual intimacy with his wife in the year before his birth, so many believed that Pythagoras was an immaculate conception or the son of a god. Thus Pythagoras, like Jesus, was known as a "Son of God."[3]

After graduating from the Eleusinian Mystery School, he traveled to Egypt, where he spent years in the Mystery Schools of Isis in Thebes. Pythagoras also studied under learned rabbis who were familiar with the secret traditions that Moses brought out of Egypt some eight hundred years earlier, and was initiated in both the Babylonian and Chaldean Mysteries.[4] Some say that while he was in Persia he trained with a master who was in the direct lineage of Zoroaster. Then he traveled to Syria and Phoenicia, where the Mysteries of Adonis were conferred on him. One of his most famous voyages was to the learned Brahmans of Elephanta and Ellora, in India, where he studied for some years. There he was called *Yavancharya,* "the Ionian Teacher," by the Brahmans.[5] There are also reports of Pythagoras training with the Druids in Britain, where he studied with Abaris, an emissary from Hyperborea, the "land beyond the North Wind." Abaris had been led to choose Pythagoras as a student by a magical golden arrow, which he later gave to his student. Abaris was an extraordinary master known as a "skywalker," a term that means he had attained the ability to fly.[6]

Figure 3.1. The master Pythagoras (illustration by Tricia McCannon)

Some say that Pythagoras's powers were shamanic, and there is intriguing evidence that he may have acquired some of his abilities from the shamans that the Greeks had encountered when they opened up trade routes to the Black Sea region in the seventh century BCE, routes that were laid down only a century or so before Pythagoras was born. Iamblichus the Neoplatonist (250–325 CE) writes that Pythagoras had the power to predict earthquakes, stop hurricanes, calm seas, and even bilocate.[7] He was considered not only a man of God, but a godlike man by many of his students, who called him "the Master" or "that Man."

Pythagoras was the first to use the term *philosopher,* derived from the words *philo* and *sophia,* "a lover of wisdom" (Sophia being the goddess of wisdom). Pythagoras believed that the true purpose of philosophy was to free the Soul from its perpetual identification with the body and the things of this world, and to awaken the consciousness of the Soul that lives within. He also believed that there is a supreme intelligence behind all things, and that the motion of God is circular,* the body of God is light,† and the nature of God is truth.[8] He believed that it is the nature of all living creatures, human, animal, and plant, to move toward this light. This is because we ourselves are made of light, and thus we are drawn to its power to help us remember the radiance of our Soul.

Pythagoras, like Orpheus, taught that the Soul is immortal and that it inhabits the body only while we are alive. It originates in the heavenly realms and returns there after death to evaluate what it has accomplished after each life is finished. This life-review process is also in accord with what modern near-death experiencers report—that shortly after passing to the Otherside they undergo a holographic life review of their former existence.

---

*The nature of God is circular, from the movement of the solar systems and galaxies to the movement of atoms. We can see this pattern in everything from tornadoes and hurricanes to the movement of the wind and water.

†Over and over again, near-death experiencers describe themselves and others as luminous beings of light.

Pythagoras and the Celestial Harmonies of the Spheres

Pythagoras finally opened his own university around the age of fifty-three, on the Isle of Crotona, a Dorian colony in southern Italy. Deeply democratic in his philosophy, he accepted people of all races into his school, both men and women. If accepted, a student then entered a five-year period of silence designed to develop the qualities of listening, humility, and a contemplative mind. Such silence also taught the student to tune in to the subtle ethereal Music of the Spheres and to learn the basics of Pythagoras's philosophy before presuming to contribute to it.[9]

Pythagoras was the first teacher to expound upon the principles of celestial harmonics known as the Music of the Spheres. These are the underlying harmonics of the universe that are largely inaudible to our outer senses. In other mystical traditions this is called the *audible life stream,* the *sound current,* the *bani,* the *vani,* and *the Word.* This celestial music has been taught by the Essenes, the Sufis, the Egyptians, the Tibetans, the Hindus, and certain sects of Christianity. However, it is largely unknown to most people because it is not taught in the exoteric churches or temples.

The Bardo Thodol is one source in which we find references to this celestial sound current. The Tibetan term *bar do thos grol* translates as "liberation through hearing in the intermediate state," clearly a reference to the Soul's ability to tune in to this celestial current immediately following death and thereby transcend rebirth.[10] Such celestial music can sometimes be heard when one is very still, as in meditation, or when one is drifting off to sleep. As we will discover later in this book, many near-death experiencers report hearing these celestial melodies when entering the dimensions of Heaven.

These sounds are connected to string theory as proposed by modern physics, which says that within the atom itself are subatomic particles that are constantly vibrating. These various parts are named *quarks, neutrinos, leptons,* and so forth, and since there are so many of them, scientists now believe that they are actually vibrating strings that create a symphony of celestial sounds, all oscillating at different frequencies. This is the "background noise" of the universe that brings matter into being. Pythagoras's sought to decode these universal patterns through music, mathematics, and sacred geometry, explaining that the laws that govern the manifestation of matter are a result of these frequencies.

As we can see, Pythagoras was ahead of his time. Much of this knowledge, which was taught secretly in the Mystery Schools of Egypt and Persia, has only now begun to resurface in our era. If taken to its natural conclusion it has the potential to help us decode the matrix upon which the universe is built. Pythagoras also taught the Golden Mean spiral on which all of creation is built, and his knowledge about music, mathematics, and sacred geometry is the basis of these disciplines today.

Euclidian geometry is also attributed to Pythagoras, for Euclid was one of his students. In addition, Pythagoras is credited with the discovery that concordant musical pitches can be expressed in simple numerical ratios. For example, a string half as long will sound an octave higher, while strings in the ratio of 2:3 sound at the interval of a fifth. This was

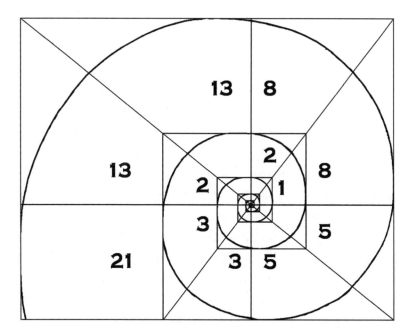

Figure 3.2. The Golden Mean Spiral

a key discovery in the history of science, for it shows how complex and logical the universe is when it is understood mathematically.[11] Today Pythagoras's teachings are the foundation of modern physics.

Pythagoras believed that numbers have a spiritual dimension. This spiritual numbering system also applies in the Kabbalah, the mystical path of Hebrew teachings. This higher knowledge of numbers was encoded in the Kabbalistic study of numerology, the Gematria, as well as in the construction of sacred mandalas in the East. Its importance was known to many initiates across the world, and in modern times these concepts were explored by psychologists like Carl Jung. The connection between numbers, sounds, and the formation of the universe is just returning to popular thought today. I believe that the power of numbers expresses certain fundamental principles of consciousness that are interwoven in the universe. Each of the nine primary numbers relates to overlighting beings whose waveform energies help to maintain and sustain the cosmos. As we shall see, this critical understanding of numbers applies to many things, from the seven chakras and seven dimensional planes, to the creation of the nine angelic hierarchies.

The Great Chain of Being

Pythagoras believed that the Soul travels into the physical world to experience many aspects of creation, including existence in the mineral, plant, and animal kingdoms. This is part of the Great Chain of Being (discussed in detail in chapter 10) that culminates in our ascension to the angelic kingdoms. He believed that once a Soul achieves the rank of human being, it no longer needs to be reborn as an animal, although it is clear that there are many human beings in the world who are far crueler than any animals I can name.

This philosophy of an upwardly moving spiritual evolution is universally embraced by millions across the world. Herodotus writes that the Egyptians were the first to assert that when the body perishes, the Soul enters another form, passing through many different kinds of beings on its journey to enlightenment. In the early stages of our incarnational cycles we may choose to have a life as a marine animal or an aerial creature; then we progress to a terrestrial animal, until we eventually become fully human. However, even human evolution is just a step toward reclaiming our godlike nature. Empedocles (490–430 BCE), a pre-Socratic Greek philosopher, wrote: "I was once already boy and girl, thicket and bird, and mute fish in the waves. All things doth Nature change, enwrapping souls in unfamiliar tunics of the flesh. The worthiest dwellings for the souls of men."[12]

The Story of Cerridwen and Gwion

The transmutation from one form to another is portrayed in the charming Welsh tale of Cerridwen and Gwion. Our tale begins with the Mother Goddess Cerridwen, who had an ugly son. Dismayed at what appeared to be his luckless future, she decides to make a magic elixir that will grant her son wisdom. She hires a young innocent, a lad named Gwion, to stir this brew, and he is told that he must stir it for a year and a day. Yet days before the brew is ready, three drops of elixir spill onto Gwion's hands. Without thinking, Gwion licks his fingers, and the perfect wisdom of the magical elixir flows into his mind. Immediately, Gwion becomes conscious. When he does, he realizes that Cerridwen will know what has happened to the brew and she will be furious. So Gwion flees.

Just as Gwion had expected, when Cerridwen discovers that he has received the potency meant for her son, she becomes enraged. The tale then goes on to tell us how Cerridwen, in various disguises, chases Gwion throughout the many kingdoms of the world. First Gwion turns himself into a fish, but Cerridwen pursues him by becoming an otter. Then he transforms himself into a rabbit, but she becomes a greyhound. Next Gwion becomes a bird, but Cerridwen becomes a hawk, flying ever more swiftly than he can. Finally Gwion turns himself into a piece of corn, thinking that Cerridwen won't notice him. But the goddess transforms herself into a hen and gobbles him up. Then, to her surprise, Cerridwen becomes pregnant with a child who is, of course, Gwion reborn. In this tale, the Mother Goddess then gives birth to the famous bard Taliesin, who becomes the Celtic teacher of Merlin the Magician. Taliesin, who is really the enlightened Gwion, becomes the most famous of all of the Druid bards, known even today for his wit and wisdom.

This intriguing tale is an encoded story about the Soul's evolution through time. It is a parable of the long journey we each make through the realms of form, taking first one disguise and then another.

The evolutionary journey of the Soul may explain why many of us have natural affinities for certain animals—birds, cats, wolves, eagles, ravens, dragonflies, dolphins, whales, hummingbirds, or bees. Earlier in our reincarnation cycle we may have actually been these animals, and thus we naturally gravitate toward them, even now when we are in human form. This can also explain our affinities for certain trees or plants or gemstones, even in this lifetime—perhaps millions of years ago we experienced some aspect of their consciousness when we were passing in and out of these forms.

Empedocles explains: "The cycle of birth through plant and animal form is meant to culminate in the world of men. The most advanced souls are reborn as prophets, minstrels, physicians, and leaders, and from these arise as gods, highest in honor."[13] While those of us raised in more restrictive theologies may find the idea that we were anything other than human in previous lifetimes to be a fanciful stretch of the imagination, modern embryologists have now discovered that every human child formed in the womb morphs through various animal archetypes before ever becoming human.[14] Is this merely a reflection of earlier stages of biological evolution, or could it also reflect the spiritual evolution of our Soul's journey?

The Many Inside the One

Today we are taught that human beings are the pinnacle of God's creation. We are also told that animals only exist to serve our needs, and thus we often treat them deplorably. We have been assured by patriarchal institutions that animals have neither feelings nor Souls, but this is not true. Everything in the universe has consciousness.

This is the first of the seven Hermetic Laws of wisdom written by Thoth, the Egyptian god of wisdom. Everything in the universe is part of the One Great Soul and thus it is alive. Paracelsus, the great Renaissance physician and philosopher writes, "There is nothing dead in Nature. Everything is organic and living, and therefore the whole world appears to be a living organism."[15] Who can doubt that plants have feelings when researchers have now done studies proving that they respond in positive ways to harmonious music and the people who lovingly take care of them, and react in strongly negative ways to people in their environment who have been violent? And what pet owner can ever doubt that animals have both feelings and thoughts? Anyone who has ever had a beloved cat or dog, bird or horse, knows that they form friendships, loyalties, and emotional bonds with those who care for them and with each other. In fact, it is the power of love itself that awakens every creature to a higher octave of vibration, quickening our spiritual evolution.

Madame Blavatsky, founder of Theosophy, speaks of this in her epic *The Secret Doctrine:*

> Everything in the Universe, throughout all its kingdoms, is conscious: i.e., endowed with a consciousness of its own kind and on its own plane of perception. We men must remember that because we do not perceive any signs—which we can recognize—of consciousness, say, in stones, we have no right to say that no consciousness exists there. . . . Nature taken in its abstract sense, cannot be 'unconscious,' as it is the emanation from, and thus an aspect (on the manifested plane) of the Absolute consciousness. Where is that daring man who would presume to deny to vegetation and even to minerals *a consciousness of their own.* All he can say is, that this consciousness is beyond his comprehension.[16]

The Greeks agreed with her. Here is a maxim from the Greek Mystery Schools: "Consciousness sleeps in the stones, dreams in the plants, awakens in the animals, and becomes self-conscious in Man. It attains Cosmic Consciousness in the Spiritual Kingdom, and

Omniscience in the Kingdom of the Gods."[17] Pythagoras believed that every species has a seal given to it by God, and that the physical form of each species is the impression of this seal on the wax of physical substance. Thus every individual body is stamped with the dignity of its divinely given pattern. He said, "There is one cosmos made up of everything, and one God immanent in everything, and one substance and one law, and one Logos common to all intelligent beings, and one truth."[18] Pythagoras believed that ultimately the human being will reach a state where she can cast off her gross physical nature and function in a body of spiritualized ether.[19] This is the light body, known to ancient adepts as the *Nuri Sarup*,* the sparkling astral body that many near-death experiencers discover when they emerge on the Otherside. Not only do they discover that they are radiant with living light, they also find that the appearance of this body can be altered at will according to the wishes of the individual. This is why people who return from the Otherside often speak about meeting loved ones who now look young and beautiful. This light body is only one of our seven subtle-energy bodies, although it is the one that we will graduate to when we leave this Earth. Pythagoras believed that once we pass through this human stage of evolution, we will ascend to the realm of the immortals where we ultimately belong. This is the loka, or dimension, of the gods.

Remembering His Past Lives

Pythagoras claimed that he remembered many of his own past lives, just as Buddha claimed that he remembered some six hundred of his.[20] Thus one of his titles was *Mnesarchides,* meaning "one who remembers his own origins."[21] In one past life he had been a Trojan warrior called Euphorbus, the son of Panthus, who perished by the hand of King Menelaus during the ten-year siege of Troy. In another lifetime he was Hermontimus, a prophet from the city of Ionia. In still another lifetime he was a humble fisherman. Then there was his life as Aethalides, the

---

*The Sanskrit word *Nuri* means "light" and *Sarup* means "body."

son of Mercury, the god of wisdom.* In that life Pythagoras received the gift of remembrance from the god of wisdom himself, giving him access to the memories of all of his past lives—a powerful gift indeed!

Pythagoras also remembered what he had experienced in the celestial realms between physical lifetimes.[22] This explains why the Oracle of Delphi had foretold the importance of his birth. The life and teachings of Pythagoras laid the groundwork for the wisdom teachings of Socrates and Plato, both of whom believed, as he did, in the eternal nature of the Soul. This great spiritual master understood not only the structure and function of the various subtle-energy bodies, but also the infrastructure behind the visible and invisible realms. He taught the connection between music, poetry, mathematics, sacred geometry, physics, nature, and the entire structure of the cosmos. To this day, some 2,500 years later, his knowledge has not been surpassed.

As a clairvoyant, I know that most of us have had scores of lives here on Earth, and this planet is only one of many possible worlds in the physical universe, let alone the other dimensional realms. While the ancient teachings believed that the greater life cycle of most human beings consists of about eight hundred physical lifetimes, during that time the human spirit, having passed through hundreds of different races and forms, has extracted from such environments that which it requires in the form of instruction and experience. Hall noted, "Having completed this cycle the Soul then either rests in a superior state until a more advanced chain of worlds is prepared for its future growth, or returns again to this inferior world to serve as an instructor to a less developed humanity."[23] As a trained past-life regressionist in the field of hypnotherapy for over twenty years, I know the power of experiencing one's own personal history firsthand. It can be life-changing. This is part of the reason why I continue to do readings and healings for people all over the world. The power of understanding our Soul's larger journey can be of enormous value in helping us call back our higher awareness, for it explains aspects of who we are at the most fundamental level that would otherwise not be understood.

---

*The Greek god Mercury is also the Egyptian god Thoth, known in Greece as Hermes Trismegistus, or Thrice Great Hermes.

The Wisdom of Socrates

The wisdom of Socrates and Plato lies at the heart of the Greek Mysteries. Their philosophies were central to Hellenistic thought for almost five centuries and were the cornerstone of the Neoplatonic movement in the first four or five centuries following Jesus.

Like Pythagoras, Socrates (469–399 BCE) studied for many years in Egypt, and when he returned to Greece he established his own academy in Athens that used the Socratic method as the primary means of teaching. This method posed questions to his students about the nature of reality; it was designed to not only develop logical thought, but also to awaken memories hidden in the Souls of his students. Later, Socrates's student Plato would employ this same technique in his writing style, using dialogues between a student and teacher to pose questions about the nature of reality. Understandably, Socrates, and then Plato, were greatly influenced by Pythagoras, and while we have no books today that are directly attributed to Socrates, there are some 250 manuscripts written by Plato. In several of these, Socrates teaches in the first person, giving us ample opportunity to discover what he taught through

Figure 3.3. The great philosopher Socrates (illustration by Tricia McCannon)

Plato's writings. The books that include Socrates' discourses include *The Republic, The Timaeus, Phaedo, Lysis,* and *Charmides.*

Socrates believed that the universe is divinely created, and that all creations share the concept of an immortal Soul.[24] He believed that the Soul is innately endowed with all knowledge because in the heavenly realms the truth is never hidden. He held that when the Soul enters the body its memories become veiled by amnesia; however, through open discourse and reflection it is possible to recover this "forgotten" knowledge. Thus the Socratic method was used to stimulate memory through inductive inquiry.[25] According to Plato, Socrates taught that "the soul, then, as being immortal, and having been born again many times, and having seen all things that exist, whether in this world or in the world below, has knowledge of them all; and it is no wonder that she should be able to call to remembrance all that she ever knew about virtue, and about everything . . . for all enquiry and all learning is but recollection."[26]

Notice that Socrates refers to the Soul as feminine, a belief that existed for centuries before the takeover by the patriarchy. Socrates goes on to remind us that "if the truth of all things always existed in the soul, then the soul is immortal. Wherefore be of good cheer, and try to recollect what you do not know, or rather what you do not remember."[27]

The Transmigration of the Soul

At the center of Platonic thought is the concept of reincarnation and the principle of karma, the spiritual law of cause and effect. Jesus taught this same principle in the statement "Whatever a man sows, this he will also reap" (Galatians 6:7). This means that what we do in this lifetime will have consequences in the Afterlife and also in our next lifetime. This universal law allows each Soul to learn from our mistakes by personally experiencing the very things that we have said and done to one another.

Knowledge of both karma and reincarnation as the mechanisms for Soul evolution is ancient. These two concepts were central to the Egyptians, Celts, Saxons, Sumerians, Persians, Greeks, Romans, Druids,

Norse, Finnish, Danish, Prussian, Teutonic, Laplander, and Lithuanian peoples. A hundred years after Jesus, the Roman philosopher Marcus Cicero (106–43 BCE) wrote: "The ancients, whether they were seers, or interpreters of the divine mind in the tradition of sacred initiations, seem to have known the truth when they affirmed that we were born into the body to pay the penalty for sins committed in a former life."[28]

Belief in reincarnation has been found among Scythians, Africans, and Pacific Islanders, as well as tribes in North, South, and Central America.[29] It lies at the heart of Hindu, Buddhist, Shinto, and Moslem religions, and was part of the original teachings of Jesus (a subject discussed at length in my last two books). Unitarian minister Reverend W. R. Alger tells us that "no other doctrine has exerted so extensive, controlling, and permanent an influence upon mankind as that of the *metempsychosis,* the notion that when the soul leaves the body it is born anew in another body; its rank, character, circumstances and experience in each successive existence depending on its qualities, deeds, and attainments in its preceding lives."[30]

Statistics show that those who have embraced the belief in reincarnation are usually well-educated, traveled, and affluent professionals.[31] "The thread of firm belief in rebirth has woven its long web, unbroken, from the dawn of time to the pragmatic present. It has circled the earth again and again, touched nation after nation, leaving not one. Consider also that it has never been upheld by the bigoted nor by agencies of persecution, but invariably by the educated, the open-minded, the wise, the good and the mystical."[32]

American philosopher Ralph Waldo Emerson writes: "It is the secret of the world that all things subsist and do not die, but only retire a little from sight and afterwards return again. Nothing is dead; men feign themselves dead, and endure mock funerals . . . and there they stand, looking out of the window, sound and well, in some strange new disguise."[33] The great Russian writer Leo Tolstoy says, "As we live through thousands of dreams in our present life, so is our present life only one of many thousands of such lives which we enter from the other more real life, and then return after death. Our life is but one of the dreams of that more real life, and so it is endlessly, until the very last one, the very real, the life of God."[34]

Benjamin Franklin remarks, "When I see nothing annihilated, not even a drop of water wasted, I cannot suspect the annihilation of souls. . . . Thus finding myself to exist in the world, I believe I shall, in some shape or other, always exist; with all the inconveniences human life is liable to, I shall not object to a new edition of mine; hoping, however, that the errata of the last may be corrected."[35] And finally, American novelist and poet Louisa May Alcott writes: "I think immortality is the passing of the soul through many lives or experiences, and such as are truly lived, used, and learned, help us go on to the next, each growing richer, happier and higher, carrying with it only the real memories of what has gone before."[36]

In the Hebrew faith, reincarnation was embraced by both the Pharisees and Essenes, two of the three sects of Judaism at the time of Jesus; however, the doctrine was edited out of the New Testament by Catholic *correctores,* scribes appointed to censor entire sections of the gospels for the Church's own political and financial purposes.[37] Yet references to reincarnation can still be found when one looks closely. For example, when the Apostles ask Jesus about the identity of John the Baptist, they say, "Is he Elijah come again?" Jesus answers by saying, "I say to you that Elijah has also come, and they did to him whatever they wished, as it is written of him" (Mark 9:13). Here Jesus is telling us that John is Elijah returned.*

Flavius Josephus (37–100 CE), a Hebrew historian who chronicled the history of the Jews fifty years after Jesus, writes: "Do ye not remember that all pure Spirits when they depart out of this life . . . obtain a most holy place in heaven, from whence, in the revolutions of ages, they are again sent into pure bodies?"[38] The Zohar, one of

---

*One of the greatest errors the Church ever made was to remove the concept of reincarnation from the Bible. This principle was originally part of the foundational teachings of Jesus, along with the law of karma, but was suppressed by the Fifth Ecumenical Council in 558 CE, almost six centuries after Christ. Though this gathering was later declared illegal, the damage was done. In my previous two books, *Return of the Divine Sophia* and *Jesus: The Explosive Story of the 30 Lost Years and the Ancient Mystery Religions,* I explain in depth why this doctrine was erased by political factions within the Church, and the devastating impact it has made on our understanding of the universal laws of life.

the holiest of Hebrew teachings and the foundational work of the Kabbalah, reminds us:

> All souls are subject to the trials of transmigration; and men do not know the designs of the Most High with regard to them; they know not how they are being at all times judged, both before coming into this world and when they leave it. They do not know how many transmigrations and mysterious trials they must undergo.
>
> Souls must reenter the absolute substance whence they have emerged. But to accomplish this end they must develop all the perfections, the germ of which is planted in them; and if they have not fulfilled this condition during one life, they must commence another, a third, and so forth, until they have acquired the condition which fits them for reunion with God.[39]

As a clairvoyant who has read for people all over the world, I know that all of us have lived before. Each Soul has a unique energy signature that is different from every other being. When I do readings I am able to trace this energy signature up into the higher worlds and open up my client's Akashic Records to discover the deeper history of her Soul. Each one of us has a spiritual past with many complex layers. This includes lifetimes spent in other dimensions and on other worlds, many times in bodies that are similar, if not identical, to our human one. We also have energetic alliances with animal groups, religions, philosophies, and tribal groups, along with occupational preferences that can be reflected in our current lifetime. In addition, some Souls have spiritual alliances with certain masters, angelic groups, or gods or goddesses based on their past-life history. These alliances are wellsprings to help us on our path to enlightenment, and when we are ready, these beings can assist us in our spiritual evolution. Having traced the records of many thousands of people to discover how their past-life history is linked to their present life, I know well how the seeds of karma can flower into the blessings, challenges, and circumstances of the present.

The Legacy of Plato and the
Neoplatonic Movement

The golden age of Greek philosophy lasted for over nine hundred years, beginning around 600 BCE and continuing well into the fifth century CE through the Neoplatonic period. Before Socrates, this age of spiritual inquiry and discovery was brilliantly expressed through philosophers like Xenophanes (570–475 BCE), Heraclitus (535–475 BCE), Anaxagoras (510–428 BCE), and Hippocrates (460–370 BCE). There was also the philosophy of Pindar (522–483 BCE), the paradoxes of Zeno (490–430 BCE), and nine volumes of history written by Herodotus (485–425 BCE), a virtual travelogue of the customs and beliefs of many lands. There was also Parmenides (late sixth or early fifth century BCE), who asserted that Earth was round; Archytas (428–347 BCE), a contemporary of Plato who invented the screw and crane; and Democritus (460–370 BCE), who discovered the atom almost five hundred years before the birth of Christ.[40] This laid the groundwork for Plato's Academy, which endured for nearly four hundred years in Greece, coming to an end in 83 BCE. Plato's philosophy continued to thrive in the Roman era, melding Christian thought with the birth of Neoplatonism around 193 CE, and then lasting for another three hundred glorious years into the Christian era.

Neoplatonism was a movement that sought to reconcile all religions and philosophies under one great system of truth, to "restore to its purity the wisdom of the ancients."[41] This, they believed, was the true objective of Jesus, the master teacher. Thus Neoplatonists were known as *Philalethians,* or "lovers of truth," for their doctrine wove together both Christian and Platonic philosophies in a powerful synthesis of wisdom that incorporated science, logic, mysticism, and metaphysics. Neoplatonists taught alongside many Church Fathers as well as rabbis and Mystery School teachers.[42] Bertrand Russell (1872–1970), the famous British mathematician and philosopher, writes of these great men and women: "The greatest men, who have been philosophers, have felt the need both of science and mysticism. The attempt to harmonize the two was what made their life."[43] Platonic thought inspired many great minds because it focused on the liberating power of truth. Plotinus (205–270 CE), one of the most renowned of the Neoplatonists, has this to say about the Soul's journey while here on Earth:

> The soul, still a dragged captive, will tell of all that man did and felt; but upon death there will appear, as time passes, memories of the lives lived before, some of the events of the most recent life being dismissed as trivial. As it grows away from the body, it will revive things forgotten in the corporeal state. And if it passes in and out of one body after another, it will tell over the events of the discarded life. It will treat as present that which it has just left, and it will remember much from the former existence.[44]

Unfortunately, this enlightened age was brought to its knees by the rise of the Roman Catholic Church in the third century after Christ. In the strong-arm shadow of its political and military might, the Church began an agenda of suppression of all philosophic and scientific discourse other than its own dogma, and over a thousand years of darkness was ushered in. Eventually, with the destruction of the Knights Templar and the Cathars in the 1200s, this race to destroy all the so-called heretics culminated in six painful centuries of witch hunts and the violent Inquisition, in which all spiritual inquiry other than the doctrine of the official Church became punishable by death.

Now let us turn to the exploration of those people in modern times who have had the rare experience of crossing over to the Otherside and returning. Let's find out what they report from their own firsthand experiences.

PART 2
THE LANDSCAPES OF HEAVEN

I feel my immortality oversweep all pains, all tears, all time, all fears—and peal, like the eternal thunders of the deep, into my ears, this truth— thou livest forever!

GEORGE GORDON, LORD BYRON

4

The Isles of the Blessed

Life is eternal, and love is immortal; and death is only a horizon; and a horizon is nothing save the limit of our sight.

ANONYMOUS

So let us look now at the evidence for the continuation of the Soul after death. To discover this we must take a look at the land-scapes of Heaven and find out what both ancient and modern accounts tell us about this Paradise. Like many people today, the ancient world believed in the concept of Heaven and Hell as well as the many inter-mediate zones, or *bardos,* that lie between these two. Yet unlike what is taught by the patriarchal religions, which claim that this in-between state is a permanent place, the ancient sages knew that these dimensions are only temporary abodes for the Soul, just as our lives on Earth are only temporary.

This world of shining light known as Heaven has been called by many other names: the Far Country, the Summerland, Shambhala, Valhalla, New Jerusalem, and Avalon. In Hindu teachings it is known as Svarga. To Mahayana Buddhists it is Sukhavati. Theosophists call it Devachan, the land of devas and gods, also known as "the Shining Land."[1] This is a specially guarded place in the higher octaves of the mental plane where all sorrow and evil are vanquished by the great spiritual intelligences who oversee human evolution. It is a place inhabited by human beings who have attained a level of purity that lifts them from the world of conflict. In the next few chapters we will consider the remarkable stories of people who have traveled into these celestial realms and visited the realms of the Afterlife.

The Elysian Fields

The Greeks called Heaven the Elysian Fields, a vast paradisiacal land on the western margins of Earth, encircled by a stream called Oceanus, which may be another name for the great Cosmic Sea. This vibrant land glows with light and is reserved for only the good, the pure, and the noble. Similar to modern-day near-death accounts, or NDEs, the deceased person meets with his or her loved ones on the Otherside, where they take up residence in a beautiful, pastoral countryside. The Elysian Fields are the immortal lands of bliss where those who have lived lives of goodness are transported without ever having to taste the bitter sting of death. This realm is identical to the Field of Reeds in Egyptian cosmology, a Paradise of shady trees, magical forests, and pastoral gardens, all blooming in a perpetual season of spring. Here Souls experience friendship, joy, peace, and love without the heartache, pain, and struggle that we know so well in the physical world. This echoes a famous nineteenth-century folk song that compares our world with this celestial one:

> *I am a poor wayfaring stranger, traveling through this*
> *world of woe.*
> *And there's no sickness, toil or danger, in that bright*
> *world to which I go.*
> *I'm going home to meet my father, I'm going there no*
> *more to roam.*
> *I'm just a-going over Jordan, I'm just a-going over*
> *home.*

◌

I know dark clouds will gather round me, I know my
*   way is rough and steep,*
But golden fields lie out before me, where God's
*   redeemed shall ever sleep.*
I'm going home to see my mother, she said she'd meet
*   me when I come.*
*I'm only going over Jordan, I'm only going over home.**

The Greeks believed that this paradisiacal realm was ruled by the titan Kronos, the father of Zeus, whose name symbolizes time. The word *chronometer* comes from Kronos; thus he represents the vast cycles of time through which the Soul must pass in its many cycles of life, death, and rebirth. This is the Wheel of Karma, where each Soul is transformed, giving us multiple chances to perfect our inner nature. As its ruler, Kronos has the ability to allow us to view our past and future incarnations, as well as to suspend time.

Like most cultures, the Greeks believed that the Soul is judged at the end of every lifetime, and the decider of one's fate is the wise King Rhadamanthys. Similar to Osiris in Egypt, Jesus in Christianity, and the Hindu god Yama, god of death, the Greeks believed that Rhadamanthys dwelt in Paradise. Rhadamanthys was said to have been the son of Zeus and Europa, the god of the sky and the goddess of Earth, a merger of the male and female cosmic forces that rule the universe. The Neoplatonic teacher Lucian of Samosata depicts Rhadamanthys as presiding over a company of heroes on the Isles of the Blessed, and in his epic poem *The Aeneid,* Virgil reports that Rhadamanthys was a judge in the Tartarus section of the Underworld. In Homer's epic poem *The Odyssey* we read, "The immortals will send you to the Elysian Plains at the ends of the

---

*"A Poor Wayfaring Stranger" is an American folk song written by an unknown composer in the 1800s. It is considered one of the top 100 folk songs of all times, listed in the Roud Folk Song Index of 25,000 songs. It may well have emerged from the rich creative legacy of black slaves suffering in the South before emancipation, but its theme is a universal one that we can all relate to.

earth, where fair-haired Rhadamanthys is. There life is supremely easy for men. No snow there, nor ever heavy winter storm, nor rain and the Ocean is ever sending gusts of the clear-blowing west wind to bring coolness to men."[2]

Pindar, the ancient Greek poet, writes how each Soul stands before the judge of the dead before being sentenced to its fate: "And those that have three times kept to their oaths, keeping their souls clean and pure, never letting their hearts be defiled by the taint of evil and injustice, and barbaric veniality, they are led by Zeus to the end: to the palace of

Figure 4.1. Theseus and Ariadne in the labyrinth with the Minotaur (illustration by Tricia McCannon)

Kronos, where soothing breezes off the Ocean breathe over the Isle of the Blessed."[3]

Plutarch claims that Rhadamanthys married Ariadne, the spinner of the red thread of fate. Ariadne was the daughter of King Minos of Crete, the princess who helped the hero Theseus escape from the Minotaur in the underground labyrinth. In the language of the Mysteries these stories signify a deeper truth. Theseus, like us, must escape from the labyrinth of our ever-repeating cycles of reincarnation. To do so we must each conquer our own animal nature, symbolized by the Minotaur. The way we do this is by aligning with the goddess who holds the red thread of fate, a symbol of our higher destiny. By following her toward a higher purpose or goal, we escape the sevenfold labyrinth of the lower worlds, becoming free of the Wheel of Time. The number seven is significant in all esoteric traditions, for it symbolizes not only the seven chakras and energy bodies we must master, but also the seven dimensional realms of the time-space lokas.

The Fields of Asphodel

The Greeks taught that between each lifetime the Soul visits a sacred meadow called the Fields of Asphodel, or the Asphodel Meadows. This meadow was named after a lovely white six-petal flower associated with the mourning of the dead. This small flower is a diminutive version of the six-petal lily we use at Easter today and is much like night-blooming jasmine. Like the lily, the asphodel's six petals remind us of the Merkaba field used to travel into the higher realms. The asphodel flower, like the lily, was thought to be a symbol of rebirth.

The Asphodel Meadows acted as a magical borderland of neutrality between Heaven and Earth. It was said that in this meadow were two pathways—one that led upward to the Elysian Fields, or Heaven, and one that led downward to the realm of Hades. The Greeks believed that at the time of death the Soul journeyed there, taking the path that was most appropriate to the life it had lived. The Soul also returned to these meadows when it was ready to come back to Earth and begin a new life.

Tibetan Buddhism calls this intermediate state the *bardo* plane.

Figure 4.2. The six-petal asphodel flower

The term *bar do,* from the Sanskrit *antarabhava,* means "transitional state," "in-between state," and "liminal state," refers to it being an intermediate dimension between earthly life and the other dimensions.[4] In Homer's epic the *Odyssey,* the poet relates the story of how Odysseus sailed beyond the dawn sky to the edge of Earth, finally arriving at a place where the sun never shines. There Odysseus entered a misty meadow filled with asphodel flowers, a grove of trees, and the junction of two rivers. Odysseus suddenly realizes that he has arrived at the Fields of Asphodel, the gateway to the Otherworld. This is the decision point of the Afterlife for the Soul.[5]

In Greek cosmology, the Soul returns to the Asphodel Meadows before each new lifetime. There it has a choice to drink from one of two pools: the River of Lethe or the Pool of Mnemosyne. Lethe is the pool of forgetfulness, while Mnemosyne is the pool of remembrance. Orphic mystics claim that less aware Souls drink from the River of Lethe, choosing amnesia before every lifetime, while initiates are taught to drink from the Pool of Mnemosyne, thus retaining the memory of who they are from lifetime to lifetime, as well as their purpose in entering each new life.

While today all of this might seem like fanciful mythology, what it reveals about our ancestors is their knowledge of the many dimensional planes of the inner worlds, especially the lower, middle, and higher registers of the astral plane reported by modern near-death experiencers.

As we shall discover, all of these various levels are dimensions within the astral plane known as the *kamaloka;* and it is our state of consciousness that determines where in the astral plane we will go upon death. While many of these realms are places of peace, joy, and light, there are yet higher and lower planes of Heaven that the Soul can visit.

The Landscapes of Hell

If a Soul does not go to one of the regions of Heaven, then it might wind up in the Underworld, a place also called Hades, Hel, or Acheron. This is where we get the modern word *Hell* today. Lamenting the fate of those who are consigned there, Plato writes, "To go to the world below, having a soul which is like a vessel full of injustice, is the last and worst of all the evils."[6]

Tibetan Buddhism names six dimensional planes, or lokas, that the Soul might incarnate into, all six of which are considered realms of samsara or suffering. These are: the realm of the gods, the realm of the demigods, the realm of the humans, the realm of the animals, the realm of the *pretas* or hungry ghosts, and the Hell realm. Each of these realms has an excess of either suffering or pleasure, except the human realm, which has an equal amount of each, and is thus believed to be con-

Figure 4.3. The six-petaled matrix of life

ducive to future spiritual growth. In their illustrated commentary on the Tibetan Book of the Dead, students of Eastern spirituality Stephen Hodge and Martin Boord note, "An excess of suffering prevents people from ever giving thought to anything else since their minds are overwhelmed by pain, while an excess of comfort and happiness dulls the mind and gives no motivation for change."[7]

These six lokas can be seen as embodying psychological states, given that the Buddhist idea is that all things are shaped and formed by the mind. Hodge and Boord go on, "It is said that a predominance of any one particular type of negativity results in rebirth in the most appropriate mode. Thus, pride leads to rebirth as a god, jealousy as a demigod, attachment as a human being, stupidity as an animal, greed as a hungry ghosts and hatred as a hell denizen."[8] In theosophical and Hindu teachings, these lokas or dimensions exist at higher and lower frequencies, providing steps of consciousness for each Soul's spiritual evolution. These are the various lokas or dimensions where the Soul takes birth and acquires experience. However, just like in our own realm, the time that a Soul spends in these dimensions is limited, whether it be a hundred years or a thousand.

At the center of these six lokas lies Paradise, the Buddhist nirvana, the Holy of Holies, the Far Country, the Summerland, or bliss, the central realm of Heaven. Looking very much like the petals of the Flower of Life, the six lokas or planes of incarnation sit around it. This plane of shining light is thought by most spiritual traditions to be the highest realm that the Soul can attain throughout its many incarnations, for this is where our Soul's eternal essence dwells in its angelic form, even while another part of us takes birth in the worlds below.

The realm that we call Hell is a lower region of the astral plane. It is a land of darkness, gloom, black houses, black roads, and black holes in the earth.[9] The Hebrew name for this region is *Sheol,* a place of negative self-delusion where the Soul is so lost in Shadow that the light from the higher realms cannot break through. This is because these Souls have imprisoned themselves with dark thought forms through their own choice. Sheol is thus a self-created prison that does not allow us to feel the love around us. In this delusionary realm we are not in touch with the light within, so of course it feels cold and bleak, forlorn and hopeless, until we are willing to turn to the light. Then our guides can pull us upward into the higher realms.

In this Hell realm the Soul experiences the torments of the *Rakshasas,* mythological demonic beings found in both the Hindu and Buddhist scriptures, sometimes called "man-eaters." These frightening spirits can drive a Soul mad with anger, fear, judgment, pride, and egoic vanity. As we shall see, these are all creations of a person's mind that has been steeped in ignorance and delusion. In truth, these furies are only aspects of the Shadow self that the Soul has given into while living here on Earth. These negative forces drove the person during his earthly life, and they continue to plague his Soul once it passes to the Otherside. This is certainly a strong argument for letting go of the destructive emotions of bitterness, rage, resentment, regret, vengeance, judgment, violence, and self-righteousness while we're still in our physical form, for these states of consciousness cannot only trap us in this world, but also in the next.

This lower realm of the astral plane is a nightmare land, and many of us may have accidently wandered into this frightening realm or an adjacent one during the course of our convoluted dreaming life. However, contact with the lower astral planes can only happen when one's thoughts and feelings fall into such decline that we consistently feel trapped in the negative emotions of anger, hatred, fear, loneliness, depression, or despair. This lowers our vibration. Then we may find ourselves dreaming in one of the lower levels that lie just above Sheol. In these realms what we see around us is merely a reflection of our own resentments, fears, and anxieties; however, none of what we see is real. It is only a projection of our own negative thoughts and emotions. This is critically important to remember so that we do not give it power. Thus, while any of us can fall into periods of grief, sadness, or depression over the course of a lifetime, it is important to remember that while we are living in this world we must maintain a positive focus. We must choose not to feed our darker thoughts, for then you will only give more power to the Shadow.

One way of changing this negative energy is by focusing on spiritual affirmations or maxims as the ancient philosophers did. Another way is through prayer and forming a connection with the powerful life-affirming grace of the spiritual masters who serve this light, and with the angelic forces that are never far from us, but who work by invitation only. Another way of counteracting the Shadow is by reading spiritual literature on a daily basis. Writings that are transmitted from the higher realms have a vibration that will pierce the darkness of pain, grief, and sorrow and lift you into the higher vibration of love. The more you can focus your thoughts in this direction, the quicker you will transform your own emotions.

Releasing the Etheric Double at Death

In Greek cosmology it was believed that to enter the realm of Hades the Soul had to cross the River Acheron. As movies such as *Clash of the Titans* depicted, the Greeks believed that the Soul had to be ferried across the river by Charon the ferryman. His price was a small golden coin called an *obolus* that was placed on the eyes or in the mouth of the deceased person. Virgil's *Aeneid* says that for hundreds of years there were paupers gathered on the shores of the River Acheron, stuck between the worlds. These people did not have a coin to give to Charon to help them on their passage across. Some Greeks even made a practice of offering libations to these unhappy spirits to prevent them from haunting the living. These are the *pretas* in Tibetan Buddhism, the hungry ghosts whose cravings and needs keep them perpetually trapped in the lower astral plane. Greek cosmology also taught that there was a guardian of Hades. This was Cerberus the three-headed dog who stood on the far side of the river. Like the loyal Basenji dog Anubis in Egypt, he conducted Souls to the Halls of Judgment. Once the Soul passed beyond this point, it had officially entered the Land of the Dead.

Theosophical wisdom, much of which is based on the bardo teachings of Buddhism, teaches that once a person dies there is a period of time during which the subtle-energy bodies detach from the physical body. While some parts of us travel up into the middle or higher regions of Heaven, the etheric sheath that acts as an interface between spirit and matter often remains on Earth for a time, although it is said to detach from the body during the first thirty-six hours after death. This etheric double is the body closest to the physical world, exactly mirroring the structure of the physical body it served. When we are living, this etheric double is blue gray in color and extends about an inch from the body, mimicking its shape and appearance. If the person is buried, then this etheric double may float over the grave for a time until it slowly disintegrates; but if the body is cremated, the etheric double breaks up very quickly, having lost its physical center of attraction. This is one reason, among many, why cremation is preferable to burial as a way of disposing of the bodies of the dead, for it frees the Soul from any connection with the etheric double, giving it nothing to tether it to Earth. If the etheric double does not disintegrate properly, it can become a Shade. In theosophical literature a Shade is an aspect of the astral body that can sometimes form from lower mental attachments. It appears as an exact duplicate of the physical person, complete with all its idiosyncrasies. It is not a hungry ghost, but rather a trapped portion of the etheric double, or subtle energy field that connects the Soul with the physical body.[10]

The Five Rivers of Hades

The Greek Mysteries taught that in Hades there were five separate rivers, each representing one of the five negative emotions that can bind the Soul to the lower astral realms. These rivers were Cocytus, the river of lamentation, said to mostly be for traitors who were filled with regret; Phlegethon, the river of fire, said to be for sinners being punished in the heat of their own unbridled passions; Lethe, the river of forgetfulness, where we fall into unconsciousness and oblivion; Styx, the river of hate; and Acheron, the river of sorrow and woe into which all the other rivers empty. These rivers represent the five most negative states that keep us trapped in a dark state of consciousness: the emotions of sorrow, grief, anger, forgetfulness, and hatred. These are the life-smothering feelings that keep us stuck in a state of self-blame, judgment, self-righteousness, vengeance, and regret—a reminder to those of us still in the land of the living to dispel these dark emotions while we still have the chance.

Figure 4.4. Crossing the River Styx (engraving by Gustave Doré)

What I find most intriguing about this cosmology is that it was the river of hate, the River Styx, that formed the boundary between the upper and the lower worlds. This tells us that it is the choice between love and fear that finally divides the realms of darkness from the world of light. To be free of this Shadow within we must first let go of any hatred of ourselves or others. This is the true power of forgiveness.

5

The Book of Life and Death
in the Halls of Amenti

Every soul comes into this world strengthened by the victories and weakened by the defeats of its previous life.

ORIGEN

While Greek cosmology developed over many centuries, they originally received their teachings about the Afterlife from the Egyptians. Egyptian cosmology is recorded in the Egyptian Book of the Dead, an ancient funerary text also known as the Book of Emerging Forth into the Light. It describes how the newly departed Soul, led by Anubis, the faithful part-canine servant, boards a vessel called the Boat of a Million Years. It then travels through the Duat, a term that refers to the crossing of dimensions, accompanied by a group of powerful gods on its way to the Halls of Amenti. There in the Halls its life is recorded in the Book of Life during a ceremony called the Weighing of the Heart. At that point it is decided whether the Soul can go into Heaven. However even to get to the Halls of Amenti, the Soul had to make the voyage in the Boat of a Million Years and face a series of trials and tribulations. In the boat with Anubis was the sun god Ra, who symbolizes the radiant light of the Soul that lives within us all; Thoth, the initiator of the Mysteries, who represents the wisdom of the Soul, a quality we need to get into Heaven; and Isis, the goddess of compassion and Great Mother of humanity, who gives us the power to open our hearts and heal ourselves.

Beside Isis stands Ma'at, the principle of cosmic truth and cosmic law. Those who murder, steal, rape, and lie do not live in accordance with this higher law. They are in service to the little self and have forgotten that what we do to others, we also do to ourselves. Since we are all aspects of the One, when we wrong one another, we also wrong ourselves. This is experienced directly in the life review when the Soul enters Heaven. In this place of ultimate reckoning, we meet a great

Figure 5.1. Anubis, the Way-Shower into the inner realms (illustration by Tricia McCannon)

being of light and often wind up judging ourselves for our own wrong-doings because we can clearly see and feel the error of our ways.

Finally, at the front of the boat is Set, the little self or ego, who tries to steer the ship with his oar. Set represents the Shadow within each of us. In Egyptian mythology Set is the imperfect god who covets his brother's land and tries to take his brother's wife. He was known to lie, cheat, kill, and steal for his ambitions; and then he murdered his brother Osiris, the lord of light. Set's original name was Satu, perhaps the origin of the name Satan today. Set is the small personality self that tries to steer our life. He is the inner Satan who has only his own self-interest in mind. Although this Shadow must also travel with the Soul toward the light of Heaven, his role is a limited one, as we shall see shortly.

As the Boat of a Million Years sails through the Duat, it traverses the darkness of the starry realms. Like the dark tunnel encountered by modern near-death experiencers, this phase of the journey is dangerous, for the Soul must do battle with Apophis, the many-headed serpent

*Figure 5.2. Crossing the Duat in the Boat of a Million Years
(illustration by Tricia McCannon)*

that lurks in the fog. Apophis represents all of the negative personality traits, emotions, and thought forms that we have not yet conquered in our lifetime, including lust, greed, addiction, fear, anger, vanity, self-judgment, shame, and guilt.

Comparisons to the Tibetan Book of the Dead

This encounter with the dreaded serpent Apophis brings to mind the Bardo Thodol, commonly known by its translated title as "Liberation through Hearing during the Intermediate State" or more commonly as "The Tibetan Book of the Dead." This text is among the many treasures attributed to the eighth-century CE "Precious Guru" Padmasambhava, who secreted it in various locations throughout Tibet. At the time he concealed these teachings Padmasambhava foretold that these texts would be revealed later, at an appropriate time. These treasure teachings were revealed in the fourteenth century by Karma Lingpa in a cave in the Gampo hills of central Tibet, and they were first made available to the West in English in 1927 by the American Theosophist Walter Evans-Wentz. Since then these teachings have been published in various book editions (going by different titles).

Like other great cosmologies, the Tibetan bardo teachings state that there are several stages to the journey once the consciousness of an individual passes out of its physical existence. The first stage lasts for three and a half to seven days, during which time the person's consciousness becomes aware that it has died. This is why traditionally there was a mourning period of three to seven days before the body was buried, the equivalent of the Jewish custom of "sitting Shiva," saying prayers for the passage of the Soul. This is also why funerals often take place three to seven days after a person has died. During this time the tethers of the etheric double are gradually being shed.

The Bardo Thodol tells us that during the next seven days the person's consciousness encounters forty-two benevolent beings of light, called the *peaceful deities*. At this time it is given repeated chances to recognize that the light from these great beings is actually an emanation of that person's own essential Buddha nature. Similarly, the Egyptians write about forty-two "Assessors" that are present for the Soul's life review. Since there is some accord with this number, I imagine that these forty-two Assessors, a number reported in both Tibetan and Egyptian practices, are the same benevolent emanations. If one's consciousness has enough awareness to recognize itself in these loving lords of light as facets of its own enlightenment, then it is finally liberated from the cycle of samsara. In effect, it reunites with its higher, Angelic Self and becomes self-realized. This is a remarkable revelation!

However, most of us do not ever recognize our celestial Self, believing that everything we encounter is outside ourselves. Instead, we project our beliefs onto this world, believing that we are meeting a spiritual figure like Jesus, Buddha, or our own Guardian Angel. Most of us are so steeped in our belief system, laden with fears, thought forms, and karmic patterns, that we completely miss this opportunity. Tibetan wisdom reports that when we are approached by these brilliant emanations of light, at the same time a far dimmer light is presented to us. This dimmer light emanates from the six illusionary planes where the Soul may continue to take birth if it does not become enlightened. Surprisingly, most Souls flee from the brilliant light and are instead drawn to the dimmer light, in turn causing the Soul to be drawn down into yet another cycle of incarnation in the lower worlds.

In Tibetan teachings, if the person's consciousness does not choose to follow these forty-two peaceful deities, it then encounters fifty-eight wrathful deities over the next seven days. If the Soul realizes that these wrathful deities are merely illusions of the mind, or projections of its own fears and paranoia, then it has another chance to become self-realized. However, most of us do not see through these frightening apparitions, and thus we are drawn to one of the intermediate regions of the astral plane. There we will spend some time before eventually reincarnating in one of the six lower dimensions or lokas.

Winning against Apophis

While traditional Buddhism interprets these peaceful and wrathful deities as projections of our own enlightened potentials, the wrathful deities seem reminiscent of Egyptian cosmology in which the Soul must face a series of frightening obstacles in its journey through the Underworld. These include crocodiles that lurk in the underbrush, a lake of fire, and of course the frightening figure of the many-headed snake Apophis. The crocodiles represent those unacknowledged fears that lurk in the shadows; the lake of fire is our refusal to turn toward the shining light of our own being; and Apophis is the beast that would steal the heart of the Soul as it makes its way toward Heaven. Apophis represents the unhealed aspects of the Shadow, which may appear wrathful, blaming, aggressive, addictive, or even seductive. Religious philosopher Jeremy Naydler gives us insight into the deeper meaning of this journey in *Temple of the Cosmos.*

> The journey through the Underworld is a purgatorial journey. In the course of it, the ba [or Soul] must free itself of all those elements in its nature that are inconsonant with Ma'at. And this process of becoming free is pictured as involving three stages: first of all, the negative energy presents itself to the traveler as an autonomous force. . . . Second the traveler and opposing force engage in a struggle. The opposer wants to steal the traveler's heart, take away the traveler's magic power, or kill the traveler's soul—that is, to cut the ba off from all contact with its spiritual source. The aim of the traveler, by contrast, is not to kill or eliminate the opposer, but rather to master it. [This is] . . . the third stage of the process. For in accomplishing this difficult feat, one actually wins for oneself—for one's higher purpose—all the negative energy by which one was initially opposed. This appropriation of negative energy—the transformation of one's demons into beneficent daemons, as one modern psychologist has put it—is crucial to the whole notion of journeying through the Underworld, in contrast to merely stagnating in it.[1]

In the Egyptian Book of the Dead we learn that during this fateful voyage, no matter how hard Ra and Set battle against Apophis, it is impossible for them to win against these negative forces. To succeed, the Soul and the ego (Ra and Set) must have the help of the Christed

Self. In Egyptian cosmology that Christed aspect is represented by Osiris, the great humanitarian god of regeneration. Calling on Osiris would be the same as calling on the power of Jesus or Buddha today. In Egyptian cosmology, Osiris sits in the Halls of Amenti, the antechamber of Heaven, as the Lord of Light and giver of grace. Followers of Osiris called themselves Christians long before the time of Jesus, believing in the transforming power of the KRST, or anointed and perfected human. In my many years of research I have come to believe that Osiris is an earlier embodiment of Jesus, for both avatars are incarnations of what in Hinduism are called the Four Kumaras, four sages (*rishis*) who roam the universe and periodically come to Earth to uplift the world.[2] This Christed aspect is the cosmic Soul or living Atman, the divine Purusha that lives within us all.

In the great Mystery traditions, the story of Set and Ra doing battle with Apophis is in reality about how our human ego can only get so far without the higher Self to help it. As the Boat of a Million Years travels throughout the twelve hours of the night, it reflects the sun's voyage through the Underworld. Ra represents our conscious Self, while Set represents the little ego. Both struggle against the chaotic Apophis, who represents the unhealed Shadow within. Yet no matter what they do, they cannot seem to win. Finally, in the sixth hour of the night, when all seems lost, Osiris arrives; he symbolizes the Inner Master or Christed Self. It is only then that the battle begins to change. Through the appearance of this higher light, the Shadow is finally defeated, and Set, the ego of the little self, is slain. Now light triumphs over darkness, and ignorance is vanquished. The Soul has "died to its old self." This is why spiritual initiates were called the "twice born," echoing the words of Jesus, who tells us: "Except as ye be born again, ye cannot see the Kingdom of Heaven" (John 3:3). Over the course of the next few hours, the Soul undergoes a profound transformation, eventually emerging as a butterfly. This is the newly awakened Angelic Self. Naydler notes, "The rebirth of Ra corresponds to the initiation of the Underworld traveler into the exalted state of consciousness that characterizes those who achieve an inner identification with the *Khu* or radiant Higher Self in themselves."[3] In this way, the journey through the Underworld was essentially a journey toward joining with the higher Self, and the vital eternal core of who we are.

Rivers of Light and the Boat of a Million Years

The metaphor of a boat that travels between dimensions is also found in other spiritual traditions. Celtic lore describes a celestial boat that takes the deceased to Paradise, called Avalon. This is why the bodies of ancient kings were set loose upon the sea in boats; a warrior would shoot a flaming arrow into the boat as the king's spirit was released from this world. Dante's *Divine Comedy* also depicts a celestial boat overseen by an archangel, which transports the Soul into the higher heavens. What are these rivers? There are several possibilities:

First, we have reports from near-death experiencers (NDEs) of tunnels that seem to effortlessly transport the newly deceased from Earth into the Chikhai bardo. According to Buddhist teachings, this is the primordial Clear Light that we first encounter when we pass to the Otherside. These tunnels seem like wormholes, rivers of energy that scoop the Soul, or in the case of Tibetan teachings, the consciousness of the person and deposit it in the Afterlife. In Egyptian lore this boat first takes the Soul to the Halls of Amenti, the antechamber of Heaven. This is where the Soul experiences its Life Review, or in Egyptian teachings, the Weighing of the Heart ceremony. Here the heart of the deceased is taken out and weighed against the feather of Truth, and Thoth writes the results of that person's life in the Book of Life. If you have lived a happy life, a forgiving life, then your heart is "light as a feather." But if you have a hard heart or a heavy heart, then you have not learned the lessons that were before you, and must return to Earth to start again.

People who have had NDEs or undergone deep hypnotherapy about their time spent on the Otherside are those who have accessed the superconscious mind and are thus able to report on what occurs when we enter these realms. They claim that the spiritual realms are striated with translucent layers of light. These vast circular traveling paths appear to be magnetic in nature. They look like stratified clouds of varied luminescence, described as beautiful, curving waves of nonmaterial energy.[4] These highways of light are similar to the ley lines we find on Earth. Ley lines, which appear to be magnetic, can be dowsed; they generally follow the course of underground rivers and mineral deposits. Similarly, in the spiritual realms these sweeping rivers of energy appear to be magnetic and are produced through sound. People who have died and returned frequently report hearing music as they are being transported along these highways. In fact, the practice of meditating on these cosmic sounds is one way to tune in to these higher realms, and may be why chanting has always been integral to many spiritual practices. Using such tones or frequencies raises our vibration and opens the way into the higher worlds. So in these inner realms our ability to travel from place to place is done on these highways of circular light.

Here is an account from a man who crossed to the Otherside and was taken to meet his Soul family:

> I am riding on a wave . . . a beam of light . . . it's similar to the bands of a radio with someone turning the dial and finding the right frequency for me. . . . I must go with the wave bands of light . . . the waves have direction and I'm flowing with it. It's easy. They do it all for you. . . . My mind is in tune with the movement. . . . I flow with the resonance . . . the wave beam . . . vibrates . . . I am locked into this, too . . . it's part of my own tonal pattern—my frequency.[5]

These vast spirals are depicted in Gustav Doré's illustrations of the celestial realms. References to these curving pathways are found in some of the most esoteric literature on the planet. This quote is from the Hermetica, an Egyptian-Greek wisdom text from the second and third centuries AD that is mostly presented as dialogues in which a teacher, generally identified as Hermes Trismegistus or "thrice-greatest Hermes," enlightens a disciple:

> In a sense, the Cosmos is changeless because its motions are determined by unalterable laws which cause it to revolve eternally without beginning and end. Its parts manifest, disappear and are created anew, again and again in the undulating pulse of time. Through

the process of time, life within the Cosmos is regulated and maintained. Time renews all things in the Cosmos by the circling process of change. . . . Time is like a circle, where all the points are so linked that you cannot say where it begins or ends, for all points both precede and follow one another forever.[6]

Hermes, or Thoth, created the Mystery Schools across the world many thousands of years ago in an effort to raise humankind's consciousness. He was a great advocate of the eternal nature of the Soul. Here is another excerpt, this one from an esoteric journal of his travels into the inner realms, called *The Emerald Tablet:*

Once I stood in the Halls of Amenti and heard the voice of the Lords of Amenti saying in tones that rang through the silence, words of power, mighty and potent. Chanted they the song of the cycles, the words that open the path to beyond. Aye, I saw the great path opened and looked for an instant into the beyond. Saw I the movement of the cycles, vast as the thought of the Source could convey . . .

Seek ye, O man, to learn the pathway that leads through the spaces that are formed forth in time. . . . Aye, time which exists through all space, floating in a smooth, rhythmic movement that is eternally in a state of fixation. Time changes not, but all things change in time. For time is the force that holds events separate, each in its proper place. . . . Aye, by time ye exist, all in all, an eternal One existence. Know yet that even though in time ye are separate, yet still are you One in all times existent. . . . Yet only by curves could I hope to attain the key that would give me access to time-space. Found I that only by moving upward, and yet again by moving rightward, could I be free from the time of this movement.[7]

The Life Review

Once the Soul has entered the Halls of Amenti, it has its Life Review. While the idea of being judged on the Otherside is nothing new, this is not a final Judgment Day as depicted by the Abrahamic religions; it is actually an evaluation of the life we have just completed, witnessed by the loving presence of the higher Self. This life review is holographic in nature and has been reported by many near-death experiencers across the world. In Egyptian cosmology, it is Anubis, the Opener of the Ways, who leads the Soul through the darkness into the light. Here, at the gates of Heaven, before the throne of Osiris, the heart of the deceased is weighed on the balance scales of life against the feather of Ma'at. This Weighing of the Heart ceremony cannot be underestimated, for the

Figure 5.3. Ma'at, the goddess of cosmic law
(illustration by Tricia McCannon)

power of Ma'at or cosmic truth is the principle of karma itself.

Karma is the mechanism by which the Soul learns that what we sow in this life is what we shall reap, whether in this life or the next. This is the most efficient way that we can experience the consequences of our actions. Channeler and author Patricia Cota-Robles refers to it as the "Law of the Circle":

> The Law of the Circle is accurate to the letter, and we are all subject to this Universal Law. . . . As Children of God, we are responsible for how we choose to use every atomic and subatomic particle and wave of our Life force. With every thought, feeling word, or action we are co-creating patterns that are either adding to the Light of the world, or to the Shadow. Depending on the frequency of vibration we send forth, our co-creations will either be a blessing, or cause a problem for ourselves and all life on this planet. . . . This is how we learn to become co-creators with our Father-Mother God. The Law of the Circle will eventually return to us every electron of Life force that we have ever sent forth. This process allows us to experience what we have created through our free-will choices, and it gives us the opportunity to transmute our mis-creations back into Light.[8]

The principle of Ma'at essentially represents divine order and the principle of love, designed to bring us to a place of mastery and Oneness. Love is the law, and the law is love, so whatever we have cultivated in life—a kind heart, a loving heart, a forgiving heart—we shall also reap. Then we are welcomed into Heaven through the light of our own vibration. However, if we have had a hard heart, a bitter heart, an unforgiving heart, then we cannot hold the frequency of love. This means we must repeat our life lessons until we have finally mastered them and completed the Circle of One.

The Akashic Records

The results of the Weighing of the Heart ceremony are recorded in the Book of Life by Thoth, the god associated with wisdom and writing.

Figure 5.4. Thoth, the Egyptian god of wisdom, holding the Book of Life (illustration by Tricia McCannon)

He records them in the Akashic Records, which are the etheric testimony of everything that has ever happened; this includes the progress that each Soul makes in every lifetime based on the purity of its heart. We can think of the Akasha as the cosmic memory bank of God. The word *Akasha* comes from the Sanskrit *akasa,* meaning "space," "sky," or "ether" (i.e., the plenum that supports the All). Hinduism explains that the Akasha is formed when Brahman, the Creator, mixes with the illusory veils of the divine Mother aspect, Prakriti, who has created the universes of matter. This matter is the playground of the Soul; however it is shrouded in maya, or illusion, causing us to misperceive the pure light of the higher reality and our connection to it. From the Akashic field all of the elements are born. These elements form the foundation of the dense lower, physical worlds, and even the subtler regions of Heaven. In fact, everything that we interact with, including our subtle-energy bodies, is a mixture of these four elements, all part of the perishable aspects of Prakriti in the manifest worlds. The Upanishads teach that through the Akasha and the four elements the spirit of God descends into the realms of relativity.[9]

So the Akasha is constantly helping to create and then record everything in these manifest realms, like the memory banks of God. Thus our individual Soul records are recorded and then stored in the Akashic Library, where they can be viewed as a kind of living picture book. These are called the Books of Life. Some report seeing these Books of Life as actual volumes in a library. Others experience them as living movies of vibrating holographic particles that the Soul can enter into when being viewed. This allows the Soul to reexperience the conditions of any given lifetime so that it can more completely feel the consequences of its actions. This Akashic Book of Life contains all the minutia of our many lives and is connected to our causal body, a subtle-energy body that records every positive thought, word, feeling, or deed that we have ever expressed. It is referred to by spiritual masters as our "storehouse of good," referring to its ability to retain the wisdom we have acquired in all lifetimes. Once we attain self-mastery, this storehouse is then released to us by our divine I AM Presence.[10]

Most of us have heard of the I AM Presence. But what is it?

Theosophical teachings tell us that it is the permanent atom of being, or God particle, that each Soul begins its existence with. This is the portion of the Divine that is individualized for each person, and it cannot be destroyed. It becomes the cause out of which the effect proceeds, and is the permanent atom of your being that is linked to the Father-Mother God. So this is the divine core of your own being, which is released to us after we have achieved mastery through our own personal effort. While each lifetime that we have is designed to assist the Soul in making progress toward this goal, once we have incarnated on Earth, our free will makes the decision of how we respond to these various life tests. We can either make choices that move us forward, or slide backward into selfish, ignorant behavior. Egyptian sages believed that striving for spiritual knowledge in every incarnation would advance us greatly on the spiritual path. Ultimately, however, these sages knew that it is only by means of the heart that true spiritual progress is made, for this opens up our access to the Divine. This is why in the Egyptian Book of the Dead it is the heart that is measured on the balance scales of life after each lifetime. And the questions that they asked basically came down to: *Have I been kind? Have I been loving? Have I shown compassion to my fellow creatures, human and animal alike?*

Ammit the Devourer

If the Soul has made no spiritual progress during the course of a lifetime, then that particular life has no value in the overall plan of the Soul's evolution. So in Egyptian cosmology an embittered, impure heart is eaten by Ammit, known as the Devourer of the Dead and the Eater of Hearts.

In illustrated editions of the Egyptian Book of the Dead we see this strange chameleon creature, Ammit, a female demon, sitting below the scales of justice. Part lion, part hippopotamus, and part crocodile, this mythical animal embodies the three largest man-eating animals known to the Egyptians. If the heart had been cruel or selfish, Ammit would devour it. The idea of such a creature could, no

Figure 5.5. Ammit, the Eater of Hearts (illustration by Tricia McCannon)

doubt, be frightening, and this was the reason why this tale was told. To the common folk, Ammit was reason enough to live a good and virtuous life, yet she was not a force to be worshipped. In fact, quite the opposite: Ammit embodied all that the Egyptians most feared, and it was said that if she ate your heart you would be doomed to a life of restlessness as a hungry ghost on the lower astral plane. At the very least, the Soul has to learn its life lessons all over again. While Ammit is no doubt a mythical being, the importance of living a virtuous life is not a myth.

This Weighing of the Heart ceremony is very much like what modern-day near-death experiencers report in terms of encountering a magnificent being of light and undergoing a life review. During this review they become totally aware of how they might have lived a better life, and many return from such encounters with a renewed sense of purpose for their lives. This intriguing cosmology tells us that when we turn away from the lessons of love and kindness, then that lifetime is wasted. When a Soul lives a life of cruelty, abuse, violence, self-indulgence, bitterness, anger, or addiction, it is bound for a time to the worlds of Shadow. Ultimately, what matters most is the love that we share with one another.

The Great Work of Soul Transformation

In ancient Egypt, each person was believed to have nine subtle-energy bodies that comprised each human incarnation. Three of these bodies are linked to our physical/emotional self, three are linked to our emotional/spiritual self, and three are linked to our mental/spiritual self. The bodies linked to our physical/emotional self are the Khat or Shat, the physical body; the Ren, the cell-self, which gives us our instincts for survival; and the Khaibit, which represents our unprocessed emotional Shadow. This may be similar to the Unconscious Mind where we store our deepest fears and personality patterns. As we have seen, the Shadow can drive us to drink, smoke, overeat, or engage in all sorts of negative behaviors, activities that bind us to the lower astral realms.

The second triad represents our emotional/spiritual aspects. It consists of the Sekem or keeper of our vital life force energies; the shining Akh of the illuminated mind; and the Ka, which is described as a part of the self that guides the fortunes of the individual in each life. The Ka is not an element of the personality itself, but is said to be a spiritual twin, similar to a daemon or spirit guide. This spirit is said to guide the person's fate, and was even depicted in Egypt as a second person or "double" in Egyptian paintings. Egyptian wisdom taught that everything that exists has its "double," including plants, animals, and objects, so this may be like an overlighting spirit or an astral double. Naydler tells us that the Ka is associated with a person's fate, and that it is also connected to the goodness of the heart.

The final triad of energy bodies, our mental/spiritual self, consists of the Sahu or spiritual body; the Khu or radiant higher Self; and the Ba, which is our spirit or Soul essence. The Ba was often depicted traveling to and from Heaven with a hawk's body and a human head. Naydler explains, "The Ba seeks out the spiritual world in which the gods reside like a falcon soaring toward the sun. . . . Because it belongs to the eternal heaven world, one can strengthen one's Ba during life by steeping oneself in matters of the spirit. Thus the Old Kingdom sage Ptahotep says, 'The wise feed their ba with what endures.' The nature of the Ba is that it is drawn to what is eternal, for this is its place of origin, its home."[11]

While a large portion of the Ba remains in Heaven as the Angelic Twin (a subject discussed at length in chapter 13), the Soul sends a portion of its energy into the lower realms to take on human form here on Earth. In so doing, it hopes to use this time on Earth to bring back wisdom that can integrate when that life is over. However if our personality becomes too mired in the lower passions, then the human self makes no progress for the Soul; it has forgotten its true reasons for being here. However, if we have lived a life of goodness, worth, and value, then these other subtle aspects of the personality will naturally gravitate to the higher realms, joining with the Ba as it reaps the lessons of its most recent life. Egyptian wisdom teaches that if we have lived a virtuous life, then we will rejoin our higher Self in Heaven.

In these higher realms everyone lives with an awareness of the Oneness of life, so the Soul is free to gauge its progress with complete honesty. Thus we choose our next life based on the spiritual progress we hope to make rather than on any creature comforts the world might provide. This begins the alchemy of transforming the little self, or ego, into the divine Self. This is what the masters call "the Great Work." Each life is just another chance to learn the lessons of Spirit, but how well we do is up to us. The circumstances of each life are chosen by ourselves and by our guides based on what we most need to learn, our choices made in former lives, and our progress in our lessons here in Earth school.

6

Glimpses of the Afterlife

It is the secret of the world that all things subsist and do not die, but only retire a little from sight and afterwards return again. Nothing is dead; men feign themselves dead, and endure mock funerals . . . and there they stand looking out of the window, sound and well, in some strange new disguise.

RALPH WALDO EMERSON

So let us now look at the evidence for the continuation of the Soul after death by considering the firsthand accounts of those who have died and returned. Perhaps the first written account we have of someone who died and returned from the Otherside is 2,500 years old and is found in Plato's *Republic*. It is the story of a Greek warrior named Er, who was killed in battle but returned some twelve days later to find himself on top of a funeral pyre with other dead soldiers. Er relates the story of what befell him during those twelve days, and his account sounds amazingly similar to modern-day reports of near-death experiences (NDEs), as well as hypnotically induced trance experiences of the Otherside, both of which we will examine in this chapter.

In the Greek legend, Er at first found himself out of his body, in a place where many Souls traveled through various passageways that led from Earth to the Otherside. This was very similar to the dark tunnels that many people who have died and returned report seeing. In Er's account, when these Souls arrived, they were judged by divine beings who could see at a glance, in some sort of display, all the things that the Soul had done during its earthly life. This is the life review that so many NDEs report. Er was not judged, however. Instead, he was brought before a council that informed him that he had been chosen as a messenger between the heavenly realms and the people of Earth. He was to return to Earth and tell the living what he had seen. Once Er was back, he had no memory of how he had returned. He merely woke up and found himself on the funeral pyre. Plato begins his story in this way:

> Well, I will tell you a tale . . . of what once happened to a brave man, Er, who . . . was killed in battle . . . on the twelfth day after his death, as he lay on the funeral pyre, he came to life again, and then proceeded to describe what he had seen in the other world . . .
>
> Each soul, as it arrived from the earth, wore a travel-stained appearance . . . and those who had descended from heaven were questioned about heaven by those who had risen out of the earth; while the latter were questioned by the former about the earth. Those who were come from earth told their tale with lamentations and tears, as they bethought them of all the dreadful things they had seen and suffered in their subterranean journey [on the Earth] . . . while those who were come from heaven, described enjoyments and sights of marvelous beauty [from their time in heaven].
>
> Er saw many Souls going up towards heaven, while others descended below the Earth to reap the consequences of their negative deeds. These Souls were going to the lower, higher, and middle registers of the Astral plane. Those who had lived good lives of average thought were sent to the middle realms. Those who had lived pure, highly conscious lives, were sent to the higher realms. And those who had lived lives of brutality, violence and wrong-doing, were sent to the lower realms. However these Souls did not remain

there permanently. Once the Soul's learning was complete it got a brand new body and returned to Earth.

Plato then reports that the Souls who were about to enter their new lives were addressed by the overseeing guides in this way before they departed: "Ye short-lived souls, a new generation of men shall here begin the cycle of its mortal existence. Your destiny shall not be allotted to you, but *you shall choose it for yourselves.* . . . Virtue owns no master. He who honors her shall have more of her, and he who slights her, [shall have] less. The responsibility lies with the chooser. Heaven is guiltless."[1] Here the guides are saying that each of us is the author of our own fate. No matter what the conditions of our birth, it is the Soul that has chosen its circumstances, and no one else. Regardless of our race, body type, gender, or economic status, we have selected these conditions before ever incarnating on Earth.

Er then told us about the Souls who were lined up to choose their next life. In this group he saw the Greek hero Odysseus:

It was a truly wonderful sight, he said, to watch how each soul selected its life—a sight at once melancholy, and ludicrous, and strange. The experience of former lives generally guided [the Soul's] choice. . . . It so happened that the soul of Odysseus had drawn the last lot of all. When he came up to choose, the memory of his former sufferings [told in the epic saga of the *Odyssey*], had so abated his ambition that he went about a long time looking for a quiet retired life, which with great trouble he discovered lying about, and thrown contemptuously aside by the others. As soon as he saw it, he chose it gladly, and said that he would have done the same if he had even drawn the first lot.[2]

Hypnotherapy Reveals the Journey of the Soul

While this account is astonishing, what is even more remarkable is that modern hypnotherapists Michael Newton, Brian Weiss, and Dolores Cannon have all described clients who have experienced the same kind of events while under hypnosis. Dr. Newton is a master hypnotherapist and the author of four insightful books on the Afterlife. Dr. Weiss is a psychiatrist and the author of several best-selling books on this subject, including accounts of clients who have reunited as soul mates and healed long-lasting emotional issues using past-life therapy. His books are verbatim testimony of the power of love in transforming our lives. Hypnotherapist Dolores Cannon has conducted over a thousand between-life and past-life regressions, exploring the mechanisms behind the scenes that guide the Soul in each life. She authored nineteen books, some of which are dedicated to the cycle of dying, being in Heaven, and then choosing to return to Earth.

Newton's entry into the world of metaphysics, like Weiss's, happened quite by accident. Both therapists discovered that by using hypnotherapy, they could get to the root of a client's problems, which stemmed from traumas in their past lives. Newton had his first glimpse into the Afterlife after he instructed a female client to go back to a time when her problem first started. To his complete amazement, she began to relate a past life when she had been a male lawyer in New Orleans during the 1930s. In that life her original Soul contract had been to protect the innocent from the Mafia. But he compromised his integrity (as a male lawyer) out of greed and began working on behalf of the criminals instead of his clients. Eventually, the Mafia framed him, and in despair he took his own life. Stunned by this turn of events, Newton then instructed his client to see what had happened after "he" died. To his astonishment, Newton heard an account of the deceased lawyer's fate as he was taken to the Otherside. First the lawyer was met by his spirit guide and went through a life review. Realizing that he had failed to live up to the moral commitments he had made for that life, he was sharply disappointed with himself during his life review. The lawyer also realized that he would have to return in another life to learn this lesson all over again. Once Newton's client emerged from hypnosis, she realized that she had once again started to fall into the same pattern of letting greed and ambition overtake ethics. This session allowed her to see and address the many problems she had in her current life and make a critical course correction.

Newton was so intrigued by this experience that he soon began taking other clients back to their former lives. In those past-life experiences he would follow the Soul over to the Otherside after the person died. He became fascinated with the descriptions of the landscapes of Heaven and discovered how the roots of many of our present emotional problems are found in our Soul's past lives. Over time, Newton became focused on discovering the mechanisms that steer our lives and the specific features of the Afterlife.

The Ring of Destiny

Some of Newton's clients reported going to a place called the Ring of Destiny. It is described as an enormous bubble, a sphere surrounded by a shimmering wall of light with curved screens. These screens transmit a panoramic view of the Soul's upcoming lifetime. This Ring of Destiny is overseen by advanced spiritual beings known as the Lords of Karma, who allow the Soul a preview of its possible life choices. Eastern wisdom calls the Lords of Karma *maharajas,* or great Souls. They are the ones who carry out the practical working out of the *Lipikas,* or Keepers of the Karmic Records—those masters who are aware of the progress that each Soul is making from lifetime to lifetime.[3]

According to Theosophy, the Lipikas *are* the Lords of Karma:

> Mystically, these Divine Beings are connected with Karma, the Law of Retribution, for they are the Recorders or Annalists who impress on the (to us) invisible tablets of the Astral Light 'the great picture—gallery of eternity'—a faithful record of every act, and even thought, of man, of all that was, is, or ever will be, in the phenomenal Universe. As said in *Isis Unveiled* (I:343), this divine and unseen canvas is the BOOK OF LIFE. . . . The Lipika . . . project into objectivity from the passive Universal Mind the ideal plan of the universe, upon which the 'Builders' reconstruct the Kosmos after every Pralaya.[4]

So for simplicity we can simply call them the Lords of Karma.

Clients report that even before entering the Ring of Destiny the Soul has already decided, with the help of its guides and a Council of Elders, what it wants to work on in its next lifetime. Based on this, the Lipikas, or master Souls who operate the Ring of Destiny, choose two or three possible scenarios where the Soul might accomplish its goals. Let's imagine for a moment that a person wants to have a lifetime dedicated to self-expression through music. This Soul might be given a choice of three different lifetimes, each with its own positive and negative challenges. The first might be as a classical pianist in England, the child of a wealthy musical couple. In this life she would have the money, support, education, and opportunity for a successful musical career, but her emotional life might be rather distant and unsatisfying because of her career-minded parents. Her second choice might be as a poor Latino boy in the ghetto of Los Angeles, a child with a broken home and little money, but deep feelings of compassion and angst. This child might be destined to be discovered on the streets and become a superstar, but then he would have to deal with the temptation of drugs, fame, and success, as well as a newly rich but emotionally broken family. Perhaps the third choice might be as a black child in Africa. In that life the boy or girl would never be rich or famous, but he or she would have the support of a strong, loving community and the chance to become a shaman as well as a musician. So every life has it pros and cons, and no life is without its challenges. There are many roads to the same destination.

The Role of Free Will

Over the course of thousands of hypnotherapy sessions, Newton discovered that he could place his clients in a deep somnambulistic state wherein the person did not recall what was said in trance even after he or she returned to normal waking consciousness. Cannon also perfected this method of putting her clients into a deep somnambulistic state, which allowed them access to detailed memories of their former lives. Both teachers have now trained hypnotherapists all over the world in these past-life regression techniques, and the consistency of these between-life reports is seamlessly corroborative, no matter what the dominant culture

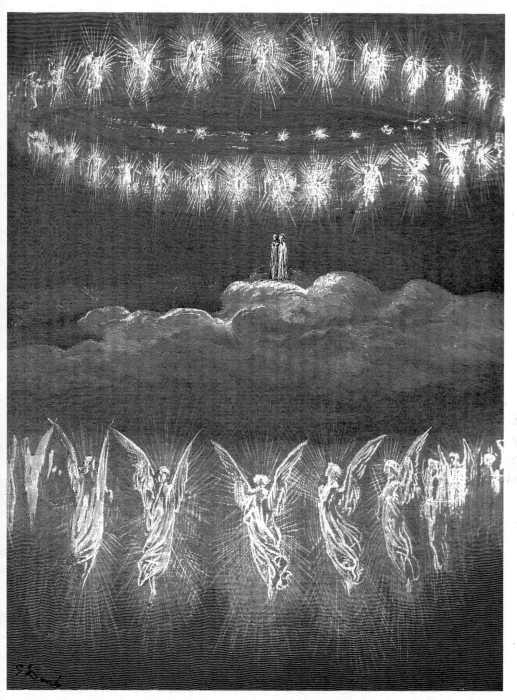

Figure 6.1. These vast circular paths are part of the structure and beauty reported by many people who have gone to Heaven and returned (engraving by Gustave Doré)

or religion of the client may be. Subjects who have been thus regressed uniformly report that in the Ring of Destiny they can control the movement of the screens with their minds. They can slow down the scenes of a possible lifetime or they can speed them up. They can move these panoramic scenes backward or forward, stopping at major turning points along the way. These are the points where important decisions are made.

Some people report seeing lines of energy converging along various places on the screens, as if they are traveling along the corridors of time. Each Soul has the power to enter a scene by freeze-framing it so that it can experience the scene in more detail.[5] This phenomenon accounts for the moments of déjà vu that most of us have experienced at one time or another in waking life, why certain experiences feel so familiar to us—because we *have* previewed them before, in the viewing room of the Ring of Destiny. Here is one such account by a woman who suffered a stroke in 1976 that was precipitated by a brain tumor. In this excerpt she is already with her spirit guide. She tells her guide that she would like to see how she came to select this particular life, and her guide then shows her a scene:

> Seated in what seemed to be a waiting area, I observed that there were five beings around me. Two of them were in a teaching capacity and were strong spiritual beings, and three of them were lesser spiritual beings. They were guardian angels, or whatever, and the three lesser ones were there to learn—sort of angels-in-training.
>
> In this pre-mortal environment I saw that I was making all the decisions for my life, the things that I chose to go through. These were things that I wanted to accomplish in order to learn various lessons. There were different choices available to me. I knew, for example, that I was going to be the oldest of the children in my family. There was a choice between three fathers and two mothers; I would have learned equal lessons from all of them. I knew that I would have a physical crisis and would be miraculously healed, and I would have a second health crisis which I would survive. My life on earth could be prolonged, I understood, by living so as to be in a helping capacity—helping others.[6]

Here is another account, this one from Dr. Newton's files, which I have condensed for brevity. In this hypnotherapy session the person is already in the Ring of Destiny:

Dr. Newton: After you have made the decision you want to come back to Earth, what happens next?

Subject: Well, when my trainer and I agree the time is right to accomplish things, I send out thoughts . . . my messages are received by the coordinators who actually assist us in previewing our life possibilities at the Ring.

Dr. Newton: All right, let's go to the Ring together on the count of three. When I am finished with my count you will have the capacity to remember all the details of this experience. Are you ready to go? One, two, three! Your soul is now moving towards the space of life selection. Explain what you see.

Subject: I . . . am floating towards the Ring . . . it's circular . . . a monster bubble . . . there's a concentrated energy force . . . the light is so intense. I'm being sucked inward . . . through a funnel . . . it's a little darker. The Ring is surrounded by banks of screens. I am looking at them. They appear as walls themselves, but nothing is really solid . . . it's all . . . elastic . . . the screens curve around me . . . moving.

Dr. Newton: What happens next?

Subject: They are . . . not reflecting anything yet . . . they shimmer as sheets of glass . . . mirrors. I feel a moment of quietness— it's always like this—then it's as if someone flipped a switch on the projector in a panoramic movie theater. The screens come alive with images and there is color . . . action . . . full of light and sound. I am hovering in the middle, watching the panorama of life all around me . . . places, people . . . I know this city! [It is] New York.

Dr. Newton: I'll come back to New York in a few minutes. Right now I want you to tell me what is expected of you in the Ring.

Subject: I'm going to mentally operate the panel . . . a scanning device in front of the screens . . . It's as if I'm in the cockpit of an airplane. I know it sounds crazy, but . . . I will help the controllers change the images on the screens by operating the scanner with my mind. My commands . . . are registered on the panel so I can track the action.

Dr. Newton: Why are you doing all this?

Subject: I'm scanning. The stops are major turning points on life's path—ways involving important decisions . . . possibilities . . . events which make it necessary to consider alternate choices in time . . . the lines of energy are . . . roads with points of colored light as guideposts which I can move forward, backward, or stop.

Dr. Newton: All right, you are moving along the track, scanning scenes and you decide to stop. Tell me what you do then.

Subject: I suspend the scene on the screens so I can enter it . . . now I have direct access to the action.

Dr. Newton: In what way? Do you become a person in the scene, or does your soul hover overhead while people move around?

Subject: Both. I can experience what life is like with anyone in the scene, or just watch them from any vantage point . . . part of me stays at the controls so I can start up the scene again and stop it anytime.

Dr. Newton: Can you divide your [Soul] energy?

Subject: Yes, and I can send thoughts back to myself. Of course the controllers are helping too, as I go in and out of the screens . . .

Dr. Newton: It seems to me when souls are in the Ring of Destiny they use time almost like a tool.

Subject: As Spirits, we do use time . . . subjectively. Things and events are moved around . . . and become objects in time . . . but to us time is uniform. When making contact [in the Ring in viewing future lives] the Soul in residence is put on hold for a moment. It's

Figure 6.2. The immensity of the heavenly landscapes moving in circles (engraving by Gustave Doré)

relatively short. We don't disturb life cycles when tracking through time . . . My choices of life environments are not unlimited. As I said, I probably won't be able to see all of a scene in one time segment. Because of what they don't show you, there is a risk attached to all body choices.

Dr. Newton: If one's future destiny is not fully preordained, as you say, why call this space the Ring of Destiny?

Subject: Oh, there is destiny, all right. The life cycles are in place. It's just that there are so many alternatives which are unclear.[7]

These kind of reports have been found in the files of many hypnotherapists around the world; I have similar accounts in my own files. Those who remember visiting the Ring of Destiny tell us that while they are shown the major obstacles that they will face in the life ahead, the outcome is not always revealed. This part of our life is obscured because these difficulties are designed to test the Soul's ability to find a solution once we are in the actual life experience. While our circumstances are designed to help us learn certain lessons, how well we handle these events is up to us. This is the all-important action of free will. As one of Dr. Newton's subjects explains: "The Ring sets up different experiments [for us] to choose from. On Earth we will try to solve them."[8] This means that while life challenges like illness, handicaps, and difficult family dynamics are all chosen by us before we begin a new life, once we are here our conscious free will is operational, and we have no memory of our previous choices. Dr. Newton writes about the role that our freewill choice plays:

If everything was preordained, there would be no purpose or justice to our struggle. When adversity strikes, it is not intended that we sit back with a fatalistic attitude and not fight to improve the situation by making on-site changes. During our lives all of us will experience opportunities for change that involve risk. These occasions may come at inconvenient times. We may not act upon them, but the challenge is there for us. The purpose of reincarnation is the exercise of free will. Without this ability, we would be impotent creatures indeed."[9]

More Accounts

Let's return to Plato's *Republic* again, to the story of the Greek warrior Er, whose experience mirrors similar accounts that crop up in virtually every culture of the world. They are found among the peoples of Egypt, Siberia, Finland, Bolivia, Argentina, and among North American native peoples. There are also strikingly similar near-death reports coming from Hindu, Islamic, and Tibetan Buddhist texts; modern-day NDEs describe reunions with departed relatives, feelings of immense joy, and the recognition that there is a borderline or separation between our world and the Otherside, between the dimension we live in on Earth and the Otherside.[10]

Plato concludes Er's story with an account of the Souls who are preparing to descend to Earth to begin new lives:

> Now when all the souls had chosen their lives . . . they all traveled into the Plain of Forgetfulness . . . and took up their quarters by the bank of the River of Indifference . . . each, as he drinks, forgets everything. When they had gone to rest, and it was not midnight, there was a clap of thunder and an earthquake: and in a moment the souls were carried up to their birth, this way and that, like shooting stars.
>
> Er himself was prevented from drinking any of the water; but how, and by what road, he reached his body, he knew not; only [that] he knew that he suddenly opened his eyes at dawn, and found himself laid out upon the funeral pyre.[11]

Plato concludes with these words of wisdom to his student, Glaucon:

> And thus, Glaucon, the tale has been saved and has not perished, and will save us if we are obedient to the word spoken; and we shall pass safely over the River of Forgetfulness and our soul will not be defiled.

Wherefore my counsel is that we hold ever fast to the heavenly way and follow after justice and virtue always, considering that the soul is immortal and able to endure every sort of good and every sort of evil. Thus shall we live, dear to one another . . . and it shall be well with us, both in this Life and in the pilgrimage of a thousand years which we have been describing.[12]

Let's examine a few other accounts. There is the story of the British admiral who narrowly escaped drowning in the Portsmouth Harbor in 1795. His account was published in a local newspaper, and it too included a life review: "In short, the whole period of my existence seemed to be placed before me in a kind of panoramic review, and each part of it seemed to be accompanied by a consciousness of right or wrong, or by some reflection on its cause or consequences; indeed many trifling events which had been forgotten then crowded into my imagination, and with the character of recent familiarity."[13]

Then there is the account of a famous nineteenth-century Swiss geologist and alpinist Albert Heim (1849–1937) who sustained a twenty-meter fall from a mountain following a failed attempt to catch his hat. In his fall, he had a near-death experience. Over the next twenty-five years Heim collected accounts from other climbers who had fallen or had similar near-fatal experiences. To his surprise, he found twenty such people. They reported hearing celestial music, experiencing an expanded sense of time, being enveloped in a calming peace, and achieving a clarity of mind that made their encounters indelible. They claimed to have experienced a life review, and also claimed that when they died they felt no pain from the injuries their bodies had sustained at the time of their deaths.[14] Heim published his research in 1892 and thus became the first person in modern history to publish a collection of what would later be referred to as NDEs.

Of his own experience Heim wrote, "I saw my whole past life take place in many images, as though on a stage at some distance from me. I saw myself as the chief character in the performance. . . . Everything was beautiful and without grief, without anxiety, and without pain. . . . I felt no conflict or strife; conflict had been transmuted into love."[15]

Near-death experiences include every culture, ethnicity, gender, age, and religion. They also occur among people with no spiritual beliefs at all, and this is a strong argument for our existence as an immortal being of light. At death the Soul shifts from one dimensional level to another, depending on its level of consciousness in life; and what we have learned in each life goes with us until we discover how to permanently abide in the vibration of love. For millennia some of the greatest thinkers in the world have contemplated these Mysteries and have had profound things to say about the nature of the Soul. Origen, a third-century AD Greek scholar, ascetic, and early Christian theologian, writes:

It can be shown that an incorporeal and reasonable being has life in itself independently of the body . . . then it is beyond a doubt [that] bodies are only of secondary importance and arise from time to time to meet the varying conditions of reasonable creatures. Those who require bodies are clothed with them, and contrariwise, when fallen souls have lifted themselves up to better things, their bodies are once more annihilated. They are ever vanishing and ever reappearing.[16]

The following comes from Madame Helena Blavatsky, the Russian spiritual initiate occultist and the founder of Theosophy:

That which is part of our Souls is eternal . . . . Those lives are countless, but the Soul or spirit that animates us throughout these myriads of existences is the same; and though "the book and volume" of the physical brain may forget events within the scope of one terrestrial life, the bulk of collective recollections can never desert the divine Soul within us.

Its whispers may be too soft, the sound of its words too far off the plane perceived by our physical senses; yet the shadow of events that were, just as much as the shadow of the events that are to come, is within its perceptive powers, and is ever present before its mind's eye.[17]

The Astonishing Case of George Richie

The extraordinary case of George Richie opens in 1946, at the close of World War II. Some years later, in 1978, Richie told his own story in a powerful little book titled *Return from Tomorrow.*

The story begins when George was a twenty-year-old army soldier preparing to leave his barracks in Texas to visit his family in Richmond, Virginia, at Christmastime. George came down with a case of double pneumonia and was admitted to the hospital, where his temperature rose to a whopping 106.5 degrees and he was declared dead. Next thing he knew, George found himself standing outside of his body by the hospital bed. At first he didn't realize that he was dead. In fact, he thought that he had just awakened in the hospital. Since it was Christmas, and he was hoping to get back to see his family, his thoughts turned toward his desire to visit them.

Suddenly, George found himself flying at the speed of thought across the night landscape. Below him he could see towns and villages passing by, and it soon occurred to him that he had no idea where he was, so he descended to the ground to ask a pedestrian. To George's surprise, the man he approached was not able to hear him. Confused, George spotted the bright neon sign of a bar and ducked inside, hoping to get someone in there to tell him where he was. But again, no one in the bar seemed to be able to hear him or see him for that matter. Growing alarmed, it suddenly occurred to George that he might be dreaming or out of his body—that the inert body he had left behind on that hospital bed might have actually been his.

In a panic, George now found himself racing back along the same aerial path that he had just taken, flying back toward the hospital, crossing hundreds of miles in mere moments. But once he arrived he realized that he had no idea which room his body had been taken to since he had been unconscious with fever. For the next few hours George searched diligently through all the hospital rooms, looking at body after body of sick young men, until at last he found his own body covered by a white sheet. The only way he knew it was his body was because his arm was sticking out of the covers and he recognized the ring he had been wearing.

I backed towards the doorway. The man in that bed was dead! . . .
But if that was my ring, then, then it was me, the separated part of
me, lying under that sheet. Did that mean that I was . . . ?

It was the first time in this entire experience that the word
"death" occurred to me in connection with what was happening. But
I wasn't dead! How could I be dead and still be awake? Thinking.
Experiencing. Death was different. Death was . . . I didn't know.
Blanking out. Nothingness. I was me, wide awake, only without a
physical body to function in.[18]

Then a great light filled the room and a luminous being appeared.
George believed this to be Jesus, for this being radiated an all-
encompassing love. In this radiant presence George saw the details of
his life quickly pass before his eyes in a life review:

How this was possible I didn't know. I had never before experienced the kind of space we seemed to be in. The little one-bed
room was still visible, but it no longer confined us. Instead, on all
sides of us was what I could only think of as a kind of enormous
mural—except that the figures on it were three dimensional, moving and speaking. . . . There were other scenes, hundreds, thousands, all illuminated by that searing Light, in an existence where
time seemed to have ceased. It would have taken weeks of ordinary
time even to glance at so many events, and yet I had no sense of
minutes passing.[19]

During this life review George realized that much of his life had
been wrapped up in anger, self-centeredness, and self-aggrandizement.
With crystal clarity he saw that

every detail of twenty years of living was there to be looked at. The
good, the bad, the high points, the run of the mill. And with this
all-inclusive view came the question. It was implicit in every scene
and, like the scenes themselves, seemed to proceed from the living
Light beside me.

What did you do with your life?

It was obviously not a question in the sense that he [the luminous Being] was seeking information, for what I had done with my life was in plain view. In any case this total recalling, detailed and perfect, came from Him, not me. I couldn't have remembered a tenth of what was there until He showed it to me.

What did you do with your life?

It seemed to be a question about values, not facts: what did you accomplish with the precious time you were allotted? And with this question shining through them, these ordinary events of a fairly typical boyhood seemed not merely unexciting, but trivial. Hadn't I done anything lasting, anything important? Desperately I looked around for something that would seem worthwhile in the light of this blazing Reality.[20]

Although George found nothing of any redeeming value about his own choices in life so far, this luminous presence offered to take him on a journey to reveal the spiritual state of other Souls that had gone to the Otherside. During this extraordinary tour George was shown two lower levels of the Afterlife, and then finally taken to a higher realm of radiant light. These three levels corresponded to the lowest, lower, and middle registers of the astral plane.

The Lower Astral Realms

To his surprise, George found that the two lowest levels of the astral plane seemed to be superimposed over our earthly world yet separated from it in vibrational density. These realms appeared to be dark and gloomy, devoid of all light. This was the Underworld, the dimensional plane where our emotions and desires create our reality, binding us to our own negative thought forms. The lowest level lies below the crust of the Earth, while the next level up seems to be superimposed over our physical world. Since each of these various dimensional planes vibrates at a different rate of speed, people in one state are largely unaware of those in other states. In chapter 4 we briefly spoke about the existence of seven dimensional planes, from the highest to the lowest. The number seven has been taught in many esoteric traditions, although sometimes the number of the dimensions is said to be as few as five and as many as twelve. Often these seven dimensional realms are depicted in a series of concentric circles, with the highest and finest vibrating plane at the center, and the coarsest dimension being the outermost ring. It is these two outer rings that George first visited, dimensions that are inhabited by Souls stuck in delusions and negativity.

The first of these dismal places was the seedy bar that George had visited earlier, where he had been neither seen nor heard by the living. This was the realm of the hungry ghosts, the *pretaloka* spoken of in the Tibetan Book of the Dead. According to this ancient text, this plane emits a dull red light. In this seedy bar George watched as many disembodied spirits tried to take a drink, but soon he realized that without bodies they could never satiate their thirst. Frustrated by their futile attempts to drink, these restless spirits had become hungry ghosts, trapped by the cravings they were enslaved by in their earthly lives, whether drugs, alcohol, cigarettes, narcotics, or sexual activity. But now, in the realm of the pretas, they had no way of assuaging their cravings. Death did not cure whatever addiction was operating during their earthly life, since addiction is an illness of the mind as much as it is of the body. George watched as these troubled spirits tried to jump into the bodies of the still living, vicariously feeding off that person's desire and ability to actually drink. If a hungry ghost is successful in attaching to a living human being as a host, then it brings its own cravings, disturbed thoughts, and wounding patterns into the life of that person.

The luminous guide then directed George to view some of the spirits that had committed suicide. These Souls were trapped in futility and regret. As soon as they had left their bodies they realized that they had made a mistake. Filled with sorrow, they followed their family members around apologizing; however, they could not get through the numbing clouds of grief that enveloped their relatives. So these suicide cases became trapped in guilt and regret. They could not move on because they could not forgive themselves for what they had done. George realized through these revelations that each of us has a chosen life span. When we cut it short by committing suicide, then our problems are compounded. This is because we have broken multiple Soul contracts with those we have promised to interact with in this lifetime, whether it be children, spouses, parents, or those we might have helped. In some cases, the Soul is doomed to wander in these lower astral realms until the term of their original life contract is up.

Next, the luminous presence took George to an even darker astral realm. This was the lowest level of the astral plane, which was heavier and gloomier than the first. Tibetans call this the Hell realm for it is filled with only a dim, smoky light. George found himself on a dark blue open plain, where he saw hundreds of angry ghosts locked in battle with one another. These fighting hell-realm inhabitants are called titans in the Tibetan bardo teachings. Everyone here was experiencing some form of emotional trauma, hurling themselves at one another in a frenzy of impotent rage. Tibetan texts tell us that those who dwell in this plane, because of the karmic effects of selfishness, are consumed by the belief that others are their enemies.[21] Soon George realized that some of these spirits were so caught up in anger, blame, and self-righteousness that they were oblivious to all the other Souls around them, so they were boxing at shadows, completely absorbed in their own self-created hells.

> Up to this moment, the misery I had watched consisted in being chained to a physical world of which we were no longer a part. Now I saw that there were other kinds of chains. Here there were no solid objects or people to enthrall the soul. These creatures seemed locked into habits of mind and emotion, into hatred, lust, destructive thought patterns . . . and the thoughts most frequently communicated had to do with superior knowledge, or abilities, or the background of the thinker. "I told you so!" "I always knew!" "Didn't I warn you!" were shrieked into the echoing air over and over . . . in these yelps of envy and wounded self-importance I heard myself all too well.[22]

Eventually, George realized that in these lower dimensions there is no faking that you are more evolved than you really are. He also saw that like attracts like, so those who are caught up in their own emotional or mental venom attract others who are just as hate-filled as they are, and all these Souls settle in the same dimension. He called this the "Society of the Damned."[23] Theosophical writer Annie Besant (1847–1933) describes these levels in her book *The Ancient Wisdom:*

The first, or lowest division is the one that contains the conditions described in so many Hindu and Buddhist Scriptures under the name of "hells" of various kinds. It must be understood that a man, passing into one of the states, is not getting rid of the passions and vile desires that have led him thither; these remain, as part of his character, lying latent in the mind in a germinal state, to be thrown outwards again to form his passionate nature when he is returning to birth in the physical world. His presence in the lowest region of kamaloka, the astral plane, is due to the existence of his *kamic* [desire] body of matter belonging to that region, and he is held prisoner there until the greater part of that matter has dropped away, until the shell composed of it is sufficiently disintegrated to allow the man to come into contact with the region next above . . .

It is, in fact, the lowest slum with all the horrors veiled from physical sight parading in their naked hideousness. Its repulsiveness is much increased by the fact that in the astral world character expresses itself in form, and the man who is full of evil passions looks the whole of them; bestial appetites shape the astral body into bestial forms, and repulsively human animal shapes are the appropriate clothing of brutalized human souls. No man can be a hypocrite in the astral world, and cloak foul thoughts with a veil of virtuous seeming; whatever a man is, that he appears to be in outward form and semblance; radiant in beauty if his mind be noble, repulsive in hideousness if his nature be foul. It will be readily understood then, how such teachers as the Buddha—to whose unerring vision all worlds lay open—should describe what was seen in these hells in vivid language of terrible imagery, that seems incredible to modern readers only because people forget that, once escaped from the heavy and unplastic matter of the physical world, all souls appear in their proper likenesses and look just [like] what they are.[24]

Over this darkened field of Souls George then saw a great host of hovering light beings. These were the angelic guides of those Souls who were trapped in Hell. These Angels waited, hoping to lead their charges out of their self-made prisons, but their charges were unable to perceive their light because they were too absorbed in their own dark dramas. But once a trapped Soul began to ask "Is there a better way, another way?" then a ray of light would descend, freeing the Soul from its prison.

These two lower realms are in the bottom three rungs of the astral plane—the kamaloka in Tibetan teachings. The word *kama* means "desire," telling us that the astral plane is a place created by the thoughts, emotions, and desires of those who live there. While the higher levels of the kamaloka reflect our own higher or more positive states of consciousness while on Earth, the lower regions are places that the Soul is drawn to because of its negative consciousness. These darker emotions can include anything from addictions to the coarse emotions of anger, greed, grief, sorrow, regret, lust, vanity, or fear, emotional states known in Eastern teachings as "the passions of the mind."

As one of the lowest subdivisions of the astral plane, the pretaloka, the realm of hungry ghosts, is the habitat of beings who have physically died but are still encumbered by their base animal nature. These hungry ghosts are written about in many ancient texts as posing a threat to the living. Many of these spirits still have unresolved addictions like smoking, drinking, drugs, or addictive sexual proclivities, but their addictions may also be to violence, abuse, or anger, or the judging of others. These Souls have managed to trap themselves with their own negative thought forms, and thus they are stuck in a place of unconscious behavior. Once they learn to purify their thoughts and turn away from the darkness, they can then pass on to more illuminated regions.

While these hellish regions are not places any of us would want to inhabit, it is important to realize that they are not permanent destinations for any Soul. They are temporary habitats reflective only of the imbalances that a person has chosen to hold on to, thus sabotaging themselves. Once the Soul lets go of these negative patterns it is free to move into the higher realms. The implications of this are enormous. It means that when we die, it is the vibrational density of a person's emotional body that determines which region of the astral plane the Soul will be drawn to. Furthermore, ancient wisdom teaches us that whatever we give our time and attention to in a given lifetime is what we cultivate in our subtle-energy bodies. So just as an athlete might spend years developing his muscles, the time that we spend devoted to developing our mental, spiritual, and emotional natures during each earthly life directly affects the direction our energy body takes when we die. Tibetan teachings also say that our focus at the time of death also effects our destination, so placing our attention on the Divine allows any fear to drop away.

Understandably, only those Souls who are involved in the coarsest activities are drawn to the coarsest regions, because that is what they vibrate with. This means that those who are obsessed with money, power, and the material world do not get very far in the higher planes, for the spiritual regions are not interested in such things. However, Souls who have chosen to focus on the more enduring qualities of love, honor, and service, and have lived a life of compassion, learning, and generosity, will naturally gravitate to the more refined levels of the astral plane. Besant writes about the passing of the Soul through the various stages of the kamaloka:

A spiritually advanced man, who has so purified his astral body that its constituents are drawn only from the finest grade of each division of astral matter, merely passes through Kamaloka without delay, the astral body disintegrating with extreme swiftness, and he goes on to whatever may be his boon, according to the point he has reached in evolution. A less developed man, but one whose life has been pure and temperate and who has sat loosely on the things of earth, will wing a less rapid flight through Kamaloka, but will dream peacefully, unconscious of his surroundings, as his mental body disentangles itself from the astral shells, one after the other, to awaken only when he reaches the heavenly places.

Others, less developed still, will awaken after passing out of the lower regions, becoming conscious in the division which is connected with the active working of the consciousness during the earth-life, for this will be aroused on receiving familiar impacts, although these will be received now directly through the astral body, without the help of the physical. Those who had lived in the animal passions will awaken in their appropriate region, each man literally going "to his own place."

The case of men struck suddenly out of physical life by accident, suicide, murder, or sudden death in any form, differs from those of persons who pass away by the failure of the life-energies through disease or old age. If they are pure and spiritually minded, then they are specially guarded and often sleep out happily the term of their natural life. But in other cases they remain conscious—often entangled in the final scene of earth-life for a time, and unaware that they have lost the physical body—held in whatever region they are related to by the outermost layer of the astral body. Their normal kamalokic life does not usually begin until the natural web of earth-life is outspun, and they are vividly conscious of both their astral and physical surroundings.[25]

Here Besant is speaking about someone who has just experienced sudden death such as an automobile accident or a random shooting, where there was no preparation for death. These Souls are suddenly thrown out of the body and can, for a time, be unaware that they have died. This is one of the many reasons why prayers are so important, particularly in the case of an accident, other kinds of sudden death, or even suicide. Once these Souls realize that their physical life has ended, then for a time they may continue to hover around the people who are familiar to them, trying to communicate. However, as soon as the Soul is ready to let go of its attachment to the human world, their spirit guides will take the Soul into the higher planes of light.

Some years ago I read for a woman whose long-term lover had just committed suicide. Let's call her Paula. Her lover had been a prominent lawyer who was trapped in a loveless marriage. As much as he struggled, he wasn't willing to leave the world of ambition, success, and social obligations that he had built for himself in order to follow the callings of his heart. Caught between the longing of his Soul to grow and the obligations and reputation he had established in the material world, he saw no way out, so he jumped from a hotel window while on vacation with his selfish, materialistic wife. Understandably distraught, Paula came to see me immediately. We discovered that for the first five days after his suicide this man was in a place of great regret and darkness. I told my client to immediately get him on every prayer list she could think of so that he could move into the light. As a result, hundreds of people who had been shocked by his sudden suicide started praying for him. Within six days of his death, on the day of his funeral, he passed over into the light, forgiving himself for his errors and moving on to spiritual therapy on the Otherside. This is the power of human prayer.

The Higher Worlds

After George Richie visited the two lower levels of the astral plane, he was then taken to the higher realms by his spirit guide. There he beheld a radiant landscape with sunny parks, enormous buildings, and people dressed in long, flowing clothing. Unlike the darkened realms, this land had a perpetual, unwavering light and was permeated with a deep sense of peace. Light seemed to radiate from everything—flowers, trees, people—as if they were lit from within. George hovered above this celestial landscape, seeing buildings as large as universities and a study center with curving staircases, wide corridors, and high ceilings. From a distance he beheld a Crystal City of light but was told by his spirit guide that he would not be allowed to enter there.

At last, George was returned to the hospital where his body lay. There, his guide explained that it was not yet time for George to die. Suddenly, he found himself back in his body, very much alive. It took George many months to recover from his illness; however, these profound events completely changed his life. Not only did he heal his anger issues with his family, but these near-death experiences awakened within him a strong desire to help others. In the years that followed

George became a doctor, a psychiatrist, and finally a writer, spending the rest of his life in service to humankind.

The NDE Movement

The George Richie case is one of the most powerful twentieth-century accounts of a near-death experience, yet the publication of his story was preceded by Raymond Moody's seminal book *Life After Life* in 1975. Dr. Moody, a professor of psychology at the University of West Georgia, was so intrigued with the George Richie case (Richie had not yet published his memoir) that he shared this story with his students at one of his lectures. Afterward, one of them approached him and began to share his own NDE. For Moody, this was the beginning of a lifelong study that was to culminate in a number of amazing books.

Moody was the first to record the various stages of the near-death experience in detail for Western readers. Over the past thirty-five years he has written fourteen books on this subject, identifying fifteen different stages that people go through when they cross to the Otherside. Other researchers have expanded or contracted this list, knowing that while many have experienced some of these stages, most near-death experiencers do not experience them all. (In the next chapter I provide a list of seventeen stages of the near-death experience.)

If Raymond Moody was the father of the modern NDE movement, there have been a number of other powerful investigators who have followed suit. Paul Perry, Melvin Morse, P. M. H. Atwater, Kenneth Ring, Elisabeth Kübler-Ross, Kimberly Clark-Sharp, and Gloria Chadwick are among the most well-known researchers, having chronicled thousands of NDEs in their various books on this subject. Craig Lundahl, the chairman emeritus at the Department of Social Sciences at Western New Mexico University, and Harold Widdison, a professor of medical sociology at Northern Arizona University, have also done their own near-death investigations, which are presented in their book *The Eternal Journey*.

There have also been medical doctors who have addressed the skeptics' claims that the near-death experience is merely the reflexes of a dying brain that has been deprived of oxygen—one of the more specious theories put forth to debunk the phenomenon. Sam Parnia is one of them. He is currently one of the leading experts in the world on NDEs. Parnia is the founder of the Human Consciousness Project at the University of Southampton, England, an assistant professor of medicine at Stony Brook University School of Medicine, and consults for Cornell University. Beginning in 2008, Parnia and his colleagues undertook the AWARE (AWAreness during REsuscitation) study, looking at some 2,060 cases of cardiac arrest at fifteen American, British, and Austrian hospitals. Among them were 330 survivors, 140 of whom were interviewed. Fifty-five of the 140 subjects reported that during the time when they were being resuscitated they experienced a brilliant flash of light, joy, peacefulness, and separation from their bodies. In his 2007 book *What Happens When We Die: A Groundbreaking Study into the Nature of Life and Death,* Parnia documents the many physical stages the body goes through as the Soul moves in and out of these higher states.[26]

Along these same lines, French anesthesiologist and intensive-care physician Dr. Jean Jacques Charbonier has addressed the near-death experience from a biochemical perspective, assuring us that these experiences are not the result of random neurons firing in the brain of the dying patient. Dr. Charbonier has written a number of books about the survival of consciousness after death. His work is based on studies carried out over the past thirty-five years by many scientific teams across Europe. In his latest book, *Seven Reasons to Believe in the Afterlife,* Dr. Charbonier proves that biochemistry alone is not enough to induce these experiences. He disproves the notion that NDEs are caused by the loss of oxygen to the brain or the surplus carbon dioxide that skeptics claim produces the sensation of seeing a being of light. The brain, he says, represents a set of structures that are optimized to create, record, and change patterns, but the brain is only a link between the Soul and the physical body. When we die, our consciousness continues, even when our brain is no longer functioning. Dr. Charbonier reminds us that many people who have returned from death have been brain-dead for long periods of time—many hours, in fact. Yet even when the brain ceases to function, consciousness continues, as we will soon see.

The Remarkable Story of Dannion Brinkley

Today there are over 16 million people who have reported near-death experiences, but the case of Dannion Brinkley is perhaps one of the most extraordinary. In 1975 Brinkley had his first of three near-death experiences, which he recounts in his 1994 book *Saved by the Light*. This book not only became an international bestseller, it spawned a TV movie of the same name.

Trained as a sniper for the U.S. intelligence community, Brinkley believed he was a true American patriot doing the best he could for his country. Raised in Akin, South Carolina, in the fundamentalist faith of the Deep South, he was completely unprepared for the extraordinary experience that would await him when he was struck by lightning while talking on the phone. So severe was the electrical current that coursed through his body that his six foot two frame was thrown into the air and his shoes were left smoldering on the bedroom carpet. Like other NDEs, Brinkley immediately found himself swept up in a tunnel:

> I actually didn't move at all: the tunnel came to me. There was the sound of chimes as the tunnel spiraled toward and then around me. . . . I looked ahead into the darkness. There was a light up there, and I began to move toward it as quickly as possible. I was moving without legs at a high rate of speed. Ahead the light became brighter and brighter until it overtook the darkness and left me standing in a paradise of brilliant light. This was the brightest light I had ever seen, but . . . it didn't hurt my eyes in the least.[27]

Next Brinkley met a great light being whose love completely enveloped him. Then his life review began, and he got to take a look at all the good and bad that had happened in his life.

> When I finished the review, I arrived at a point of reflection in which I was able to look back on what I had just witnessed and come to a conclusion . . . I felt a deep sense of sorrow and shame. I expected a rebuke, some kind of cosmic shaking of my soul. I had reviewed

my life and what I had seen was a truly worthless person. What did I deserve, if not a rebuke? As I gazed at the Being of Light, I felt as though he was touching me. From that contact I felt a love and joy that could only be compared to the nonjudgmental compassion that a grandfather has for a grandchild. "Who you are is the difference that God makes," said the Being. "And that difference is love . . ."

As the Being of Light moved away, I felt the burden of this guilt being removed. I had felt the pain and anguish of reflection, but from that I had gained the knowledge that I could use to correct my life. I could hear the Being's message in my head, again as if through telepathy. "Humans are powerful spiritual beings meant to create good on the earth. This good isn't usually accomplished in bold actions, but in singular acts of kindness between people. It's the little things that count because they are more spontaneous and show who you truly are."[28]

The Council of Light

Brinkley's first book is remarkable for many reasons. First, his was the only NDE account that displayed virtually all of the stages of an NDE outlined by Raymond Moody. Second, Brinkley's life review was a profound wake-up call. He experienced all of the suffering he had caused the families of those men that he had killed in the line of duty, and this realization transformed his life. Finally, he was taken into a Crystal City with many cathedrals, a place that Brinkley unabashedly calls "Heaven," where he was greeted by beings who comprise a powerful Council of Light:

> These cathedrals were made entirely of a crystalline substance that glowed with a light that shone powerfully from within. . . . It had spires as high and pointed as those of the great cathedrals of France, and walls as massive and powerful as those of the Mormon Tabernacle in Salt Lake City. The walls were made of large glass bricks that glowed from within. . . . This place had a power that seemed to pulsate through the air. I knew that I was in a place of learning. . . . I was there to be instructed . . .

The place reminded me of a magnificent lecture hall. . . . The wall behind the podium was a spectacular carousel of colors. . . . Its beauty was hypnotic. I watched the colors blend and merge, surging and pulsing the way the ocean does when you are far out at sea and look into its depths. . . . In the next moment the space behind the podium was filled with the Beings of Light. They faced the benches where I was sitting and radiated a glow that was both kindly and wise.[29]

There were thirteen elder beings on this Council who glowed with a deep blue light. They had come to deliver a message for mankind, communicating telepathically through images as they instantly conveyed an entire volume with a single thought.

I could ask any question and know the answer. It was like being a drop of water bathed in the knowledge of the ocean, or a beam of light knowing what all light knows. I had only to think a question to explore the essence of the answer. In a split second I understood how light works, the ways in which spirit is incorporated into the physical life, why it is possible for people to think and act in so many different ways.[30]

These thirteen light beings showed Brinkley twelve boxes filled with future events that might unfold over the next few decades, especially if human beings did not change their present course. These events even included a third world war that could be set in motion from 1994 to 1996, but the light beings reminded him that we each have the power to change our collective future by changing our actions in the present. "If you . . . keep living the same way you have lived the last thirty years, all of this will surely be upon you. If you change, you can avoid the coming war."[31] Altogether, Brinkley remembered 117 of these prophecies when he returned to normal waking life; today, a hundred of these events have already come to pass.

This was to be the first of three near-death encounters that Brinkley would experience over the next few years, each one transformational.

It took him a year to recover from the shock of having his electrical system fried by lightning, but once he was back on his feet he left his government position and set up a national hospice program for veterans, to help his military comrades make peace with their lives before they passed over to the Otherside. He calls it the Twilight Brigade. Today this program has enlisted over fifty-five hundred volunteers and helped thousands of soldiers cross over to the Otherside. This humanitarian movement has freed many Souls from being trapped in the lower astral planes by releasing them from guilt, anger, shame, fear, and regret, feelings that many people experience at the end of life, particularly warriors who have seen battle. Ironically, Brinkley named his umbrella organization Compassion in Action, or CIA.

Over the next twenty-five years Brinkley underwent two more NDEs. The second one occurred during a massive heart surgery designed to repair the damage caused by the lightning strike. The third was an operation to relieve pressure on his brain that had occurred for a similar reason. In his second encounter with the Council of Light he was told that they were pleased with what he had accomplished in the intervening years. But during his last encounter Brinkley was taken to the lower levels of the astral plane and shown the vast number of Souls trapped in a hellish realm of their own making. Like George Richie, Brinkley witnessed people imprisoned in the angst of negative emotions, unable to move on until they could let go of these self-sabotaging emotions and beliefs.

The NDE "Wake-Up Call"

The importance of right thinking, right action, and right living while on Earth cannot be overstated. And acquiring as much spiritual wisdom as we can during any given lifetime can propel us forward on the path to emotional healing and spiritual enlightenment. It is also important to stay as clear as possible with yourself, including your daily thoughts, emotions, and habits, particularly when a Soul approaches the doorway of death. Today, with the increased use of alcohol, pharmaceuticals, and mind-numbing drugs, many people are no longer mentally clear when they die. Dementia and Alzheimer's also contributes to this, as does the amount of aluminum and other heavy metals in our environment, which is sharply rising in our foods. These mind-altering substances not only disconnect us from our clarity of mind, they exaggerate any paranoia we may have taken on about death, dying, or a fear of the Afterlife.

Furthermore, while many religions do great good for the living, the erroneous dogmas of blame, shame, guilt, and damnation that they teach do not do us any favors when the end comes. In fact, they keep the Soul bound in the lower astral realm of regret. Likewise, the enormous amount of violence and pornography we see on television and on the Internet negatively programs the subconscious mind not only during our dreaming life, but in the Afterlife as well. We must understand that the astral and mental planes are highly responsive to the direction of our thoughts and emotional states, so what we focus on expands, whether it be worry, fear, poverty, regret, or lustful passions. This is why books like the Tibetan Book of the Dead were first written—to focus the dying person's attention on the Divine. The purer our thoughts and the lighter our hearts, the farther we will go when we cross over. Not only should we free ourselves from the fears and negative habits we have acquired while we're still alive, we must also forgive all those who have wronged us, not only for their sake, but for ours. Once we realize that in the astral and mental planes our thoughts and emotions are what we will create or attract, magnetizing us to the various registers of the astral plane, then it is clear that focusing on beauty, harmony, love of others, love of self, and an appreciation for the goodness of life can only lift us into the higher spheres. By remembering that the universe is conscious and that like attracts like, we begin to understand the wonderful consequences of living a virtuous life in the here and now.

It is also important that we remember to pray for those Souls who have passed to the Otherside, for some of them may need our prayers, especially those who have died in trauma or in inner conflict. The love and forgiveness we send to these Souls has the power to break up the darkness that surrounds them. Our prayers can help them break out of their energetic prisons, and when they emerge on the Otherside their beloved guides will be waiting. Souls who die in pain, confusion, or the ravages of addiction are often taken to a kind of rehabilitation center on the Otherside before they are even allowed to see their loved ones. There, their auras are bathed in the flow of celestial light that can help heal the rips and tears that have formed in their subtle-energy bodies and restore the brilliance of their light. Then they are given a long time-out. During this period they are in serious therapy so that they may once again learn to have faith in their ability to create a different kind of life. Then, when they are finally ready, they are given another chance at a human life.

Dr. Eben Alexander's Account

In recent years, one of the most moving accounts I have read of an NDE comes from a self-professed atheist and neurosurgeon Eben Alexander. Dr. Alexander's NDE was precipitated when he suddenly contracted bacterial meningitis and fell into a weeklong coma. His team of medical doctors expected him to die because his brain registered absolutely no activity. However, inwardly his consciousness was taken to the extraordinary realms of Spirit. After five days in a coma, Alexander made an astonishing recovery that was calculated at a million to one by his doctors. When he returned to life he related stories of the vast vistas where he had traveled while his brain had registered no activity.

In his first book, *Proof of Heaven,* Alexander relates what happened to him as he was pulled out of the lower astral plane by the power of love. First, he found himself in a lower level of the astral plane that he calls "the earthworm's view." This was a brown loamy area surrounded by other spiritually unconscious people. These people were not bad; they had just been living lives of spiritual darkness. Oblivious to the passage of time, he at last heard celestial music that broke through the murky darkness:

Something had appeared in the darkness.

Turning slowly, it radiated fine filaments of white-gold light, and as it did so the darkness around me began to splinter and break apart.

Then I heard a new sound: a *living* sound, like the richest, most complex, most beautiful piece of music you've ever heard. Growing in volume as a pure white light descended . . .

The light got closer and closer, spinning around and around and generating those filaments of pure white light that I now saw were tinged, here and there, with hints of gold.

Then, at the very center of the light, something else appeared. I focused my awareness hard, trying to figure out what it was.

An opening. I was no longer looking at the slowly spinning light at all, but *through* it.

The moment I understood this, I began to move up. Fast. There was a whooshing sound, and in a flash I went through the opening and found myself in a completely new world. The strangest, most beautiful world I'd ever seen. . . .

Below me there was countryside. It was green, lush, and earthlike. It *was* earth . . . but at the same time it wasn't. . . .

I was flying, passing over trees and fields, streams and waterfalls, and here and there, people. There were children, too, laughing and playing. The people sang and danced around in circles, and sometimes I'd see a dog running and jumping among them, as full of joy as the people were. They wore simple yet beautiful clothes, and it seemed to me that the colors of these clothes had the same kind of living warmth as the trees and the flowers that bloomed and blossomed in the countryside around them.

A beautiful, incredible dream world . . .

Except it wasn't a dream.[32]

He then describes how he fell back into this darker vibration again until finally a beautiful young girl riding on a butterfly came to find him. She pulled him up from this loamy darkness into the light. Later he was to discover that this girl was his deceased sister whom he had never met because he had been adopted as a baby. This girl had come to retrieve her brother through the power of light and sound. Together, they found themselves riding on the back of the butterfly over the shimmering countryside:

Without using any words, she spoke to me. The message went through me like a wind, and I instantly understood that it was true. I knew so, in the same way that I knew that the world around us was real—was not some fantasy, passing and insubstantial. The message had three parts, and if I had to translate them into earthly language, I'd say they ran something like this.

"You are loved and cherished, dearly, forever."

"You have nothing to fear."

"There is nothing you can do wrong."

The message flooded me with a vast and crazy sensation of relief. It was like being handed the rules to a game I'd been playing all my life without ever fully understanding it.[33]

Passing through the deep blue skies of this beautiful countryside, Alexander saw brilliant orbs of light flying through puffy pink clouds. He knew that these were advanced beings, like Angels. "A sound, huge and booming like a glorious chant, came down from above, and I wondered if the winged beings (the angels) were producing it . . . it occurred to me . . . that if the joy didn't come out of them this way then they would simply not otherwise be able to contain it."[34] He observed that in this world his senses were not isolated from one another—he could *hear* the silvery bodies of the beings that flew above him, and *see* the joyful perfection of the songs they sang. "It seemed that you could not look at or listen to anything in this world without becoming a part of it— without joining with it in some mysterious way."[35] In this world everything was a part of everything else, even though at the same time things were distinct and separate. "Thoughts entered me directly. . . . solid and immediate—hotter than fire and wetter than water—and as I received them I was able to instantly and effortlessly understand concepts that would have taken me years to fully grasp in my earthly life."[36]

In time, Alexander found himself drawn into a higher level of Heaven as he followed this celestial music upward. Eventually, he was pulled into even higher dimensions, where he encountered the presence of the Source. He came to an immense pitch black void that felt like a womb, which was "brimming over with light." He describes this as "The

*Figure 6.3. Dante and Beatrice observe the passage of Angels in Heaven
(engraving by Gustave Doré)*

Creator, the Source who is responsible for making the universe and all in it. This Being was so close that there seemed to be no distance at all between God and myself. Yet at the same time, I could sense the infinite vastness of the Creator, could see how completely minuscule I was by comparison."[37] Alexander calls this Source "the OM," for this was the sound that permeated everything. This being, he explains, expresses all of the same human qualities that we possess—warmth, pathos, compassion, curiosity, irony, and even humor—but in a far greater measure.

He also learned that our universe is one of many, that there are countless dimensions in Creation that cannot be understood from the lower dimensions. He realized that the only way to truly know these worlds is to enter them and experience them for ourselves. These worlds are all part of the same overarching reality, and none of them are truly separate from us except through our inability to perceive them.

Alexander was then shown that evil had only been created to allow us to experience the power of free will. Without this ability to choose, there would be no growth. For all the bad things in the world, he realized that the power of love was overwhelmingly stronger than the power of hate, and that it would ultimately triumph.

Needless to say, this experience profoundly changed Alexander when he returned to the land of the living. Today his many activities include working with sound therapists to try to re-create the celestial music that he heard in Heaven, a music that allowed him to pull himself up into the higher realms. It is his hope that he can give others an experiential glimpse of the heavenly realms that await them once they cross over.

My Personal Experience
Returning from the Dead

The last near-death experience I want to share with you is my own.

In August 2003 I had been in the hospital for about a month as a result of a strange *E. coli* infection. *E coli* exists in the intestines of all of us; its job is to break down food, but if it gets outside of the intestines it can kill you. In my case it had gotten into my fallopian tubes, and the doctors discovered that I had a tumor the size of two tennis balls there.

Since fallopian tubes are only the size of a piece of string, this infection was really serious: if the tube burst, I would die.

During the four-and-a-half-hour surgery to remove this infection, I died on the operating table and crossed over to the Otherside. While I do not remember moving through the tunnel of light, I found myself standing before five luminous beings of light. This Council of Elders sat above me at a semicircular table in a round, high-domed chamber. Luminous, but human in shape, I could see no facial details because they were made completely of light. They bathed me in waves of unconditional love, filling the room with their wisdom, joy, and approval. I was immersed in their healing energies as they acknowledged me for all of the thousands of people I had helped using my clairvoyant and healing gifts, and I felt received at the very deepest level of my being. Since I had never really felt understood or accepted in my family of origin, which was a very traditional Christian family, this was a profoundly healing experience for me. If these higher beings could see who I was and find me worthy, then what my family thought didn't really matter.

I told them then that I wanted to come "home," meaning that I did not want to return to Earth. I wanted to stay there in my celestial home. Like many of us, I had gone through my own very difficult passages in life—spiritually, emotionally, and financially—and I didn't want to go through any more. I had already had three major health crises as a result of helping to transmute karma for large groups of people, and each time I had been overwhelmed by the effort it took for me to get back on my feet. While the work I had done had been spiritually important, helping millions of Souls trapped in the lower astral plane to make their way toward the light, each one of these transmutations had resulted in near fatal events for me. These medical "hiccups" had cost me tens of thousands of dollars in hospital bills, and the last thing I wanted to do was return to my body and spend another few years digging my way out of medical debt.

As I stood there before the Council of Elders, luminous beings of light who are sometimes called the Lords of Karma, I was completely enveloped by their love. I realized then that these beings saw the purity of my heart and my willingness to serve. Not only that, I realized that

I had stood before them many times before. This was the very same Council that had sent me down to Earth. They knew *exactly* who I was and what I had come to do, even if I couldn't remember. My life was part of a greater plan. Standing in the blaze of their love, I also realized that I had been taught to judge myself far too harshly. Growing up in a perfectionist family and a judgmental religion, I had developed a strong inner critic that was constantly picking at what was wrong with me. But these incredible beings were not judging me; they loved me unconditionally. It was I who was judging myself. I realized then that the things that matter the most about our life are:

> *Who loved you?*
> *Who did you love?*
> *Who helped you?*
> *Who did you help?*
> *What positive difference did your life make*
>   *as you passed through this world?*

These are the most powerful matters in any life. In Heaven, no one cares whether you drive a new car, how pretty you look, or how much money you have in the bank. They only care about the purity of your heart. This is the gold of Heaven. This assembly of wise beings knew that I had spent my life in service to the Divine, and they bathed me in waves of appreciation and love for how well I had done.

I am tired, I telegraphed back to them. *I just want to come home.*

Then they asked me a question that changed my life: *What will happen to all those Souls you said that you would help if you return home now?*

I contemplated this question in silence. I realized then that each of us makes a contract before we ever come to Earth. We each have certain things we want to accomplish, challenges we have agreed to take on, people we want to help, tasks we are committed to finishing. This may be as simple as inspiring others with your voice, your dance, or the kindness of your heart. It could involve raising children, saving animals, protecting the land, or fighting for justice, equality, or freedom. It could mean discovering a new medicine, bringing forth an ancient teaching, helping the elderly, or standing up for women's rights. I saw that while each of us has our karmic challenges, we also each have a dharmic purpose, something larger than us, a spiritual purpose, if only we step forward to claim it.

I knew in that moment that I would return to Earth to complete my mission. From the perspective of Heaven, fifty years on Earth is but a blink of an eye. And whatever we do not complete in one life we return to do in another. If we let circumstances defeat us or cash in our chips too soon, we'll regret it when we reach the Otherside.

The next thing I knew, I woke up in the intensive-care unit.

Let me say that even though I had made the decision to return, it was hard for me to want to come back from that beautiful place. In fact, I had no desire to live at all when I returned. Like many of us who have touched the hem of Heaven, once we are back from the celestial realms this 3-D world seems very unimportant. From this higher perspective we realize that every one of us will achieve enlightenment one day, though it may take a million years, or for some, a billion or more. From this perspective we know that our loved ones back on Earth will make it, even if we are removed from the equation. However, as I stood there before that luminous Council of Elders, I knew that when we decide to come back to Earth we make a soul contract. This contract is intertwined with those of the people around us, so if we leave the body before it is time, we will affect many others. Our lives do matter—not only to us, but to all of the members of our spiritual family who have agreed to incarnate along with us.

Through this experience I came to be a friend of death. I realized that dying is but a doorway to a golden world beyond our own. And in this knowledge I am reminded of the words of Mozart, a child prodigy who came to believe that his own genius had come from previous lives. "As death, when we come to consider it closely, is the true goal of our existence, I have formed during the last few years such close relations with this best and truest friend of mankind, that his image is not only no longer terrifying to me, but is very soothing and consoling! I thank my God for graciously granting me the opportunity of learning that death is the key which unlocks the door to our true happiness."[38]

7

The Seventeen Stages of the Near-Death Experience

I look upon death to be as necessary to the constitution as sleep. We shall rise refreshed in the morning.

BENJAMIN FRANKLIN

While it is clear that the near-death experience is universal, there are many stages that one may experience between the earthly life and a life in the paradisiacal realms. The following seventeen steps are the ones most often reported in near-death experiences. We will take a look at each of these stages through the personal accounts of those who have experienced NDEs.

The Seventeen Stages of the NDE

1. The Soul finds itself outside of the body looking down at its lifeless form.
2. The Soul observes events nearby that it could not otherwise have known.
3. The Soul hears a whooshing noise and sees a spiraling dark tunnel.

4. The Soul is caught up in this tunnel and pulled upward.

5. At the end of the tunnel the Soul beholds a dazzling being of light.

6. The Soul experiences a rapid life review.

7. The Soul feels supreme compassion from this being of light as it realizes the errors of its ways on Earth and the connectedness of us all.

8. The Soul meets loved ones who have crossed over before it.

9. The Soul is allowed to make, or prevented from making, a more prolonged visit to the Otherside.

10. The Soul is shown some of the territory of Heaven.

11. The Soul hears celestial music that seems to permeate these inner realms.

12. The Soul beholds the Crystal City of light.

13. The Soul meets with an angelic Council of Elders, or Council of Light.

14. The Soul receives a revelation or a profound teaching.

15. The Soul is then given the chance to return to Earth.

16. If the Soul does not wish to return to Earth, it is shown the impact its death will have on others should it decide to cut its life short, thereby encouraging the Soul's return to physical form.

17. The Soul realizes that it must finish its original Soul contract and agrees to go back to Earth.

The Tunnel of Darkness and the Welcoming Party

When a Soul leaves its body, it often finds itself watching over its own physical death with a mixture of curiosity, detachment, or concern. Some people recall floating above their body, watching doctors and nurses scrambling to save their life. Some report standing outside of their body, trying to figure out why no one seems to be able to hear them. Then, shortly afterward, the Soul hears the sound of a rushing wind, sometimes described as a whooshing sound or a chime. This seems to signal the appearance of a transport system into the bardo, or intermediate realm between this world and the next.

Almost immediately a spiral of energy envelops the Soul and he or she is propelled through a tunnel often described as having a dark-grayish atmosphere. Some report sensing other people or animals moving around them in their peripheral vision. These may be beings who have died at the same time and are making their own transition, or perhaps the tunnel is like a wormhole or elevator that transports the Soul through the various regions of the astral plane, like moving upward on a glass elevator. Some believe that the grayish atmosphere that surrounds this transport system is really a fog of dense thought forms that surround the Earth, a fog composed of all the many centuries of negative emotions that we have created. As the Soul is pulled up, it sometimes senses other spirits residing in this fog.

At the end of the tunnel the Soul sees a brilliant beam of light. Tibetan Buddhists call this the Clear Light, but it is also known as the Dharmakaya, or "Truth Body," which meets the Soul at the time of death. This brilliant light is actually the person's own higher Self that has come to greet them. It is the pure white fire being of our Angelic Twin (a subject we shall take up in greater detail in chapter 13). Since few people recognize this as their higher Self, they often return from their NDE to report that this radiant light being is either an Angel or a spiritual teacher like Jesus.

Directly afterward the Soul emerges from the dark tunnel into a misty landscape. This is the first intermediate bardo; it is described as being filled with celestial music and prismatic light. At this point the Soul is often met by friends waiting for its arrival. These Souls are part of the welcoming party that have somehow been alerted that the newly deceased is arriving in Heaven. Here is an account from a fifty-three-year-old woman whose near-death experience was caused by a vascular tumor lodged at the base of her brain:

> The more I approached the light, the more I began to see people I recognized. I was impressed by the fact that these people had a marvelous look about them. My grandmother didn't look like an

old woman; she was radiant. Everyone looked young, healthy, and strong. I can say that they were of the light, as if they were wearing clothing made of light, and as if they themselves were made of light. I was not allowed to go very far—they were keeping me close to them. I wanted to know more about the music, about the sound of a waterfall, about the birdsongs I was hearing, and I wanted to know why they wouldn't let me go farther.[1]

Here is another account of a Soul's arrival that also includes a life review:

I came out of this tunnel into a realm of soft, brilliant love and light. The love was everywhere. It surrounded me and seemed to soak through into my very being. At some point I was shown, or saw, the events of my life. They were in a kind of vast panorama. All of this is really just indescribable. People I knew who had died were there with me in the light, a friend who had died in college, my grandfather, and a great-aunt, among others. They were happy, beaming.[2]

Meeting the Being of Light

Next, the Soul beholds a brilliant being of light who emanates an all-encompassing love. Some near-death experiencers believe this being of light is Jesus, Mary, or Buddha. Others think it is an Angel. In India some have claimed it is Yama-Raja (Lord Yama), the Hindu Lord of the Dead, said to greet the Soul on the Otherside. While it is certainly possible that this is Jesus, Mary, or Buddha, it is also possible that our belief systems color our interpretation of who we interpret this luminous figure to be. In truth there is a deeper explanation.

The Tibetan Book of the Dead essentially tells us that this secondary Clear Light is the Soul's Angelic Twin, which has come to meet the personality self. In Egyptian teachings this may be equivalent to the Khu, or "shining body." This is the pure White Fire being that eternally resides in the higher realms, even while some part of the Soul has partaken of its journey in the realms of illusion. Gnostics called this the Angelic Twin.

If the Soul recognizes this being as none other than itself, then it is immediately liberated from samsara, the wheel of life, death, rebirth, and suffering. This recognition is actually a profound revelation, for it reveals the depth of who we really are. If we are, in fact, pure angelic beings who eternally reside in the celestial kingdoms, then this means that one day we shall all return to this place of remembrance. All of our many lifetimes are simply ways that we entertain ourselves and learn throughout time. When we hear the profound awe that Souls experience when they first encounter this being of light, and the unconditional love that it projects to its less-than-perfect human self, then this realization puts an entirely new spin on the idea of a life review. In essence, our divine Self is saying, "How did *we* do? Did *we* bring back some wisdom from *our* journey?"

This encounter with our own light-being self is a critical moment, for the recognition that this is our eternal twin can catapult us into Paradise, or as the Tibetan Buddhists call it, spiritual liberation. However, this recognition of the true Self rarely happens because of our own feelings of unworthiness as well as the deep programming by our various religious dogmas. Our inability to perceive clearly is due to an impure emotional and mental state that has become polluted in the human condition. So if the Soul does not recognize its Angelic Twin as itself, then it passes onto the next stage of the journey.[3] However, if the Soul is able to raise its vibration to recognize this higher Self, which is basically in Christ consciousness, then we are liberated from the wheel of endless rebirth and can step outside of time and space. At this point the returning Soul is bathed in an outflow of unconditional love from its higher Self, enveloping the returning personality self in a deep sense of peace.

Here is an account of one such meeting with this light being. Alice was rushed to the hospital in a coma, while her Soul watched from above as the doctors scrambled to save her life:

> Then I was aware of an Immense Presence coming toward me, bathed in white, shimmering light that glowed and at times sparkled

like diamonds. Everything else seen, the colors, beings, faded into the distance as the Light Being permeated everything. I was being addressed by an overwhelming presence. Even though I felt unworthy, I was being lifted into that which I could embrace. The joy and ecstasy were intoxicating. It was explained that I could remain there if I wanted; it was a choice I could make.[4]

This next account comes from Dannion Brinkley, who describes meeting this shining being of light—our true Self, which is called the *Nuri Sarup* (Light Body or Radiant Form) by mystics—in the first of his three near-death experiences: "I looked at my hand. It was translucent and shimmering and moved with fluidity, like the water in the ocean. I looked down at my chest. It too, had the translucence and flow of fine silk in a light breeze. The Being of Light stood directly in front of me. As I gazed into its essence I could see prisms of color, as though it were composed of thousands of tiny diamonds, each emitting the colors of the rainbow."[5]

Like many other near-death experiencers, Dannion reports seeing rainbows. These are mentioned repeatedly in Tibetan texts as well. They remind us of the Norse legends of a Rainbow Bridge said to connect the realms of Heaven and Earth. In Norse mythology this bridge links Middle Earth, or Midgard, with the higher worlds. It is part of the Tree of Life, called Yggdrasil in Norse mythology—the tree that connects all the dimensions.

The Life Review

In the presence of this great being of light the Soul then beholds the events of its former life. These events flash before its eyes. Tibetans call this life-review process "the Mirror of Karma."[6] Some have described it as being like a holographic movie, as if they are suddenly watching their life on a large television screen. Events not remembered for decades are suddenly there instantaneously, in minute detail, highlighting key points of one's life. As the Soul watches, it feels the emotions of all those whom their life has affected, feeling keenly how their deeds have inflicted joy or pain on others. This creates a profound sense of clarity about the merit of the life they have just lived. Could they have made other choices? Could they have done better? Here is a condensed excerpt from a Soul experiencing the life review:

> When the light appeared, the first thing he said to me was, "What do you have to show me that you've done with your life?". . . And that's when these flashbacks started. I thought, "Gee, what is going on?" because all of a sudden, I was back early in my childhood. And from then on, it was like I was walking from the time of my very early life, on through each year of my life, right up to the present . . . The scenes were just like you walked outside and saw them, completely three dimensional, and in color. And they moved. . . . It was like the little girl I saw was somebody else, in a movie, one little girl among all the other children out there playing on the playground. Yet, it was me . . .
>
> Now I didn't actually see the light as I was going through the flashbacks. He disappeared as soon as he asked me what I had done, and the flashbacks started, and yet I knew that he was there with me the whole time, that he carried me back . . . because I felt his presence, and because he made comments here and there. He was trying to show me something in each one of these flashbacks.
>
> All through this, he kept stressing the importance of love. . . . He showed me some instances where I had been selfish to my sister, but then just as many times where I had really shown love to her. . . . He pointed out to me that I should try to do things for other people, to try my best. There wasn't any accusation in any of this, though. When he came across times when I had been selfish, his attitude was only that I had been learning from them too.[7]

Such a life review is profoundly transformational, for it allows the Soul to see its life against the yardstick of love. Notably, it is the Soul that judges itself most harshly during these sessions; those people who have experienced an NDE and returned to tell about it often make powerful changes once they are back, choosing a path of greater service.

Here is an excerpt from a woman who died when her fallopian tube ruptured during an ectopic pregnancy. In this account she stands before the being of light and undertakes her review: "This Presence could see into my mind, and there was no way I could hide any thoughts. Gently I was encouraged to understand how my mistakes had hurt others by experiencing what others had felt as a result of my actions. I was confused, as it all seemed so strange. The word *death* was never mentioned, yet somehow I came to understand that I was in that place of spirits where the newly dead move on to."[8]

A man who died of cardiac arrest after a traffic accident and returned to tell about it says, "I was in a light of love and this light was alive. It was speaking to me. I was shown my whole life, everything good and bad that I had done. My life passed by at high speed before my eyes in great detail and I was shown, as an overlay, the hands of a clock moving backward at dizzying speed. No one was judging me. It was I, myself, who was judging all of my actions."[9]

And here is yet another account:

I first was out of my body, above the building, and I could see my body lying there. Then I became aware of the light—just light—being all around me. Then it seemed there was a display all around me, and everything in my life just went by for review, you might say. I was really very, very ashamed of a lot of the things that I experienced because it seemed that I had a different knowledge, that the light was showing me what was wrong, what I did wrong. And it was very real.

It seemed like a flashback, or memory, or whatever was directed primarily at ascertaining the extent of my life. It was like there was a judgment being made and then, all of a sudden, the light became dimmer, and there was a conversation, not in words, but in thoughts. When I would see something, when I would experience a past event, it was like I was seeing it through eyes with omnipotent knowledge, guiding me, and helping me to see.

That's the part of it that has stuck with me because it showed me not only what I had done, but even how what I had done had affected other people. And it wasn't like I was looking at a movie projector because I could feel these things, there was feeling and particularly, since I was with this knowledge. . . . I found out that not even your thoughts are lost. . . . Every thought was there. . . . Your thoughts are not lost.[10]

Considering the power of these life reviews, we can understand now why the great Mystery Schools required each of their students to write a "Philosophic Will"—basically, a way of reflecting on what good they had done in life as part of the preparations for entering training. Imagine if each of us did a life review once a year, what a difference it would make when we pass over to the Otherside!

Landscapes of Light

Many near-death experiencers never go beyond the stage of the life review, and so they only make it to the first bardo. Afterward, the person is returned to her body to continue her life on Earth. However, some Souls go beyond this point, and are allowed to travel farther. Then the person returns with stories of dazzling landscapes of light. It seems that the deeper one penetrates these realms, the more substantial the visions become. Often these radiant vistas seem to invoke a deep sense of recognition, as if the Soul has been there many times before. Here is an account from a woman who returned after days in a coma to tell of her experience:

I found myself in a place of such beauty and peace. It was timeless and spaceless. I was aware of delicate and shifting hues of colors with their accompanying rainbows of "sound," though there was no noise in this sound. It might have felt like wind and bells, were it earthly. I became aware of other loving, caring beings hovering near me. Their presence was so welcoming and nurturing. They appeared formless in the way that I was accustomed by now to seeing things. I don't know how to describe them. I was aware of some bearded male figures in white robes in a semi-circle around me. The atmosphere became blended, as though made of translucent clouds. I watched as these clouds, and their delicate shifting colors, moved through and around us.[11]

Here is another account from a woman who died of an asthma attack and returned:

When I came out of the tunnel, I was in a pearly, misty place. . . . It was then that I thought, *I've died.* . . . At that instant I was in a different level. Here, all was soft gold, including me. . . . All of life's fears and worries seemed so unimportant, so absolutely nothing to worry about, and all behind me stretched infinity, that all the people I'd ever known, knew now, and even would know were there, all made out of this golden "light," all made of the same stuff, and so truly, we are all one. I saw this like a liquid golden ocean out of which each person rose, made of the ocean, in their own individual shape, but all one originally, basically many loved ones were there, and endless joy.[12]

Dannion Brinkley describes being pulled upward into the light to begin his journey through the Summerland:

We began to move upward. I could hear a hum as my body began to vibrate at a higher rate of speed. We moved up from one level to the next, like an airplane climbing gently into the sky. We were surrounded by a shimmering mist, cool and thick, like fog off the ocean. Around us I could see energy fields that looked like prisms of light. Some of this energy flowed like great rivers, while some eddied like tiny streams. I even saw lakes and small pools of it. (Up close these were clearly fields of energy, but from a distance they resembled rivers and lakes, the way you would see them from an airplane).

Through the mist I could see mountains the color of deep blue velvet. There were no sharp peaks and craggy slopes with jagged edges in this mountain range. The mountains were gentle, with rounded peaks and lush crevices that were a deeper blue. On the mountainside were lights. Through the mist they looked like houses turning on their lights at twilight. There were many such lights and I could tell by the way we swooped down and accelerated that we were headed directly for them. . . . Like wingless birds we swept into a city of cathedrals. These cathedrals were made entirely of a crystalline substance that glowed with a light that shone powerfully from within.[13]

A similar description of this land of light comes from a woman whose heart had stopped from an allergic reaction to an anesthetic:

I found myself in a beautiful landscape. The grass is greener than anything seen on earth, it has a special light or glow. The colors are beyond description. The light is brighter than anything possible to imagine. In this place I saw people that I knew [who] had died. There were no words spoken, but it was as if I knew what they were thinking, and at the same time I knew, *that they knew,* what *I* was thinking. I felt a peace that passed all understanding. I felt as if I wanted to stay there forever, but someone, I felt it was my guardian angel, said, "You have to go back, as you have not yet finished your term.[14]

This next NDE excerpt comes from a woman mourning the death of her aunt. When she suddenly dies herself, she gets to meet her aunt on the Otherside, giving her a powerful sense of closure. After returning to her body, she says, "I know that mountains and valleys, rivers and lakes, trees and flowers, are more real there than here, and best of all, our loved ones live to love and welcome us home when we are called upon to change to a higher life."[15]

This following comes from Arthur, who was a staunch materialist as a young man. This changed, however, on a road trip taken in 1932. Arthur's friend was driving the car when it suddenly skidded over a three-foot-high ridge of oiled gravel outside of Los Angeles. The car flipped over in a series of violent somersaults, and Arthur and his friend were catapulted through the cloth roof of the car before it smashed into a ditch. The driver escaped without injuries, but for a time Arthur found himself in the beauty of the Far Country:

> Gradually the earth scene faded away, and through it [the cloth roof] looked a bright, new beautiful world—beautiful beyond imagination! For half a minute I could see both worlds at once. Finally, when the earth was all gone, I stood in a glory that could only be heaven. In the background were two beautiful, round-topped mountains, similar to Fujiyama in Japan. The tops were snowcapped, and the slopes were adorned with foliage of indescribable beauty. The mountains appeared to be about fifteen miles away, yet I could see individual flowers growing on their slopes. I estimated my vision to be about one hundred times better than on earth.
>
> To the left was a shimmering lake containing a different kind of water—clear, golden, radiant, and alluring. It seemed to be alive. The whole landscape was carpeted with grass so vivid, clear and green, that it defies description. To the right was a grove of large, luxuriant trees, composed of the same clear material that seemed to make up everything. . . . Then I noticed that the landscape was gradually becoming familiar. It seemed as if I had been here before. I remembered what was on the other side of the mountains. Then, with a sudden burst of joy, I realized that this was my real home! Back on earth I had been a visitor, a misfit, and a homesick stranger. With a sigh of relief, I said to myself, "Thank God I'm back again. This time I'll stay!"[16]

Notably, Tibetan lamas say there are five kinds of eyes, apart from normal human eyes. These are the Eyes of Instinct, Celestial Eyes, Eyes of Truth, Divine Eyes, and the Eyes of Wisdom of the Buddhas. These five types of eyes may have to do with the vision of five of the subtle-energy bodies (astral, causal, mental, spiritual, and Soul bodies), for all of these five types have capabilities far beyond those of normal human eyes.[17]

The Crystal City of Light

Some near-death experiencers report seeing a Crystal City of light. This is one of several magnificent cities, each the center of the various levels of the astral plane. Jewish cosmology refers to this as the "City of the Just," a realm where only the noblest, most righteous Souls mingle and dwell. It is a place without hunger, war, or poverty, where we spend our days with those we love, together developing the highest qualities of our Souls. In this kingdom we live in a state of perpetual light and joy, and we can move up in vibration into even higher levels of the astral plane. These realms are equivalent to many of our religious ideas about Heaven, and these cities grow ever brighter the higher our vibration.

Some Souls are only allowed to see the Crystal City from a distance. Like George Richie, they glimpse it, but are not allowed to enter. In other cases the Soul is taken by their guide to a way station outside the city's gates. There it is determined whether the Soul has arrived prematurely (as George was), and if so, the person is sent back to Earth. Sometimes, however, the Soul is allowed to enter the city and then return, as Dannion Brinkley did. These people are those who have been chosen to go back to Earth to share their experiences with others.

Perhaps not surprisingly, some near-death experiencers report seeing lustrous gates that lead into this Crystal City, similar to the "Pearly Gates" in the old gospel hymns. There are seven of these gates, just as there are seven lower planes and seven chakras in the body. These gates are made of opalescent gems, and the buildings of the city are constructed of a translucent material that shimmers from within. Near-death experiencers report that the streets seem to be made of precious metals like gold or silver. Here are two reports of those who have been there and returned.

And then I saw, infinitely far off, far too distant to be visible with any kind of sight I knew of . . . a city. A glowing, seemingly endless city, bright enough to be seen over all the unimaginable distance between. The brightness seemed to shine from the very walls and streets of this place and from the beings which I could now discern moving about within it. In fact, the city and everything in it seemed to be made of light. . . . The beauty of the countryside was incredible, but even it could not compare with the splendor of the city because of the glow.[18]

[My guide] next led me to a city. It was a City of Light. It was similar to cities on earth, in that there were buildings and paths, but the buildings and paths appeared to be built of materials which we consider precious on earth. They looked like marble, and gold, and silver, and other bright materials, only they were different. The buildings and streets seemed to have a sheen and to glow. The entire scene was one of indescribable beauty.[19]

Some travelers describe seeing magnificent houses, and in this realm the size of a person's home depends on their generosity in their most recent life. Those who gave much to others have large homes, while those who have been more selfish live in smaller homes. Here is one account from a woman whose deceased brother escorted her through the residential part of this city:

I was surprised to see [that] while many of the homes were spacious, others were very small. Some were barely larger than a small kitchen or large bathroom. I couldn't imagine why anyone would want to live in a house so small. I asked my brother about this.

"That was all the material they sent up," was his strange reply.

"What do you mean?" I asked.

"That was all the good works they sent up," he replied, meaning that the size of a house one gets in paradise is determined by the quantity and quality of the good deeds performed [on Earth].[20]

Some near-death experiencers report seeing great halls of learning and gorgeous temples or cathedrals. Some visit vast libraries where the Akashic Records are stored. Darryl, for example, a construction worker, found himself standing before a cathedral that looked a lot like St. Marks. He reported that the building was made of translucent crystal blocks whose centers emanated a gold and silver light. He knew immediately that this was a place of learning because the information was pouring forth from the building itself:

> Buildings are perfect there, every line and angle and detail is created to perfectly complement the entire structure, creating a feeling of wholeness or inevitability. Every structure, every creation there is a work of art. . . . I was in a land where there were flowers and trees I've never seen on earth. . . . It was a land where there were living beings who had a fantastic ability to build palaces and houses with big, heavy columns, palaces and high-rise buildings, shaped in forms people have never thought of here.[21]

Larry, also a construction worker, died in an accident and then returned to report his experiences. His keen eyes brought back many details about the composition of the buildings on the Otherside:

> The room seemed to be made of crystallized marble of a soft pink hue. Another door, opposite the one [that] I had entered, opened onto a street. Several low benches of white crystallized marble were against the wall. The doorways in the room had no doors, and the window opening had no panes. . . . I felt like I had returned home. I knew where I was and where I was to go. We had only traveled a short distance down the street, when I stopped beside a building that I recognized. I had frequented it on many occasions.[22]

This account, like Arthur's story, poses the question of how a Soul could possibly recognize a landscape when they have only just arrived. This is because the Soul has been to these places before. After each life we are reborn into these heavenly realms to reunite with loved ones, assimilate knowledge, grow in spiritual service, and eventually make plans for a new life somewhere in the physical realm.

The Libraries of Learning

One of the most impressive places that some of those who have gone to the Otherside, and returned, talk about are the vast libraries of knowledge. These libraries contain the histories of all that has happened and the personal records or Book of Life of every individual Soul. Since there are billions of Souls in the world, there are also billions of books, and each book contains the Akashic Records of that individual. The books are all stored in vast libraries where Souls can go to study. So a Soul can take their Book down from the shelf and read it, or view it holographically as a movie. References to the recordings made after each life in an individual's Book of Life are referred to in the Egyptian Book of the Dead during the Weighing of the Heart ceremony. These books are vibrational recordings preserved in the larger Akashic Record, the memory particles that record all events in the universe. The Akashic Records are created by the Akasha, which is like the causal memory membrane of God that grows as a result of all of our experiences. Each individual Soul is then able to view these vast records in the many spiritual libraries found throughout the astral and causal planes.

Many Souls describe these libraries as vast rectangular buildings with glowing white transparent walls. Long rows of tables stretch off into the distance and big, thick books line every shelf. Large pedestals stand at the end of the long tables where a guide may assist a Soul with a particular lesson, and students study alone or in pairs. As one might imagine, there are countless Souls reviewing their records here. Initially, these records appear as pages, but when the book is opened they are actually vibrating sheets of energy that form picture patterns of events. Some have even described them as sheets of moving waterfalls that can be entered into with our consciousness, even while another part of us remains in the library reading.[23] These records are overseen by wise monastic beings described as archivists, scholars, or even Angels. They are quiet, focused beings who are there to assist Souls with their individual records. They may even be Lords of Karma, for it is clear that they help the Soul evaluate the choices it could have made in each lifetime. Here is the NDE account of a woman who found herself in a beautiful garden around various libraries: "I know that every single building was a different subject. All knowledge in the universe was stored in those libraries. I was excited because I wanted to go and study and read everything."[24]

These libraries not only provide a review of the life just ended, they are also used to prepare for the life to come. Here is an account from a woman who remembers studying there after a short life where she drowned herself because she had become pregnant out of wedlock in Edwardian England. In this passage she is already in the library working with one of the Lords of Karma, who shows her several alternative choices she could have made during that lifetime:

I'm in a place of study . . . it looks Gothic . . . stone walls . . . long marble tables . . . I know where I am now. It is the library of great books . . . the records . . . there is a huge open space where I see many souls at long desks, with books everywhere, but I'm not going to that room now. The old man takes me to one of the small private rooms off to the side where we can talk without disturbing the others. . . . The room is very plain with a single table and chair.

The old man brings in a large book and it is set up in front of me like a TV viewing screen. . . . He sets his scroll in front of me first and opens it. Then he points to a series of lines representing my life. . . . These are life lines—my lines. The thick, widely spaced lines represent the prominent experiences in our life and the age they will most likely occur. The thinner ones bisect the main lines, and represent a variety of other . . . circumstances . . . [and I see] crystal prisms . . . dark and light depending upon what thoughts are sent.

Now, I remember I have done this before. More lines . . . and pictures . . . which I can move forward and backward in time with my mind. . . . They form the patterns for the life pictures in the order you wish to look at. . . . He flips a page and I see myself onscreen in the village I just left. It isn't really a picture—it's so real—it's alive. I'm there . . . we are going to look at other choices. After seeing what I actually did at the pond where I took my life—the next scene has to be back at the pond on the bank. This time I don't wade in and drown myself. I walk back to the village. I'm still pregnant.[25]

Through this process the angelic archivist helped this woman play out several different versions of her life that did not include suicide, so that she could see the outcomes of other possible choices. In this way she began to see the life lessons inherent in each of her possible choices. The lesson behind this kind of exercise is clear: No matter what our circumstances in life, there is always a choice. We each have the power to change our lives, even under the worst conditions. When we can think outside the box to consider other possibilities, we can continue to find happiness and strength no matter what our life challenges may be.

The Moment of Clarity and the Great Work

In all of these near-death accounts the reports follow a certain pattern: We die and are then reborn in the world of light unless we have trapped ourselves in some lower part of the astral plane through our own negative attitudes and fears. Once on the Otherside, we regain our memories of our former state and begin to reconnect with some aspect of our true Self. From this higher perspective we can clearly see how much progress we have made. When we enter the middle and higher registers of the astral plane, we are flooded with a deep sense of connection to all living beings. In these realms we are no longer bound by our fear of death, the struggle to make a living, or the drive to become famous, so it is easier to shrug off the cloying fears of the human ego that so often seem to drive our life in the physical world.

In these higher realms, nothing is hidden to others. Not only is communication telepathic, but the Lords of Karma see all of who we are and yet love us unconditionally. In this dimension we are aware of the Oneness of life and are able to take stock of our spiritual progress without the destructive emotions of shame, fear, or guilt clouding our judgment. We are bathed in the energies of unconditional love and able to return to the warmth and comradery of our Soul family. Then, when we are ready, we will decide to try again, selecting the circumstances for our next life based on the spiritual progress we wish to make rather than on the egoic comforts of wealth or vanity that often drive a person in earthly incarnation.

Thus, step by step, life after life, we move forward on the path, transforming aspects of our human self through multiple experiences, until we are able to merge with our Angelic Twin. This is the alchemical process that spiritual adepts call "the Great Work." It is the transformation of the highest kind, where we turn the lead of the little self into the gold of the higher Self. Each life is but another chapter along the way, a chance to come a few steps closer to reclaiming our own angelic nature. How well we do with the course we have set for ourself determines whether we move forward or backward; each success or failure influences the conditions that we set up for our next life, until finally we have completed all of the lessons that we have chosen to learn here in Earth school. If we are successful, we can then select a life at an even higher level of existence, whether it is the loka of the demigods or the gods, or attaining Paradise. Later in this book we will take a look at the many life lessons that each one of us must master while living on the physical plane. But for now, let's contemplate the words of the spiritual adept Manly P. Hall, who writes about this pivotal moment when we stand before our higher Self during our life review:

We are told that between each life drama there is a moment when to man is revealed the meaning of it all. It is forgotten, however, as he assumes the unresponsive bodies that form his personality. But his moment of realization is the life-giving moment of the soul, when injustice and inharmony are swept away and man, standing free in space, secures the sweeping impersonal outlook that is inclusive and not exclusive.

Then, for a moment he sees the plan, stupendous, irresistible; he sees his place in the plan; he recognizes the inevitability of his ultimate accomplishment; he knows his God and is bathed in the effulgence of the divine reality. In the physical world he may have been an atheist, but in this supreme moment he sees, for in this moment mortality is absorbed in immortality. He transcends the mold of creation and recognizes both his origin and his ultimate [Self].

To those left behind who knew both his virtues and his faults, his broadness and his limitations, this is a great comfort; for they realize that in that moment he will know himself as he really is, and lay plans for future greatness far surpassing any achievement of the past.[26]

8

The Seven Heavens of the Astral Plane

All that we are is the result of what we have thought:
it is founded on our thoughts, it is made up of our thoughts.
If a man speaks or acts with a pure thought,
happiness follows him, like a shadow that never leaves.

GAUTAMA BUDDHA

We have now read some amazing accounts of those who have passed over to the Otherside and returned. The landscapes described are usually limited to the regions of the astral plane, for this is the first place the Soul enters after the body has died. In this chapter and in the next one we will take a look at three distinct levels of Heaven as found on the astral plane, the mental plane, and the causal plane.

While the stories we have heard from near-death experiencers are all quite powerful, describing an incredibly beautiful place, the astral plane is only an intermediate dimension that connects the physical world with higher realms of light. Beyond the astral lie the mental and causal realms, and it is in these higher dimensions that our angelic, true Self resides. The physical, astral, and four lower parts of the mental plane are known in Tibetan teachings as the *rupaloka,* or worlds of form. In each of these dimensions we find people, cities, planets, and civilizations at increasingly luminous levels of light. Space and time still exist here, but operate by a different set of laws (as we will discover later in this book). As we move up in vibration, the energy of light, or Spirit, increases, and the density of matter decreases, creating stunningly beautiful realms of perfection that are difficult for us, in our present density, to even imagine.

Beyond the mental plane lie the sixth and seventh dimensions, known in Eastern traditions as the Buddha realms and Nirvana regions. The Hebrew Kabbalah also speaks of these various realms, calling them the "Worlds of Creation," for the existence of these formless dimensions creates templates that allow the rupa worlds of form to manifest. These higher dimensions are called the *arupaloka* in Tibetan teachings; this is the dimension that lies beyond the forms of the life that we know (i.e., cities, towns, trees, buildings, and so forth). Instead, these higher realms are filled with changing geometric shapes, fractal geometries, and templates for what will eventually become the rupaloka, the realms of form. These higher dimensions are so filled with light and sound that it is difficult for us to even fathom them since, as human beings, our reference points are immersed in physical form. Yet as we will see, these are the first realms the Soul enters when it begins its downward journey from the Ocean of Love and Mercy to eventually arrive on Earth. The sixth and seventh dimensions are inhabited by millions of high-vibrating Angels, masters, and presiding deities, all of whom work for the Creator. Their jobs are to assist in co-creation and maintenance of the realms below.

The Seven Dimensional Planes
of the Astral Realm

Teachers of the ancient wisdom tell us that there are seven major dimensional planes that are each composed of seven subdivisions. Each major plane and sub-plane is then separated by different rates of vibration.

Figure 8.1. The seven dimensional realms

Theosophical teachings say that the pure light of the atom is also cloaked in a series of seven shells or sheaths, mirroring the ancient hermetic saying "as above, so below." These sheaths act as veils, with each atom acquiring its various bodies as it descends into the world of form. This is also true of each Soul, which is surrounded by a series of subtle-energy bodies like the many layers of a Russian doll, which together comprise the human aura. Because of this layering, the ancients used the image of seven (or sometimes nine) concentric circles, one set inside of the other, to describe the structure of the universe.

Within the worlds of form, which are composed of the physical, astral, and four lower regions of the mental plane, we find houses, rivers, forests, temples, animals, and humans. In the East these are called rupaloka. In the higher levels of the mental plane we move into the formless worlds, or arupaloka realms. While all of these dimensions are made out of the elements of air, earth, fire, and water, a different element predominates in each realm. In the physical world earth is our dominant element; in the astral plane, water; in the mental plane, air; and in the higher worlds of pure spirit, fire. So in each dimension the nature of these elements differs in terms of both vibration and proportion.

Because of its fluid nature, the astral plane is thought to have a predominance of water; yet to those who live there, all of the elements appear just as ours do here on Earth, being made of the various states of liquid, solid, gas, or ether. Yet this dimension is imbued with a fluidity and translucency of manifestation that far surpasses our own dense physical state. Visitors to the astral plane, such as near-death experiencers or those who have been led there in trance, often describe this realm as being starry in appearance. Objects have a luminosity that shines from within. Astral landscapes of fields and flowers, forests and rivers resemble those of Earth, but these objects exist at a more perfected level. Since spirit precedes matter, the landscapes of the astral plane were created before the physical world, so it would be accurate to say that our world is a reflection of this more rarified kingdom. In addition, each successive plane vibrates at a higher atomic rate than the one beneath it, so each *loka* expresses higher and higher levels of complexity, allowing

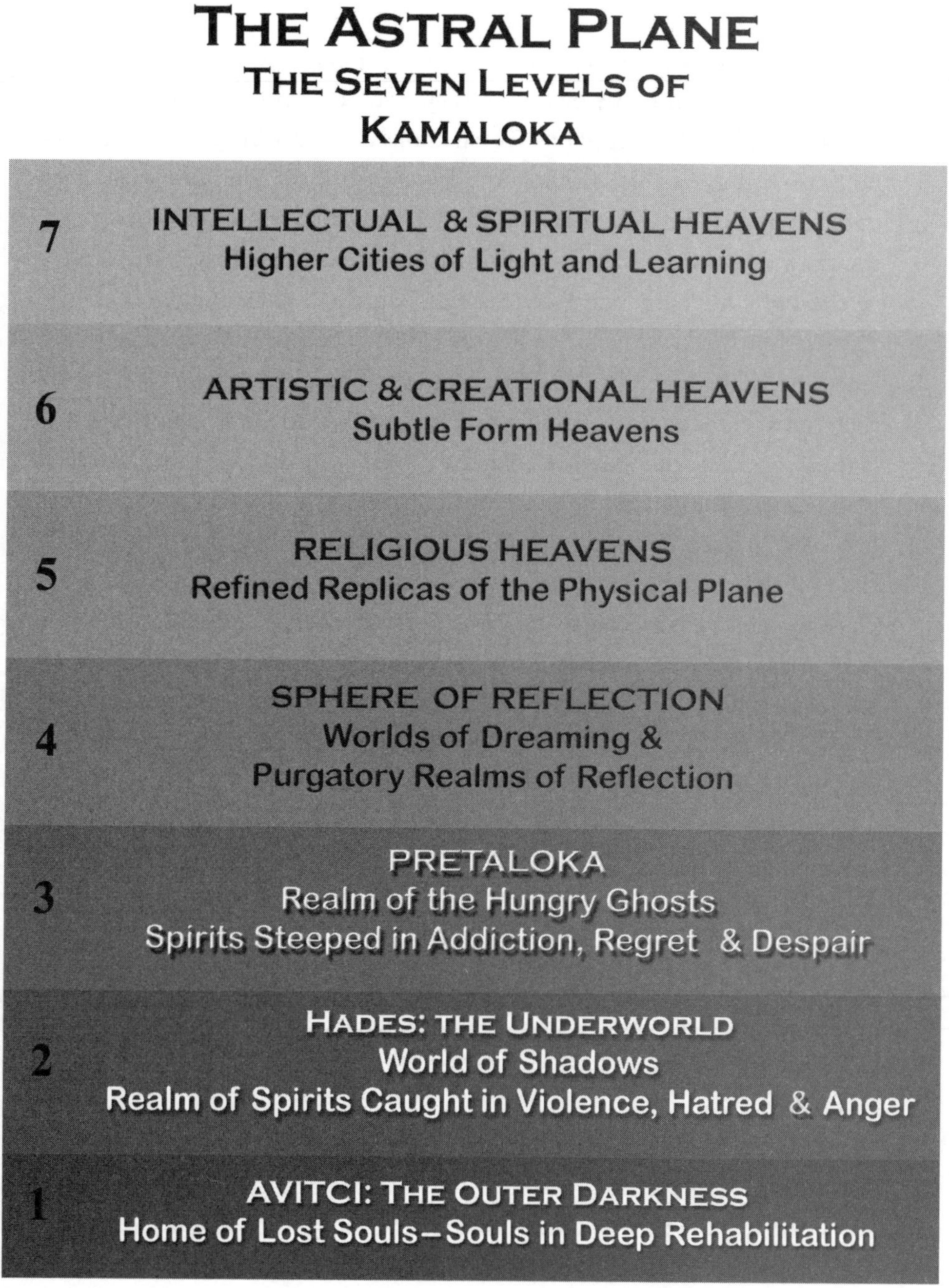

THE ASTRAL PLANE
THE SEVEN LEVELS OF
KAMALOKA

7 — **INTELLECTUAL & SPIRITUAL HEAVENS**
Higher Cities of Light and Learning

6 — **ARTISTIC & CREATIONAL HEAVENS**
Subtle Form Heavens

5 — **RELIGIOUS HEAVENS**
Refined Replicas of the Physical Plane

4 — **SPHERE OF REFLECTION**
Worlds of Dreaming &
Purgatory Realms of Reflection

3 — **PRETALOKA**
Realm of the Hungry Ghosts
Spirits Steeped in Addiction, Regret & Despair

2 — **HADES: THE UNDERWORLD**
World of Shadows
Realm of Spirits Caught in Violence, Hatred & Anger

1 — **AVITCI: THE OUTER DARKNESS**
Home of Lost Souls—Souls in Deep Rehabilitation

Figure 8.2. The seven regions of the astral plane

the Soul to have a variety of experiences, depending on its state of consciousness.

Like the physical plane, the astral dimension has seven subdivisions, each distinguished by its own vibratory level. In Buddhism, the lowest region is called *Avici* or *Avitci,* often translated into English as "incessant" or "interminable." This is the lowest realm of Hell, the place of outer darkness. This is a place of the City of Shadows where Souls are so far away from the light of their own true essence that they seem lost to the light of their true natures. There, great beings of light, called Restoration Masters, help Souls to release the hatred, cruelty, and violence that have so polluted their thinking. These Restoration Masters then reweave the light of pure Spirit back into the Soul itself, working to give each fallen Soul another chance at starting again. These lost Souls may be people like Hitler, Nero, or Charles Manson, people who have indulged in such despicable actions that they have completely misused their spiritual energies, to the detriment of the world.[1] Since Avici is a place where so many souls that have negative energy are concentrated, it appears dark to those outside of it. Other Souls are not allowed into this place where Souls who have been associated with horrors are undergoing alterations, nor would we want to visit there. It is a place of healing, but from a distance it has the appearance of a dark sea. All the light around this area is brighter in contrast because positive energy defines the greater goodness of bright light. When one looks at this darkness carefully one can see that it is a mixture of deep green. We know this is an aspect of the combined forces of the healers working there. We also know that Souls who are taken to this area are not exonerated; eventually, in one way or another, they must redress the wrongs they have perpetrated on others. This they must do to restore full positive energy to themselves.[2]

The next level up from Avici is the dark murky area that we heard about in George Richie's account. This is the realm where Souls get stuck in their own fury, hatred, bitterness, and self-righteousness, and it is described as having a muddy red light, perhaps reflective of the anger and negative emotions of its inhabitants. Buddhist texts call the inhabitants of this realm titans because of the vehemence of their anger, hatred, and fury. However, please recall that even in this place of negative emotions, the spirit guides of these Souls are ever close at hand, awaiting the moment when they will let go of their destructive creations and free themselves from the thoughts and emotions that bind them.

The third level up from this is the realm of hungry ghosts. These needy spirits are the kind of spirits that one might encounter in a haunted house, a bar, or a cellar, or as the result of a sudden and tragic accident. These Souls may simply not know that they are dead yet; they may be stuck on a treadmill of emotions and bound in grief, regret, fear, or some kind of mental or emotional addiction. They are trapped by negative belief systems, traumas, and fears and do not know how to let go.

The fourth level of the astral plane is a "sphere of reflection." This is reserved for the spiritually unawakened. These are people who simply never developed spiritually, and thus dream away most of their astral life. This is equivalent to the story that Eben Alexander told about finding himself with many other unconscious people in the dark, loamy area he described as the earthworm's point of view. Prayer can assist these Souls in beginning the upward rise into the realms of light, just as Alexander—whose family and friends were praying for him day and night—did. But our release from these lower levels where the Soul is stuck is ultimately about our decision to open our heart again and begin the journey toward the light.

How to Clear Earthbound Spirits

I have oftentimes encountered hungry ghosts throughout my many years of spiritual healing work. They can often be found hovering around nursing homes, mental institutions, battlefields, and cemeteries. Often these spirits do not know where to go or how to move on to the next plane of existence because they're stuck. Some have been there so long that they have forgotten much of who they once were, but they are still trapped in the emotions of their circumstances at death. In nursing homes and mental institutions there are many such hungry ghosts who have become deeply confused as a result of too many pharmaceutical drugs, and thus have become so disoriented that they continue to identify with the illness they suffered in their former life.

Over the years I have helped to free as many of these Souls as I can by calling on spiritual assistance from the angelic realm. There is a very specific way to clear these spirits that does not put you at risk and can assist these Souls in going over. What I mean is that since most human beings cannot see or hear these spirits, when a ghost finds someone who can, they may decide to follow that person home. Then they can glom on to the healer. If they do, they can bring their physical maladies into your energy field, and you might begin to experience pain, illness, or disharmony in these same areas of your body.

There is a right way to clear a spirit, and I will share some of that with you now. The most important thing to realize is that this is not entertainment. These are real people who have a real problem, and compassion and empathy from the healer is mandatory. Without that you are simply a sensationalist, a frightened bystander, or trying to be an amateur magician. The forces of light that you will need to contact to clear that spirit only respond to the frequency of love, so if your intent is to be of assistance, then you need to cultivate this intention in your own energy field. That way you will have the spiritual connection with the angelic forces to be able to assist these confused spirits.

The easiest and most effective way to release a spirit is to summon a powerful column of light, and connect this column to the energies of the Christ vibration. You can imagine this column being connected to the sun and to the light of the heavenly kingdoms. You will establish the column about fifty yards away from you and about a hundred feet in the air. This way it can be seen from a great distance, but does not touch the earth. The column will be spinning, much like a tornado, but without the debris or destruction. Then you call in the great Angels of healing: Michael, Raphael, Gabriel, Zadkiel, Sariel, and Uriel, and their attendant legions. These Angels will surround the entrance to the portal at the base of the column and help welcome these Souls back into the light. Spiritual guides can help to gently lift the spirits up with their arms, to reassure them that they are safe, wanted, and loved.

Then you speak to the earthbound spirits and begin to encourage them to go into the light. Many of them will be afraid. You might also ask them to look up into the light and see the faces of those who have loved them and are waiting for them in Heaven. Giving them this human connection to their past friends and families will help to allay their fears. You should also recognize that this kind of transition into the light takes courage for many of them, for this whirling column is a powerful vortex and can be quite frightening. You may also want to ask these spirits to become aware of their own spirit guides who are there to assist them in this transition. While not every Soul will have the courage to move on, the majority usually do. Whatever their choice, free will is honored in every case.

This entire process should take about twenty minutes; however, some Souls will hesitate. It is also important that you give directions to the Angels to close the portal when you finish. If you cannot wait long enough for all of these spirits to enter the column of light, then be sure to ask the Angels to close the portal within one hour, making sure that you thank them before you leave. Otherwise every ghost within a hundred miles will see your beacon and come running, and that area will be overrun by spirits for the next few days. Imagine that you have summoned a train that is destined for the higher regions. Many Souls may want to move forward, but are uncertain as to what they will face on the Otherside. Your job, as a healer, is to reassure them. Then, before you leave, be sure to tell all disincarnate spirits that if they do not wish to take the train at this time they will remain at this site. This way, you will not have a bunch of ghosts following you home.

Thoughts and Emotions That Bind Us

In the southern part of the United States there are many earthbound spirits that hover around Civil War battlefields. This is because this traumatic war pitted brother against brother, and many of those who died were emotionally conflicted. In North America I have also found many Native American warriors and shamans who are still protecting the earth, unable to abandon the land they loved to the treacherous invaders. In England and Europe I have also found an abundance of trapped disincarnate spirits because of the centuries of war fought on that soil. In England, for example, there are the ghosts of nuns, priests, and Druids who once protected the ancient sites, and some still remain to this day. In other places there are ghosts of those killed in old inns, battlefields, and monasteries that were destroyed by Henry the VIII.

In Warsaw, Poland, I immediately felt the dark energies of thousands of disincarnate spirits hovering over that city. Poland was the first country invaded by Hitler and was held hostage by the invading Nazis for over five years. Then, when World War II ended, the Communists took over, terrifying an already traumatized nation. In and around this city I found thousands of Souls who had either been shot by firing squad, or who had died trying to protect their families. Even those who had perished from natural causes had spent years living in a state of paralyzing fear. These were the brave husbands and fathers who had been afraid to act against their tormentors for fear that their families would be massacred in retaliation. This set up an internal conflict within those individuals who were not able to protect their land, yet were afraid to leave their loved ones behind. So this conflict held them earthbound for decades.

Let me share one story about clearing thousands of these traumatized spirits. For several years I traveled to Poland to teach. On one of these trips I thought that I should try to clear these many troubled spirits who had already suffered so much. One Sunday morning in May, on the day of the Assumption of the Virgin Mary, I had a dream that the Divine Mother had come to help me release these people. I was teaching a workshop that weekend, and after lunch I asked if the class would like to clear these spirits. To this suggestion they gave an enthusiastic "Yes!" That afternoon, with a hundred students, we held a powerful ceremony that sent five thousand of these Souls into the light. During the invocation, an image of the Lady of Mercy appeared above us in the tall cathedral hall where the workshop was being held. She hovered in the white column of light, rays of pink streaming from her hands, welcoming all Souls that had been trapped by the war—Poles, Germans, and Russians alike. The next time I visited Warsaw, the gray cloud that had hung over the city had lifted, and the city was free.

The common feature among many disincarnate, earthbound spirits is that the person who is trapped has died in a confused or conflicted state of mind, revealing how the power of our mind can keep us chained to old patterns. Earthbound spirits are often those that have died in a sudden death, had mental illness, were involved with drugs, or had unresolved issues, making it hard for them to pass into the light. The key elements are emotions and beliefs. Many spirits may not even realize that they are dead, or their fear of Hell may cause them to remain. Because the Abrahamic religions have taught most of us to fear God's retribution, many "God-fearing" people are afraid that they will be punished when they die. To that end, I would like to share one more ghostly encounter that reveals how our own belief systems can keep us trapped.

Some years ago I was speaking at a conference in Santa Fe, New Mexico. Afterward I decided to stay over for about a week to sightsee. I drove to Bandelier National Monument, and then north to the beautiful town of Taos. There, a friend introduced me to a gold prospector who was digging for treasure in the hills. This man—let's call him Carl—had a problem with a ghost. He explained that there was a vindictive spirit haunting the area where he was digging. When he would hang his jacket up on a tree to dig, he would find great rips in the fabric when he returned, like his jacket had been slashed with a knife. Carl wanted to know if I would come to the site and get rid of the ghost. Intrigued, I agreed to check it out.

When I arrived at the dig site the next afternoon I could immediately feel the presence of an angry spirit. So I sat down and meditated, speaking to the Soul that was trapped there. It was the Soul of a nineteen-year-old Spanish lad who had been chained to that area for over three hundred years. The young man had been part of a Spanish army of gold-hungry soldiers in the late 1600s or early 1700s that had discovered a treasure of gold. Deciding to bury the gold and return later, the men killed the youngest member of their company. This was apparently a custom that prevailed as a result of the religious beliefs of that era: by not performing the Last Rites as prescribed by the Catholic Church, this would essentially strand the murdered person, leaving his ghost to guard the treasure. So this young man, who had been raised a strict Catholic, feared that if he left this locale his Soul would go to Hell. This belief had stranded him there for over three centuries!

I explained to the spirit that he had done an excellent job of guarding the treasure, but that now he could go into the light. I told him that there were many people in Heaven who loved him and were waiting for his arrival. But the young man was afraid. He told me that unless a priest gave him the Last Rites, he feared he would go to Hell. I explained all of this to Carl, emphasizing the fact that this boy was just an innocent victim. I told Carl that if he would get a priest to perform the Last Rites for the young man, then the boy would cross over. But Carl was an opportunist. He couldn't have cared less about the plight of another Soul, particularly one he could not see. When I left the Taos area, Carl had done nothing, and even today I do not know how the situation was resolved, if indeed it ever was.

The reason why this story has remained in my mind for so many years is because with all of the thousands of Souls that I *have* helped to cross over, I could not help this one. The young man's own belief systems had trapped him. This is the power of our beliefs. Our thoughts and emotions have the power to keep us earthbound, even when we no longer have a physical body. For those who are stuck between dimensions, the situation is much harder, since the living cannot see them. However, with a little help from the living, many of these trapped Souls can be persuaded to release their fears, forgive themselves or others, and move into the light.

The Astral Heavens

The fifth sub-octave of the astral plane is dedicated to the religious Heavens. These are the regions that correspond to Heaven for all of the various religions of the world. These cities of light exist for people of good intention, but who have never expanded their horizons. These various realms have been built over many ages by the thought forms and beliefs of millions of people. Here is the Hebrew City of the Just, the Native American Happy Hunting Grounds, the Celtic Summerland, the Elysian Fields of the Greeks, the Egyptian Field of Rushes, and of course, the Christian Heaven. In these realms the overlighting deity of each of these religions faithfully appears to its followers, encouraging them, blessing them, and supporting their spiritual growth to the limits of what each Soul can understand. While this may seem a bit pandering, we must realize that millions of people still cling to the belief that their particular religious path is the only "true" path. At the higher levels, each of the great masters and teachers who have come to Earth understands that there are many paths to God, and they have no quarrel with one another. Thus each person is called to her own understanding of God in accordance with her own nature, spiritual maturity, conditioning, and willingness to open to a more universal truth.

Finally, in the two highest octaves of the astral plane we transcend the limits of religious dogma and move into the creational and spiritual levels of the astral plane. This is where those who are pure of heart, open of mind, and devout in nature are to be found. The sixth sub-octave includes luminous landscapes and rippling oceans, snow-clad mountains and fertile plains, and scenes of such beauty that even the most transcendent displays of Earth are only a shadow of its beauty. These are the artistic heavens, a place where Souls are given access to music and art, color and creation beyond anything that we know on Earth. Here individuals can make fabulous creations from thought alone, developing the Soul's ability as a co-creator with the Divine.

The seventh subdivision is almost entirely occupied by those Souls that are dedicated to the pursuit of truth. These are the philosophic heavens. Here a Soul may choose to spend years in study in the great libraries, learning the laws of science, spirituality, and philosophy. Here there are great museums of invention, and one may study the histories of thousands of other planets across the universe. These libraries can also be visited by those of us who are living in the physical realms if we are evolved enough to travel there. This can be done in meditation or in our nightly dreams. On both of these higher levels there are temples of Golden Wisdom that are overseen by spiritual teachers. I have spent many years visiting these divine places, and they are a wonder to behold.

The Qualities of the Astral Plane

Like the physical body, the astral body has a set life span, so in time, even the most confused or grief-stricken Souls will have their astral body eventually dissolve. Then the Soul awakens from the dark thought forms that have trapped it, to eventually move into the healing levels available on the mental plane. The astral corpse, which consists of fragments of the seven concentric shells that have been held together by the magnetism of the Soul, disintegrates, and the Soul is drawn upward. At the time of this astral death the Soul may find itself unconscious of its surroundings, but when it awakens, it finds itself in the subdivision of the mental world that corresponds to its spiritual development at that point in its evolution.

As mentioned previously, the astral realm, or kamaloka, is a desire realm where we are strongly influenced by our emotions. Once a Soul attains the fifth level of the religious Heavens and above, the sensitivity of the five physical senses begins to expand, allowing us to experience two or more senses at once. Thus a person can suddenly *feel-know* another person or object. One can *hear-see* the clouds, the grass, or a tree. We can *see-know* the things around us, just as one of our near-death experiencers describes feeling knowledge flowing from a temple. In addition, our astral senses are greatly expanded, as we saw in the case of Arthur, whose astral vision allowed him to see the mountains at a great distance: "The mountains appeared to be about fifteen miles away, yet I could see individual flowers growing on their slopes. I estimated my vision to be about one hundred times better than on earth."[3] Sages tell us that if one so desires, we can even see the back of an object at the same time as its front, the inside of something at the same time as the outside.[4] Thus nothing that we wish to know and have the consciousness to perceive is hidden from us. Not only that, but on the astral level we can alter our appearance through the power of thoughts and desires, so that once a person crosses over, they can make themselves younger or older, taller or shorter, or any gender they desire. However, since most of us are still governed by the thoughts that we developed while on Earth, our ability to manifest in the astral world is tied to the limitations of our belief system while on Earth. Theosophical wisdom tells us that:

> as the great life wave of the evolution of form passed downwards through the astral plane, and constituted on that plane the third elemental kingdom, the Monad [or Soul] drew round itself combinations of astral matter, giving to these combinations . . . a peculiar vitality and the characteristic of responding to, and instantly taking shape under, the impulse of thought vibrations. This elemental essence exists in hundreds of varieties on every subdivision of the astral plane, as though the air [itself] became visible here—as indeed it may be seen in quivering waves under great heat—and as if it were in constant undulatory motion with changing colors like mother of pearl.
>
> This vast sphere of elemental essence is ever answering to vibrations caused by thoughts, feelings, and desire and is thrown into commotion by a rush of any of these, like bubbles in boiling water. The duration of the form [created] depends on the strength of the impulse to which it owes its birth; the clearness of its outline depends on the precision of the [person's] thinking, and the color depends on the quality—intellectual, devotional, passionate—of the thought.[5]

The Influence of the Law of Attraction

The connection between our thoughts and our emotions and their ability to manifest our reality is taught in many great traditions. Indeed, what we think and feel defines our goals, actions, and character. Our thoughts and emotions have a direct bearing on how we create our reality, including and especially here in the physical world. Thoughts of prosperity and self-confidence translate into success, while thoughts of poverty and victimization translate into lives of frustration.

Metaphysically this is the law of attraction, meaning that what we dwell on and believe is what we will manifest in life.

Even at this earthly level of density, our mind and emotions shape our life. This combination of emotional and mental bodies is what the sages call *kama manas* (*kama,* "desire," *manas,* "mind"—i.e., the desire-mind body, or in human terms, the personal ego). Vedanta speaks of the Soul as working in the *manomayakosha,* a sheath composed of the lower mind, the emotions, and the passions. In other words, our desires direct our mind. If we are only focused on feeding our materialistic nature, then this is the direction the mind will follow. The mind, or *manas,* works like an old-fashioned recording device: any repetition of thoughts or habits cuts grooves in the mind, thereby reinforcing fears, beliefs, and habits, training the mind to react in a particular way. When our thoughts are consistently negative, then we fall into the crippling emotions of envy, doubt, blame, shame, lust, addiction, anger, low self-esteem, and victim consciousness. And if the Soul does not direct the mind to raise its attention above the mere physical, then the Soul cannot make any progress. It will stay trapped in the struggles of the physical world for eons, until it finally chooses to change its thoughts and create a different reality.

This is why we have been warned about the dangers of gluttony, drunkenness, lust, vanity, greed, anger, and unrestrained hedonism. It's not that food, sex, money, or sensuality are bad; in moderation all things have their place. The admonition to avoid excess is meant to remind us that we must feed our spirits first. When we only feed the desires of the flesh and the personal ego, then we retard our own spiritual progress. Better to feed the mind, heart, and spirit, for these things will endure long after the wrappings of the body have fallen away. The body is a holy temple where our spirit dwells, so the healthier we can keep it, the better off we will be. But the body is only a vehicle for the real work of the Soul. And so while the body is important, it is not the be-all, end-all of our existence.

Sex, which is a sacred communion that can expand our heart into a transcendent state of Oneness, is a sacrament to activate our kundalini life force, thus it should be treated with the utmost respect. This is one of the reasons why love and sex should be joined together, for this can open up the spiritual centers. For the last two thousand years the Abrahamic religions have taught guilt and shame around sex, thereby separating love from sex, and head from heart, in an effort by the patriarchy to gain control over women's reproductive rights. But the emotions of shame and guilt short-circuit our ability to trust ourselves, to step into our power, and to open up the higher centers of love. When we disconnect our sexuality from our hearts and minds, then we suppress the true gift of sacred sexuality, which allows human beings to awaken the power of Spirit within their own bodies. A true holy union of love through sex has the power to generate a profound awakening in spiritual consciousness, freeing us from the tyranny of religious-based dogmas.

So now, having traveled through all seven levels of the astral plane, let's take a look at the mental and causal levels of the heavenly worlds, where our true Self resides.

9

The Mental and Causal
Heavens

*A man is but the product of his thoughts. What he thinks,
he becomes.*

MAHATMA GANDHI

The mental plane is a vibrational leap up from the astral realms below it. As its name implies, this dimension is created by the power of our thoughts, and so the rate of atomic vibration is even faster than the realms beneath it, and thus manifestation here is as fast as the speed of thought.

Like the astral plane, the mental plane is also composed of seven subdivisions. The lower four are part of the rupaloka, the worlds of form referred to in Eastern literature as the lower *manas,* or lower mind, the part of us that is focused on logical thought, analysis, sorting, and judgment. It uses logic to argue, reason, and evaluate, and the thoughts that it produces are about concrete things in the physical. It is only when you are able to direct your mind toward more creative, abstract, or spiritual matters that it begins to nourish the development of the Soul.

As the Soul evolves this higher mental function over many lifetimes, finally taking its attention off of the survival needs of food, shelter, money, and reproduction, the mind deepens. It becomes more observant of its choices in life. It begins to witness how our own thoughts, words, and actions create the conditions of our life. Instead of merely *reacting* to the events around it, the Soul begins to discover the energies that its own thoughts have created and sees what part we play in forming the positive and negative conditions around us. This is the law of cause and effect, or karma. When this level of self-reflection sets in, then the Soul can finally begin to become responsible for itself, learning to steer the course of one's life. We can then make the choice to move away from negative situations and dramas and stop making self-defeating choices. We become co-creators of our own experiences, the architect of our own life.

Of course, from the Soul perspective this ability to see the relationship between our thoughts and what we manifest in life takes place over time. As we travel through multiple lifetimes, we may experiment with many choices, some resulting in pleasure, others in pain. This trial-and-error process eventually teaches us how to make wiser choices and becomes the voice of the conscience within the subconscious mind. The sum of these experiences is held within the Soul's memory; this leads us to avoid that which causes trouble and pain and to lead a more noble, ethical life. This is how the Soul learns. When we couple this growing inner awareness with an internalized moral compass, we call it the *conscience*. The conscience is the internal barometer that tells us what is right and what is wrong. It is the inner censor that the Soul uses to help us remember what will cause a karmic backlash and what will further the Soul's growth. The conscience is an aspect of the Angelic Twin that whispers: *Do not do that!* or *Yes, do that!* This internal guidance system is trying to help our human part remember those choices that will yield a higher spiritual reward, and to avoid those things that will only create suffering later on, in this lifetime or future lifetimes. Eventually, over many lifetimes, the Soul establishes more and more control over its mental and astral bodies, so that it is no longer ruled by desires, fears, or judgments. When this finally occurs, the Soul is no longer the victim of the constantly changing tides of the outer worlds. Instead, it becomes the human architect that learns to create its reality, not only in this world, but in the astral and mental levels as well.

Those who wish to accelerate their spiritual evolution may even learn how to direct the mind to work in a more focused way. This teaches discipline and sustained co-creative thought, something we will need when we get to the higher realms. By teaching the mind to work in a quiet, sustained manner in order to connect with the greater silence of Spirit, we learn how to direct it toward accomplishing our own objectives. This is why meditation is so important—it allows the mind to come into contact with the higher Self.

At this point the Soul can begin to explore its own dreams and creativity, expanding the power of abstract thought to enhance spiritual study. In this way the mind learns how to be still so that it can listen to the impulses coming from the Soul itself. When this connection with the higher Self is made, the baser instincts and cravings of the body begin to fall away, finally allowing the mind to become a servant of the Soul. This kind of training unfolds over many lifetimes, but in time each of us can learn how to awaken to a level of genius and insight that belongs to the Soul alone.

Devachan

An ancient name for the heavenly realms is *Devachan*, a term that means the "Shining Land" or "Land of the Gods." This Theosophical term was derived from the Tibetan term *Dewachen*, meaning "blissful land," synonymous with the Sanskrit *Sukahavti*. According to the Tibetans, *Dewachen* is the pure land of the Buddha Amitabha. It is a place where no pain or sorrow exists, and the Soul is in the companionship of those they love. In this intermediary state it resides in continuous happiness and in the fulfillment of its soul's yearnings. This is a specially guarded part of the mental plane where all sorrow and evil are excluded by the great masters who oversee our evolution. The amount of time a Soul spends in Devachan depends on the amount of material that it has created as a result of its positive actions, words, and deeds during the course of its earthly life.

This principle is reflected in the story of the woman whose brother explained to her while she was visiting Heaven that the reason there are tiny houses in Heaven is because "that was all the material they sent up." In the mental realm our dwelling places can only be built from the good actions, thoughts, and deeds that we have generated in our previous life. This well of goodness includes all the intellectual, emotional, spiritual, and moral efforts that a person has put forth, not the worldly success, wealth, or fame one acquired. Only spiritual merit matters, and thus the mental plane is built on all the many acts of kindness we have generated throughout our Soul's many lifetimes, for these purer, more noble thoughts are the true temple of God, built from the energies of pure Spirit.

The masters tell us that in earlier ages, when people's thoughts were more directed toward the enduring questions of life and the search for God, most of us spent a great deal of time between lifetimes in these heavenly realms. In fact, the vast majority of Souls spent decades or even hundreds of years between their earthly incarnations. However, today we are greatly distracted by materialism, not to mention the disturbing images of violence that we see on television daily. In this dense realm our monkey mind is rarely focused on anything for very long, jumping from the cell phone to the computer to the TV; from distracting family dynamics, to work, to the bills we didn't yet pay. Thus few of us learn the discipline of inner stillness and self-reflection. As a result, our time spent in these higher realms between incarnations may only last a few years because our eyes are not set on Heaven. The shorter our life span here on Earth, the shorter our time between lifetimes, so when children die early they return almost immediately. The longer the life span we have in this world, the longer the break between lifetimes, giving the Soul ample time to assimilate its experiences, to review past choices, and to make a plan for a new life.

Once we are in Devachan, the events of Earth seem distant and unimportant, almost as if they were but a dream that we have awakened from. I know this was true for me when I passed over because it is clear from this perspective that this dimension is a higher reality than the one we just left. From this perspective we know that whatever trouble our loved ones are immersed in on planet Earth will eventually be resolved, if not in this lifetime, then in another. From this higher perspective we understand how much of earthly life is filled with distortions and misperceptions, and how only love and the things of the Spirit are true and abiding.

In Devachan there are no barriers between one Soul and another; thus we can experience true communion with others. I believe this is one of the reasons why we long for a soul mate when we are in the human world, because in the lower earthly realm the illusion of separation from the Divine (and therefore from others) is almost too painful to bear. This is why so many people anesthetize themselves with drugs and alcohol and all the other things we become addicted to. Perhaps some deeper part of the person remembers feeling this higher union, and so missing that connectedness feels like a dull, aching, unrequited emptiness. Those who have visited Devachan, or Heaven, tell us that it is far more vivid than anything we find in this world, and that the union of hearts there is nearer and dearer than anything we know here. Perhaps this is because the physical world has two additional veils that cloak it—the physical and astral bodies—thus masking our minds and hearts from the people that we meet.

The Power of Thought

The dominant element in the mental realm is air, for this element responds to the creative impulses of the mind, allowing ideas to take shape at the speed of thought. Here on Earth I often feel frustrated by the amount of time it takes to manifest a creative idea, but in this dimension of Heaven we can create our visions with ease. In Devachan, a painter, sculptor, or musician can create exquisite works through the power of intention alone. I remember time spent in this realm where I used music to create the most incredible paintings and sunsets, by using sound to hurl colors on a canvas as large as the sky. On Earth our creations often fall short of what we have in mind, but in Devachan the beauty of our creations is breathtaking.

In many ways the world we live in now seems to be in slo-mo, and it is almost so slow that we cannot seem to make the connection between what we think and how our lives turn out. Thus it seems to take forever for us to figure out the relationship between cause and effect, that what we think and do comes back to us. Even when we have learned to focus our minds, it sometimes takes years for us to perfect our training and manifest ideas here on Earth. But in Devachan we can manifest almost instantly, and so learning how to control your thoughts is the key to being able to remain conscious in this realm after we have died.

In the mental realm the Soul learns to work with its own co-creative powers. Souls that have not yet developed the ability to use their imaginative powers will find that their time in this heavenly realm is more shallow, for it is the quality of our thoughts that determines our reality. Here the Soul gradually learns to focus its attention on directing the plasma of the universe, working *with* the life force of Spirit instead of *against* it, as we so often do on Earth. Thus the Soul learns how to shape the seeds of atomic life and assist them in growing. The Soul starts small in the beginning, learning how to assist minerals, plants, and animals with the evolution of life. But in time the Soul learns about the delicate balance of ecosystems, and under the tutelage of the masters who oversee the creation of worlds, it begins to work with other Souls to assist in larger areas of creation, such as planetary systems.

While Devachan is a realm of bliss, it is also the place where the Soul assimilates those experiences it had in the realms below, transmuting this learning into abilities it takes with it into another lifetime on Earth. Past affinities endure, so that a person who has studied a subject deeply in one life will find that he or she has an aptitude for that same subject in the present life. Those who have developed skills in music, mathematics, literature, science, healing, history, strategy, or the arts will find that these talents increase in each successive lifetime. Skills that we might need in a future life can also be studied in Devachan as well, so that when we arrive back on Earth we will find that learning those activities is easier.

Everything thought on Earth is thus utilized in Devachan. Every aspiration is worked up into power: all frustrated efforts become faculties and abilities; struggles and defeats reappear as material to be wrought into instruments of victory; sorrows and errors shine luminous as precious metals to be worked up into wise and well-directed volitions. As Theosophical writer Annie Besant says,

> Schemes of beneficence, for which power and skill to accomplish were lacking in the past, are, in Devachan worked out in thought, acted out, as it were, stage by stage, and the necessary power and skills are developed as faculties of the mind to be put into use in a future life on earth, when the clever and earnest student shall be reborn as a genius, when the devotee shall be reborn as a saint. Life then, in Devachan . . . is the land in which the mind and heart develop, unhindered by gross matter and trivial cares . . . and where the progress of the future is secured.[1]

The Four Lower Levels of the Mental Plane

Like the physical and astral planes below it, the mental plane has seven subdivisions. The four lower levels are all considered to be part of the world of form. The lowest level is the region where Souls are the least progressed. These Souls are still young, and their highest thoughts on Earth may have only been around the welfare of family and friends. This level also includes people who have admired others of a more noble character and aspired to do better. While these people may not have a lot of spiritual purity on which to build a heavenly life, still, every goodness is recorded, no matter how small. In their next life these younger Souls will be reborn with a tendency to respond to higher ideals than before.

The second level of Devachan is composed of people of all faiths whose hearts have turned toward God under any religious name. While his concept of God may be limited, still, that person has chosen to align with the idea of divinity, pouring out his love in that direction. At this level the Creator meets those Souls by whatever form and name they call the Spirit, no matter what their intellectual limitations may be. So at this level, depending on the Soul, the Divine veils itself in the familiar form of a religion, seeking to assist these younger or intermediate Souls in growing in purity and devotion.

The third region of Devachan is inhabited by noble, devoted Souls that have spent their earthly lives in service to humanity out of a desire to do good on behalf of others. These are Souls whose hearts have turned toward service, whether it be helping plants, animals, children, the elderly, or even the health of the planet as a whole. Thus it is the purity of their thoughts and hearts that draws them to this region. In future lives these Souls will be the great humanitarians.

The fourth region of Devachan is the realm of artists, thinkers, musicians, scientists, and inventors whose mental powers are focused on contemplating the deeper reflections of divinity through the many faces of nature's harmony, love, beauty, and unity. These are the inspired minds of past ages whose music, literature, artistry, and spiritual insights still inspire millions today. These are the lovers of truth who are the perfect candidates to become channels through whom the illumination of the masters flows into the world. In this realm we also find many great spiritual teachers who imbue their students with wisdom so that when these students are reincarnated on Earth they will become light-bringers for the world. These masters may then overlight those students once they reincarnate, acting as invisible guides to aid them in their mission. These illuminated masters send out telepathic dreams, inspiring their pupils with inventions, films, books, paintings, music, and ideas that assist them in the present and in their next incarnation.

The Causal Plane

Once we pass through the four lower levels of the mental plane we move into the formless, noncorporeal arupa levels. This is the realm of pure perception whose upper region is called the causal plane, although some believe that the causal level is actually part of the higher mental plane. This is the place where all of our positive experiences from every lifetime have been assimilated and contained within our higher Self. The causal body is the seed body that the Soul retains from lifetime to lifetime, building its individuation over eons. Yet most of us who live in this world are not advanced enough to attain this realm, at least not for very long, as Theosophist Annie Besant writes:

> A vast number of souls touch the lowest level of the formless world as it were, but for a moment, taking brief refuge there, since all lower vehicles have fallen away. But so embryonic are they [in their development] that they have as yet no active powers that can function independently, and they become unconscious as the mental body slips away into disintegration. Then, for a moment, they are aroused to consciousness, and a flash of memory illumines their past and they see its pregnant causes; and a flash of foreknowledge illumines their future, and they see such effects as will work out in the coming lives. . . . For here again, as ever, the harvest is according to the sowing, and how should they who sowed nothing for that lofty region, expect to reap any harvest therein?
>
> But many souls have, during their earth life, by deep thinking and noble living, sown much seed, the harvest of which belongs to this fifth *devanchanic* region—the lowest of the three heavens of the formless world. Great is their reward for having so risen above the bondage of the flesh and impassion and they begin to experience the real life of man and the lofty existence of the soul itself, unfettered by vestures belonging to the lower worlds.[2]

In the three upper levels of the mental plane the Soul learns through direct knowing. It discovers the underlying causes behind all things, which may have been previously concealed by the irrelevant details of the lower realms. Later, when the Soul returns to the physical world, this knowledge may be revealed in those intuitive flashes that seem to transcend logic or reason. In these realms, the truly conscious Soul studies its own history to discover the convoluted threads that are part of its master plan.

The higher a Soul goes in these formless regions, the more advanced it becomes in understanding. This means that when that Soul eventually returns to Earth it is no longer drawn into the petty dramas and struggles of the material world, because it is more attuned to the pursuit of truth that is found in a spiritual or intellectual life. At this level a Soul may also learn to mitigate any past negative deeds, thus reducing the karmic obstacles it will encounter when it returns to a human life. This connection with the higher Self also allows it to make a more purposeful plan for future lifetimes. Plus, this connection with the causal Self allows it to imprint its newly acquired physical, emotional, and mental bodies, which change with every new incarnation, with a strong sense of purpose. Consequently, Souls that have attained this level are born with noble spiritual aspirations that make it almost impossible to choose an ordinary life.

The Sixth and Seventh Octaves of the Mental/Causal Realm

Those Souls that achieve the sixth level of the mental/causal plane have made a connection with the mind of God. From this point on, the Soul has gained insight into the deeper questions that confound the ordinary rational human mind. Paradoxes are resolved in ways that formerly did not make sense. These Souls become the channels for spiritual, creative, and archetypal wisdom. At the sixth level, the Soul has reached a point where it is in constant communion with the masters. Many of the great spiritual adepts make their home in the seventh octave, although others are stationed at various levels throughout both the astral and mental planes. Thus the Soul often becomes a student of one of these great teachers on the inner planes, and if this Soul decides to return to Earth in service to humanity, these teachers, in spirit form, will volunteer to serve as guides to assist that person on her journey.

The seventh level of the mental/causal plane is the dwelling place of the great Councils of Light and the master initiates who have served the evolution of humanity for eons. These spiritual adepts have gone through their own cycles of incarnating in former ages of the world, finally achieving the wisdom that we are still working to attain. From this higher dimension these masters pour down spiritual, moral, and intellectual inspiration, communing with those receptive Souls who yearn for this connection. This last subdivision of the mental plane is where we sense the illusory nature of duality, for once a Soul passes into the Buddha and Atman realms, the reality of Oneness can never be doubted. While, to a certain degree, individuation still remains, it does so in the context of the overall understanding that all is One.

Heaven's Number-One Principle

The great master Jesus taught, "There are many mansions in my Father's house" (John 14:2). Jesus was referring to the many dimensional levels within the kingdom of God. He also told us that "the Kingdom of Heaven lies within" (Luke 17:20–21), pointing out that our access to these heavenly realms is within our own power to perceive them. Thus attaining Heaven has to do with one's state of consciousness. We achieve that by focusing on those things that bring us closer to the light. This is done over time by maintaining noble thoughts, performing compassionate deeds, and remembering how to live with a forgiving heart. The more we practice these principles, the higher our consciousness, both in life and on the Otherside.

The first of Thoth's seven Hermetic laws teaches us that the universe is mental, or conscious. When we apply this principle to what we have learned about the inner realms, we can begin to see how our thoughts have a direct effect on our reality—not only in this earthly world, but in all the dimensions. What we believe shapes our thinking. This, in turn, shapes our emotions and our actions, as well as our sense of personal identity. Our thoughts also shape our relationship to the rest of creation as well, seeing others as friends or enemies, part of our tribe, or something to be feared. Remember that Jesus taught that those who judge others will be judged in return. Those who harm others will also be harmed. Those who spread love will then be loved. And those who seek to find the beauty in others will discover that their inner beauty grows stronger every day.

This also means that through our thoughts, words, actions, and energies, we have the power to heal others, harm others, and create a better world. This means that we must learn how to focus on the things that bring us happiness and inner peace. Realizing this, we can choose to open a path before us that will change our lives and accelerate our journey home. We can learn to sow the seeds of humility, kindness, and service in our daily life, for it is these actions that will bring us to greatness.

PART 3
OUR GENESIS MATRIX

That which is part of our Souls is eternal. . . . These lives are countless, but the Soul or Spirit that animates us throughout these myriads of existences is the same; and though "the book and volume" of the physical brain may forget events within the scope of one terrestrial life, the bulk of collective recollections can never desert the divine Soul within us. Its whispers may be too soft, the sound of its words too far off the plane perceived by our physical senses; yet the shadow of events that were, just as much as the shadow of the events that are to come, is within its perceptive powers, and is ever present before its mind's eye.

HELENA BLAVATSKY

10

The Great Chain of Being

When I see nothing annihilated, and not even a drop of water wasted, I cannot suspect the annihilation of Souls. . . . Thus finding myself to exist in the world, I believe I shall, in some shape or other, always exist; with all the inconveniences human life is liable to, I shall not object to a new edition of mine; hoping, however, that the errata of the last may be corrected.

BENJAMIN FRANKLIN

So now let us consider how Creation unfolded. From the original outpouring of light from the Creator came a great stepping down of frequencies that in turn created a vast hierarchy of dimensional planes and beings, each endowed with a spark of the pure white light of the Creator.

The Great Chain of Being concerns the two waves of Creation that brought the universe into being. These are the involutionary wave and the evolutionary wave, two currents that are essential to the unfolding of awareness. As the Creator breathes out, divine consciousness flows out into the universe. This is the involutionary masculine wave that flows outward, helping to create the diversity of consciousness that goes from the One to the many. Yet to do this, the Creator must step down into denser and denser forms, moving from spirit into energy, and from energy into matter, until it finally loses awareness of its own divinity.

This stepping-down of energy is what the Bible alludes to in the account of the Fall, which actually refers to the fall in consciousness that exiles us from the full realization of our divine nature. The biblical account is an aberration of the deeper meaning of this story, whose true meaning has been forgotten or obscured. The story that we learned in the Christian religion claims that Adam and Eve were exiled from the Garden of Eden because they ate from the Tree of Knowledge. This implies that human beings should be punished for seeking knowledge. Yet nothing could be further from the truth, as the pursuit of higher knowledge is critical to becoming spiritually enlightened and free. That biblical story was generated by a patriarchal culture of priests who sought power and control and were not above using guilt and shame to get it. It was created after the release of the Jews from captivity in Babylon, and it is a distortion of the original Babylonian creation story known as the *Enuma Elish,* which tells the story of the simultaneous creation of man and woman by the Elohim, or Anunnaki gods, who took a more primitive version of humankind and accelerated its DNA to produce *Homo sapiens,* the version of humankind that we have today. In the last hundred years this story has been confirmed by the discovery of ancient cuneiform tablets found in the city of Nineveh.

And so the true fall in human consciousness is the loss of spiritual connection when we move from a state of Oneness to the amnesia and duality of the three-dimensional human world. While it is impossible for any of us to truly be disconnected from Source because the Divine lives within us, from the human perspective we believe that we are separate and alone. We have forgotten that we are actually a spark in the body of God that has chosen to move into the world of matter. Entering this realm of duality allows us to experience the enormous *contrast* of feelings produced by the absence of bliss. It is this contrast that allows us to learn what it is to feel alone and afraid; to know heartache, suffering, and loss; to experience pain, old age, and death. This becomes a tool for awakening our patience, compassion, and empathy for others.

Our descent into the lower realms also allows us to have a wide range of choices in exercising our free will. And we may choose to experience *maya*, or illusion, for as long as we wish, all in the name of *lila*, "the play of Soul." Then, when we have lapped up every possible experience, we can return to the Source and abide in the heavenly kingdoms. But to make the shift from duality to union, we must consciously align with the wave of love that reconnects us with Source. This is the evolutionary wave that flows back to Oneness. It is feminine in nature and is much like a great ocean current that unites us in the supreme light of our own true Self.

So the real meaning of the Fall is the forgetting of our own nature, just as our return is our journey back to Spirit. Physician and author Larry Dossey writes about these two energetic currents:

> If we look back on evolution as the reversal of involution, the entire process may seem more intelligible. Involution is a process of dismemberment. Evolution is a process of re-memberment in which we see the reappearance of higher-order wholes—which is what we indeed observe. Involution is a process of decreasing consciousness [as Spirit moves further into denser forms of matter]; evolution a process of increasing consciousness [as Spirit lets go of the attachment to matter], which is what the data shows. And the driving force behind the entire process is the return of Spirit to Spirit—Spirit remembering and reconstituting itself, building bigger and better brains in living organisms in this process, through which it can manifest this remembering.[1]

What is the key to making this reconnection? Mystical teachings tell us that it lies within the heart. Spiritual teacher Eckhart Tolle reminds us that "the power of the heart is the power of life itself, the power of the very intelligence that pervades and underlies the entire universe."[2]

The Hierarchy of Creation

In *The Celestial Hierarchy,* written by Pseudo-Dionysius the Areopagite, a fifth- or sixth-century CE Christian theologian, the writer compares God to a ray of primal light that can never be deprived of its intrinsic unity. Yet as the One proceeds to the "many of the manifested worlds," it leaves a portion of itself in every creature. This manifestation takes place in the worlds of time, space, and matter, which creates a veil over the divine unity as it descends toward the extremity of Creation. In the ancient world this veil was thought of as nature and was called the veil of Isis, signifying the inaccessibility of nature's secrets. "I am whatever was, or is, or will be; and my veil no mortal ever took up. I am the things that are, and those that are to be, and those that have been."[3] This stepping down of the primal Creator through the agents of light and sound creates a hierarchy of spirit and matter and consciousness that acts like a ladder, unfolding from the highest levels of light to the lowest, so that every being may be led, according to its capacity, to experience and then embrace the principles that will lead it back to unity with the Divine.[4]

The idea of the existence of a hierarchy is not just a political one: hierarchy exists in every structure of nature—forming the subatomic, atomic, organic, and molecular levels, and ranging from a single cell to entire bodily organs. From single organs these hierarchical structures cluster into organ systems, then join together to become whole bodies. From individual people we evolve into a human species, then develop into families and villages and nations. Finally, all of these come together to become the inhabitants of a planet, which along with other planets, make up a solar system. Thus there is a gradual stepping up or stepping down of complexity in the world of matter. As we move up the ladder we see increasing levels of sophistication: from the mineral kingdom to the bacterial, the plant to the animal, the human to the demigods, the gods to the great *chohans,* or masters, who oversee entire dimensional planes. Each progression upward takes us higher in awareness, but is built on the levels that exist below it. This evolutionary ladder leads us back to union with our own divine nature. Helena Blavatsky writes about this Great Chain of Being in her opus, *The Secret Doctrine:* "The whole cosmos is guided, controlled, and animated by an almost endless series of Hierarchies of sentient Beings, each having a mission to perform and who—whether we give to them one name or another, and call them Dhyani-Chohans, or Angels—are messengers in the only sense that they are the agents of Karmic and Cosmic Laws. They vary infinitely in their respective degrees of consciousness and intelligence.[5]

So as the Great Spirit breathes out, it transforms into the energy of light, sound, and consciousness. This energy is then stepped down in successive movements (or dimensions) to eventually become matter in the third dimension. This is reflected in Einstein's famous equation $E=MC^2$, telling us that energy and matter are interchangeable. So Spirit, or energy, is converted into matter when it is multiplied by the speed of light. This means that energy precedes matter, and that matter will eventually return to energy. Blavatsky explains, "The Universe is worked and guided from within outwards. As above so it is below, as in heaven so on earth; and man—the microcosm and miniature copy of the macrocosm—is the living witness to this Universal Law and the mode its action."[6] Professor Jay Williams, chairman of the department of religion at Hamilton College in Clinton, New York, reminds us that "matter, which is constantly coming into being and passing away, is the manifestation of a vibration from the Depth, vibrations which make a Mahler symphony look like one note without overtones, played on a monochord. The world we sense, according to this image, is ordered, as it is, by the great vibratory source whose ground bass is the essential pitch of the universe. Matter is the vacuum vibrating. The cosmos is a symphony."[7]

Understanding that energy and matter are interchangeable, and that energy is either being stepped up or stepped down in the great spiral of nature, we can then comprehend how the laws that govern energy might vary at each dimensional level. This means that the laws that bind this plane are different from the ones above it. This also means that the beings who inhabit each plane or dimension may have greater or lesser powers of manifestation. In this world, for example, it sometimes seems to take forever to bring an idea into form, but think how quickly this works in the world of dreams. On the astral plane the distance between atoms is more expansive, and thus the laws of density are lessened and manifestation is as easy as using one's sustained emotions and thoughts. So this means that when beings from the higher realms visit our dimension, they may appear to us to be performing feats of magic. But it is not really magic at all; it is the ability to use the higher universal laws. Similarly, human beings may appear to be capable of feats of magic to less evolved beings like cats or dogs. After all, we turn on the television with the click of a button, fly in the sky without wings, talk to people who aren't really there through a small box, and never seem to age, at least in comparison to the relatively short lives of our pets. Who we are may seem almost incomprehensible to animals. Even producing food from a can is a mystery to them. All they know is that whatever we do seems to work, even if they don't understand how.

The Laws of the Various Dimensions

As already mentioned, there are two kinds of realms: the rupa worlds of form, and the formless arupa realms. The worlds of form include the physical and astral planes, as well as the four lower levels of the mental plane. This means that in all of the worlds of form we have bodies, houses, landscapes, cities, and objects that we can interact with, although at higher or lower levels of vibration, with each plane going downward being more dense than the ones above it. For example, in our dreams it is clear that we can manipulate reality far more easily than in waking life because the astral realm is more fluid than our own. Thus as we move up the dimensional ladder consciousness exists in beings that might look fluid, able to change their shape at will, or even appear gaseous to us. In the formless realms we have changing patterns of sacred geometry, and we can see some of these geometric shapes in the artwork of Tibetan mandalas, the stained-glass windows of Christian cathedrals, the whirls and loops of Celtic and Native American art, and the beautiful spirals found in the Jewish and Islamic faiths. These sacred geometric templates are the energetic patterns that underlie the denser structures of nature. In these higher, formless realms there are no relatable objects because everything is a moving reflection of light, sound, plasma, and emanation. Professor Williams says this about the nature of atoms and the world behind them:

> Atoms, the building blocks inherited by modern science from the ancient Epicureans [of Greece], have been found to be neither indivisible nor solid. In a word, they are not atoms at all. The stuff of atoms seems to operate in a stranger world, characterized by neither space nor time nor causality.
>
> The continuity of matter, so apparent on a visible level, is entirely subverted inside the atom. Laws become probabilities; once-certain attributes become obvious illusions. The world of post-Einsteinian physics is neither a mechanism nor even a knowable reality. It is as though we see only the white caps of matter on an ocean of emptiness, whose depths are both unexplored and apparently unexplorable.[8]

Mayan elders tell us that there are forty-eight laws of physics that must be obeyed in the physical dimension, while the astral dimension has only twenty-four such laws. So things that we consider to be magical down here are business-as-usual up there. These are abilities like telepathy, flying, shape-shifting, and teleportation, which near-death experiencers often report and that some ET contactees also report from their encounters with beings from other dimensions. This is also the reason why many people who return from the higher planes after having a near-death experience report seeing loved ones who appear more youthful in Heaven. In the fourth dimension and above one can alter one's appearance at will. In this dimension telepathy is normal, and the ability to send holographic ideas allows us to receive vast downloads of information in a very short period of time. In the mental plane there are only twelve of these laws that govern energy, making these abilities exponentially stronger. In the sixth dimension there are only six laws of physics, while in the seventh dimension there are only three. These are the arupa or formless levels governed by the angelic hosts of Heaven.

Of course, while living in the physical world most of us never experience such miraculous abilities as levitation, mind-reading, or bilocation, unless like the yogis we have developed these spiritual abilities. Yet these powers are known by shamans, monks, fakirs, saints, and other holy people. In Hinduism and Buddhism the existence of such advanced *siddhis,* or powers, is readily acknowledged, and the Buddha expected his more advanced disciples to be able to attain these abilities. The Buddha had the gift of telepathy and the ability to create doubles of himself; he could levitate, walk on water, bring people back from the dead, and simultaneously shoot fire and water from his body. These abilities were also demonstrated by Jesus, who could heal blindness, control the elements, pass unseen in crowds, walk on water, and bring the dead back to life. Today we know that modern-day masters like Sai Baba also demonstrate the ability to teleport, manifest objects, and convert one type of matter into another. I personally know people who have seen Sai Baba read minds, teleport, and appropriate objects from the higher realms into this world. I have also heard firsthand stories of his ability to appear in two places at once, to open a portal between two widely separated points in space, and to send another person through this portal so that they could be at the bedside of a dying parent.

Max Planck, the theoretical physicist and Nobel Prize winner who originated quantum theory, says that he "regards consciousness as fundamental" to reality, and that "matter is derivative from consciousness."[9] Increasingly, as discoveries in physics accelerate, we are confronted by the reality that our thoughts and emotions contribute to what manifests in our world in terms of the circumstances we see around us. Richard Conn Henry, professor of physics at John Hopkins University and former deputy director of NASA's astrophysics division, states that a fundamental conclusion of the new physics is that the observer creates reality, and thus the universe is a mental construction.[10] English physicist James Hopwood Jeans (1877–1946) came to this very same conclusion: "The stream of knowledge is heading towards a non-mechanical reality. The universe begins to look more like a great thought than like a great machine. Mind no longer appears to be an accidental intruder into the realm of matter. We ought rather to hail it as the creator and governor of the realm of matter. Get over it, and accept the inarguable conclusion: the universe is immaterial-mental and spiritual."[11]

Esoteric wisdom tells us that each plane and each subplane is separated from all the others by vibrational frequency. This is why, from our respective plane, we are largely oblivious of the existence of other dimensions. To perceive them we must raise our frequency to their level through our consciousness or else they will remain invisible. Yet together these higher planes form the background of the entire universe. From these higher dimensions it is easy to gaze down into the physical realm if a being is willing to lower its vibration to a denser level. Understandably, most Souls that have attained these higher levels of Oneness would never choose to lower their vibration, yet there are advantages and disadvantages to coming to a place like Earth, where beings can experience greater and greater levels of contrast and individuation. People who are clairvoyant like myself have learned how to raise their vibration to attune to these higher realms; as a result we can perceive the energetic currents moving in the other planes. Yet what a clairvoyant sees or how accurate he or she is depends in part on how high that person's vibrational antennae is attuned.

Kenosis, the Great Outpouring

Christian theology explains the idea that the Creator pours out its own energy to create the universe in terms of *kenosis,* which means the self-emptying of one's own will and becoming entirely receptive to God's will.[12] In other words, all things are made from the substance of God, from the beauty of a sunset to a cocker spaniel, so God's consciousness exists in everything and everyone at some level. Yet as the energy is stepped down, there is a forgetting or a lessening of consciousness. This eventually creates a state of amnesia, until finally the Great Spirit enters the worlds of matter where the laws of density seem to bind its very being. This increasing density and decreasing vibration creates a sense of fragmentation, duality, and separation. However, this duality or separation is really just an illusion, since it is impossible for the Divine to ever truly be separated from itself, even though, from our limited human perspective that separation feels real enough.

The sages tell us that even in the densest realms everything we see is the play of Spirit losing itself and finding itself. What frees or binds us in any given lifetime is our own choice as to whether to align with our higher Self, which means aligning with the power of love and forgiveness. When we negate our intrinsic angelic nature we find ourselves caught up in the darker involutionary wave of the desire realm, the *tamas*. This then drags us down further, like an undertow, until we forget our divine nature—something that happens to all of us from time to time while living in this realm. This is why having a spiritual community is so helpful, for when one person falters, another is there to remind her of her basic divine nature.

Thus when we embrace the light of who we really are, our blinders fall away. This moves us forward. Thus the higher *sattva* wave of evolution sweeps us back up the ladder toward self-remembering, while the downward wave of involution of the tamas takes us on the wildest ride of our life, to the point of becoming so mired in the Shadow that we forget our own identity. Larry Dossey writes about this from the perspective of the Soul:

> Yet the agony of each level is that it appears . . . to be separated from Spirit—fallen and lost forever. But Spirit is not lost at each level, just forgotten; obscured, not destroyed; hidden, not abandoned. . . . When involution is completed, the stage is then set for evolution to begin. Some insist that the reason evolution seems to work as well as it does is that it is a precise, backward readout of the prior process of involution. In other words, evolution is simply following a blueprint of a design already laid out.[13]

Since the driving force behind evolution is the quest for reunion with the Divine, or love, it is this force that spurs us onward, whether we are a human being, an ant, or a blade of grass. The love we share with one another, even our plants, pets, and planet, has the power to accelerate everything around us. As the Soul moves closer to the light or to Source, choosing ever more sophisticated organisms to incarnate in to experience greater and greater levels of consciousness, at each successive level the Soul increases its ability to remember who it truly is, until

Figure 10.1. The dream of Jacob's ladder showing Angels going up and down is a metaphor for the Great Chain of Being that we all travel. It is the ladder that leads back to Heaven (illustration by Gerard Hoet).

finally it comes to embrace its own true Self. Once this happens, the Soul can burst free from the confines of matter, claim its evolutionary destiny, and begin to help others who are stuck on the path below. This is the true path of mastery.

The Power of the Heart

The physical world is an excellent place to learn about patience, compassion, suffering, priorities, and the consequences of our actions, but it is also a very tough training ground. The only beacon of light that can bring us through this minefield is the power of our heart. This is the one path Spirit has given us that, when all else fails, will ultimately bring us home. The heart is the gateway to remembering our Oneness. However, for many Souls who have suffered a great lack of love in their lives as a result of abandonment, loss, or abuse, opening the heart is not easy. When the heart is closed to love, we become separated from our true Self. This disconnection from the vibration of Oneness then causes us to fall into hopelessness and despair, creating greater misery as the light of our own true Self becomes clouded over. This can show up as toxic relationships, self-sabotage, depression, and sadness. We may even become so disappointed by life that we are susceptible to the millions of negative thought forms that surround us every day. This can turn the mind toward anger, bitterness, violence, and frustration, generating a self-defeating cycle of pain, arrogance, and cruelty that will never bring us happiness. This self-defeating cycle generates the Shadow, a presence that was known as the Great Adversary or the Dweller on the Threshold within the Mystery traditions.

The Shadow is the abnegation of the light that lives within us. It is fed by the monstrous illusion of fear, a word that rightfully stands for *false evidence appearing real*. The Shadow is that part of us that prevents us from connecting with our own divine essence. In religious circles this aspect became personified as Satan. By externalizing this negative force, religions claimed that any opposing group or person was being led by the devil or by heretics or infidels in service to the devil. Yet in truth we are all equally loved by God since we are all a part of the Source. If we perpetuate the myth generated by religions that the devil exists outside of us, we abdicate personal responsibility for our own unhealed, unloving state of consciousness.

When a person projects his Shadow onto another, that which he most fears about himself begins to take on a life of its own. People who cheat on their spouses usually fear that their spouses will cheat on them. Those who lie to others fear that they are being deceived. Those who fear homosexuals are often suppressing their own sexual tendencies. Terrorists who fear the domination of the West are wrapped up in trying to dominate others with their cruel deeds. And likewise Western countries that fear terrorists, are those that have been dominating others for decades and creating terror among the very countries they fear. By making another person, nation, or religion the cause of all our suffering, we cease to look at our own ignorance, prejudices, and actions. By claiming that "the devil made me do it," we avoid taking responsibility for our own unacknowledged anger, judgment, greed, lust, vanity, and self-righteousness.

Years ago, within the history of Christendom, the Church allowed wealthy people who transgressed the law for their own selfish reasons to pay a tax for their ill deeds to get off the hook. This tax was called an *indulgence;* it allowed the rich to plunder the lands of those they exploited, with only a slap on the wrist by religious authorities. This same kind of thinking is happening in parts of the Moslem world and religious Right today, where both Imams and certain Christian preachers teach a philosophy of hate against those they judge responsible for their misfortunes; in so doing, they create violence, pain, and suffering for millions. In the Abrahamic religions we see the internalized Shadow of that religion projected onto other people and groups and used to justify violence and hatred. The unacknowledged "little self" that lies within us all must ultimately be claimed and integrated into the higher Self in order to defeat the Shadow.

The third-century Christian theologian Origen, one of the most well-known of the Church Fathers, promoted the externalization of the Shadow, seeking to make it easy for the common man to understand this concept.

Plate 1. Every human being possesses seven vital energy centers, long known as the seven sacred flames, chakras, or vortex wheels. These centers are where the pranic life energy of Creation flows into our physical and subtle energy bodies, acting as a receptacle or storage cabinet for the beliefs, experiences, and traumas we accumulate in each life. Behind this meditating figure is the Flower of Life mandala, long held sacred by the ancients as one of the templates for Creation itself. Artist: Deo Sum

Plate 2. On the steps of the temple stands the Priestess, overlit by her Higher Self. Even higher above her is her angelic Oversoul whose light is as great as a luminous sun. Artist: Amorea Dreamseed

Plate 3. Each of us is an angelic being, even though we have forgotten our true nature. This beautiful illustration shows the vertical column of the Seven Chakras surrounded by angel wings, a reminder of the importance of awakening both sides of our natures and bringing them into unity to reclaim our true divine nature. Artist: Nikki Zalewski

Plate 4. The Goddess of Nature stands beside the Tree of Life, commanding the spiral ascent of the serpent beside her. This classical William Blake painting represents Nature's universal unfoldment in the sacred spiral, a pattern that can be witnessed in a thousand forms, from a pinecone to the whirl of the galaxies. "Eve Tempted by the Serpent" by William Blake.

Plate 5. The Pathway to Heaven has long been depicted as a spiral one, reflecting the patterns of nature. As the Soul moves upward on its journey to enlightenment, we encounter similar lessons again and again, until we get the lessons right. We also meet the same Souls again and again, having multiple chances to resolve our issues with them, until we finally come to unity and peace. "Jacob's Dream" by William Blake

Plate 6. The Soul crosses the bridge of darkness into the World of Light, the tunnel that leads to Paradise, Shamballa, Valhalla, or the Summerland—all names for the infinite light of Heaven. Artist: Anastasios Kandris

Plate 7. The Soul meets its Angelic Twin on the stairway to the Gates of Heaven. Here the Soul begins its life review of the lifetime just ending, seeing clearly how the Soul could have used its time in a more loving and transformative way. Artist: Bruce Rolff

Plate 8. This Bhavacakra (Wheel of Life) shows the six lokas or realms of desire. They are planes of experience where the Soul may choose to incarnate when it is in a less enlightened state. Included are the realms of devas (gods), asuras (demigods), humans, animals, naraka (hell realm), and preta (hungry ghosts realm). Artist: Stephen Shephard

Plate 9. A stained-glass window from Notre Dame Cathedral in Paris with Mary and Jesus at the center. This powerful mandala displays the same six lokas around a central image. Built between 1163 and 1250 CE, Mary has the moon at her feet, a three-pronged lily in her hand, and twelve fleur de lis insignias surrounding her. The lily and the fleur de lis are both used to represent the trinity of the Divine Father, Divine Mother, and Divine Child. The fleur de lis is also a symbol of Egyptian royalty or the Beekeepers, dedicated to preserving wisdom for future generations. Photo: Bill Perry.

Plate 10. *This gorgeous stained-glass window from the Basilica at the Monserrat Monastery near Barcelona, Catalonia, Spain, reveals the same six dimensional realms surrounding a seventh central Heaven. It is from this central realm of Paradise that the light pours down onto baby Jesus as he lies surrounded by his parents, Mary and Joseph. Above them are two flanking Angels, and below are emblems of the trinity. Each of these elements is symbolic, revealing how the union of our masculine and feminine natures leads us to oneness, and ultimately to the kingdom of the Divine within ourselves. Photo: Evoken*

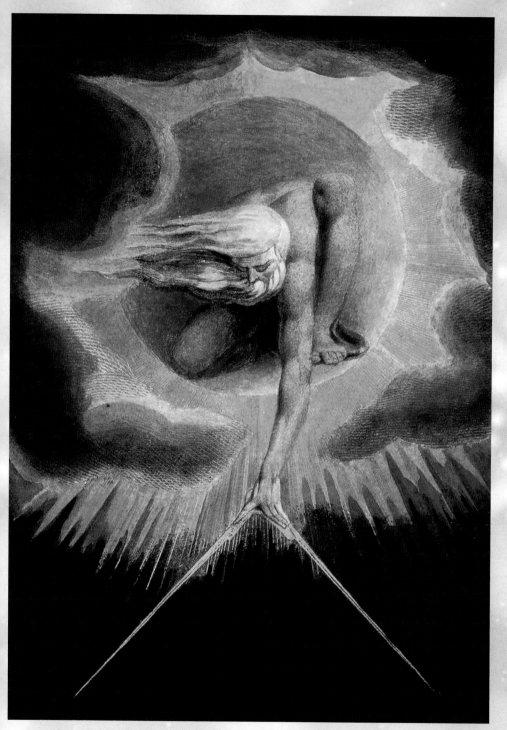

Plate 11. While patriarchical religions have long conceived of God as being male, the One is beyond gender or duality. Yet it begins creation by dividing itself into two. These are the Divine Father and Divine Mother known for centuries throughout the world. This is the first Trinity that allows the architecture of the universe to begin. *"The Ancient of Days"* by William Blake

Plate 12. The Soul atom or the "I AM Presence" is the core of who we are. It is the individual spark of the Creator that is unique to each living being. Without it, our Souls would not exist. By connecting with our own "I AM Presence," we tap into Source energy, allowing our human self to transmute negativity. Artist: Andrey VP

Plate 13. In this beautiful stained-glass window from the Church of Saint Merri on the right bank of Paris, we see Issa or Jesus, emerging from a mandorla or vesica piscis, the symbol of a master who has harmonized his masculine and feminine natures to become unified in themselves. Photo: Meunierd

Plate 14. In this biblically inspired stained-glass window, Mary the Mother emerges from the vesica piscis, arrayed in an almond-shaped envelope of light. Like Isis before her, she stands on the sickle moon with rays surrounding her. Around her head is a halo with twelve divisions, much like the twelve stars that surround Isis, marking both women as Queens of Heaven. Photo: Dawid Lech

Plate 15. This beautiful nineteenth-century painting depicts the infinite care that our loving Spirit Guides have for us. In this image we see this Angel of Protection behind her two young charges. Used by permission of Victorian Traditions.

Plate 16. *From the womb to the tomb we are overseen by our spiritual Companions. They often greet us after our Life Review and assist us in examining where we could have made more positive choices. While all of us have at least one Spirit Guide, many people have two or three. Each individual Guide has his or her own unique set of talents designed to assist us with the life plan we have made before incarnating on Earth. "Christ in the Sepulchre, Guarded by Angels" by William Blake*

But in the process he reinforced the idea that the problem lies *outside* of us instead of *within* us. Origen said that we should visualize this internal conflict as a "little devil" and "a little angel" sitting on either shoulder, and in fact some Medieval painters depicted it this way. "All men are moved by two angels," Origen wrote, "an evil one who inclines them to evil and a good one who inclines them to good. . . . If there are good thoughts in our hearts, there is no doubt that the angel of the Lord is speaking to us. But if evil things come into our heart, the angel of the evil one is speaking to us."[14] However, what is at work here is not the devil; it is the pull of two opposing currents—one that takes us away from love, and the other that brings us back into connection with our higher Self.

The Nature of Evil

Given that the Shadow, the Great Adversary, is not something that exists outside of us, does not mean that there are not negative forces in the world. So what is this evil? Evil is acting against the spiritual laws of the universe in such a way that it creates a distortion in the little self that separates us from the Law of One. The Law of One tells us that each sentient being, human, plant, and animal alike is an expression of the light of God. Thus we are all divine sparks that are evolving in consciousness, and all of us are worthy to be loved, even when our actions are based on ignorance, illusion, misaligned thinking, and bad programming. When a person gives away his power to the negative emotions of anger, fear, self-righteousness, and separation, then he has given his power to the Shadow. This moves us away from our own divine qualities of love, kindness, honor, and honesty. We fall out of alignment with Ma'at, the principle of divine truth.

People who follow the path of darkness are those who have clouded their own inner light with the illusion that we are separate from one another. This makes it easy to justify hatred, vanity, greed, pride, anger, jealousy, cruelty, judgment, torture, and egoic ambition. These Souls have fallen victim to the Shadow, the illusion of separation; they have forgotten that we all come from the same illuminated Source. They have wrapped themselves up in a shroud of delusion and called it religion or righteousness. These people are actually afraid of the light, for they fear that it will annihilate them. Yet nothing could be further from the truth, since light is the essence of our being. The pure white fire lives within all living beings, waiting only to be activated by the power of love. So in the end it is love that will free us of these illusions and help us find the true path back home.

As long as the lower worlds exist there will always be polarity: light and dark, up and down, hot and cold, male and female. It is the nature of the created universe. But in the higher rupa levels the forces of light and darkness are largely separate from each other. However, in the physical world these polarities are mixed together, so it is harder to tell the honest people from those who are steeped in lies. Any observation of the world around us will underscore this realization. We find rich, successful people doing horrible, immoral things like molesting children, while there are saints like Mother Teresa humbly going about their mission, largely unnoticed by the world. Many times the richest materialists are the shysters, con artists, warlords, politicians, and manipulators, while the wisest, most compassionate people may be the peasants, fishermen, dockworkers, or street cleaners, people who will never achieve fame or glory in this world. Professional athletes who spend their lives in violent sports are paid vast sums of money so that we can watch them destroy their bodies in public contests that we call "sport," while schoolteachers who shape the minds of our children are paid minimum-wage salaries and can barely pay their rent. So this world is one that has been turned upside down. On Earth the good, the bad, and the ugly are all mixed up together, so it takes a great deal of discernment to see what is genuine, enduring, and true. This is why Earth is such a difficult classroom to master. Only by awakening our hearts and engaging with our true Soul Self can we see past the veil of these illusions and find a way out of this minefield.

The Three Gunas

Earlier I used the terms *tamas* and *sattva,* which are accompanied by a third term, *raja.* These are the three gunas, which acccording to Hindu philosophy, are the three primal qualities at work in the universe. These are the main powers of cosmic intelligence that determine our spiritual growth in the Great Chain of Being. The Sanskrit word *gunas* means that "which binds," because when they are wrongly understood they keep us in bondage to the external world. The principle of the three gunas is not only applied to the life of an individual person, but also to entire cultures, movements, and world ages.

The highest of these energetic waves is the sattva path. This is an upward-moving energy wave that carries us back to the Source, itself. The word is derived from *sat,* meaning "holy," so a sattva culture is one whose art, music, architecture, and literature are all oriented to the Divine. Sattva cultures manifest during golden ages, in which people live lives of goodness, integrity, and alignment with the light. Many eras of the Egyptian and Hindu civilizations, for example, were oriented toward these principles, creating architecture, art, and customs that were in harmony with the forces of the Divine. These cultures also taught the principles of the Afterlife, thereby helping people achieve mystical states of consciousness to advance their individual enlightenment and secure a higher place in Heaven.

The energy of the raja guna is horizontal in nature. It produces a materialistic society that is rich, opulent, diversely creative, and deeply invested in the physical world. It is based on the belief that "bigger is better." This path often believes that the physical world is all there is, and thus the level of true spirituality is limited. Yet raja cultures are highly creative ones, much like our own, giving Souls the chance to express themselves in new and creative ways in this world of form. From pet rocks to blenders, from wild fashion jewelry to Hula-Hoops, from jukeboxes to computers, raja cultures produce a huge smorgasbord of ideas. Raja cultures also contain a subcurrent of spirituality that is usually expressed through religion or humanitarian causes, yet the real keys to spiritual enlightenment are often concealed or obscured. These cultures focus on mastering the physical world and profiting from it, much as we, in the West, do today.

The third guna is the downward-pulling tamas energy that leads us away from the light. This is the path of selfishness, brutality, and violence that feeds on the misery of others. This path is consumed by the emotions of fear, hate, jealousy, prejudice, lust, self-righteousness, and accusative thinking. People who are immersed in this wave of energy may be obsessed with horror movies, pornography, drugs, crime, obsessions, fetishes, the sex trade, and even child abuse. A tamas culture is also fascinated with the darker elements of the Underworld such as werewolves, vampires, and monsters. It breeds greed, cruelty, chaos, and addiction, and ultimately traps the Soul in the bowels of the lower astral plane. These people choose angry, discordant music, obsessive thinking, and violence. Nazi Germany, for example, became a tamas culture of control, prejudice, oppression, and murder. Today, when we look at the horrendous oppression being played out in the Middle East, we can see the tamas current at work—in the bombings of terrorist groups, daily acts of violence, and the suppression of women. Tamas cultures pull the Soul away from the harmony of its own eternal nature, dragging us downward as they seek to extinguish our connection to the light.

Most of the United States and Western Europe are primarily rajaistic cultures that have been focused for decades on the accumulation of material wealth and the perfecting of the human body. In these cultures, mainstream scientists are encouraged to believe only in the physical sciences. Fortunately our scientific paradigm is now beginning to shift toward a recognition of the role that nonphysical energies play in the creation of the universe. In our rajaistic culture we have mostly good-intentioned churches, mosques, and synagogues that exist as altruistic forces trying to uphold some semblance of morality and assist people in times of need. Yet how many times have we found our preachers, priests, and televangelists caught up in greed, power, and illicit sexual activities, while showing no true wisdom or helping people find true spiritual enlightenment? And how many powerful multimillionaires continue to be focused on power, greed, and material wealth, to the determent of our environment, our animals, and the common man? These are the negative expressions of this current.

Today, even though we live in a rich, opulent raja society, there are also other, even darker subcurrents in motion. While the tamas component of society may at first seem to be fun, pushing our boundaries with

Sattva Guna
Upwardly moving
wave
connecting
us with the Divine

INVOLUTIONARY WAVE OF SPIRIT
Taking us out
into forgetfulness
in the
material realms

Raja Guna
Horizonally moving
wave taking us
into materialism

EVOLUTIONARY WAVE OF SPIRIT
Taking us back
into remembrance
of the light of
our own being

Tamas Guna
Downwardly moving
wave connecting us
with darkness,
death, and
negative karma

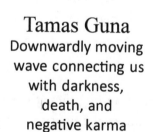

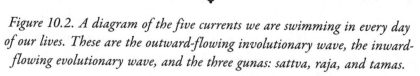

Figure 10.2. A diagram of the five currents we are swimming in every day of our lives. These are the outward-flowing involutionary wave, the inward-flowing evolutionary wave, and the three gunas: sattva, raja, and tamas.

horror movies and a fascination with zombies and vampires, it is also seen in the daily dose of robberies, shootings, and killings viewed on the television each night. It is also expressed in the increase in sexual addictions and perversions, the proliferation of pornography on the Internet, and in the horrendous increase in the sex-slave trade that is being run by the darkest and most debased of people.

Make no mistake, there is also a strong sattva current operating in our raja culture. This is found in the growing number of people who have chosen to align with life-affirming causes and who are committed to spiritual awakening and the care of Mother Earth. These people are behind many of the great charities of the world that are trying to protect the rights of animals, end hunger and cruelty, and improve educational opportunities. They are the individuals who are growing organic food, developing clean energy sources, committing to ecological balance, supporting women's rights and minority rights, and working in general for spiritual growth. They are the doctors, nurses, chiropractors, naturopaths, yoga teachers, and healers who are dedicated to practicing holistic methods of health and healing. These members of society are attuned to the planet and to climate change. They are not interested in the paradigm of war and are, instead, busy building lives based on kindness, authenticity, and service. They see the interconnectedness of all living beings and are committed to restoring our planet to wholeness.

The Big Picture

Understanding these three energetic currents as well as the involutionary and evolutionary waves that are part of the Great Chain of Being is a powerful way to make better choices in life, for these are the background energies against which the Soul plays out its existence. And finding your own personal balance within these changing tides is fundamental to living a happy life. Remember, it's not about creating an excess of any one current; it's about creating balance in your life. For example, if a person's working life is focused only on rajaistic activities like sales, marketing, production, accounting, import, export, or the manufacturing of goods, then in her free time she needs to do something different.

She needs to fill herself up with sattva activities that inspire or uplift the spirit. Maybe this means gardening, camping, hiking, meditation, working with animals, reading a spiritual book, or attending a spiritual retreat. Another person may already be immersed in sattva activities on a daily basis; perhaps she is a healer or yoga teacher, a counselor, or does spiritual readings. So when she is free she may want to go shopping, see a good movie, or read a romantic novel. She might even want to see a vampire movie. Remember, it's all about finding a healthy balance in one's own life.

By understanding the energy signatures of these three gunas, we now have a yardstick to gauge our daily decisions. What are we feeding ourselves with our choices each day? What part of us is still caught up in anger, conflict, or negative struggles with others? Do we spend most of our time feeding our spirit or focusing on our negative thought forms? By stepping back and answering these questions honestly, we can then choose to take a different direction, and thereby learn how to strike a balance in life. Remember, what we spend our time doing in this lifetime will ultimately expand us or limit us, not only now, but in the heavenly worlds—and also in our next lifetime.

Because we live in a primarily rajaistic society I know that sometimes it feels that we must fight tooth and nail to find the time to reclaim that connection with our higher Self, whether it is through meditation, taking a spiritual workshop, reading a book, or simply sitting down to journal or record our dreams. But remember, God is only as far away as our next breath, and in every moment we can choose to tune in and align with our higher Self. Then we have the power to not only transform our lives, but also to enlighten matter itself.

11

Divine Origins

To conceive of Atum is difficult. To define him is
impossible.
The imperfect and impermanent cannot easily apprehend
the eternally perfected.
Atum is whole and constant. In himself he is motionless,
yet he is self-moving.
He is immaculate, incorruptible, and ever-lasting.
He is the Supreme Absolute Reality.

HERMETICA

So let us now imagine how you might go about creating the cosmos. If you were the one and only for all eternity and there was no one else but you to create from, how would you set things in motion? After all, there is no blueprint to create galaxies, solar systems, oceans, plants, people, or animals. There is only you. So the Creator did the only thing it could: it began by dividing itself in two so that it could behold itself. Taoist wisdom tells us, "The Tao produced One: One produced Two: Two produced three: Three produced all things. All things leave behind them the Obscurity (out of which they have come), and go forward to embrace the Brightness (into which they have emerged), while they are harmonized by the Breath of Spirit."[1]

These two essential aspects are the Divine Mother and the Divine Father, pure emanations of love and wisdom, truth and power, who have been honored by civilizations throughout the ages. While these divine parents may have gone by many names in different ages and cultures, I call them Auriel and Rigel, for that is how they first introduced themselves to me nearly thirty years ago. Auriel, the Divine Mother, is the emanation of unconditional love. Her symbols are the pink rose and the sacred heart. She is the velvet cloak of the green rolling hills, the vault of the stars at night, and the whisper of your heart when it yearns for union. Eastern traditions call her Aditi, the First, the All Mother, Begetter of the Universe. She is the white dove of peace that brings the Holy Spirit, and the homing beacon in every heart that calls us home. She is, indeed, the very fabric out of which the universe is made.

Rigel, the wise Divine Father, is the Great Eagle whose wings span the cosmos. He is the blue flame of burning truth, power, and wisdom whose wings turn the universe. An image of the Great Eagle is engraved on hundreds of temples and cathedrals across the world, symbolizing the Divine Father Who Sees the All. In Native American cultures he is the Great Thunderbird or Eagle. In Egypt he was known as Heru, or Horus the Elder, an aspect of the divine masculine who is beyond the worlds of form.

It is from this name, Heru, that we get the name *Jeru*salem, since in the ancient world the letter *H* was used for *J* in the Hebrew language. In Rome, the eagle represented the "God Most High" and became the

Figure 11.1. The Great Eagle

emblem of the emperors. Because of the eagle's association with the virtues of wisdom, strength, and reverence, this symbol was later adopted by a number of nations in their coat of arms, including Poland, France, Germany, Romania, Russia, Iceland, Austria, Yemen, Mexico, Moldova, Nigeria, Ghana, Syria, Albania, Armenia, Indonesia, Zambia, and the United States.

The United States chose this symbol because it was revered by the Iroquois Confederation, from whom Thomas Jefferson got the structure for our legislative branch of government. Among virtually all Native American peoples eagle feathers are the most sacred of healing tools, for the eagle represents a state of wholeness that is only achieved through understanding and initiation rites. Even today, the highest rank a Boy Scout can hold is that of Eagle Scout. Yet the symbol of the eagle was already known to our Founding Fathers, whose roots lay in the mixture of Freemasonry and Rosicrucianism that blended the wisdom of ancient Egypt with the teachings of Christ. As we can see, the deeper meaning of this symbol goes back tens of thousands of years, even to the time of the Anunnaki gods who once helped to settle this planet.*

The Masculine and Feminine Principles

Knowledge of the Divine Mother and Divine Father is known throughout the cosmos, although few of us have learned how to honor the

---

*The eagle and the hawk were the foremost symbols of the Anunnaki leadership, the tall, long-lived beings who helped foster humanity for thousands of years. These are the beings historically referred to as "the gods." In Mesopotamia, the leader of this group, Ninurta, chose the eagle as his symbol, and in Egypt the hawk and falcon were the symbols of the gods Ra, Horus, and Osiris. While the history of the Anunnaki gods deserves a book all of its own, suffice it to say that these world civilizers oversaw the birth of human civilization for tens of thousands of years, only moving away from human affairs sometime between 2100 BCE and 500 BCE. They are responsible for many of the mysterious ruins we find today such as Stonehenge in England, the Great Pyramid of Giza, the monuments of Easter Island, Gobekli Tepe in Turkey, and Puma Punka in South America. Like modern humans, the Anunnaki were scientists, doctors, astronauts, and physicists, and had great knowledge of the metaphysical underpinnings of the universe; thus they chose the symbol of the eagle or Divine Father to represent the concept of God the Father.

Divine Mother in our patriarchal age. Yet in the mystical teachings of the Kabbalah these are the first two expressions of the One who existed before all things, Kether. In the Kabbalah the divine pair is known as Chokmah, wisdom, and Binah, understanding—the Father and Mother of the All. In Hinduism this is Vishnu and Lakshmi, the divine couple that resides in the Cosmic Egg that floats on the waters of the deep. They are the two great principles of love and truth. Tibetan wisdom calls them the great Mother-Father God Samatabhadra and Samatabhadri, or Yab-Yum, the intertwined masculine and feminine energies in Tibetan practice. Tibetan Buddhism refers to these two great principles of wisdom (feminine) and skillful means (masculine), symbolized respectively by the ritual implements of the bell and the dorje that animate the universe. Like us, one part of these divine beings eternally resides in the Cosmic Sea, while another part is woven into the fabric of the cosmos.

In Hinduism these two complementary forces are Shiva and Shakti, the male and female expressions of kundalini, or the life force. Shiva, it is said, chases Shakti throughout time, pursuing her as long as the universe exists. When he catches her, Creation will roll back on itself, returning to a primordial state of Oneness. In this moment it is said the universe will vanish, for it is through the duality of these two primordial beings that the subject and the object are created, making it possible for the lover to behold the beloved. In the Zoroastrian hymn the Ahunavaiti Gatha we read:

In the beginning there was a pair of twins, two spirits, each of a peculiar activity; these two spirits united, create the first; one, the

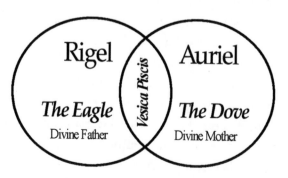

Figure 11.2. The union of the Divine Mother and Divine Father that form the Cosmic Egg

reality; the other, the nonreality. . . . And to succor this life *Armaiti* (the Divine Mother) came with wealth, the good and true mind: She, the everlasting one, created the material world. . . . All perfect things are garnered up in the splendid residence of the good Mind; the Wise and the Righteous, who are known as the best beings.[2]

In Taoism these two forces are depicted by the yin-yang symbol, the path to union that expresses itself as the two genders of every species, the poles of the planet, the valences of atoms and batteries woven into the fabric of the universe itself, because nothing in creation can exist without these two complementary energies. In Egypt they are known as Isis and Osiris, said to have been created long before they came to Earth as the eternal sister and brother, the wife and husband, the two halves of a single whole. They are the divine twins who are both separate and joined as long as the universe is in form. Jesus speaks of them as the "Abba-Amma" God behind Creation itself.[3]

The Dot within the Circle

Behind these two powerful energies is the one primordial presence, that of Source. The Supreme Creator has been called by many different names: Atum, Saguna Brahman, Sugmad, YHVH, Allah, the Logos, and the Infinite, to name a few. But whatever name we use, this divine intelligence is the Source of all things. Its consciousness seems to spring from nothingness, and it manifests in countless forms, forms so small and so grand that you may hold it in your two hands or see the vastness of its reflection spread out against the majesty of the night sky. Its consciousness exists in everything, whether multiplied or divided, and it surrounds us in both the visible and invisible realms. In the Hermetica, an ancient Greek-Egyptian wisdom text, the purported author Thoth asks: "Do you think Atum is invisible? Nothing is more visible than Atum. He created all things so that through them you could see Him. This is Atum's Great Heart—that He manifests Himself in everything."[4]

The Upanishads remind us: "Manifest, near, moving in the secret place, the great abode herein rests all that moves, breathes, and shuts

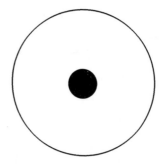

Fig. 11.3. The ancient symbol for God, the Sun, and the singularity, surrounded by Creation

the eyes . . . Luminous, subtler than the subtle, in which the worlds and their denizens are fixed. That this imperishable Brahman . . . that deathless Brahman is before, Brahman is behind, Brahman to the right and to the left, below, above, preceding: this Brahman truly is the all."[5]

Thus the ancients chose the symbol of a circle with a dot at the center to represent this first cause (see figure 11.3 above). In later centuries this representation became the astrological symbol for the Sun, the giver of light and life, not only because it sits at the center of our solar system, but because nothing would exist without this light. In Dante's *Paradiso*, the third part of his *Divine Comedy*, the saintly Beatrice tells Dante that the heavens and all of nature hang from this one eternal point.[6] "Manifesting as the formless dot, the beginning of all things is a state of Oneness which man calls unity. All things in the world today have one natural origin. All things began as one which came forth out of No-thing, the Unmanifest, by the 'elongation of the dot.'"[7]

The Kabbalah refers to this primordial atom or supreme intelligence as the "Unknowable Ain." The Ain is the heart of the Great Mysteries, and today physicists are using this same symbol to represent the concept of the Singularity and the Event Horizon. These are scientific names for the One who creates the many, for they are irrevocably linked to each other. From the One comes the circular expanse of the universe. Eventually, the many will discover that this One lives within the center of their being. "This great unborn Soul is the same which abides as the intelligent [Soul] of all living creatures. . . . Subduer of all, Ruler of all, the sovereign Lord of all . . . Upholder of worlds, so that they fall not into ruin."[8]

Manly P. Hall reminds us,

> All things move and evolve as diversity in unity. . . . Realizing the fundamental unity of all forms and all life manifesting through infinite diversity, infinite time, and infinite space, the student can understand the ancient occult demand for brotherhood. If all things are individualizing sparks from one neutral source, then each is a brother to everything else. Man is not to coalesce with, but to cooperate with all living things. . . . The unity buried in this diversity, and hence unrecognizable by the young soul, is seen in its true aspect as the sole reality by him who has raised his spiritual consciousness above the plane of matter.[9]

Ancient Egyptian sages referred to this creative force as Tum or Atum, the first primordial drop in the Cosmic Ocean that set everything in motion. This is the primordial atom, the Word that moved across the waters of the deep, creating ripples like a pebble thrown into a pond. These ripples flow out from the center in concentric waves, like a great beacon of sound, moving at tremendous speed to create the expanse of all dimensions.

The Nine Dimensions

Both Hebrew and Christian theology adopted the image below, placing God at the center of the universe in a hierarchy of ascending and descending planes. Entities closer to the center, they believed, are closer to the presence of God, while those on the edges are farther from the light of the Divine. This same principle can also be found in the microcosmic and macrocosmic layers of an onion, the rings of a tree, the orbital planes of an atom, and the structure of the solar system.

Thus the masters taught that the Word brought all things into being. "In the beginning was the Word and the Word was with God, and the Word was God. . . . All things were made through Him and without Him nothing was made that was made" (John 1:1–3).

Many ancient wisdom teachings believed that there are seven of

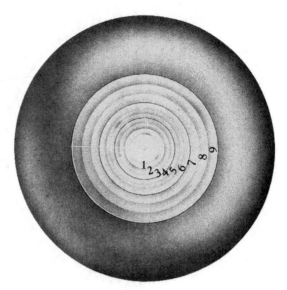

Figure 11.4. An ancient depiction of the nine dimensions nested inside one another. Many ancient traditions have used this image of concentric circles to represent how the various planes are layered, separated only by the vibration of their frequency.

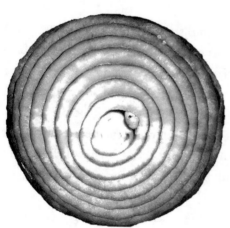

Figure 11.5. There are nine or ten layers inside an onion, reflecting this same implicit order. Like a transmitting beacon of sound and light, these rings radiate out from the center.

these vibrational dimensions nested inside one another, and each plane was believed to have seven sub-octaves. Other cosmological systems claimed that there are as many as nine, ten, or even twelve dimensional planes with their respective sub-octaves, some vibrating at such exquisite levels of purity that they can hardly be perceived. Throughout time, the knowledge of these inner planes has been encoded into different symbols, key among them being the seven-layered labyrinth inscribed on the floor of many ancient temples, as well as the beautiful Chartres Cathedral in France.

Figure 11.6. The classic labyrinth was constructed with seven rings or dimensions that the Soul must traverse in its descent and ascent to and from Heaven.

This labyrinth represents the Soul's journey into and out of the worlds of form. At the center of the journey sits the Flower of Life, leading to the activation of the six-dimensional rainbow body of light. Only here, at the center, can we connect with Heaven, a realm that sits at the center of the six lokas, or planes, as described in Tibetan wisdom. It is in this place of centeredness where we access the heart, where our Angelic Self resides, and it is only this connection that will free us to make the journey out of the world of duality. We are reminded:

This involution of the life of the Logos as the ensouling force in every particle, and its successive enwrapping in the spirit-matter of every plane, so that the materials of each plane have within them in a hidden, or latent condition, all the form and force [of the Divine]—the possibilities of all the planes above them as well as those of their own—these two facts make evolution certain, and give to the very lowest particles the hidden potentialities which will render it fit—as these forces become active powers—to enter into the forms of the highest beings. In fact, evolution may be summed up in one phrase: it is latent potentialities [within every being] becoming active powers.[10]

Multiple Dimensions, String Theory, and Parallel Worlds

Theoretical physicist and futurist Michio Kaku is the cofounder and popularizer of string field theory, which proposes that there are multiple universes and dimensions beyond the one we know. He writes about these various dimensions in his book *Parallel Worlds: A Journey through Creation, Higher Dimensions, and the Future of the Cosmos.* Until recently, Kaku tells us, scientists viewed the idea of a multidimensional reality with great suspicion. "But recently the tide has turned dramatically, with the finest minds on the planet working furiously on the subject. The reason for this sudden change is the arrival of . . . 'String Theory' and its latest version, 'M-theory,' which promises not only to unravel the nature of the multi-verse, but allows us to 'read the Mind of God.'"[11] String theory is actually a scientific description of the ancient philosophical concept of the "music of the spheres," the biblical Holy Word, or the audible life stream known in Sanskrit as *shabda* ("speech-sound," as in the sacred syllable *Om*). Dr. Kaku tells us that "string theory and M-theory are based on the simple and elegant idea that the bewildering variety of sub-atomic particles making up the universe are similar to the 'notes' that one can play on a violin string, or on a membrane such as a drum head. (These are not ordinary strings and membranes; they exist in 10 and 11 dimensional hyperspace.)"[12]*

Physicists have traditionally viewed electrons as being point particles that are infinitesimally small. This means that they had to introduce a different point particle for each of the hundreds of subatomic particles they found, which is very confusing. But according to string field theory, if we had a super microscope that could peer into the heart of an electron, we would see that it is not a point particle at all, but a tiny vibrating string; it only appears to be a point particle because our instruments have been too crude. This tiny string, in turn, vibrates at different

---

*Dr. Kaku goes on to tell us that M-theory could very well stand for "membranes, magic, mystery," or even "Mother," an apt description of the many ways in which this secret information has been considered by the sages of the past.

frequencies and resonances. If we were to pluck this vibrating string then it would change mode and become another subatomic particle, such as a quark. Pluck it again and it turns into a neutrino. In this way we can explain the blizzard of subatomic particles as nothing less than different musical notes of a string. We can now replace the hundreds of subatomic particles seen in the laboratory with a single object: the string.

In this new scientific vocabulary, the laws of physics, carefully constructed after thousands of years of experimentation, are nothing more than the laws of harmony one can write down for strings and membranes. The laws of chemistry are the melodies that one can play on these strings, and the universe is a symphony of strings. And the "mind of God" that Einstein wrote so eloquently about is cosmic music resonating throughout hyperspace.[13]

Esoteric wisdom says that this divine melody, or *shabda,* is the modulating frequencies of the sacred sound that set everything in motion. As we shall see, these modulations are part of the functions of the Seraphim, who, along with the other orders of Angels, ultimately create the templates for all the structures of the universe, informing the structure of energy as it descends into the worlds of matter.

This torus (see figure 11.7 on facing page) is both the infinity symbol and the ouroboros,* the ancient symbol of the snake or dragon biting its tail. All of these symbols were designed to depict the circular nature of the universe.

Jill Purce, a British voice teacher and family constellations therapist, writes about how this waveform pattern is created by the unformed waters of the Cosmic Egg turning in to behold itself:

These same vortical [spiral] laws govern the movements of water, which composes nearly three-quarters of our physical bodies. Water

---

*The ouroboros symbolizes something constantly re-creating itself, as in the eternal return and the idea of primordial unity related to something existing from the beginning with such force that it cannot be extinguished. This symbol first emerged in ancient Egypt and India and has frequently been used in religious, alchemical, and mythological symbolism. It is associated with Gnostic, Hermetic, and Hindu wisdom. Carl Jung interpreted it as an archetype of the human psyche, and Jungian psychologist Erich Neumann believes that the ouroboros represents the pre-ego "dawn state" of the connected but undifferentiated state of humankind.

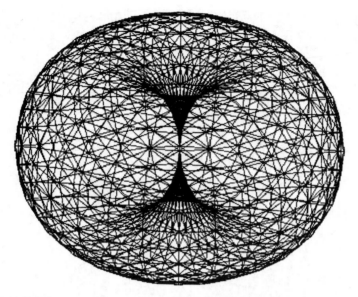

Figure 11.7. The torus may very well be the shape of the universe according to the latest physics, for it is the perfect circle turning in and out on itself.

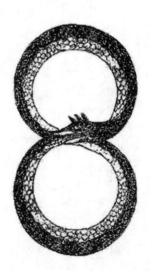

Figure 11.8. This infinity symbol shows a snake biting its own tail, a variation on the ouroboros and representing the recurring cycles of time and the cyclical motion of the Creator.

is the pure, potential, and unformed matrix from which all life takes its being . . . [the Cosmic Sea, or plenum]. It is from the involution of the unformed waters that the egg crystallizes by turning in upon itself—of energy, of matter, or of consciousness; and all these are one and the same.

Figure 11.9. The celestial circle of Heaven, called the Empyrean
(illustration by Gustave Doré)

This order, reverberating down into the microscopic and subatomic levels, both structures and reflects our consciousness. The full significance of this organization, which was obviously known to the Greeks, since their word *kosmos* means 'order,' is again being demonstrated by physicists, who say that matter actually consists in its own movement and organization. Similarly, the growth of human consciousness is the continuous refining of its own organization, the ordering of its individual microcosm.[14]

This means that as we evolve, we move up the spiral ladder of consciousness in the unwinding or activation of our own DNA. This spiral movement can also be found in our sympathetic and parasympathetic nervous systems, acting as a stairway to Heaven. William Blake, the British mystic and painter, portrays this beautifully in his image of the Soul's ascent into the heavenly realms, as seen in color plate 5.

The Eagle, the Sacred Masculine

So how does this spiral come to exist? It is the Divine Father's waveform on which the universe is built. Madame Blavatsky writes, "To reach the knowledge of that Self, thou hast to give up Self to Non-self, Being to Non-Being, and then thou cast repose between the *wings of the Great Bird*. Aye, sweet is rest between the wings of that which is not born, nor dies, but is the AUM throughout eternal ages."[15] What is Blavatsky speaking of? It is the wings of the Great Eagle. Other mystics have

Figure 11.10. Rigel the Great Eagle, symbol of Father God who sees all things

acknowledged this eternal presence, the winged one that I have come to know and love as Rigel.

To Zoroastrians, this Divine Father is the Hawk, an aspect of the sacred masculine that never comes into the worlds of form, but who sends aspects of himself into the lower dimensions through the solar lords, the Seven Holy Kumaras. Only four of these seven beings ever incarnate in the physical world; the other three remain in the higher dimensions to oversee the evolution of billions of worlds. The four incarnate Kumaras are known as the "deathless ones," the sons of God in Vedic literature. These are the great solar lords who come from age to age and are associated with the torch of illumination, the staff of wisdom, the Tree of Life, the trifold Flame of the Sacred Heart, the ankh (or cross), and the scales of justice. We find these symbols linked to divine teachers such as Lord Krishna, Jesus (or Lord Issa), Mithra, Quetzalcoatl, Hermes, Rama, Thoth, Osiris, Horus, Moses, Pythagoras, Tammuz (or Dumuzi), and Orpheus, to name a few. *The Chaldean Oracles of Zoroaster,* fragmentary texts from the second century AD, begin in this way:

> But God is He having the head of the Hawk. The same is the first, incorruptible, eternal, unbegotten, indivisible, dissimilar; the dispenser of all good; indestructible; the best of the good; the Wisest of the wise; he is the Father of Equity and Justice, self-taught, physical, perfect, and wise—He who inspires the Sacred Philosophy.
>
> Theurgists assert that He is a God and celebrate him as . . . a circulating and eternal God, as understanding the whole number of all things moving in the World, and moreover infinite through his power and energizing a spiral force. The God of the Universe, eternal, limitless, both young and old, having *a spiral force.*[16]

The Spiral of Creation

To the Greeks, the Fibonacci sequence is the mathematical blueprint on which the universe is built. This is the sweep of the Eagle's wings moving through the universe, an expression of pi, the mathematical constant that forever builds upon itself.

Figure 11.11. The sacred spiral
of pi is seen as the vortex of
life as it moves the planet.

Figure 11.12. The spiral permeates creation. Here it is shown in a pinecone,
a snail's shell, and a galaxy.

Jill Purce writes, "This simple two dimensional spiral has a number of remarkable properties. It both comes from, and returns to, its source; it is a continuum whose ends are opposite and yet are the same; and it demonstrates the cycles of change within the continuum and the alternation of the polarities within each cycle. It embodies the principles of expansion and contraction through changes in velocity, and the potential for simultaneous movements in either direction towards its two extremities."[17]

When we stand back and look at the world around us, we can see the curl of this spiral mirrored in the wind and water currents, the spiral of smoke, and the interstellar gas that forms the galaxies. It is found in the coils of a pinecone, the unfurling of a rose, the whirling pattern of our fingerprints, and the way hair grows out of the crown of our head. It is found in things as grand as hurricanes and as mundane as water going down a drain. These are all the manifold expressions of the Eagle's wings.

The Fibonacci sequence begins with the number 1, then moves to 2, and then each additional number is generated when the last two numbers are added together. Thus the sequence moves from 1 to 2, then to 3, then to 5, to 8, 13, 21, and so on. From God's point of view, this makes perfect sense. First the one divided itself in two. It then created the Cosmic Egg in which the Divine Mother and Divine Father reside. This generates the *vesica piscis,* a shape that is the intersection of two discs, or the number 3. This is the doorway where Spirit can move into the worlds of matter. It is also the shape of the Cosmic Egg, a subject we will come to shortly.

Next, the Divine Daughter and Divine Son were born as mirror expressions of their parents. This generates the number 5. Then came the overseers of magnetic fields, electrical fields, and mineral fields,

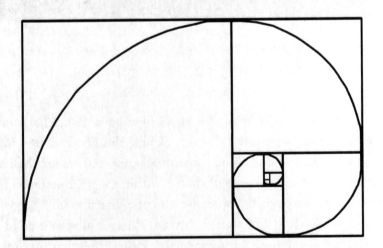

Figure 11.13. The Fibonacci sequence as the template for creation

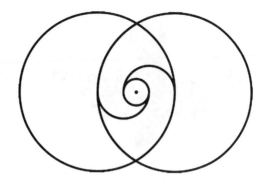

*Figure 11.14. The separation
and merger of the two divine
forces that set Creation in
motion through the doorway
of the vesica piscis*

which generates the number 8. These numbers are not simply mathematical formulas, but the first great intelligences that derive from the One. They are the interpenetrating waveforms that hold the universe together; I know them as the "Council of Nine," the nine primordial waveforms that create, maintain, and sustain the cosmos. Eventually, these highly sentient beings stepped themselves down into smaller subsets, creating the nine orders of Angels, the nine Sephirot on the Kabbalistic Tree of Life, and the trillions of life-forms found in the world around us. This is also why the number 9 is intrinsic to Creation. For example, there are only nine primary numbers before we return to the number 10, thus regenerating the entire sequence of numbers. A circle measures 360 degrees, which, when added together makes the number 9. It takes nine months for the human gestation cycle, and some of the most sacred numbers spoken about in Revelations, like 144,000, add up to the number 9.

The Dove, the Divine Mother

The dove is the symbol of the creatrix from whom all expressions of the Divine Mother flow. She is the heart of unconditional love. Her symbols are the pink rose and the dove, the bringer of peace. She is the homing beacon who leads us back to our center, the principle of love made manifest in the adamantine particles of love that comprise the atoms of the universe. She is the Holy Spirit permeating the universe.

This divine presence has been known by countless names in different

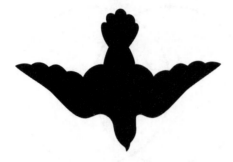

Figure 11.15. The dove of peace is a symbol of the Divine Mother and the Holy Spirit as she descends into the world of form

cultures: Lakshmi, Hathor, Nuit, Aditi, Armaiti, Venus, Aphrodite, and Durga, to name a few. In Egypt she is Isis, she of ten thousand names and ten thousand faces. In Britain she is Brigit, the bringer of light. In China she is Quan Yin, the Mother of Compassion. And in Japan she is Amaterasu, Mother of the Sun. In Native American culture she is White Buffalo Calf Woman, the teacher of balance. And in India she is Sita, the pure devoted wife. To the Hebrews she is Sophia, the Mother of Wisdom. And in Christianity she is both Mary, the Mother of Compassion, and Mary Magdalene, the "disciple who knew the All."* She is known to me as Auriel.

Finally, after nearly 1,500 years, the true wisdom of Mary Magdalene is being brought to light in our time, redeemed from the scandalous lies heaped on her by the early Church, which claimed that she was a prostitute. Nothing could be further from the truth! Not only did Mary Magdalene train as a priestess of Isis at the same time that Jesus studied in Egypt, Gnostic Christians believe that she is an incarnation of the Divine Daughter, Sophia, the female Christ who has been denied for some two thousand years, a daughter of wisdom and love. Today it is profoundly gratifying to see so many people awakening to her beauty, for Jesus revealed to his Apostles that he would not return until the sacred feminine has been re-enthroned in the world.[18] It is perhaps for this reason that the feminine energy continues to be maligned and sup-

---

*Issa, the Arabic name for Jesus, called Mary Magdalene "the one who knows the All" and "disciple of disciples." To discover more about who she is and the critical importance of the role she was asked to play, please refer to my previous book *Return of the Divine Sophia.*

pressed in the world today because her emergence poses a threat to the entrenched patriarchy, so it pushes back.

The Great Cosmic Egg

Through the separation of the divine couple, who are nevertheless joined in their essence, the vesica piscis is formed. This becomes the great Cosmic Egg, another name for the primordial drop that floats on the Cosmic Ocean. The vesica piscis is also the one emblem that Jesus left to represent the heart of his teachings. In Christian theology it became the Ichthys, or "sign of the fish," representing not only this sacred union, but the dawning of the Age of Pisces. It is created through the merger of our male and female natures, which opens our inner sight and allows us to see the Kingdom of Heaven.

Later in Church iconography the vesica piscis was adapted into the mandorla, the aureole that surrounds the entire figure of Christ and other sacred personages, considered the doorway through which these holy ones emerge. Numerous stained-glass windows depict Jesus, Mary, or the Madonna and Child within the mandorla. This is also the shape of the Tisra Til, or Third Eye, which allows us to see into the inner worlds. Hermetic wisdom tells us that this primordial shape is the shape

Figure 11.16. The Ichthys is the one hermetic symbol left to us by Jesus. It forms the vesica piscis, or seed syllable of Creation, which is the primal sound. This powerful symbol is created by the union of the male and female, forming the doorway through which spirit comes into matter. In the brain this union of both hemispheres allows the opening of the third eye.

of our auric field. This auric egg has many subtle-energy layers and is composed of the emotional, astral, mental, causal, etheric, and spiritual bodies. The vesica piscis is not only the shape of a candle flame and a drop of water, it is also the shape of the eyes, the windows to the Soul. It is the shape of all seeds whose blueprints produce the millions of species of plants. In fact, this shape reminds us of the small kernel of wheat that the Eleusian Mysteries used to represent the Soul itself. It is also the shape of a woman's yoni from which the child emerges at birth, as well as the shape of the opening at the end of a man's phallus, where the seed of life emerges. This shape is also created by the spiraling of our DNA.

From this primordial seed issues the power of the Word that brings the universe into being. This is the Logos or template of Creation itself. In the Hermetica we read: "I saw in the darkness of the deep, chaotic water without form, permeated with a subtle intelligent breath of divine power. Atum's Word fell on the fertile waters making them pregnant with all forms. Ordered by the harmony of the Word, the four elements came into being, combining to create the brood of living creatures."[19]

Some call this the eternal *Hu* or sacred *Om,* the male and female aspects of the Word. This is the sound that near-death experiencer Eben Alexander heard in Paradise, a sound that he identified with the Divine Mother. The Buddhist mantra *Om Mani Padme Hum* contains both of these seed syllables, describing the first unfolding stages of Creation. First there is the sacred *Om.* Then comes the Divine Mother (or in Latin, *Ma*ter and in Spanish, *Ma*dre), and then the Divine Father (the Latin *Pa*ter and the Spanish *Pa*dre). Finally, there is the creation of the perfected human (in English, the *hum*an being), which is none other than the Adam Kadmon of the Kabbalah. The beautiful Buddhist mantra *Om Mani Padme Hum* is translated as "the Jewel in the Lotus," a reflection of the Great Mystery hidden within the Cosmic Egg. Many believe that this powerful mantra sums up the teachings of Buddhism, for it reflects the integration of duality and polarity—the universal and individual, through and into each other, like metaphysical mirrors. Its power is said to be activated by a fifth element, *shri* or *hri,* which refers to divinity itself. At the center lies the unknowable One, what

Figure 11.17. The divine couple that lives within the Cosmic Egg that floats on the Ocean of Love and Mercy (illustration by Sylvia Laurens)

the Zohar, the foundational work of the Kabbalah, calls the *Ain,* the wisdom of the *Ain Soph,* and the divine child of light called the *Ain Soph Aur.* This is the first created Soul, the Atman or Isvara of Hindu teachings. This is Sat Nam who holds the holy name of the indwelling Christ.

The Balance of the Universe

The dance of sacred union is mirrored in other ancient symbols. One of the most beautiful is the Star of David, a Hebrew symbol that fits perfectly over the Flower of Life. The Star of David is composed of two intersecting triangles, one pointing up, the other down, representing the union of spirit and matter, masculine and feminine.

In Hermetic wisdom the Star of David represents the merging of the four alchemical symbols representing the elements air, earth, water, and fire. These four elements represent respectively our mental, physical, emotional, and life-force natures, generating the shape of the legendary, alchemical philosopher's stone that extends life and symbolizes enlightenment and bliss. When these four elements are in equilibrium, the Soul has achieved mastery over itself.[20] Thus the Star of David not only represents the activation of the spiritual Buddha body found in the sixth dimension, but the four elements that make up the entire cosmos.

Figure 11.18. The Hebrew Star of David within the Egyptian Flower of Life

**THE FOUR ELEMENTS
MERGED IN UNION**
AS THE
DIVINE MOTHER & FATHER

*Figure 11.19. It is the merging
of all four elemental forces that
leads to mastery*

FIRE

WATER

AIR

EARTH

Fire and air are masculine elements, while water and earth are considered feminine. These four elements exist in everything in various proportions, and the ancients believed that each dimension has a predominance of one over the others. The third dimension is the realm of earth, while the astral plane is akin to water. The mental world is ruled by air since thoughts rule manifestation, and the higher planes exist as brilliant realms of fire and light. The Hermetica reminds us: "By Atum's will, the elements of nature were born as reflections of this primal thought in the waters of potentiality. These are the primary things: the prior things: the first principles in all the universe. Atum's Word is the creative idea—the supreme limitless power which nurtures and provides for all the things that through it are created."[21]

All that we see and all that we don't see comes from the Divine Mother and Father, or the emanating principles of truth and love. These overlapping energies form the Eye of God, the doorway through which Spirit moves into the world of matter. This is known as the Eye of Ra or Eye of Horus. Ra is the doorway of light, while Horus is the doorway to truth.

These two names, Ra and Horus, symbolize the awakening of the

Figure 11.20. The Eye of Horus

Figure 11.21. A NASA image of the energy field of the Milky Way as seen in a spectral photograph that displays the red shift. This astonishing image is but one of many Cosmic Eggs in the galactic ocean.

two hemispheres of our brain that, when combined, allow us to open our inner sight, a portal to the doorway of Heaven, the gateway where each Soul stands at the moment of Creation. Thus many cultures use the All-Seeing Eye to represent the omniscience of the Creator itself.

Furthermore, as we look out into the cosmos, we find that each galaxy is enveloped in an energy field that looks like a Cosmic Egg.* So all of these millions of galaxies recently discovered by modern sci-

---

*The egg-shaped appearance that surrounds all galaxies can be seen in photographs that include the red-shift spectrum of light.

ence reveal a plethora of Cosmic Eggs floating in the great sea of the cosmos—the exact image once shared by sages in the mystical literature of the Vedas.

Behind the vesica piscis is a great primordial intelligence. This is the being that I call Domalar, one of the nine intelligences of the Council of Nine. She is the place of endless possibilities, the merging of Spirit with matter that allows life to come into being in the worlds of form. The Hermetica reminds us that "the Cosmos which our senses perceive is a copy and an image of this eternal Cosmic Mind, like a reflection in a mirror. . . . From its first foundations there has never existed a single thing which was not alive."[22] And thus from the microcosm to the macrocosm, this living template permeates the entire universe.

The Son of God Begotten

From this first trinity that includes the Divine Mother, the Divine Father, and Domalar, their place of union, the Son and Daughter are born. The Son is often described as a solar male, while his sister, the Daughter, is his lunar reflection. Yet in truth all of these beings are beyond the kind of duality that we humans ordinarily perceive. As a result, there are both lunar and solar aspects to each of them, because, while they exist to create balance in the world, they themselves are whole and complete beings. In some cultures we find goddesses like the Egyptian Sekhmet or the Japanese Amaterasu, who are solar females. Likewise, there are expressions of the lunar male like Thoth and Khonsu in Egypt, and Nannar in Sumeria.

In the incoming Age of Aquarius these male and female aspects of the Divine will return to balance once again, both in the world at large and in our personal expression in the world. The astrological sign of Aquarius is known for its androgynous qualities; it is ruled by the elements of air (or understanding) and ether (or Spirit), so as this age unfolds, our societies will move back into balance, with both genders being honored. Over the last two thousand years, during the Age of Pisces that is just ending, the male principle was symbolized by the solar lion as "the Light of the World," while the Daughter was marginalized, maligned, and forgotten. But these two beings, the Son and Daughter of God, are embodied in the trifold flame of the Sacred Heart and represent our own potential for divine union. This trifold flame is composed of the pink/rose ray of the Divine Mother, the blue/violet ray of the Divine Father, and the golden ray of the Holy Child.

In Egypt the solar male was epitomized by Osiris, and later by Horus, his son, while Isis, the Mother of Wisdom, was the female expression of the Christ energies. The Inca called the solar male Inti, just as he was Lugh to the Celts, and Helios to the Greeks. Christians refer to him as Jesus (or the Arabic Issa), the living Christ. When this Christed energy is ignited it moves up the spine, igniting our halo and signaling the merging of our little self, or personal ego, with our Angelic Twin, the higher Self. The ancient symbol for this activation is the caduceus, the staff of enlightenment, a symbol brought to humanity by Thoth, the founder of all the Mystery Schools. Traditionally this staff was only carried by master initiates who had attained this state.

Today the caduceus is used as the emblem of healing in medicine, yet what it really illustrates is the awakening of the sympathetic (masculine) and parasympathetic (feminine) nervous systems moving up the spine. When joined, these two currents activate the central nervous system that conducts kundalini energy up the spine to the crown, awakening the pineal gland in the center of the brain. This, in turn, awakens our inner sight, allowing the Soul to have access to the higher realms of light.

Figure 11.22. The caduceus, the staff of enlightenment

The Daughter of God Not Forgotten

The Daughter is known in the Talmud as the Shekhinah, the Breath of God. Her symbol is the snake, the perfect emblem for the sine wave on which all light and sound must travel—the carrier of the Holy Spirit through space and time. Her movement is found in the rhythm of our heartbeat, the graph of our brainwaves, the oscillation of magnetic fields, and the rising and falling ocean tides. The Shekhinah carries the light of her Brother and the sound of her Mother, allowing all worlds to come into existence. She is the intelligence hidden in our undulating DNA and the delivery mechanism through which sound, light, and movement travel through space.

In ancient traditions this undulating energy was symbolized by the snake, the symbol of mystical wisdom. In Egypt she was called Uchat Buto, "Ancient of Ancients." In North, South, and Central American cultures she was the Grandmother Snake, bringer of enlightenment, still revered by ayahuasca shamans today.

In Mesopotamia we find statues of priestesses holding two serpents,

Figure 11.23. The snake as a symbol of the Shekhinah

one in each hand, symbolizing the two nervous systems used in the process of enlightenment. This tubular serpentine shape can also be found in the human body as the esophagus, the intestines, and the male and female organs of procreation. Carl Jung wrote that the snake is the "word-creating Spirit concealed or imprisoned in matter," the oldest symbol in alchemy. When she transforms into the winged serpent she becomes the Morning Star, an emblem of the Soul's discovery of its true angelic nature.[23] This is also the shape that is created as our solar system moves around the galactic center, inscribing a large cosmic serpent reminiscent of the ouroboros, which was the symbol used by the ancients to represent the passage of time.

It is unfortunate that in the last two thousand years the real meaning of the serpent has been demonized by the dualistic, fear-based dogma of the patriarchical religions. Yet when we stop to think about it, the snake is the only animal that is reborn while still alive—the perfect symbol for our own process of spiritual initiation. Today, humanity is beginning to emerge from the fear-based misogyny of millennia of

Figure 11.24. The spiral movement of the planets around the Sun is reminiscent of the snake.

male-dominated religion, yet when we look around us we can see that there are still places where women are intellectually and socially controlled, killed, or repressed by their male "masters." Nevertheless, any true look at the universe has always and will always include both the Divine Male and the Divine Female as equal partners in Creation. The more we can return our own lives to this balance, the faster we will restore this broken world to wholeness.

12

Angels, Devas, and Mortals

The highest revelation is that God is in everyman.

RALPH WALDO EMERSON

Belief in the existence of Angels is found in many cultures and religions around the world, including the Greeks, Persians, Hebrews, Hindus, and Buddhists. Angelic beings are found in Native American culture as well as in Christian and Islamic theologies. The word *angel* is derived from the Greek *angelos* and the Hebrew *mal'akh,* meaning "messenger."[1] Yet these high-vibrating beings have also been referred to as *devas, suras, archangels, daimones, orishas,* and *devs* by other cultures. The word *deva* comes from *div,* meaning "to shine"— perhaps a reference to the brilliant light of their auras or energetic appearance. This brilliant light is seen by many, even when they choose to cloak themselves temporarily in human form. Vedic scholar Jeanine Miller (1930–2013) writes, "Devas are the luminous energy principles behind all phenomena, whether of Nature or of the Cosmos, hence they can be thought of in terms of the regents of the universe, the custodians of the One law, the Cosmic Order which they establish throughout manifestation."[2]

Like all higher beings of light, Angels express the harmony of cosmic law and the pattern of divine order and Oneness that is eternal in the upper dimensions. In fact, their job is to establish this cosmic order in both the higher realms and in the worlds of space and time. The Rig-Veda, the foundational source of an ancient Indian wisdom meaning wisdom or gnosis, teaches that the essential nature of these beings is "law-abiding, born in law, sublime fosterers of law, [and] haters of falsehood" (Rig-Veda VII.66.13ab). Angels are the "herdsmen of the Supreme Law, whose decrees are truth" (Rig-Veda V.63.1ab). Thus it is the task of the Angels to fashion the blueprint of the Logos in all the worlds below. Miller writes:

> The devas' solidarity, their essential righteousness, their concerted activity are their peculiar characteristics that eminently mark them as the agents of the One Law by which, through which, and in which, they live and move and perform their varied tasks. The rishis and ancient sages, conceived of an impersonal eternal Law to which all, even the most exalted of beings are subservient. That Cosmic Order is the "song" of the cosmos. So the devas revel in the sacred song of the Cosmic Order.[3]

Because Angels are linked to the melody of the Word, the celestial sound current, Vedic sages believed that they could be summoned with the use of certain songs or prayers or mantras. Thus many spiritual paths have employed the use of holy hymns, sacred chants, and musical poems, which adepts believe create a "flashing song" of brilliant light that draws them into our realm, especially when these prayers are combined with a pure heart. This is how the great sages attuned themselves to the higher realms through chants and songs dedicated to the celestial hosts, using the illuminating power of the Word to milk the nectar of Heaven.[4]

The Qualities of Angels

Anyone who has ever encountered an Angel can testify that their frequency is much purer than that of a human being. This is because their foundation lies in the celestial worlds, and thus they are in harmony with the Logos and the Music of the Spheres. Existing in the sixth and seventh dimensions, they are actually frequencies of moving light and sound. That is why the appearance of an Angel is often accompanied by music or the sound of chimes. We are reminded that "Angels themselves differ in appearance according to the Order to which they belong, the functions which they perform, and the level of evolution at which they stand."[5]

Angels are not burdened with the additional energy bodies that humans have (described later in this chapter), and thus are not driven by the same egoic appetites. They do not have mental, astral, emotional, or physical bodies, or the inherited genetic patterns that lie at the heart of our cellular memory. They do not have a primitive reptilian brain, an emotional limbic system, a physical body to feed, or a dualistic bicameral brain like we do. So understandably they are light-years ahead of the common human being. Angels have only acquired two of the seven subtle-energy bodies that we have: a diamond body and an etheric body; this allows them to directly transmit vast amounts of information in milliseconds. Human beings, on the other hand, have five additional energy bodies, the net result of which is to submerge us in duality.

Angels' ability to send and receive information almost instantly is a function of the brilliant diamond body of the seventh dimension, which has the power to travel at the speed of thought, perceive in 360 degrees, and visit any plane of reality. Their six-dimensional Buddha body emanates joy, peace, and bliss. It can energetically merge with the subtle-energy fields of all living things—vegetable, animal, mineral, human, or planetary—directing an empathetic life force to another.

Philosopher and mystic Emanuel Swedenborg (1688–1772) writes: "The wisdom of the angels is indescribable in words. . . . Angels can express in a single word what man cannot express in a thousand words. . . . For in every single word spoken by angels, there are arcana of wisdom in a continuous connection to which human knowledge never reach." He goes on to explain: "Those who are in heaven have more exquisite sense, that is, a keener sight and hearing . . . the light of heaven, since [it] is Divine truth, enables the eyes of angels to perceive and distinguish the most minute things. Moreover their external sight corresponds to their internal sight or understanding; for with angels one sight so flows into the other, as to act as one with it."[6]

The Archangels

Within the angelic kingdom there are the great Archangels, or Dhyani-Chohans as referred to in Theosophical literature. These are the emissaries of light, such as the Archangels Raphael, Michael, and Gabriel, who have never descended into mortal form, but have and will ever remain at the side of God, helping to oversee our human evolution. They may also be great Souls that have already completed their entire evolutionary program in an earlier cycle of time. Thus these beings have acquired a consciousness that is far closer to God-awareness. In this way these great beings of light operate much like spiritual laws, having become direct extensions of the will of God. These beings are the overlighting intelligences that assist in the running of the universe.

"Fundamentally," clairvoyant Geoffrey Hodson tells us, "these Beings are directors of universal forces, power agents of the Logos . . . [God's] engineers in the great creative process, which is regarded as continuous."[7] According to ancient wisdom there are several types of posthuman entities. These include the Archangels, the Lords of Karma, the Mind-born Sons, the Sons of Light, the Builders, the Lords of Light, and the Planetary Angels. The highest Archangels have achieved such a level of enlightenment that they are put in charge of enormous universal forces, galaxies, and the flow of incoming rivers of light. "Those of the first group build or rather rebuild every [planetary] system after the Night [of God] when all manifestation goes into a dormant state. The second group of Builders is the Architect of our planetary chain exclusively, and the third [group] the progenitor of our humanity—the Macrocosmic prototype of the microcosm."[8]

Angelology

Today there seems to be some confusion about whether the Angels we read about in the Bible were really etheric spiritual beings or the physical "messengers of the gods" (i.e., the ETs who visited our planet in previous ages). So let me take a moment to address this matter. The "gods" that we are referring to are the extraterrestrial visitors known as the Anunnaki (or Anakim). Their sojourn on our planet has largely been hidden from the public for the past two thousand years, yet their arrival on our planet and their interactions with us are recorded in history, myth, and legend, and in recent times much of the historical information about these beings has begun to surface.

These tall, long-lived world civilizers came to colonize our planet eons before our human history began, and because their countenance is far more radiant than ours, they have been known as "the Shining Ones." These cosmonauts could fly, and many of their aerial vehicles look quite similar to those of modern-day UFO accounts. These spaceships are depicted in hieroglyphs, bas reliefs, paintings, tapestries, and murals across the world. Accounts of these "gods" are also found in Norse, Greek, Roman, Egyptian, Indian, Native American, Chinese, Australian, Mayan, Incan, and Celtic cultures.

Over the past two centuries, archaeology has unearthed thousands of clay tablets written in cuneiform from the ancient lands of Sumeria, Chaldea, Assyria, and Persia (modern-day Iraq, Syria, Turkey, and Iran), all documenting human interactions with the Anunnaki. These discoveries have the power to rock the very foundations of traditional religious theology, and so their existence should not be swept under the rug. And while this is not the subject of this particular book, it is relevant because these gods are linked to what are commonly known as Angels in the Old Testament—great winged beings who were commissioned by the Anunnaki to act as messengers between them and humans, thus blurring the line between beings who originated from another part of the universe and the higher beings of light who come from the spiritual dimensions.

After nearly thirty years of research I am now convinced

that both of these groups of beings exist. The Angels of the Old Testament appear to be a group of luminous physical beings sent by the Anunnaki gods to deliver messages to humankind—messages that were often moral or inspiring, but also assisted with the implementation of law and the infrastructure of civilization, especially once the gods began to withdraw from human interaction. The second is a group of spiritual beings who were sent by the spiritual hierarchies from the fourth and fifth dimensions. Their only interest in humanity is the preservation of knowledge and upliftment of our spiritual evolution. While these spiritual beings are certainly capable of manifesting a human form if needed, they are not physical beings, nor are they subject to the passions of a physical or emotional body. As a mystic and historian who has had interaction with both of these groups since I was a child, I understand that it's easy to get the two mixed up. The focus of this book, however, is on the higher angelic beings of light who function as selfless expressions of spiritual law. It is the job of these Angels, devas, and spiritual teachers to oversee the evolution of planets like this one and to act as guardians for humanity as we awaken over time. These angelic beings honor the free will of all human beings and do all things in accordance with divine will.

Because of this confusion, however, the development of angelology has been a mishmash of different sources reported by those who have had encounters with both groups. These accounts go back to the time of Enoch many thousands of years ago. Some of these encounters even made their way into the Zohar, the Old Testament, the Koran, and the Vedas, each a holy book that lies at the heart of our various religions. This makes it even harder to sort out the mystical encounters with beings from the higher realms from our ancestors' past encounters with sophisticated space beings. Author and researcher Malcolm Godwin writes about this confusion in the development of angelology:

> The evolution of the idea of a unique angelic species can be viewed
> from countless angles. Historically speaking, for instance, they are

clearly the hybrid result of an extraordinary Hebrew program of cross-breeding original Egyptian, Sumerian, Babylonian, and Persian supernatural beings. This genetic interaction of ideas produced the outward appearance of the winged messengers of God which we know of today. By the 1st century after Christ, this essentially Jewish creation was adopted, almost wholesale, by the new religion, and six centuries later by the Muslims. Since then, that fundamental angelic form has undergone no radical alterations.[9]

In his book *Angels: An Endangered Species,* Godwin tries to untangle the mystery of Angels from historical, scientific, and philosophical perspectives, but unless one has had a direct encounter with these beings this is a difficult task. Throughout history, many people such as myself have had these kinds of direct transmissions from beings who dwell in the higher realms, and have received gnosis* as a result. Some of them have sought to convey the things they have learned to others and in so doing were heralded as saints, prophets, oracles, or madmen, depending on the times. Certainly hundreds of rishis, yogis, mystics, rabbis, priests, nuns, and spiritual initiates have also had their own transcendental experiences with the nonphysical realms and received great wisdom as a result. The Indian rishis, for example, whose spiritual sight was hereditary, would enter into communion with the devas and find that they could approach the "thousand-branched Tree of Life" to apprehend the functions of the great powers at work in the cosmos.[10]

Some of these groups, like the Essenes, sought to consciously establish contact with these spiritual hierarchies so as to accelerate their own spiritual enlightenment. In the Essene Gospels of Peace, a little-known group of writings hidden in the Vatican and only made public in the twentieth century as a result of the scholarship of a priestly candidate named Edmond Szekely, we learn that Jesus taught his followers how to establish communion with fourteen different Angels. These are clearly Angels of a spiritual kind, since each Angel he mentions works with the elemental forces of nature. Jesus taught his followers how to energeti-

---

*Gnosis is the direct transmission of wisdom or knowing, as opposed to linear thought.

cally connect with the Angels of the sun, the earth, the waters, the air, and the Angel of Mother Earth. These are the overlighting devic presences that work within the realms of nature to help sustain the worlds of form. Here is a small excerpt from one of these prayers: "Angel of the Sun! There is no warmth without thee, No fire without thee, No life without thee. . . . Holy messenger of the Earthly Mother, Enter the holy temple within me and give me the Fire of Life!"[11]

So we can see that Jesus knew about and worked with the spiritual beings who oversee the kingdoms of nature, but are these beings different from the Angels of the Old Testament? As confusing as angelology is for both historians and UFOlogists, for those with inner sight there is no question that such higher dimensional beings exist. The list of those who have had encounters with them is long and includes people like Emanuel Swedenborg, Hildegard van Bingen, Joan of Arc, Socrates, Carl Jung, Padre Pio, and Dorothy MacLean, cofounder of the Findhorn community in Scotland. The list also includes Joseph Smith, founder of the Church of the Latter Day Saints; Saint Francis of Assisi, who received the stigmata from a flaming Seraphim; and Mohammed, the founder of Islam, who claimed that he was visited by the Archangel Gabriel. In fact, so powerful was Mohammed's encounter that the Quran has made the existence of Angels one of its six articles of faith.[12]

Speaking from personal experience I can tell you that such powerful encounters can completely transform a person's life, yet they take place at a subtle-energy level that is beyond and behind the physical world. Madame Blavatsky writes about these angelic beings in her opus *The Secret Doctrine:* "The Hermetic philosophers called Theoi, gods, Genii and Daimones (in the original texts), and by other names. The Daimones are—in the Socratic sense, and even in the Oriental and Latin theological sense—the guardian spirits of the human race; those who dwell in the neighborhood of the immortals, and thence watch over human affairs.[13]

Barbara Martin, a lifelong clairvoyant, writes about her own encounters in *Communing with the Divine:*

> Countless sages and mystics have claimed direct contact with
> these Holy Ones. . . . They work to uplift humanity and form the

evolutionary link connecting us to God. These exalted beings work on different levels of unfoldment, which is why it's called a hierarchy, yet all work in perfect harmony with one another. Together they form the evolutionary chain that links all life from the simplest amoeba to the most radiant archangel . . . God works through these wonderful beings, guiding and steering the entire process of evolution.[14]

Our Angelic Origins

For many centuries religion has taught that Angels and humans are essentially two different species. In other words, a human being can never evolve into an Angel, and vice versa. While it is easy to understand how we might believe this to be true—after all, the nature of human beings is concrete, limited, and mortal, and that of Angels is ethereal, transcendent, and immortal—this is, in fact, not the case. In reality, each one of us begins our journey in the devic or angelic kingdom. Ancient wisdom confirms this:

> To many of us it is a familiar thought that men and angels belong to a composite body, that they work together to fulfill the purposes of nature law and human evolution. But to many of us it is quite a different matter to begin to realize that each man is not only human, but is also devic in the most profound aspects of his nature. He is indeed man and deva in his own right, and these two inseparable parts of himself constitute the whole individual, one part totally unable to function without the other.[15]

The Soul descends from the Cosmic Ocean, or Ocean of Love and Mercy, where it has been in total Oneness, but now it is challenged to begin the journey of learning individuation. When this Soul, in the form of a pure white flame, begins its descent from the Ocean of Love and Mercy, it first enters the sixth and seventh dimensions. At this point it has no experience of life, nothing that marks it as separate from any other spark in the body of God. It is only aware of the one eternal reality that connects us to the whole, but it has a limited awareness of anything other than swimming in the Cosmic Sea and its desire to serve the universal plan. Thus in order to grow the Soul must acquire a series of subtle-energy bodies that will allow it to build its own experiences, just as we must have a physical body to participate on this plane of existence. In the seventh dimension the Soul acquires a Soul or Diamond body, and then, in the sixth dimension, it takes on an etheric or Buddha body, sometimes referred to as the "rainbow body" because of its brilliant colors. In these two higher dimensions it also acquires a devic matrix.

Devas are associated with Angels, yet the devic kingdom also includes trillions of other diverse beings, from the smallest plant elemental to the fairies, from personal Guardian Angels to the largest Archangel. But since these beings have not obtained mental, astral, or causal bodies, they are not anchored in the third or fourth dimensional realms as we humans are. Their Souls are anchored in the fifth, sixth, and seventh dimensions, even though they may be on assignment in the lower realms. With some exceptions these beings are invisible to human beings unless they wish to be seen or a person has developed her inner sight. Theosophist Maria Parisen writes, "Each entity from the smallest to the highest has its own particular work to perform, and just as the most exalted Deva uses His mighty intelligence in the forming of world destinies, so the little Nature Spirit uses his intelligence in directing the processes of the [mineral, animal and] vegetable kingdoms."[16]

Like a great symphonic orchestra with millions of instruments, these devic beings serve the divine plan, each according to its own nature, spiritual maturity, and ability to channel divine forces. Thus a deva may appear as a whirling gas cloud, a plasma being, or the translucent intelligences that surround the world of nature. In time it learns to direct the life-force energies of a tree, a forest, or a mountain, overseeing the worlds of nature to sustain and amplify existing universal templates. This capacity to direct the energies of the universe is gained over time, so in the beginning a deva may only be able to encourage the life force in a flower, a stone, or a bush, but over time its ability to work in larger ways increases.

A Slice from the Soul Records
of a Devic Spirit

Hypnotherapist Dolores Cannon writes about the journey of the Soul through the devic realms in the past-life regression sessions she has done for a number of people, some of whom report lives on other planets as well as lives in the celestial realms before ever coming to Earth. In *Legacy from the Stars* she shares the account of a young man whose sessions involved past lives in the devic kingdom. There he found himself spending thousands of years helping to maintain the energies of a star, acting as a plasma being who converted the noxious fumes of a planet into a breathable atmosphere, and learning how to transform the denser energies of matter like rocks. In one session he found himself in a classroom being taught by a higher being who was teaching the devas how energy moves from thought to gas, then to denser matter, and finally to rock. When asked why the physical world had to be formed, this is what he said:

> Because that is God's plan that spirit take the body of form. And that the Soul experience form. . . . There must be spirit in matter. God must be experienced in matter. . . . We are learning that each form, each level is just a denser form of spirit. Matter, I mean, ether, God . . . Life force must be in everything. Everything must be alive. . . . Spirit must be able to live in the rocks . . . in those forms. . . . Not alive, not as my soul. The life force is thinner. It keeps what I am alive.[17]

When this being was asked about the purpose of evolution, he replied:

> To be, to know, in a moveable being. This is why I am, is to express, to know in a movable being, not as a rock. . . . I feel that I am to know simplicity, and also complexity. I must know how to put things together for a greater purpose. . . . I must embrace the larger thing that I am. I am a little point, and I must expand myself to embrace all of God. I must learn to love

more. . . . I think I am to grow into a larger form than what I am now, in this life . . . more like an angelic larger form, where I will touch and teach and help and be with smaller forms, like a guardian angel. . . . I think that is my destiny, to do this. I am created to do this.[18]

So in the sixth and seventh dimensions the Soul starts out as a simple devic spirit serving in one of the four elemental kingdoms: air, earth, fire, and water. This is our devic matrix. Then slowly we gain more complexity, learning how to direct the universal energies of the God force toward their life-affirming end. This apprenticeship of individuation and co-creativity takes place over billions of years, until the Soul is finally ready to acquire a causal body in the fifth dimension. Once this happens, the deva or Angel is born as a more individuated Soul in the fifth dimension, having its other subtle-body sheaths slowly built around it. In this dimension it acquires a causal body, a mental body, and then an individual ego. This allows it to more fully experience the formless levels of the mental plane and then to finally begin its descent into the worlds of form in the fourth and third dimensions. Depending on how long the Soul remains in the fifth dimension, its various experiences will help to shape many things about its character and the path that lies ahead of it, strengthening certain affinities for music, dance, arts, color, plants, flowers, or even healing. Other Souls may develop an affinity for observing the stars, the celestial web of life, or studying the laws of the universe. Still another Soul might become strong in the attributes of courage, justice, law-making, or wisdom. These affinities depend on the length of time a Soul stays in the fifth dimension, and the experiences it begins to have.

During the time that the Soul is in the fifth dimension, it joins a Soul family. This family usually consists of some eight to twenty members who start at approximately the same degree of spiritual development. This group has one or more Guides assigned to it whose job is to personally help that circle of Souls in their evolution.

Eventually, after millions of years, the Soul will decide to enter life in the fourth and third dimensions. In the fourth dimension or astral plane, the Soul will acquire the addition of two subtle-energy bodies—the astral body and emotional bodies. These two bodies are very intertwined and deal with our relationship to our sense of self-worth and our relationships with others.

Eventually, the Soul will become bold enough to take on a physical body, encouraged and guided not only by its personal guides, but also by a circle of advanced spiritual beings. This is the Council of Elders who will oversee its long evolution and with whom the Soul will meet at the end of every lifetime. This Council works with the Guardian Angels and the Soul to determine the Soul's goals for every lifetime. All of these wise, patient beings are part of our spiritual support system who oversee the evolutionary journey of each individual Soul. We could also call them the Lords of Karma, for they are involved in overseeing our evolutionary journey for hundreds of lifetimes. Some have called them the Council of Elders, the Council of Light, or the Lords of Karma, yet all of these are different names for the same wise spiritual beings who help to guide our personal development.

Once the Soul has entered the physical realm, it begins to experience the million and one emotions that will flood it as it embarks on its Course Curriculum, acquiring the countless experiences that will allow its greatness to emerge. In this process the Soul forgets who it really is until finally, by its own free will, it chooses to begin the journey back up the spiritual ladder, to remembrance and union. Professor John Algeo, former vice president of the Theosophical Society in America, explains it thus:

> We humans, far from being the crown of evolution, as we are wont vaingloriously to imagine ourselves, are actually the nadir of spiritual development. As the most individual of all beings, we are the most separate from the divine Unity, and thus the farthest of all beings from our common source. In us the monadic development reaches its lowest point. Our future is to reestablish connections, to forge the links that will bind us back to the Unity, to become One—consciously, deliberately, of our own free will. At the Omega

point of evolution, we are to merge without losing our identities, to recreate the Unity, but then a Unity that knows itself and has chosen its state.[19]

In time, over hundreds of incarnations on this planet and others, we move forward as a conscious seeker of the light. Eventually, as a result of our experience of suffering, we learn to become a willing servant of the Divine, having forged the steel of our own free will into a complex multidimensional being of light who has acquired enough mastery to become a fully evolved spiritual master. Madame Blavatsky writes:

> In sober truth . . . every "Spirit," so-called, is either a disembodied or a future man. As from the highest Archangel down to the last conscious Builder, all such are men, having lived eons ago, in other Manvantaras [world ages*], on this or other Spheres; so the inferior, semi-intelligent and non-intelligent Elementals, are all future men. That fact alone—that a Spirit is endowed with intelligence—is proof to the Occultists that that being must have been a man, and acquired his knowledge and intelligence through the human cycle."[20]

And so while devas and humans often seem to be quite different, in truth what we have are beings who are at very different phases of their evolution. Nature spirits have not acquired an ego yet, and the other complexities of human layering have not been given to them.[21] They are at the front end of the involutionary wave, in the early stages of individuation, while human beings are in the middle of their journey. Eventually that devic being will take birth as a human being in the third dimension, acquiring additional subtle-energy bodies along the way to make this happen. Over time the Soul will acquire more and more complexity and learn greater individuation through the power of

---

*A Manvantara is the period of time between the breathing-out of God that creates the entire universe, and the breathing-in of God that brings all things back into stillness. What Blavatsky is saying here is that some of the most powerful Angels are actually fully enlightened beings who are carryovers from previous universal ages.

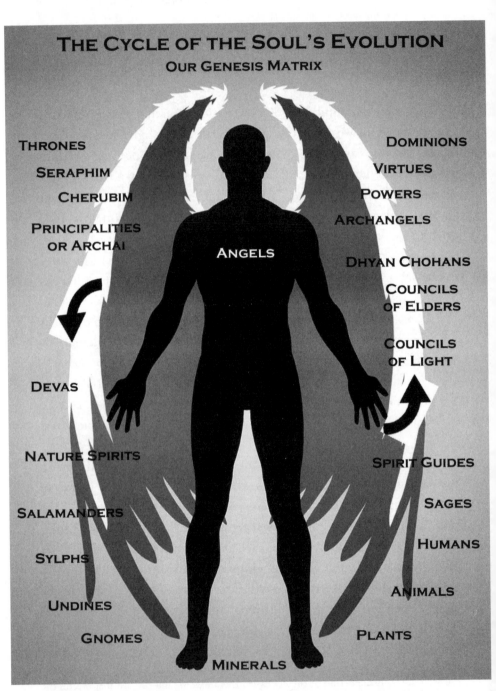

Figure 12.1. *The involutionary and evolutionary circle of the Soul's descent and ascent from a place of semi-aware angelic intelligence to a place of mastery, truly claiming our angelic inheritance*

free will. Ultimately, as a human being, it begins the journey toward self-mastery, finally graduating from Earth school. Thus human beings are at the outermost realm of the involutionary wave, preparing to begin their return back home to Source. We ordinary people are caught equally between the two waves of Creation, exactly in the middle of our journey, while the mystics and masters among us have already moved into union with the Source.

The Devic Kingdom

Up until about two hundred years ago the existence of the devic kingdom, as well as the vast realm of nature spirits that people had encountered living so close to nature, was widely acknowledged. But as our scientific, technological societies have grown more and more mental and less and less heart- and spirit-based, we have gotten out of touch with this realm. In fact, all three of these kingdoms, human, plant, and devic, were meant to work together in harmony. Today, however, we believe that fairies, pixies, elementals, Angels, and other such creatures are but the stuff of fairy tales. Yet all these ethereal beings actually support humans in symbiosis, for they are the hands and feet of the Creator in the realms of matter.

Theosophist and clairvoyant Geoffrey Hodson (1886–1983) first began to share his discoveries about the devic kingdom in a little book called *The Kingdom of the Gods*. Published in 1952, the book depicts his paintings of these nature spirits, revealing visions of the radiant devic energies that oversee mountains, islands, and forests. Being made of energy and light, these devic spirits often take on the shape of the plant or mountain, mirroring the very form of energy they serve. A tree elemental, for example, might appear as a tall, radiating being with large, extended arms. A bush elemental might look fat and round. A mountain elemental might be tall and pointed or wide and jagged. These are the translucent beings that I first saw as a child in the forest across the road from my parents' home, elementals that I describe in my first book, *Dialogues with the Angels*. These devic spirits are part of the psychospiritual fabric of the causal realm that nourishes the infrastructure of nature. Here is a short excerpt from Hodson's book that describes observing an overseeing mountain elemental:

> The appearance of these Beings is most magnificent. In height, colossal, often ranging from thirty to sixty feet, the mountain God is surrounded on every side by outrushing brilliantly colored auric forces. These flow out from the central form in waves, eddies, and vortices, varying continuously in color, in response to changes of consciousness and activity. The face is generally more clearly visible than the rest of the form, which not infrequently is veiled by the out flowing energies . . . Whilst in man the heart and solar plexus chakras are distinct, in mountain and other Gods, they are sometimes conjoined to form a brilliant force center, often golden in color, from which many of the steams of power arise and flow forth. On occasions these streams take the form of great wings stretched out for hundreds of yards on either side of the majestic figure.[22]

Depending on whichever element they are associated with, these devic spirits have been called *gnomes* (earth), *undines* (water), *sylphs* (air), and *salamanders* (fire). The Greeks referred to them as *dryads* (trees), *naiads* (water), and *oreads* (mountains). Celtic people have their sea kelpies, forest brownies, and village leprechauns. Some see them as fairies or "little people." It is clear from this list that there are many categories of devas, from the simplest elemental who assists in the growing of a plant, to the larger formless (arupa) devas that move through the pure elements of water, fire, earth, and air. Many of these Souls will evolve into fairies on their way to eventually becoming human, but while in a humanoid shape these beings assist with the tasks of nature.

Scholar Jeanine Miller writes about how the Vedic seers were aware of these benign helpful nature spirits: "Everything in the universe pulsates with deva life, whether this be the intelligence that energizes deva substance or that substance which responds to the impact of divine Intelligence, the call of the high devas and evolutionary life."[23] To the ancient philosophers, "Fire, air, water, earth, were but the visible garb, the symbols of the informing, invisible Souls or Spirits, the Cosmic Gods."[24] Madame Blavatsky reminds us that "we live and have our being in the Elements, hence in the very substance of the devas, for without air or water we cannot survive, and earth is obviously our habitat."[25]

When the Soul first begins its journey into the sixth and seventh dimensions, it gains experience by aligning with one of the four elemental kingdoms. This allows it to begin to individuate over time. Most Souls have spent three, four, or five billion years in the devic realm long before coming into the denser physical realms as a human being. As an elemental the Soul's essence is anchored to the higher worlds, even though it may have been on assignment in the third, fourth, or fifth dimensions. In this way, through the different elements that it experiences, the Soul begins to acquire certain affinities. These affinities then become a part of the Soul's matrix, manifesting in talents, interests, and energetic alignments once it takes birth in the human realm. Understandably, the longer a Soul spends in any of these elements, the greater the gifts it receives from them.

When I do a reading for a client I first begin by taking a look at the age of the Soul. I want to know which of the nine angelic orders it was created in, for this tells me the path of its greatest happiness. Then I look at its experience in the various elemental realms. This reveals a great deal about the natural talents of that person and how he has best expressed himself in the world of matter. It also guides me in looking at the major themes, latent talents, and even why the person may be strong in some ways and weak in others. In addition, I want to know the age of the Soul and its spiritual maturity, for as we shall see in chapter 15 (page 323), there are beginner, young, intermediate, advanced, and master Souls. Each has its own strengths and weaknesses.

The following lists the various spiritual gifts and affinities associated with each of the four devic kingdoms. Most Souls have only experienced two or three of these kingdoms and the order in which they experienced that element, as well as the amount of time spent in that element; makes a powerful difference in how these gifts are expressed in an individual's life.

The Water Kingdom

The water element is perhaps the first element linked to Creation and thus it is profound and primordial, since water represents the vast plenum from which all things arise. Thus it is the task of water spirits to nourish all the kingdoms of nature, to care for and tend to all of life. Thus water is constantly pouring out its essence to reveal the principle of love at work in the cosmos. The task of water spirits is that of the Great Mother as she performs her work of bodybuilding under the impulse of divine desire. This is the feminine element at work.[26]

To me, water is the most essential of all of the elemental realms. When this element is used as a palette for creative expression by the Soul it teaches empathy, compassion, and sensitivity. The spiritual gifts acquired from this element are clairsentience and clairaudience. Clairsentience is the ability to sense someone else's energy empathetically. This ability is ruled by the third chakra and gives one the ability to feel the subtle-energy field of others that extends from the living body. Because this element gives the Soul an innate sensitivity to feelings and emotions, it is perfect for healers, therapists, and people whose careers are attuned to the bioenergetic fields of others. This ability can also be used to sense the subtle energies of an animal, a place, or a person.

Water spirits have clairaudience. This is the ability to hear the sound currents that run behind the manifest universe. Clairaudient people are often musicians, poets, composers, or writers. They may become speech or music therapists. If you have this ability you may find yourself humming a tune that you picked up in your sleep or occasionally hearing melodies that come from the inner planes. Clairaudience can result in many wonderful gifts expressed through the flow of music, poetry, singing, composition, or writing. Such attunement to sound currents gives the Soul the ability to receive automatic writing, to have dialogues with one's spirit guides, or to channel information from the higher regions. Water spirits also have a strong connection to the creative arts. This includes skills related to the flow of energy such as dance, qigong, tai chi, sports, or simple grace. These gifts express themselves in professions that deal with painting, makeup, beauty, fashion, color therapy, or interior decoration. Many water spirits are naturally talented dancers, musicians, or artists.

The challenges of this extremely sensitive element are such that if water is not grounded by earth, it can soak up the negative energies of others like a sponge. This can cause a person to put on weight, feel drained, or get sick if continually exposed to a negative environment. Water spirits who are incarnated as humans should take at least a five-minute shower each morning to cleanse their energy field from their dreams and fluff their auras. When exposed to many random people such as in a mall, they should take an evening bath using Epsom salts and several drops of the essential oil of lavender; this will help to cleanse their energy field. If a water spirit is in a relationship with a partner who is negative it's best that she not sleep with her partner because she will inadvertently take on his negative energy while trying to clear his field during sleep. This will leave her exhausted in the morning. To recharge, she should spend time in the garden or woods, beside a stream, beach, or waterfall, and arrange to get some couples therapy or get out of the relationship altogether. Otherwise, she can become toxic with negative energy that is not her own.

The Earth Kingdom

Souls who have come through the earth kingdom are naturally attuned to the earthworks of matter. These Souls are grounded and have a natural ability to work with their hands. They are often able to shape physical matter in very practical ways. This talent can be used for making things, like becoming a woodworker, a blacksmith, an herbalist, or a builder. This ability to channel energy through the hands can also be used for healing, and earth spirits and water spirits are some of the most powerful and sensitive of healers.

Earth spirits are usually very practical people, and their creative abilities are channeled in very three-dimensional ways. Theirs is the world of grounded practicality, so they are often contractors or architects, auto mechanics or machine manufacturers, farmers, ranchers, carvers, sculptors, or construction artists, shaping the world in very foundational ways. Having earth in one's matrix is highly grounding and will always help a Soul manifest its life in a more substantial way. Because earth spirits have natural talent with their hands, they are not only natural healers, they may also be gardeners or landscapers. These are people said to have a green thumb. Earth spirits have a natural feeling for plant devas, natural medicine, food, and cooking, and many of the various expressions of earth. Thus they may become fabulous chefs, naturopaths, or herbalists. Since they naturally gravitate to the substances of the earth, these people may become veterinarians, forest rangers, farmers, ranchers, protectors of wildlife, zoologists, or choose to raise animals. Earth spirits also have a natural ability to communicate with gemstones and crystals and the energies of Earth herself. They may decide to become blacksmiths, metal workers, sculptors, engineers, or jewelers. They may become geologists or seismologists, land surveyors or cartographers—all careers that work with charting the energies of the planet.

Earth spirits are also natural warriors since this link to the land drives them to protect. These are people who not only build cities and fortifications, they also make weapons and go into battle to defend the cities. In this way they use their talents to either protect, kill, make, create, solve practical problems, or attune to and heal others, aligning with the natural energies of the land.

Because earth spirits are grounded and concrete, they are not abstract thinkers. You would not normally find an earth spirit reading a book like this one unless they have one of the other elements in their matrix. They are not intrinsically spiritual and are rarely interested in philosophy or religion. Metaphysical concepts are not important to them except as they might be applied to solve a practical earth-based problem. Their spirituality comes through touch and connecting with the land, the animals, and the plants, and in this they are supreme.

The Air Kingdom

Unlike earth spirits, air spirits are focused on the world of ideas; thus they are often inventors, philosophers, mathematicians, scientists, theologians, teachers, and high creatives. Since air is the one element that penetrates the other three elements—earth, water, and fire—air spirits are natural diplomats and natural intermediaries between all other elemental realms.

The spiritual gift of air is clairvoyance, or the ability to see with the inner eyes. While all Souls possess the innate ability to develop the clairvoyance, clairaudience, clairsentience, and claircognition, in most of us these inner senses are merely slumbering potentials. Those Souls who have come through the various devic kingdoms and developed affinities for each of these gifts will always have an easier time accessing their respective abilities than someone who has not. Thus it is easier for an air spirit to awaken his or her inner sight as a clairvoyant, a psychic, a seer, or a mystic than it is for a Soul who has not come through the air kingdom.

Air spirits are able to easily download ideas from the mind of God if they practice meditation, dream journaling, or higher alignment. These are genius concepts that already exist at the higher realms, and these holographic ideas can be brought into the physical world by those who are attuned to receiving them. This gives air spirits a natural edge as inventors and high creatives, and they are often quite active in their dream state. They may be moviemakers, photographers, creative directors, artists, entertainers, and art directors. They may be storytellers, comedians, writers, or novelists, and they can quickly think on their feet. Once these Souls develop their spiritual abilities through meditation or lucid dreaming, the sky is the limit in terms of accessing their higher creative powers.

A drawback is that air spirits can be too mental, living in the head and not being grounded in the body. They can sometimes be so mental that they become disconnected from their emotions and the practicalities of daily life. They can forget to eat or shower, gather books around them like an old library, wear rumpled clothing. Balance is clearly needed for them to become grounded and to reconnect their mind to their heart.

The Fire Kingdom

Fire spirits are extremely creative Souls, for fire is the second element that brought the world into being. Some spiritual paths believe that it was the first element to emerge from the Cosmic Egg; an event that science calls the Big Bang. Fire spirits are highly intelligent, charismatic, and dynamic, and can be warlike and aggressive. They are impatient and can run circles around a slow-moving earth spirit. They have a powerful curiosity about everything, particularly sex, which is a conduit for fire energy or the kundalini. This curiosity also includes any subject that has to do with action, power, violence, dynamism, life or death, or the use of the sexual life force.

On the minus side, fire is not naturally compassionate, empathetic, or patient, so it can be self-centered, egotistical, and highly destructive. When there is too much fire in someone's Soul matrix he may struggle with anger, aggression, or self-sabotaging behavior. However, when combined with the softer elements of water or earth, fire can express itself in more balanced ways. In the right measure fire is leadership-driven, shamanistic, alchemical, creative, and enlightened. Taken to its highest level it brings creativity, brilliance, knowing, high charisma, and the power to create alchemical transformation in the healing of others.

The Elemental Matrix

As we can see, the elements that a Soul accumulates in its earlier devic stages can play a crucial role in the direction in which it later evolves. Souls that have a lot of water must learn to ground more solidly in the earth. Souls with too much fire or air must learn to open to the sensitivity and emotions of water and to use the earth as an anchoring point for their quickness of thought. Souls who have too much earth must learn to increase the properties of air and water, thought and feeling, in their natures. While some Souls have only had the experience of working with one of these elements, most Souls have evolved through two or even three elemental kingdoms, making them ever more complex in their composition.

In *The Secret Doctrine,* Madame Blavatsky speaks of these same elemental affinities: "The meaning of this is that as man is composed of all the Great Elements: Fire, Air, Water, Earth, and Ether—the Elementals which belong respectively to these Elements feel attracted to man by reason of their co-essence. That element which predominates in a certain constitution, will be the ruling element throughout life."[27] Each element thus contributes to the matrix of the individual Soul, but too much of any one element can create an imbalance in life. So doing our best to cultivate the strengths of each of the four elements can ground us, inspire us, and motivate us as we move through the human world.

In addition, it is important to know that the length of time a Soul spends in each element has a direct bearing on that Soul's abilities. A person with three billion years in water will be far more clairsentient and clairaudient than someone with only one billion years. Plus the order in which the Soul experiences these elemental kingdoms has an impact. If a Soul ended its time in the devic realms in the element of earth, it will naturally be drawn to earth matters as it moves into its incarnations in the fifth, fourth, and third dimensions. If a Soul ended its time in fire, then the Soul will find itself swept up in the passions of war, sex, conflict, impatience, leadership, and creative brilliance. Once we begin to rearrange these elements in both duration or sequence, the permutations of the Soul's evolution become ever more complex. The best healers, for example, always have water and earth in their matrix. This combination gives the Soul the empathy to perceive the wounds of another person and the ability to transmit healing energies to those wounds through their hands. When you add to that the element of fire, you have the power to facilitate miraculous healings.

Entertainers often have water or fire in their matrix because the element of water pushes them toward emotional expression, while fire feeds their longing to be seen on stage. Those Souls with water, earth, and air in their matrix might easily become statesmen, philosophers, or diplomats because this combination creates a sympathetic spirit of idealism, kindness, and practical groundedness.

The Seven Subtle-Energy Bodies

After the Soul descends from the sixth and seventh dimensions, it then acquires the additional energy bodies that allow it to become human. The first and most important is the causal body, the energy body that it will sustain from lifetime to lifetime. The causal body contains all of the Soul's past-life records and is directly linked to the higher Self. Then comes the mental, astral, and emotional bodies. Lastly comes the etheric double that overlays the physical body, helping to maintain the person's physical vitality. This etheric double is an energetic replica of the physical body that extends about an inch beyond our skin. When we are sick it become gray and contracts. When healthy, it is a blue-gray color that shines with vibrancy.

While we are in the physical world each of these subtle-energy bodies serves a specific purpose, but when we die all of the lower bodies gradually dissolve as we reintegrate with our causal body and higher Self.

Why do we need these subtle-energy bodies? Well, just as you might need a space suit to go walking on the moon, so too must the Soul obtain bodies of greater and greater density to travel into the realms of matter. Each of these subtle-energy bodies is not only connected to one of the seven dimensions, it is also connected to the seven chakras, the subtle-energy centers that run along the spine. Ancient teachings describe these seven chakras as "portals" or "gates of enlightenment." They are the means by which the Soul becomes linked to a physical body, stepping down the energy of Spirit into the matter.

In addition, each chakra is connected to certain organ systems as well as to their corresponding emotions and thoughts. And any unhealed wounds from the present life or from any of our past lifetimes may choose to reside in any of the various organ systems. These negative energies trapped in one or more of the chakras can eventually make their way from the subtle-energy levels into the physical body and manifest as physical, emotional, or creative energy blockages. By clearing away these old energy patterns, whether they are the result of traumas, vows, beliefs, bindings, or negative emotions like anger or fear, we

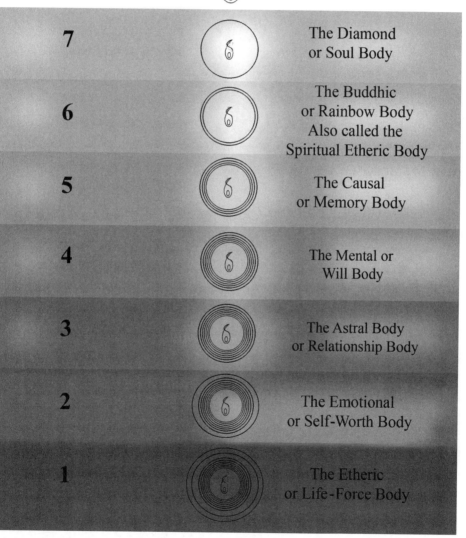

The Creator

The Seven Subtle-Energy Bodies of the Soul

The Flame of the Soul

7	The Diamond or Soul Body
6	The Buddhic or Rainbow Body Also called the Spiritual Etheric Body
5	The Causal or Memory Body
4	The Mental or Will Body
3	The Astral Body or Relationship Body
2	The Emotional or Self-Worth Body
1	The Etheric or Life-Force Body

Figure 12.2. The seven subtle-energy bodies that the Soul acquires as it descends into the world of form

THE SEVEN CHAKRAS
& SEVEN ENERGY BODIES

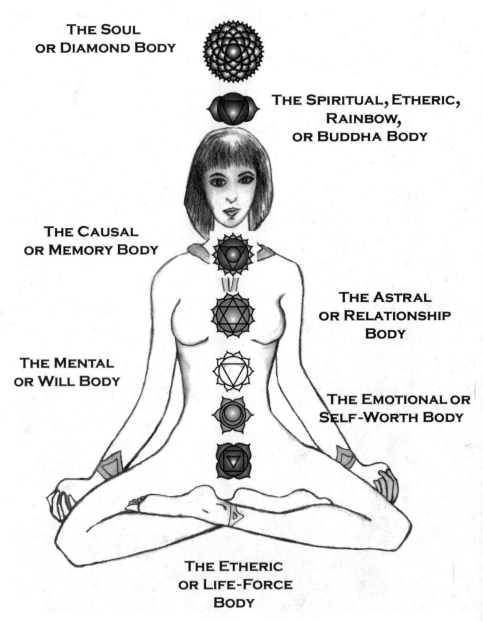

THE SOUL
OR DIAMOND BODY

THE SPIRITUAL, ETHERIC,
RAINBOW,
OR BUDDHA BODY

THE CAUSAL
OR MEMORY BODY

THE ASTRAL
OR RELATIONSHIP
BODY

THE MENTAL
OR WILL BODY

THE EMOTIONAL OR
SELF-WORTH BODY

THE ETHERIC
OR LIFE-FORCE
BODY

Figure 12.3. The seven energy bodies and their connection to the various chakras (illustration by Tricia McCannon)

can restore the body to harmony and mend the traumas of the Soul. Thousands of people have undergone this kind of deeper spiritual transformation with therapists like Brian Weiss, Michael Newton, Dolores Cannon, and myself, hypnotherapists trained in these matters. These patients can attest to the power it has to bring real and lasting healing.

The Diamond or Soul Body

This body is so named because of its flaming brilliance and radiant facets. These facets are the incarnational aspects of wisdom that we acquire during our long journey through the dimensional realms. The diamond body is linked to the flame of white fire of our higher Self. This diamond layer is the first covering we take on as we begin our journey into the lower worlds; thus it is directly linked to the higher Self and the crown chakra, being closest to the Soul itself. The diamond body is masculine in nature, just as the Soul is feminine. It has the power of direct knowing and the ability to receive genius ideas directly from the mind of God.

The Buddha or Rainbow Body

The Buddha body, also called the *rainbow body,* is the bliss body that is activated in deep meditation. It is a luminous, rainbow-colored body that is feminine in nature and linked to the brow chakra, helping us to connect with our higher Self. Through the Buddha body we can open up our spiritual gifts of clairvoyance, clairaudience, clairsentience, claircognitive abilities, and lucid dreaming. This body is linked to the development of our intuitional, creative thinking in the feminine part of the brain. Since our culture is primarily left-brain, linear, and male-dominant, this means that we must begin to develop these inner spiritual gifts when we awake and harmonize the feminine side of our natures.

The Causal or Memory Body

The causal body is a multifaceted force field that contains the memory of the I AM presence. This energetic sheath is essentially the Soul's journal, for it records all that has ever happened to the Soul from the fifth dimension downward. The causal body is connected to each person's

Book of Life. This body also contains the blueprint of our current life mission. It is blue, highly structured, and is connected to the throat chakra and our self-expression. This part of who we are remains consistent between various lifetimes, absorbing the wisdom that we bring back to it after each lifetime. The causal body is the "seed" body of our individuation, until such time as we can more fully inhabit our higher Self.

The Astral or Relationship Body

The astral body is located at the heart chakra and is directly linked to all of our relationships as well as to our ability to open our heart to love. It is feminine in nature, multicolored and pastel, and changes from moment to moment depending on how open we are. It is linked to the thymus gland, the lungs, the heart, and prana, or the life force itself. This subtle-energy body is also linked to our ability to breathe deeply, either letting love in or keeping love out. When we have issues with our lungs or heart it may have to do with the ways in which we have held on to our sorrow, grief, or resentment; this affects not only our health, but all of our relationships. The heart center has long been called the Hermetic center, for it is at the center of the seven chakras and is vital to our spiritual path.

The Mental or Will Body

The mental body is masculine and golden and is linked to the third chakra, located at the solar plexus. This body sorts, organizes, and weighs information to manifest our reality; however, this can only happen with the right use of will. In other words, since our beliefs strongly affect how we think, feel, and act, if our minds do not create a foundation of healthy belief systems, then our life may reflect these poor choices. The true intent of the mental body is to keep our Christed Self connected to the mind of God and for us to learn how to use our creative faculties of thought to co-create with the Divine. The mental body contains the functions of the rational mind and the subconscious mind, which may or may not be in agreement. By clearing out the blocks in the subconscious mind and creating life-affirming beliefs in the conscious mind, these two aspects of the mental body can begin to work together to help us manifest a happy, successful life. Then once a person makes the choice to align her personal will with her higher Self, the mental body becomes linked to the brow chakra. "My will to thy will," is a powerful affirmation for creating this kind of alignment. This means that you align your conscious will with the I AM Presence, getting the "little self" out of the way so that the higher Self can come through. When properly employed, the mental body is a powerful tool to support our manifestation of a positive reality.

The Emotional or Self-Worth Body

This subtle-energy body is feminine, fluid, and multicolored, changing from moment to moment with our moods. It is connected to the second chakra and deals with our sense of individuality, creativity, and prosperity. It also deals with sexuality and self-worth. In the physical world the emotional body is strongly connected to a person's boundaries and self-esteem. When abuse happens in childhood, this can directly affect our sense of self-worth. Depending on the level of abuse—physical, verbal, or sexual—the damage done to this energy body can create a lifetime of repair work to heal. This is one of the many reasons why child abuse is such an enormous transgression against society and against that individual, for whatever we experience in childhood shapes us at a fundamental level of the personality.

The Etheric or Life-Force Body

This highly structured masculine energy body is an exact double of our physical form. It is blue and extends about an inch beyond the surface of the skin. It is directly connected to the flow of vital energy, the force of Spirit itself, and the physical health of all of our organs. When a person is sick, this body turns bluish gray and contracts to about half an inch above the skin. As a reflection of a person's primary life force, this field is connected to the first chakra, located at the perineum between the legs. This power center deals with life-threatening issues and can shut down when a person is faced with danger, death, or other life-threatening traumas. Our sense of self-worth resides here, linked to the flow of kundalini and life force. In the many years of my healing work with clients, I have seen many negative beliefs stored here: emotions of fear about whether we deserve to be alive, or whether we should remain invisible in order to stay safe. This energy center has enormous bearing on one's overall health and can be highly compacted when there have been lifetimes spent in prison under persecution, or when we've been told that there is something wrong with us, causing us to make ourselves as small as possible in order to survive.

The Ego

The human ego is different from the true Self or I AM presence. This little self has strong ties with the mind and emotions, which are linked to our second and third chakras. The human ego deals with self-worth, identity, sexuality, boundaries, prosperity, and the sense of right and wrong. While the I AM presence is immortal, the human ego is not. On Earth this little self allows us to develop individuation and learn choices until we choose to become aligned with our higher Self. When this happens, then these two aspects of who we are can begin to work in harmony, and the ego then becomes subsumed by the Soul itself. Until then, the little self is mired in the belief that we are abandoned, cut off, and separate from the Divine. It is this illusion that causes our insecurities, fears, and lack of self-esteem, which we project onto others. These negative emotions lie at the heart of our personal and social problems and must be overcome for the Soul to align with the Angelic Twin's true evolutionary plan.

The Function of the Ego

Despite what we are often taught, especially in certain Eastern religions, my guides have made it clear to me that it is not our job to destroy the little self. The ego will dissolve naturally when the time is right. The ego is a tool that human beings need to survive in this world of matter until such time as we can live fully from the higher Self. It is our task to become a parent to this little self, to remind it that it is safe, loved, and not alone, just as we would a beloved child. Like a good parent, the Soul must remind the little self that none of us have ever been abandoned by Spirit, but have each chosen to enter this world to embark on this amazing adventure called life. Then the little self will begin to feel safe again. It will realize it is not alone and begin to consult the Soul, eventually turning the reins over to the Soul's greater wisdom. Then together, these two parts can work in unison to steer the chariot of life back in the direction of the Soul's evolution instead of succumbing to the fears, insecurities, and negative thoughts that lead us into the shadows.

∾

Whatever traumas your subtle-energy bodies have been through, they can be brought back into balance, for these are merely the vehicles through which the Soul processes its many life experiences. Each of these bodies can be positively or negatively programmed, either consciously or unconsciously, by the words and actions of those around us. Thus what we believe and what we tell ourselves about who we are and our relationship to the world has a huge influence, affecting the circumstances that we attract or create. In part 4 we will take a deeper look at these archetypal patterns and how we can begin to heal them. But for now let us turn to an extraordinary concept known in esoteric circles as the Angelic Twin.

13

Meeting Our Angelic Twin

The soul comes from without into the human body, as into a temporary abode, and it goes out of it anew passing into other habitations, for the soul is immortal.

RALPH WALDO EMERSON

The concept of the Angelic Twin is found at the most esoteric levels of many world traditions, including the Jewish sect known as the Essenes, which Jesus belonged to; the early Christian Gnostics, who upheld the true teachings of Jesus; ancient Egyptian teachings; and the hidden teachings of Catholic theology. In essence, this concept holds that each of us has an angelic counterpart abiding in the celestial realms. The life that we are living now is but an extension of this higher, pure white-light being that has decided to extend a portion of itself into the worlds of form. It is this divine light-filled Angelic Twin that greets the Soul when it reaches the Otherside and asks us for an accounting of the progress we have made after each lifetime.

In the Egyptian Book of the Dead we find several references to this pure white-light being in the symbols of the gods Ra, Horus, and

Osiris. The sun god Ra is said to represent the radiance of the Soul itself. Then there is Osiris, god of the Afterlife, resurrection, and regeneration, who is the risen lord of light who meets us in Heaven. Osiris was said to be the "Ba of the world," the Soul of perfected humanity. He is the being that each Soul is brought before when the heart is weighed against the feather of Ma'at. Then there is Horus, the great restorer of truth who overturns the egoic aspects of Set. Set symbolizes the little self. Finally, there is the ever-renewing phoenix or bennu bird associated with all great world saviors. Legends of the phoenix tell us that he is a flaming being of light who descends from the higher worlds to sing his song of glory. He perishes in the flames of this world, only to be reborn, time and time again. This amazing symbol of the Soul's constant renewal on the wheel of life, death, and rebirth applies to the Christ within each of us. Thus it is not surprising that the phoenix is associated with Jesus, Horus, and Osiris, because it represents the inner beauty of the true Self.

Here are a few excerpts from the Egyptian Book of the Dead found on a papyrus in the grave of Ani, the royal scribe of Thebes, overseer of the granaries of the Lords of Abydos and scribe of the offerings of the Lord of Thebes. In these passages Ani has already made his way to Heaven and hopes that his Angelic Twin will come to meet him. Then he can become one with Horus or Osiris and receive the kingship of his own Soul, symbolized by the ever-renewing bennu bird:

May the soul of Osiris Ani, the triumphant one, come forth with thee from heaven. . . . May he cleave his path among the never resting stars in the heavens. . . . May I, even I, arise . . . like a hawk of gold coming forth from his egg [the auric cocoon or Cosmic Egg]. May I fly and may I hover as a hawk. . . . May I rise, may I gather myself together as the beautiful golden hawk which hath the head of a bennu bird. . . . May I become a shining one therein. . . . I, even I, am Horus who dwells in splendors. I have gained power over his crown. I have gained power over his radiance, and I have travelled over the remotest parts of heaven. Horus is upon his throne. Horus is upon his seat. My face is like unto that of a divine hawk [Horus].

. . . I have risen up in the likeness of a divine hawk, and Horus hath set me apart in the likeness of his own soul.[1]

In this passage, Ani has gained access to his Angelic Twin. He has achieved his end: to become one with the sky god known as the "son of truth" and the upholder of Ma'at. This Egyptian teaching tells us that it is our Angelic Twin who greets us upon our return to Heaven. This is the great being of light that we first encounter during our life review, as reported by near-death experiencers. In other words, this magnificent Angel of light is not Jesus or Buddha, but the Christed aspect of our own Oversoul.

Gnostic Christians also embrace the idea that each person has an Angelic Twin, an aspect of oneself that never leaves the higher dimensions. This wisdom was taught by Jesus, but it was suppressed by the Catholic Church. Gnostic cosmology states that the entire universe is an emanation of the original Oneness. This Oneness divided itself into a plurality, thus creating a vast hierarchy of worlds and beings that issued forth from that original point of light. These trillions of Angels inhabit the transcendent regions of glory and beauty and are benignly disposed toward human beings who aspire to union with God; thus they wish to help us on our path.

The "Fallen Angel"

Gnosticism also teaches that some of these cosmic spirits became estranged from the Source, such that in time they began to look upon themselves as self-existing rulers in their own right. These are the prideful beings that Jesus called *archons,* found in the third- or fourth-century CE Gnostic text known as the Pistis Sophia. One of these great Angels became so arrogant that he asserted that there were no other gods before him. This is the source of our legends about Lucifer, a great Angel who became darkened as a result of his arrogance. The Gnostics believe that this being is Jehovah, the deity of the Old Testament. Jehovah claimed to be the ruler of the gods, who "shall have no other gods before me." While this might be blasphemous in some circles, the

Gnostics may have been correct. After careful study it appears that the Jehovah of the Old Testament may well have been the Roman god Jove. Jove, or Jupiter, was in essence the Sumerian god Ninurta, the powerful thunderbolt-wielding son of the god Enlil, known throughout the Greek world as Zeus, king of the gods.*

Regardless of who this "fallen Angel" really is, Gnostic Christians believe that it is this negative energy that has trapped us in the endless karmic cycles of oppression, blame, shame, guilt, and illusion. This same kind of masculine dominance was also expressed in the heavy-handed

---

*A serious study of the Sumerian tablets of the city of Nineveh reveals that the Anunnaki gods came to Earth over four hundred thousand years ago and were responsible for the creation of *Homo sapiens*. Among the three most powerful of these gods was Enlil, who was put in charge of all the others. His eldest son, Ninurta, the thunderbolt-wielding god, had been promised dominion over all of Earth by his father; and once the elder gods retired, Ninurta was promoted to kingship, becoming Zeus, "the god most high" for millennia. However, once the gods began to withdraw from the affairs of human beings some four thousand years ago, Ninurta did not want to relinquish control. Falling into conflict with some of the other gods, particularly Marduk (Mars), Ninurta took control of the leadership of a group of refugees known today as the Hebrews. Leading them out of Egypt through his chosen ambassador, Moses, Ninurta sought to forge these people into an army to serve his own purposes. From Old Testament accounts it appears that he was quite active with this group for several centuries; however, it is equally clear from his on-again, off-again relationship with his people that he was eventually pulled back by the other gods and may have eventually left Earth, leaving humans to rule themselves. Once this overlighting deity was gone, the priests of Jehovah began to wield their own power, weaving stories of their flight out of Egypt and their interaction with this god into the version of the Old Testament that we have today. Then, down through the centuries, the stories, the history, the customs, and the folklore produced by these events culminated in our understanding of Judaism, Christianity, and Islam today.

While this interpretation that Jehovah may have been a long-living extraterrestrial whose appearance was accompanied by roaring flames, billowing clouds, and radiation burns may overturn the history that most of us have been taught, it actually has a great deal of validity. I chronicle some of this in my book *Return of the Divine Sophia*, where I explain how the early Gnostics came to regard the leader of the extraterrestrial gods as a tyrant. Of course, looking back, Ninurta, or Jehovah, may only have claimed to have been "the god most high," reserving the title of Supreme Creator for God (big *G*). Yet the priests of Jehovah claimed that this was God Almighty, setting in motion the birth of the three Abrahamic religions we have today, which are all based on our misperception of these events.

political control exercised for centuries by the Roman Catholic Church, just as today we find it in the actions of fundamentalists of all religious stripes.

The Gnostics, being true disciples of Jesus, believe that the world was created by a Mother-Father God, or as Jesus called it, the "Amma-Abba." This Divine Mother/Father occasionally sends aspects of itself out into the world as the Divine Daughter and Divine Son. Some two thousand years ago these aspects became embodied in the figures of Jeshua (or Issa) and Mary the Magdala, or Mary the Great. Gnostics believe that we, as human beings, are caught between the light of the Creator and the tyranny of the artificial systems imposed upon us by the dark Angels who have tried to enslave us. Gnostics say that because we are trapped in the illusions of the lower worlds, the Mother God placed within us a homing device so that we could find our way out of this darkness. This "spark of holiness" is centered in the heart, and thus it is through the power of love that we can find our way out of this illusionary prison. It is love that will awaken us from the lie of separation and dualism, free us from the cycle of samsara, and lead us back into merger with our Angelic Twin. Stephan Hoeller, author and scholar of Gnoticism, explains: "Inspired and urged on by wise and helpful angels from above, and shackled and enslaved by tyrannical and unwise angels from below, we undergo troubled dreams as we strive to shake off our intoxication induced by the deceptions perpetrated by the tyrant angels. The knowledge that awakens us from the illusory dreams is not arrived at either by moral rectitude or by cognition of philosophical means, but through interior, revelatory experience."[2] In Gnostic Christianity this awakening is called *gnosis,* a direct transmission of wisdom that reunites the human little self with its Angelic Twin, the higher Self. Later, the Church would alter this concept, changing the words of Jesus to tell us that each person has a "Guardian Angel" watching over him or her.

Our Divine Twin

Gnostic Christians believe that a meeting between a human being and his or her divine counterpart is a cosmic event, an encounter so powerful that it can repair the illusion of separateness and lead the person out of darkness. This is reflected in the Gospel of Thomas, when Jesus tells us: "When you make the two into one, and when you make the inner [Self] into the outer [self], and the outer [self] into the inner [Self], the above [being] as the below [human being] . . . then you shall enter the Kingdom [of Heaven]" (Thomas 22:9–21). This powerful statement lies at the heart of all Jeshua's teachings, and Gnostics are focused on help-ing their students achieve this state of Oneness while still living in the physical world. Hoeller, an ordained priest in the American Catholic Church and a holder of the English Gnostic transmission in America, cites a story found in the Nag Hammadi Library about a visit received by Jesus at a very early age. The storyteller is Mother Mary, and the visi-tor looked exactly like Jesus would look when he became a man. This visitor inquired where he might find "Jesus, my brother." Then, when the two finally met, the older Jeshua embraced the younger Jeshua and they became one.

Similarly Mani, the third-century CE Persian prophet and Gnostic, tells us that when he was twelve years old he too had a vision of his godlike twin, an Angel who came from the "Gardens of Light." This Angelic Twin urged Mani to withdraw from the religious sect he had been raised in and prepare himself for a spiritual mission. At the age of twenty-four his Angelic Twin appeared again and instructed him to go forth and share his teachings. Finally, when Mani was about to undergo martyrdom later in life, his Angelic Twin appeared one more time. This time it united with him and bore him up to Heaven. Historically, we know that even while Mani was undergoing torture in prison, he insisted that he had no human teacher at all but had received all of his teachings directly from his Angelic Twin.[3]

The Sacred Marriage

The merging with one's Angelic Twin is the true meaning of sacred marriage, the reference to the marriage of a bride and a groom that Jesus speaks about so often in the New Testament. The Nag Hammadi Library texts, discovered in 1945, reveal this rite of sacred union as the culminating fulfillment of the Mysteries instituted by Jesus for the liberation of the Soul. In later centuries the Church suppressed the original teaching and derailed its true meaning. The Church even dared to claim that Jesus was the bridegroom and the Church was the "bride of Christ," thus demanding that people join the Church. But the true bride is each one of us, and the true groom is in fact our Angelic Twin, our Christed Self that lives within each of us. In the Gospel of Philip we read:

> It is the holy in the holy. . . . Everyone who will enter the bridal chamber will kindle the light. . . . But the mysteries of this marriage are perfected rather in the day and the light. Neither that day, nor its light ever sets. If anyone becomes a son of the bridal chamber, he will receive the light. If anyone does not receive it while he is in these places, he will not be able to receive it in the other place. He who will receive that light will not be seen, nor can he be detained. And none shall be able to torment a person like this, even while he dwells in the world.[4]

In another biblical passage we read: "Bridegrooms and brides belong to the bridal chamber. No one shall be able to see the bridegroom with the bride unless one becomes one."[5] And in yet a third passage we hear Jesus's words on the day of the Eucharist: "You who have joined the perfect, the light with the Holy Spirit, unite the angels with us also, the images."[6] In all of these references Jesus is saying that our human self is only an image that our Angelic Twin has projected onto the canvas of time and space. In other words, our true Self is really a perfected angelic being.

Valentinus, a second-century CE Gnostic prophet, adopted Jesus's teachings on sacred union into one of his Mystery rites, hoping to help others make contact with their Angelic Twin. After Jesus's teachings Valentinus called this rite "the Bridal Chamber," for it represented the highest spiritual initiation a Soul can have while still living on Earth. So great was this event that it was actually celebrated as a wedding feast. Gnostic theologian Clement of Alexandria describes this powerful sacrament, saying the Gnostics "then lay aside their souls, and at the same time as the woman receives her bridegroom, each of them receives his bridegroom or angel."[7]

The Myth of
the Guardian Angel

The Catholic Church altered the Gnostic teachings about the Angelic Twin, saying instead that each person has a personal Guardian Angel. In doing so they concealed the deeper truth that a part of us is eternally in Heaven and never leaves it. Ancient teachings tell us that only about a third of who we are ever incarnates on Earth. The rest remains in the higher worlds, or may send another portion of itself to take incarnation in other dimensions or other worlds. Thus it is possible to be having more than one lifetime in the third, fourth, or even fifth dimensions, while the greater part of who we are remains in Heaven. By concealing this inner teaching of Jesus, the Church maintained its power to excommunicate a Soul, holding the threat of purgatory or Hell over its head. Instead the Church taught that the Guardian Angel presents the person's Soul to God at the gates of Heaven—an image reminiscent of Horus presenting the deceased to his father Osiris in the Egyptian Book of the Dead. While having an intermediary to argue a Soul's worth in Heaven may sound reassuring to some, it completely misses the point, which is that each of us is in essence already an angelic being. The core of who we truly are is that pure white light, and the union we seek is with our own higher Self, which already resides in Heaven. If this deeper wisdom was taught by religious authorities, then it would place the responsibility for spiritual growth squarely on the shoulders of the individual and take power away from outer authorities. This is something that religions do not seem to be interested in doing. In truth, it is only our own ignorance, false beliefs, and negative thoughts, words, and actions that can keep us from this divine reunion.

This single realization has the power to liberate humanity from centuries of mistaken thinking—and the belief that we are not worthy. When we can truly embrace the idea that we ourselves have chosen to come into this world to learn, then we can really get down to the business of using the life we are living now to further our spiritual evolution. This, in turn, leads us to embrace the cherished aspects of the being within, reminding us, as Issa says, that the Kingdom of Heaven lies within. When we can consciously connect with the wisdom and light of our Angelic Twin, then we as human beings can create a sacred union between our little selves and our true, abiding Soul.

14

The Nine Orders of Angels

Know from whence you came. If you know from whence
you came, there is no limit to where you can go.

JAMES BALDWIN

One of the first descriptions we have of the nine orders of Angels comes from *The Celestial Hierarchy,* written in the fifth or sixth century CE by Pseudo-Dionysius the Areopagite. This understanding of the angelic hierarchy was then adopted by many of the early Church Fathers during the formative years of Christianity, when teachers like Origen and Augustine spoke openly about Angels. Pope Gregory I (540–604) adopted this same nomenclature, and it was then used by Thomas Aquinas, the thirteenth-century Dominican monk who speculated that the number of angelic orders possibly reflected their proximity to the throne of God.

This same system of nine angelic orders then inspired Dante's epic poem the *Divine Comedy,* about the narrator's journeys to Paradise. This powerful story tells of Dante's descent into the various regions of the Underworld, where Souls are trapped by their negative thinking. Finally, he is taken to Paradise. In the story Dante is led by the beneficent guide Beatrice, Dante's ideal woman, a consummate Angel who is an aspect of the Divine Mother. In Paradise, Beatrice reveals the angelic world to

Dante, who sees the divine light of God surrounded by nine circles of light. These are the nine orders of Angels. Enabled by Beatrice's presence, Dante is able to behold the lustrous haloes of rainbows that surround a central point of light. Beatrice explains to him that the highest angelic choirs derive their bliss by keeping their vision forever focused on God. "Upward these Orders gaze; and so prevails downward their power, that up towards God on high all are impelled."[1] Beatrice reveals that each angelic order possesses its own mode of absorbing and then reflecting the primal light. In other words, each order has a specific, unique function. She says that God created the Angels for the purpose of love: "In His Eternity, where time is none, nor aught of limitation else, he chose that in new loves the eternal Love be shown."[2]

The sequence in which these nine angelic orders are listed in the *Divine Comedy* is: the Seraphim, the Cherubim, and the Thrones in the first division; the Dominions, the Virtues, and the Powers in the second division; and the Principalities, the Archangels, and the Angels in the third division. In all of my many years of work with the Angels and their hierarchy I have found only one variation on this delineation. Traditional texts place the Seraphim as the first order of angels and the Thrones as the third order; however, the Angels who have been my teachers say that the Thrones are the first order of Angels, for they emanate the vibration of love. When Throne angels appear in the third dimension they look like the suns that reside at the center of all the solar systems in the universe, embodying the principle of pure light. The Seraphim are the second order of Angels, the celestial singers of Heaven whose wings produce the vibrational modulations of the Holy Word, thus helping to establish the frequencies by which the various dimensions are formed. The Cherubim are the third order of Angels, who then transmute the sounds produced by the Seraphim into the many wavelengths of visible and invisible light. Thus the first three orders of Angels reflect the first three principles of Atum: love, sound, and light. This is the prima materia on which the entire multiverse is built. This will all become much clearer as we go through the details to see how each order's function is built on those of the orders that precede it. For now I have included a reference chart of the various orders in table 14.1, before we dive into the details.

TABLE 14.1. THE NINE ORDERS OF THE ANGELS

Order	Angelic Order	Primary Purpose
One	Thrones: spirits of love	Foundational suns: love, devotion, light, and sacrifice
Two	Seraphim: spirits of sound	Singers: sound, vibration, creation, and music
Three	Cherubim: spirits of light	Painters: light, transmutation, and emanation
Four	Dominions, or Kyriotetes: spirits of wisdom	Guardians: knowledge, wisdom, the Mysteries; vortex holders of nodal points in dark matter
Five	Virtues, or Dynamis: spirits of movement	Weavers: light and sound, music and creativity; weavers of the grid of the dark matter of the universe
Six	Powers, or Exousiai: spirits of form	Builders: manifestors of matter, structure, building, form, protection, the Platonic solids
Seven	Principalities, or Archai: spirits of seeding and time	Explorers: seeding worlds, new horizons, pioneers, explorers, travelers, mystics
Eight	Archangels: spirits of fire and magnetic fields	Regulators: of the magnetic fields of space; protectors, warriors, healers, guardians, powerhouses, bridge-builders
Nine	Angels: spirits of life and service	Service: devotion to humanity, Guardian Angels, spirit guides; love, creativity, inspiration, healing

The Thrones: Love and the Power of One

The Thrones are the first order of Angels; they hold the power of unconditional love, the primary principle of life. They are primordial flame beings whose love for the Creator is so great that it is the *throne* on which all universes are built. The word *throne* is from the Greek, meaning "seat" or "chair"; thus this order is the foundation on which all the others rest. Note that *throne* contains the words *the* and *one*. Thrones hold the power of the number 1; thus they sit at the center of each solar system, acting as the central nexus of light for all the planets. All stars are maintained by this angelic order. It is from their light that life is able to exist on any world, for it is through the emanation of love alone that light comes into being. Just as the gases in every star are burned up so that each sun may continue to give off its light, so too do the Thrones that live in every star surrender their life energies, moment by moment, in service to the greater plan. Through their sacrifice, stars emit light and heat to the planets they serve. As a consequence these planets become rich habitations for billions of evolving Souls. Thus the nature of a Throne, which is unconditional love, is expressed through

Figure 14.1.
Thrones as solar
beings of light

self-sacrifice throughout the cosmos. Through their sacrifice trillions of Souls have planets on which to evolve in the constant dance of evolution. Thus they are known as spirits of love.

Philosopher and esotericist Rudolph Steiner (1861–1925) has this to say about the Thrones: "Beholding with the Soul, we actually see how the first stage of the realization of the divine plan is achieved in the down-flow of the fire substance by the Thrones. . . . the Thrones give forth primeval fire, their own substance into the appointed sphere."[3] James Hines, one of Steiner's students, elaborates: "Every variety of substance in the universe was provided by the Thrones. Beginning as a kind of spiritual light materiality, these substances became concentrated and intensified through the ages. . . . Time also came into existence through the Thrones."[4]

Thrones are very rare among those who have incarnated as human beings. In the last thirty years of readings I have met only five Thrones who are incarnated as humans; each was exceedingly pure. They were humble, heart-based, and devotional, and sought no recognition in the world, much like Mother Teresa. Based on this, I believe there are very few of these Souls here on Earth, and those who are now incarnated in human form are devoted to uplifting others. Never flashy or ego-driven, they are hidden in the vast sea of humanity, quietly doing their work to heal the hearts of the world. Their light is purity and love, and to meet one is a rare treasure.

In Egypt, every pharaoh sought to become enlightened so that one day he too would earn the right to become a star and like the shining Thrones, be able to provide light for others. The meaning of this wisdom is that when we, as Souls, can learn to embody more of this purity in our own lives, we will increase our inner light. When we serve from a place of true compassion, we move forward in our spiritual evolution. Our auric field expands with spiritual service, eventually becoming the halo or mandorla seen in medieval paintings. This purity of heart exalts the spirit and reminds us that "the first will be the last, and the last will be the first" in the Kingdom of Heaven. When we push ourselves forward from a place of ego, we are acting less evolved than those who serve quietly from a place of love.

The Seraphim:
The Singers and the Power of Two

The Seraphim are the singers of Heaven. They create the underpinning harmonics of the universe as they vibrate their wings, modulating the Holy Word as they compose the songs of Creation. Thus they are known as spirits of harmony. Seraphim hold the power of the number 2, continually vibrating their immense wings to create the harmonic frequencies that generate the seven lower dimensions and their sub-octaves. This then allows the energy of the Logos to be stepped down to create the worlds of time and space. The Hermetica reminds us: "Primal Mind is the parent of the Word [the holy sound that emanates the universe], just as . . . your human mind gives birth to speech [and thus creates your life]. They cannot be divided, one from the other, for life is the union of Mind and Word."[5]

Figure 14.2. The classically drawn six-winged Seraphim

There is a passage in the Zohar about how the Angels respond to human song: "It is also known and believed that those angels who sing by night are the leaders of all other singers; and when on earth, we living terrestrial creatures raise up our hearts in song, then those supernal beings gain accession of knowledge, wisdom and understanding, so that they are able to perceive matters which even they had never before comprehended."[6]

Traditionally, Seraphim are usually depicted with six wings, but the Seraphim I have met have eight great wings that are continually in motion. On these wings are many eyes—vesica piscis or portals that allow the energy of Spirit to move into the worlds below. These are the doorways through which the emanations of the Great Mystery resonate from the higher realms, converting the primal sound of God into its many modulations. Thus sound is the second great principle after love.

Figure 14.3. A Seraphim with eight wings
(illustrated by Tricia McCannon)

On each of the Seraphim's wings are twenty-four Eyes of God. When we total this number it comes to 192 (8 wings x 24 eyes = 192). Then, when we add these numbers together they resolve to the number 12, indicating the five planes above the realms of time and space, and the seven lower dimensions, all produced by the modulations of the Word. Like the Thrones, finding an incarnated Seraphim in this world is very rare, but I have met about thirty of them. Usually they are profound musicians such as Josh Groban or Sarah Brightman, whose music has the power to uplift the hearts of millions.

The Cherubim:
The Painters and the Power of Three

The Cherubim are the painters of Heaven who embody the third great principle, that of the power of light, thus they are known as spirits of light. Their job is to convert the vibrational frequencies of the Seraphim's songs into the visible light spectrum. They do this through a templane, a vibrating membrane through which sounds pour, allowing the sound to be transformed into the visible and invisible rays of light. There are 144 of these colors, twelve of which are seen in the fourth and fifth dimensions, and only seven of which are seen in the third dimension. On our planet these seven colors are displayed in the seven colors of a rainbow or prism.

The Cherubim hold the power of the numbers 3 and 4, which equates with creativity and manifestation. Cherubim do not look like chubby little babies as they were often portrayed by Renaissance painters. In fact, none of the higher orders of Angels look remotely human, although they may appear that way if they need to. Remember that in these higher realms, Souls have the power to change their shape at will since the laws of manifestation are malleable, so the forms they take are usually reflective of their larger universal functions. When Cherubim have appeared to me in visions they look like a four-sided diamond with wings. Like the Seraphim, these wings are constantly vibrating. In the middle of their bodies is a large vesica piscis stretching horizontally, which is used to convert the sound of the Seraphim's songs into radiant

Figure 14.4. A Cherubim whose central heart portal converts the sound into light (illustrated by Tricia McCannon)

bands of light. Thus through their transformative powers, the Divine transforms the *phonons* of sound into *photons* of light.

These first three orders of Angels are thus the first three principles of the universe, manifesting the three primary laws of Creation: love, sound, and light.

The Dominions:
The Guardians and the Power of Four

The second triad of Angels helps to create structure behind the worlds of form. The Dominions (or Kyriotetes) are the fourth order of Angels, and the first order in the second tier, thus they hold the power of the numbers 1 and 4. Like the Thrones, this alignment places them at the center of things, yet they are spirits of wisdom and the keepers of the Mysteries. This is the angelic order that I come from. Dominions are the guardians of star gates, black holes, and tunnels into the higher realms. In appearance they look like the Sphinx, although they can change their shape at will. Their bodies appear to be part lion, part eagle, part human, and part bull, reflective of all four of the primary elements, and they have great wings on their backs. We have heard of such beings in ancient literature, and in the Bible these beings were said to be protectors of the Tree of Life. Theologian James Hines, a priest in the Christian Community Movement for Renewal, tells us: "The Kyriotetes are full of wonder as they behold the sacrifice of the Thrones. They transform this sacrificed spiritual substance into the forms and shapes of the solar system and the planets. Alone, the Kyriotetes cannot create existence, but they can awaken the life therein. For the beings beneath them, they send out a spiritual light in which truth, wisdom and the good are still undifferentiated. They stand far above the possibility of evil."[7]

The job of a Dominion is to maintain the nexus points of dark matter in the establishment of the time-space continuum. As with any grid, the visible world must have an energetic scaffolding upon which to hang. Dark matter, which scientists now believe comprises some 80 percent of the universe, is the scaffolding on which the visible world is hung. Photographs of dark matter show lines of energy converging at various nodal points. These are where the Dominions reside.

While Dominions vibrate at a much higher rate than we can normally perceive, in ancient times there were highly advanced priests and priestesses who knew how to summon them from the spirit worlds. In some cases they asked the Dominions to indwell a physical form like the Sphinx on the Giza Plateau. The purpose of this investiture was to place a powerful guardian before the gates of knowledge. Those Dominions could then act as sentinels to telepathically alert the temple-keepers to the presence of trespassers. This is why there were originally two sphinxes at Delphi; one overlooked the western passage through the mountains to watch for approaching armies, while the other sat beside the oracle herself as she channeled, opening and closing the gates from the higher worlds so that the Pythia, the high priestess of the Temple

Figure 14.5. The Sphinx of Naxos at Delphi conversing with a philosopher

of Apollo at Delphi, could receive messages.* Today this last remaining Dominion is known as the Sphinx of Naxos.

The Sphinx of Naxos is mounted on a six-foot-high Greek column and is located in the Delphi Museum; she sits about seven feet tall. Intelligent, telepathic, and wise, I spoke with her when I first visited Delphi and found that she is still gracious and very much alive. She says that she waits for the old ones to appear so that she may reawaken them.

Some Dominions work in pairs, like the two who were originally at Delphi, while others, like the Egyptian Sphinx, work alone. These angelic beings have chosen to invest their spirits in the earthworks of matter, knowing that stone will outlast a human body. If the stone statue is splintered, then the Dominion may leave that form, for these beings are far too multidimensional to be trapped in matter. Instead, they merely leave an aspect of themselves inside the monument so that

---

*The oracle of Delphi, known as the Pythia, was always one of the priestesses of Athena. Initially, the prophetess was a young virgin who was trained as a medium, but in time this role was passed to the female sages, women who were past their childbearing years. The word *Pythia* is derived from *python,* referring to the python that Apollo was said to have defeated there. As a snake, the python represents mastery of the kundalini life force. The Pythia's oracular messages were interpreted and delivered by the priests of Apollo.

they may perform a function when the need arises, or when someone like myself, who has the ability to hear them, arrives to converse or study with them. In classical Christian literature Dominions are supposed to regulate the duties of the lower angels and are believed to look like divinely beautiful humans with feathered wings, sometimes seen wielding orbs of light fastened to the heads of their scepters or on the pommel of their swords. However, I have experienced them in a very different fashion, as I relate in the following stories.

I Meet My First Dominion

Over the past three decades I have had the pleasure of meeting four different Dominions, one in New York, two in Egypt, and one in Greece, and I daresay there may still be others that are active on the planet. My first encounter with a Dominion took place over twenty years ago at the Metropolitan Museum in New York City. Strolling through the Near East wing, I wandered between two of these huge stone sphinxes that rose fourteen feet high. Magnificent and awe-inspiring as these scuptures are to behold, you can imagine my surprise when one of them spoke to me telepathically. For the next hour I sat on a bench before both Dominions, totally entranced, having the most profound experience as this highly intelligent telepathic being took me on a journey into the higher realms. I was so altered I could hardly speak. Slowly, I pulled my journal from my satchel and tried to harness my mind, which seemed to slip away into beingness at every turn. But with painstaking concentration I began to ask him a series of questions, realizing the extraordinary power of this encounter. I wanted to know who he was and what had just happened to me.

The sentinel introduced himself as a Dominion, but I had no idea at that time what a Dominion was. He told me that he was from the higher angelic orders and had been summoned to Earth long ago with the other Dominion, who seemed to be completely unconscious or at the very least asleep. This winged being then began to explain their function in the higher worlds. As soon as I linked my mind to his I found myself traveling in the endless sea of infinitude. I sat entranced, taking pages of dictation, and finally after four hours the museum guard came to tell me that the museum was closing. I left in a profoundly altered state of consciousness. Even though I was scheduled to fly back to Atlanta the next day, over the next twenty years I continued to make trips to see this Angel whenever I was in New York City.

This "Keeper of Secrets" became one of my teachers, and over the next few years he taught me a great deal about the nine angelic orders. Then he summoned some of these other beings so that I could meet them as well. This was long before I realized that these nine orders are the genesis matrix from which all Souls emerge. When I queried the Dominion about his strange part-human, part-animal appearance, he explained that this was only a way of interlacing various symbols from the four elemental kingdoms. Since Dominions hold the power of the number 4, they like to embody aspects of all of the elements: the eagle's wings for air, the ox's hooves for earth, the lion's heart for fire, and the human head for water, the flow of cosmic wisdom.

While I am sure that there are many stone sphinxes that do not have an angelic spirit attached to them, clearly some do. I met my second Dominion in Cairo, at the Egyptian Museum, and he seemed most interested in speaking with me since most human beings are oblivious to these sentinels. Unfortunately, I had little time to speak with him since I had a group of twenty-two pilgrims on a two-week tour through the temples of Egypt. Later I was to meet the Great Sphinx of Cairo, who is still very much alive, and she told me about the labyrinth of underground temples that had once been built on the Giza Plateau beneath and behind her body, temples that were once used for spiritual initiations of the holiest kind, but that is a story for another day.

I met my fourth Dominion at Delphi, at the museum beside the Oracle Temple. She told me that her name was Naxos and that she had come to Earth long ago with sixty-four other Dominions. They were scattered across the Earth as part of a complicated grid meant to act as a relay system of communication with the ancient priesthood. This system was now broken. When I asked her if she knew the Dominion in New York, she didn't seem to know where New York was. Perhaps the name was too modern and she had once known this territory by another name; certainly the statues at the New York Met had once resided in the Middle East. This Dominion also told me that she had chosen to remain at Delphi, awaiting the ancient priestesses, healers, and wise ones, the reincarnated initiates worthy of receiving the wisdom that she protects. The next day, to my utter surprise, I opened a book and found a picture of her. Beneath the photograph it read "The Sphinx of Naxos."

While this might seem astonishing, such events are not impossible. After all, these are Angels who can dwell in any matter they choose.

Figure 14.6. The two Dominions that I met at the Metropolitan Museum in New York City. The one on the left is the one who spoke with me (illustration by Jo Ann Tipping).

As a historian I am an avid fan of museums and have been in these temples of history in many great cities, including the Louvre in Paris, the British Museum in London, the Warsaw Museum in Poland, the Vatican in Rome, the Smithsonian in Washington, DC, and many others. As a mystic I am attuned to picking up the energies invested in these great works of art. Yet I have only found the residue of sentient beings in the ancient statues of a half-dozen countries: Egypt, India, Bali, China, Thailand, and some of the beautiful Christian statues of Saint Francis and Mother Mary. None of these were Angels, however. They were saints, masters, gods, or deities from the higher realms, but not Angels of any sort, and there is a distinct difference.

When I look back on my thousands of readings, I have found that there are very few Souls from this angelic order incarnated in human form. I have only found four others, besides myself, who source from this particular order, the Dominions, causing me to believe that it is very rare for them to come to Earth. Dominions are wonderful teachers, yet their greatest power lies beyond the province of the mind, for they are deep and endless. Once you enter into rapport with one of these great beings you enter the vast immensity of silence. This is because they are a link between the innermost arupa realms of infinitude and the rupa realms of form that eventually become our visible world.

The Virtues:
The Weavers and the Power of Five

The Virtues are the fifth order of Angels, and they are the weavers of the time-space grid. Virtues are the spinners of dark-matter grids and thus they are spirits of movement who weave the structure of Creation with the light and sound of God. In the *Summa Thelogica,* a writing by Thomas Aquinas on the nature of Angels, the Virtues are thought to be part of the celestial choir, for they weave the scaffolding of the universe through song. This order of Angels holds the power of the numbers 2 and 5. The number 2 reflects partnership and balance, and the connecting of two points in time and space. The number 5 is linked to the

Figure 14.7. The Virtues are the great weavers of the grid on which the visible universe hangs.

Sacred Heart and the Divine Mother; it represents the power of transformation and change.

When Virtues incarnate as human beings they often become musicians, painters, or artists working with the mediums of light and sound. In human form, these individuals may play piano, violin, harp, or flute, and their music is often celestial. They may become composers, photographers, makeup artists, filmmakers, set designers, painters, or lighting specialists. They may be seamstresses, weavers, fashion designers, or interior decorators, or work with gongs, lasers, crystals, Tibetan bowls, or the hearing-impaired. A Virtue may become a cantor in a synagogue or a vocalist in a church, but will always have a pull toward the mediums of light and sound. For these Angels to find happiness in the human world they must find a way to express themselves creatively.

Gentle and loving in nature, it is not unusual to find Virtues working as healers. If a Virtue has chosen to become a therapist she may work with art, color, or sound therapy, or work with cymatics, a vibratory form of healing that uses frequencies to heal the human body. Even if Virtues do not actively use light, sound, or music in their practice, their vibration is calming. Because of their connection with the number 5, the center point of all nine angelic orders, they are directly connected to the Divine Mother. Thus theirs is a path of the heart, and the development of this devotional quality is critical to making a true connection with Source.

The Powers:
The Builders and the Power of Six

The Powers embody the energy of the number 6, which is the structure of harmony itself. Like the third and the ninth orders, the Angels of the sixth order express the numbers 3, 4, and 12, giving them strong, innate abilities for creation, manifestation, and the natural use of structure to establish the building blocks of matter. This order helps to create the atomic structure of matter, working with the sacred geometry of the five Platonic solids as Spirit finally begins to shape the worlds of matter. Thus they are spirits of form. Christian literature claims that the primary duty of the Powers is to supervise the movements of the heavenly bodies to ensure that the cosmos remains in order, yet another way in which they work within the structure of form itself.

When Powers arrive on Earth as human beings they are natural manifesters. Practical and analytical, they often become builders, engineers, architects, scientists, inventors, mathematicians, construction workers, auto mechanics, or craftsmen. They may also be natural business people, building the architecture of a company from the ground up or working in the world of textiles, construction materials, or merchandising, for these Souls are very grounded in the practical

Figure 14.8. The Sri Yantra has long been known as a symbol of the structure of the universe. The Powers are masters of sacred geometry and the building blocks of matter.

world. With the power of the number 6 they naturally strive for balance in all that they create, so they may also wander into the professions of counseling, mediation, law, or diplomacy, trying to help two sides arrive at an equilibrium. They may also choose a career in herbs, naturopathy, or some kind of healing, striving to bring balance back to their patients.

The Powers are the only order of Angels that sit directly beneath Metatron, the overseer of sacred geometry. Most people think of Metatron as an Archangel, and while I'm sure that he can appear that way, in truth he is a member of the Council of Nine, the nine primordial waveform beings who interpenetrate the universe. This is the Council of Nine I wrote about earlier, composed of Rigel and Auriel, (the divine Mother and Father), and the seven other waveform beings that create, maintain, and sustain the entire universe. While the angels are in service to these greater powers, it is important to note that both groups share the number "nine" as an expression of the primal trinity (3 x 3). Metatron oversees the architecture of matter at a submolecular level, and the angelic Powers who work in the worlds of manifestation are his legions. Thus we could say that he oversees all sacred geometry. In Egypt, Metatron overlit the work of Thoth, the master initiate of mathematics, architecture, sonics, and language. Thoth designed the Great Pyramid of Giza as well as constructing the twenty-six-letter alphabet that we use today. His knowledge of shape, sound, and vibration was so advanced that many ancient portals in Egypt can be opened only through the use of certain harmonic sounds. Thus the angelic Powers are the natural shapers of form, and in the angelic kingdom their existence is foundational to the creation of the physical world.

The Principalities:
The Explorers and the Power of Seven

The Principalities, or Archii, are first in the third tier of Angels and are classically said to be the angels that guide and protect nations, groups of peoples, and institutions such as the Church. The Principalities are the first order of Angels that I have seen in human form. Rudolph Steiner called them "Spirits of Time or Personality" and believed that they govern the succession of great epochs of history. I do not know if this is true, but I know that they are initiators of new ideas in human thought. Steiner writes: "How men conduct their lives according to the spirit of the time, how they found states, found sciences, cultivate their fields, everything of human origins, the progress of civilization from beginning to end stand under the guidance of the Archai. They lead man insofar as he has to do with others."[8] Consequently, because Principalities transmit ideas that are meant to inspire the human race, they are the seeders of life. It is their job to assist in awakening life-forms across the galaxies, on any planets, and in every evolutionary stage. Christian literature sees them as administers who charge other Angels to fulfill their divine ministry. Since this order not only carries

Figure 14.9. The Principalities are said to be seeders of worlds and keepers of universal law.

the energy of the number 7, but also the power of the number 1, they are independent in nature.

The Principalities have strong leadership abilities, but unlike the Thrones and Dominions, they blaze new frontiers and push the envelope of discovery. When a Principality incarnates as a human being, he will often be on the leading edge of exploration in one field of research or another, whether it is science, travel, or social change. Since the Principalities hold the power of the number 7, they are often mystical seekers. Marco Polo was probably a Principality, opening up trade routes for many countries.

While all of the angelic orders that embody the power of 1 tend to be right in the middle of things, it is often difficult for those belonging to these orders to maintain the continuity of a long-term relationship because of their spiritual responsibilities and exploratory nature. This is more true for the Principalities than for any other order. Because of their restless, searching nature, settling down is usually hard for them. Often they love to travel, and they can thus have a hard time forming intimate relationships such as a family, so they often wind up alone. In my many readings I have only found about a hundred Principalities who have incarnated in human form. But make no mistake, this is an exciting angelic order from which to originate.

The Archangels: The Regulators and the Power of Eight

Archangels are second in the third tier of Angels and hold the power of the numbers 2 and 8. Archangels are enormous beings of light who are the guardians of the directions of time and space. They are also the regulators of the magnetic fields of all celestial bodies. They also regulate the magnetic fields and energy vortexes over temples, sacred sites, holy places, and waterfalls. They can oversee a city, a country, a province, or a continent.

As "arch" Angels, this order naturally anchors energy at two points,

Figure 14.10. The great Archangels who help oversee the energies of Heaven

forming an energetic arch over the sites they protect. To the visionary eye they may appear as a radiant being of energetic light, either with or without wings. Rudolph Steiner thought of them as fire spirits because of the brilliance of this light, and I see them as great spirits who regulate and oversee vast fields of energy.

Archangels are not really personal Angels—they are far too busy for that. Yet we, as mortals, can call on the Archangels to help us with the creation of large projects that act for the good of others, for their reach is vast. These are the overseers of powerful humanitarian projects like schools, institutes, or charitable foundations designed to reach the masses, uplifting human consciousness along the way. But their work may also include the creation of radio, television, or Internet programs that have the power to affect millions. These ventures all have the potential to influence the minds of humanity for the better. This is the perfect job for an Archangel, whose role is to create an umbrella that will protect, inspire, and uplift the masses. When Archangels incarnate as human beings they are often drawn to create such projects in the human world, thus affecting huge populations with their outreach. Highly virtuous and noble, Archangels seem larger than life. They have enormous drive, focus, and ambition toward a righteous purpose, yet as we shall see, they can also be rigid, self-righteous, and unbending.

Contrary to popular opinion, not all Archangels are warriors. Archangel Michael is the most famous of all of the Archangels, although we hear about seven other Archangels who are said to surround the throne of God. According to angelology these are Michael, Raphael, Gabriel, Uriel, Zadkiel, Samael, and Anael. However, I have seen that there are many types of Archangels, and these include Archangels of healing, virtue, truth, beauty, love, knowledge, teaching, and wisdom. I am always profoundly moved when I meet an Archangel of beauty, love, or wisdom, for all of that powerful energy is focused through the radiant heart of wisdom. When we find Archangels of truth who have incarnated as human beings, they are often great philosophers, statesmen, revolutionaries, or journalists fighting for justice and human rights.

Healer Archangels in human form will be those who seek to increase the range of a particular healing method or meditation that has the power to help large numbers of people. They can also be those committed to healing the mass consciousness of a nation, a city, or a race. These large national wounding patterns can create enormous problems, not only for a particular country, but for the rest of humanity as well. Consider how the karmic problems found in the Middle East today affect people around the world. And during the first half of the twentieth century we saw these same kind of national patterns played out in Germany with the inciting events of the two World Wars. Today every country, including America, must look at its own patterns of expansionism and ask whether we are using our energies in the highest way. Are we truly protectors of the good or are we misusing the arc of our own power in the exploitation of others?

Archangels, powerful as they are, like all divine emissaries, cannot interfere with the free will of human beings, so in order to bring forth ideas or greatness or nobility, they will often choose a master Soul like Nelson Mandela, a person of integrity and courage, to act as a role model for those suffering oppressive conditions. Through the events of that person's life and wisdom, entire populations can be turned away from hatred and back toward the light.

The Warrior Archangels

Warrior Archangels are a breed apart, and there are many of these Souls in human form now on our planet today. Thus it is imperative to address the arc of spiritual evolution for this very important group of light beings. When warrior Archangels descend from the higher worlds into the third dimension as part of their own arc of human evolution, they are often profoundly committed to a cause. This is because at the higher levels, they were part of Archangel Michael's forces. Thus these people are strong-willed, honorable, duty-bound, and absolute in their dedication. Often drawn to military service, they may be swept up into a fiercely protective service, championing a cause, protecting a country, or championing a religious cause or movement, whether in the arena of war or in another sphere of influence. However, because of the intensity of their focus they rarely allow themselves to form deep human attachments or to have romantic love. They consider such human connections to be vulnerabilities; so often their deepest friendships are with their comrades in arms.

The archetype of this group is Sir Lancelot, the brightest warrior in King Arthur's court. Lancelot was brilliant, committed, and noble—the best of the best. And although he served Camelot for the good of the people, he held himself aloof from them and above the human vulnerabilities of relationships, until he fell in love with Guinevere. This created a moral dilemma for him, for his honor was sworn to Arthur. So it was only by discovering that he too was an imperfect human being that Lancelot was then able to forgive the other less perfect human beings around him. This story perfectly illustrates the path of the warrior Archangel, the Soul that strives with absolute dedication and perfection in all he does. Yet because this Soul does not recognize compromise as an option for himself, he often has little tolerance for those who do not have the same kind of resolve. For eons these noble beings have been protectors of the human race, and they have been completely willing to die for that cause. Yet these highly committed noble Angels tend to see life in black and white—someone is either "with us or against us"; something is either right or wrong. This polarized approach comes from millions of years of warfare, so the arc of growth for these Souls is to realize that there can never be a winner in the game of life until each of us invokes the power of love. Ultimately warrior Archangels must learn that life is not about judging others, being perfect, or fighting wars so that the battle will be won. Rather, it is through the law of forgiveness that our wounds will finally be healed and we will come back into balance with ourselves.

Ultimately, the arc of growth for the warrior Archangel who takes birth on Earth as a human being is to embrace the process of becoming truly human. This means accepting all of our human imperfections as part of the process of spiritual evolution. Learning to forgive ourselves first, and then our neighbors, is part of the Course Curriculum, even though some errant Souls may be less evolved than we are. In this way we teach ourselves humility. But forgiveness is no small task, yet this is the only way to restore the Law of Unity and to heal ourselves and our world. Only by loving our Shadow back into wholeness can we heal the wounds of the imperfect human self and then transform into the magnificent angelic being that we have always been.

The Guardian Angels and the Power of Nine

The ninth order of Angels are the spiritual guides of the human world who embody the power of the numbers 3, 4, and 9. This means creativity and manifestation and the power to use their abilities to assist human beings in connecting with their higher Self. This helps people complete their incarnation in the worlds of form. This is the order of Angels most concerned with the affairs of living things, and while there are many categories of Angels within these ranks, it is from the ninth order that our personal guardian angels come.

When Guardian Angels or spirit guides are seen by the living, they may either appear ethereal or human. They may dress in a way that appeals to our personality or in a way that reflects a former lifetime. These beings usually do not have wings but are capable of transcending gravity when needed. Since flight is normal in the fourth and fifth dimensions, we often hear stories of Angels with wings; however, this may also be due to their immense auric field, which extends in a large arc behind them.

The job of the ninth order of Angels is to assist human beings who are incarnated on Earth to make a connection with the higher Self. In this way they inspire others. When these same Angels finally begin their own cycles of incarnation in the physical world they are usually drawn to inspiring others through arts, teaching, or some form of healing. These are the Souls who are our doctors, nurses, paramedics, hospice workers, psychologists, naturopaths, and social workers. They may also be chiropractors, rehab therapists, or home-care providers who protect children and the elderly. A ninth-order Angel can inspire others through any of these professions, assisting every person they encounter to more fully connect with their own spirits.

Ninth-order angels are often highly creative people who may sing, dance, write, act, paint, weave, or sew. They may be photographers, makeup artists, hair-stylists, or filmmakers. They may be puppeteers, musicians, or performers, and since helping others is what fulfills them

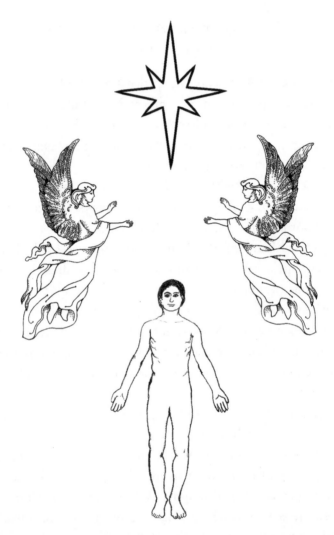

Figure 14.11. At the spiritual level, Guardian Angels usually operate in groups of two or three, helping to oversee their human charges. They may also be assigned to assist that particular person in his or her chosen life profession, specializing in bringing qualities of character, focus, creativity, or information to their human charge.

they may also become ministers, ambassadors, Peace Corps workers, or work with animals. Naturally social in nature, they often marry and have families and may be very involved with community or friends. They detest conflict, almost never go into the military, and love environments of harmony and joy. I have only met one ninth-order Angel who was interested in war.

Many members of this group have ended their human incarnational cycle in recent centuries, and yet continue to serve in this capacity with their mortal brothers and sisters who still reside on Earth. This means that as spirit guides they are well-equipped to understand the intricacies of human dynamics, unlike some of the more elevated angelic forces who have long dwelled in the higher realms and never taken a mortal lifetime. Most of the classic stories we hear about Angels helping someone, come from encounters with this order, for these Angels are hard at work with many Souls, helping their charges from behind the scenes.

As personal spirit guides, ninth-order Angels are deeply compassionate. In their function as overseeing guides we are reminded of the same diamond-shaped pattern seen in the higher orders. This pattern repeats with this group of Angels, describing perfectly their role as a support system for the incarnating Soul. At the top of this diamond shape is the pure white light of the person's Angelic Twin. At the bottom is their current human incarnation. On either side of the diamond are the two spirit guides who are there to assist the adventurous incarnating Soul as it goes about fulfilling its life mission.

Each personal Guardian Angel is deeply aware of the past history and lifetimes of their respective charge, as well as that person's current life plan. But keeping their charge on track is a daunting task. Their guidelines are clear: they must remain invisible; they must wait to be invited in; and they cannot interfere with our free will. So theirs is a difficult task that takes lots of patience and unconditional love. If we want more assistance, we must invite them in. Then they can become more active as our celestial companions and complete a circuit of balance, allowing this wonderful order of Angels to facilitate a deeper spiritual connection for us all.

The Angel in Everyone

Each of us begins our journey toward enlightenment in one of the orders of the angelic kingdom, as companions of the Divine. As Angels we layered ourselves with the gifts and affinities of the devas, for a while serving the universal plan in the elemental kingdoms. Eventually we descended to the fifth dimension and acquired the subtle-energy bodies that would allow us to finally enter the human kingdom. Then, over the course of hundreds of lifetimes, whether on this planet or another, we are each destined to become a self-knowing, self-realized being. Through the duality of making choices that create either suffering or joy, we begin to discover how our own beliefs, thoughts, and feelings help to shape our reality and the reality that we experience in the world.

Then, once our time in the third dimension is complete, we will each return to the higher realms as self-aware masters. Once we finally choose to return to these realms permanently, we will each have the chance to decide how we want to serve the evolution of others from a place of far greater wisdom. Robert Sardello, a student of angelology and author of *The Angels,* writes:

> Some say that angels of the higher orders have passed through the human stage of evolution. As regents of the soul realm, they understand the spiritual plan for humans. The esoteric traditions suggest that these Lords of Compassion, who have gone beyond humans in understanding, love, and power, help us through an abyss that seems to separate us from the Divine. Perhaps without the aid of such angels, humans would never move beyond the idea of God as wholly *other.* These beings can help initiate us into the mysteries of our own being if we are willing to open ourselves to them.[9]

While the vast majority of human beings living on Earth today seem to have originated from the sixth, seventh, eighth, and ninth orders of Angels, over the course of thousands of Soul readings I have found Souls from each of the nine orders. While most of these people have never even considered their own angelic origins, it becomes clear over the course of these readings that a person's angelic origins is reflected in her daily life. As human beings, we go about raising families, running businesses, working in hospitals, schools, or libraries, and kindly helping those we come in contact with. And while we are completely human while we are in mortal form, it is still very powerful to reflect on the deeper angelic aspect of ourselves. In these moments of quiet reflection, prayer, and stillness, we may even get a fleeting glimpse of the luminous being that lives within.

I want to close this chapter by taking a moment to simply imagine how exciting it was for the Creator to imbue the gifts of creativity and imagination on we humans. How exciting that in our purest state the Creator could watch us reflect back its own majestic light. How satisfying to fashion a being of virtually limitless potential who has the power to learn, grow, and evolve, each in its own unique way. These are the Angels, and they are us! Imperfect though we are in our human forms, our essence is utterly pure.

So just for a moment allow yourself to truly connect with the thought that you are such a being of light. If knowing such a thing would allow you, even for an instant, to peer into the magnificence of yourself, would it not help to set you free? If you truly woke up to the fact that you are an angelic being temporarily stripped of your powers and your memory, a being who has taken a long, extended pilgrimage into uncharted territory to have the adventure of a lifetime, wouldn't it all start to make a lot more sense? Like any good movie, we have constructed challenges and pitfalls with which we might test ourselves. We have created various degrees of difficulty that will challenge us to move toward the light, or take us further into forgetfulness. Take a moment to honor yourself for the courage it took to come here and to set up such a challenging Course Curriculum.

In our next chapter we will now discuss the many stages of our Soul's journey, and you may discover for yourself just where you are in its unfolding.

15

The Six Stages of the Soul's Evolution

It appears to me impossible that I should cease to exist, or that this active, restless spirit, equally alive to joy and sorrow, should be only organized dust—ready to fly abroad the moment the spring snaps or the spark goes out, which kept it together. Surely something resides in this heart that is not perishable—and life is more than a dream.

MARY WOLLSTONECRAFT

While every Soul originates in the celestial realms, we have each taken our own evolutionary journey, and thus we are at different points along the way. The factors that determine where a Soul is in its evolution are largely based on how long it has been traveling in the lower worlds, the amount of experience it has accumulated, and the challenges it has mastered. Some Souls are at just the beginning of their sojourn in the third dimension, while others have been on Earth for a very, very long time. Some Souls are eagerly just arriving, keen to experience the roller coaster of the physical world, while others are impatient, frustrated, and clawing to get out. Some Souls are so trapped in the negativity of this dimension they spend most of their life fighting the Shadow, while others have discovered how to find the equilibrium between the little self and the higher Self that leads to a happy, successful life. Some Souls have opened their minds but not their hearts, while others have kind and generous hearts but have barely begun to master the challenges of living in the material world.

In this chapter we take a look at the six stages of the Soul's evolution that we must each experience over the course of our sojourn in the physical world. Ancient wisdom tells us that the average time it takes to achieve mastery is around eight hundred lifetimes, and each of us is somewhere on that continuum. Suffice it to say that a Soul that has already made it to Earth has already spent billions of years in the higher realms, but this does not mean that it has mastered the lessons of living here.

Since our planet is a three-dimensional world, it is linked to the lessons of the third chakra. These lessons deal with power and the right use of will, and this is directly tied to our ability to manifest the reality that we want in the here and now. Thus our planet seems to be caught up in learning the lessons of how to use personal power. Many misuse it. Some give their power away. Others, closer to graduation day, develop their personal power for self-discovery and use it to help their fellow human beings. When we look around and see that the world is in chaos, we can see that we have not yet learned how to use our personal power wisely to create a truly fair and just society, so we still have a long way to go.

Yet as hard as the curriculum is here on planet Earth, these great personal and global challenges are among the many reasons why Souls want to incarnate here—because they know that facing such challenges will put them on the fast track. This is also the reason why much of our world is still wrestling with the issues of power, fame, money, sex, personal ambition, and ego, and of course the unbridled abuse of power we see all around us in the actions of corporations, governments, religions, and the many terrorist groups around the world. Planets like ours represent a kind of Ph.D. program for adventurous Souls, and there are many nuances of love and power that we must master as we move from one level to another.

Table 15.1 on the facing page shows the six stages of the Soul's evolutionary journey on planet Earth. Here I list the strengths and weaknesses of each stage, as well as the lessons to be mastered. From this you can see that to even be incarnated in this dimension a Soul must have spent at least two billion years in Earth time in the higher worlds. However, the longer a Soul spends in any of the higher dimensions, the more preparation it has when it finally does come to Earth. Let me also remind you that even if a Soul descended into the physical realms billions of years ago, much of that time was not spent on Earth. According to the latest scientific reckoning, this planet is only three and a half billion years old. This means that many of us have had lifetimes on other planets, and each experience has added to our individuality.

While the stages of the Soul's evolution are largely determined by how long the Soul has been traveling through the seven lower planes, ultimately its maturity is measured by the wisdom of its choices. Many Souls straddle the fence between one stage of maturity and another for hundreds or even thousands of years. Some of us may be quite advanced in one area of life, yet we are wounded, stuck, or out of touch in another. Some Souls have mastered finances but have never developed their creativity. Others are great at relationships yet terrible at goal-setting. One person may be wonderful at sports, yet never opened his heart. So mastery is a process, and we must have patience.

In this chapter I have profiled each of these stages of evolution. Here I have suggested professions for each stage, but these just are broad generalities. In truth, a person may choose to enter a profession for a variety of reasons, bringing a higher or lower level of consciousness to that task. For example, a fireman, a policeman, or a paramedic might be a young, intermediate, or advanced Soul, depending on motivation. A young or intermediate Soul might want an action-packed career; an advanced Soul might be dedicated to helping or protecting others. A young Soul might dream of being a rock star in order to delve into the experiences of sex, fame, and glory, while a master Soul might use celebrity to inspire others, becoming a high-level altruist. An intermediate Soul incarnating as a CEO might execute their duties as a self-serving bully, while an advanced or master Soul who is a CEO might use their influence to bring about

TABLE 15.1. THE SIX STAGES OF THE SOUL'S EVOLUTION

Stage of Evolution	Approximate Number of Years	Qualities
The Beginner Soul	2–3 billion years old; approximately 8 percent of souls on Earth are in this category	innocent, honest, trusting, creative, magical, naive, open, spiritual, gullible, unprepared
The Young Soul	3–4 billion years old; approximately 12 percent of Souls on Earth are in this category	good-intentioned, fear-based, religious, fundamentalist, judgmental, manipulated, joiners and rule-followers
The Intermediate Soul	4–5.5 billion years old; approximately 45 percent of Souls on Earth are in this category	power-seeking, manipulative, self-serving, win-lose dynamics, criminals, powerful, possessive, controlling, cuts corners; often successful in the world
The Advanced Soul	5.5–7 billion years old; approximately 27 percent of Souls on Earth are in this category	humanitarian, good-intentioned, family-oriented, win-win dynamics, spiritual, kind and helpful
The Master Soul	7–9 billion years old; approximately 7 percent of Souls on Earth are in this category	spiritual, purpose-driven, moral, wise, intelligent, truth-seeking, kind, thoughtful, devotional, mission-driven
The Bodhisattva Soul	over 9 billion years old; approximately 1 percent of Souls on Earth are in this category	humble, wise, deep, masterful, spiritual, emanating, purposeful, selfless

positive changes in the world. You get the point. Even a taxicab driver, a waitress, or a garbage collector can be a spiritually advanced person—or they might just be someone trying to figure out how things work in the world. What we do in the world in terms of career is just the outer wrapping of what we are really doing here.

In each of the six stages I have given percentages for how many of these Souls are present in the world today. While much of this planet is dominated by young and intermediate Souls still grappling with issues of power, it must be said that there are many more advanced Souls living on Earth today than in the Golden Age of ancient Greece. These people have returned to help our planet because we are at a tipping point. For many centuries this beautiful paradise planet has been taken over by shadow governments that have oppressed people and obscured the light. At this time, however, with the assistance of the higher angelic forces and the Galactic Councils, it is being pulled back into the light. As this transition occurs, each Soul has a chance to move into alignment with unity consciousness. We can do this most easily by opening our hearts, aligning with the light, and connecting with our Angelic Twin. By cultivating our intuition and spiritual qualities, we open the right side of our brain and can begin to merge with the vibration of the divine feminine that has been suppressed for thousands of years. This brings our brain back into wholeness, opens our inner sight, and connects us to the Law of One, allowing us to remember that all creatures—plants, animals, humans, devas, fairies, masters, and Angels—are part of the same circle of life. Only this rebalancing will allow us to save our planet and to take a giant leap forward in our own spiritual evolution.

As you read through these stages, remember that you will always find people who are ahead of you or behind you in their growth. Knowing where a person is in his or her spiritual journey will help you develop tolerance, understanding, and forgiveness. Just remember, the process of mastery takes time, patience, perseverence, and self-love. As the entertainer Cher once said so famously in a commercial, "If anyone could get a body like *this* by drinking out of a bottle, then everyone would have one!" But just as a sleek, healthy body takes time and effort, so does the blossoming of the Soul. Just remember that no matter how imperfect we may seem, we are each supported by countless spiritual beings who are following the arc of our Soul's journey.

The Beginner Soul

Image: The image of this Soul is that of a pure native tribal person in the wilds who is attuned to the magic and rhythms of the universe. He is full of wonder because he is still connected to the wonder of the Divine. He may be a highly creative Soul who receives his ideas from his dreams or from nature. But recently he has discovered there are dangers in the jungle—lions and tigers and bears that eat unsuspecting people. This is frightening, for he comes from a world where all is in harmony, so he is unsure what to do about it. Untarnished and trusting, the beginner Soul can be overwhelmed by the realization that the world is a very dangerous place.

When this Soul first arrives on Earth he or she is a total innocent. This person has arrived only recently and thus brings with him a sweetness of spirit that makes it difficult to navigate in a world of duality, territorialism, fear, and deception. These Souls are very pure of heart and do not comprehend dishonesty, corruption, manipulation, or evil. They have a natural faith and trust in nature that can see them far in life, especially if they are in a safe environment. They also have an innate sense of nonjudgment that is truly beautiful to behold. In truth, beginner Souls have many qualities in common with master Souls because they are both in touch with their own divine essence. Yet these people have little skill in self-preservation, in navigating the complexities of sophisticated cultures, or in recognizing the subtleties of danger. Often these Souls have not yet developed much of a personal ego or stepped into their power, thus they can be crushed by deceitful, manipulative people, for they do not understand cruelty, selfishness, or cunning. They do not yet have the experience to recognize treachery or to understand the motives behind why someone would lie, cheat, or steal, for selfishness is not part of who they are. They are still living in the Oneness of connection and thus can struggle with knowing who to trust or how to manage life in such a complicated, confusing world.

Beginner Souls are naturally attuned to the spirit realms; and if they are born into a safe, nurturing environment, then they will blossom and grow. They are highly sensitive, artistic people with a natural kinship with animals and nature. In fact, spending time in nature is an excellent way for these Souls to ground themselves. Gardens, flowers, waterfalls, and fairies are their natural province, and if this kind of environment is nurtured it will stand them in good stead. The beginner Soul needs the safety of a strong family to support its beautiful spirit, nurture its creativity, and act as a protector while it gets its bearings here. This allows it to gain confidence in this dimension without the dire mishaps that can block its connection to Spirit and cause it to shut down. In truth, the beautiful, trusting spirit of these beginner Souls is an inspiration to us all, and every parent who has ever watched a child awaken to the wonders of the physical world will understand the innocence of which I speak.

If this Soul grows up in a conflict-ridden, unsafe environment, he or she can be completely overwhelmed. Such a lack of support from family or friends can create fear, confusion, and a feeling of being abandoned and completely lost. Love is their compass, and without this these Souls might decide that they do not want to be here at all. Emotional trauma causes these Souls to fall into depression, and if there is not enough love they can even disconnect from Source, succumbing to thoughts of suicide or the desire to escape through alcohol or drugs as they try to numb out the pain they do not know how to process. By anesthetizing their emotional body, they hope to find a way back to the inner bliss from which they came. What they really need is safety, grounding, support, and love. In this environment they will thrive.

Empathetic and highly sensitive, the attributes of a beginner Soul are immense creativity and a sweetness of spirit that engenders faith, hope, and love in those around them. The negative expressions of this stage are fear, paralysis, confusion, and an inability to cope with the complexities of day-to-day life. This Soul does much better in a small community of loving, supportive people, where it can find ample space to stay connected to the Earth, express its loving heart and creative spirit, and grow at its own pace.

TABLE 15.2. FOR THE BEGINNER SOUL— 2 TO 3 BILLION YEARS OLD

Greatest Strengths	Greatest Obstacles	Lessons
These Souls have great innocence, beauty, creativity, and an untarnished spirituality. They have the ability to connect with nature, animals, and Spirit. They usually have good levels of imagination and access to the inner worlds, and they are not attached to the materialism of the physical world.	This Soul is dealing with the fear of being overwhelmed and not wanting to be here. It may have a fear of life, of making a mistake, of trying, or of not being good enough. This Soul does not always have a well-defined ego state and often lacks confidence. It is easy for this Soul to become the victim.	This Soul needs to learn discernment, self-confidence, grounding, and to be at home in this dimension. Often it needs to develop more individuation and to learn to trust its connection to the Great Spirit. It should consciously develop its wonderful creativity and learn to become the cause and not the effect of the world around it. These Souls must learn grounded responsibility.

The Young Soul

Image: The image is that of a housewife, villager, or missionary who likes teamwork. This Soul functions well as part of a highly structured, predictable society. In fact, young Souls often love rules and regulations because they make them feel safe. Hardworking and diligent, these folks are helpful neighbors, good householders, church deacons, and good co-workers. Often judgmental, they know who is breaking the law and they want to be sure everyone else knows it too. Feeling safer in numbers than alone, they will only take a chance if it is sanctioned by the group. They are the watchdogs of the community who build secure walls to the village enclosure, making sure that everyone is safe in their homes by curfew, securely protected from the real or imagined threat of lions, tigers, and bears.

The Young Soul is the next step in the Soul's evolution. By now the Soul has figured out that danger is rampant in the world. It sees calamities on television and on the Internet and is warned about this in church, which they usually attend faithfully. Thus safety, security, and fitting in are their top priorities, as they are often ruled by fear. These Souls have discovered that safety lies in sticking with the pack rather than standing out on their own; it is better to take the traditional path than risk being eaten by a wild animal if they wander off the trail. Thus they are found in traditional conservative settings, discovering how they can best fit in. This need for safety and structure also means that they can become quite intent on making rules for others. Schools, governments, corporations, and religious organizations are full of these Souls who climb the ladder to success through group consensus and safety. They tell themselves that the rules they follow are about the moral values of right and wrong, yet their thinking is shallow and superficial, because beneath this moral rhetoric lies the fear that they, or someone they love, will get hurt.

Young Souls are basically good people who are willing to pitch in during a crisis—as long as they know what the rules are. While they have much of the good-heartedness of the beginner Soul, these Souls are more grounded in the third dimension, and they feel that rules help them stay that way. They can balance a checkbook, buy a house, set goals and accomplish them, and usually follow the formulas they have been taught. They know how to get a job, get married and have a family, build their life skills, and slowly establish an ego identity in the world. Because of this they may also strongly identify with the external world of job, family, church, mosque, temple, community, or other kinds of group affiliations. They are intent on mastering the physical realm step-by-step, building confidence as they go.

Often centered in family, social, or religious organizations, these Souls rarely act outside the norm. They are not imaginative thinkers since they shy away from coloring outside the lines. When they do have an original idea they will look outside themselves for validation, just to make sure it meets with the approval of others. In career choices they tend to follow a safe, well-established path. This may mean that they become a secretary, bookkeeper, factory worker, auto mechanic, construction worker, computer person, waitress, or day laborer—all jobs that require little creativity. As a hobby they might do scrapbooking, knitting, cook-offs, bingo, join the high-school band, or play the piano at church. While these hobbies and jobs are not limited to young Souls, they provide the kind of structure in which a young Soul might begin to develop its creative thoughts and life skills.

At a leadership level their skills are usually very predictable because they like to fit in. Many times you will find young Souls intent on upholding the existing laws, so they might be policemen, preachers, lawyers, office workers, or school principals whose intentions are genuine, even if their insight into life's complexities is two-dimensional. They will do all they can to make sure these rules are obeyed, since it is only through group consensus that they feel safe. Thus those who do not conform are often judged as weird, sinful, oddball, kooky, or even downright evil. At this stage of evolution the Soul does not have true wisdom or personal power, and when it does acquire power through position it often misuses it. The fundamentalists of this world are usually young and intermediate Souls, and it is their lack of experience that drives their fear and judgment of others. As a result they are prone to projecting blame, guilt, and criticism onto other people and groups. These negative emotions can then be used by less scrupulous Souls who wish to exploit their fears and manipulate them for their own purposes.

While these Souls are basically well-intentioned, they are not yet ready to look at life in a more profound way so they seldom take time to explore their deeper emotions except within safe social parameters. Although they do not know it, the underlying emotion that runs their lives is fear. Young Souls have realized that this is a constantly changing, unpredictable world, so are trying to protect against its dangers. Young Souls do not yet see the consequences of their own negative words and actions because they are limited in experience. They may act foolishly, never realizing that the things they are doing and saying are responsible for their own problems. Since he hasn't made this connection, it is easy for the young Soul to adopt the belief that he is the victim and to blame others for his difficulties.

It is also important to know that there are young Souls who are at the end of this cycle. These Souls are moving up into the intermediate level, so instead of conforming they may be in rebellion against the very rules they upheld in former lifetimes. At this point the Soul is discovering how to listen to its inner guidance and break free from the sanctions of traditional thought. They may, in fact, be so fed up with the past that they want to break all the rules. While this can be scary, it is actually an important step forward in their evolution, for it is only by making our own personal determinations about life that we can discover what is true and what is merely propaganda. Personal experience is the key to developing one's inner value system as we learn to think for ourselves. Along the way we will eventually discover the lessons of self-responsibility, inner reflection, and spiritual autonomy; this frees us from the limitations and prejudices of others. Then the Soul can move forward in reclaiming its own sweet spirit.

TABLE 15.3. FOR THE YOUNG SOUL— 3 TO 4 BILLION YEARS OLD

Greatest Strengths	Greatest Obstacles	Lessons
This Soul has figured out how to fit into the Earth systems and is learning physical plane mastery. These are usually good, honest, steadfast people with limited imagination, limited emotional range, and limited depth of perception. They can be very responsible.	These Souls are often fear-based people who can easily become trapped by the prejudices of social systems, developing judgments and self-righteous attitudes toward others. They rarely think outside the box and often give their power away to social or religious organizations. Sometimes they are overly responsible, and sometimes they are irresponsible. Often they do not see how their own negative thoughts and actions affect others, so they are prone to projecting blame out into the world.	This Soul needs to learn to step back from the emotions of guilt, shame, and victimhood. It needs to learn the lesson of cause and effect and to take responsibility for its own life. This Soul needs to develop courage and faith in its higher Self and to think in a bigger way, expanding its horizons for new experiences. It needs to realize that life is not all black and white, right or wrong, but many shades of gray. It needs to develop faith in the spiritual world, not just in the exterior world of the senses.

The Intermediate Soul

Image: The intermediate Soul's focus is the acquisition of power. He or she may be the town mayor or councilman, appearing as everyone's friend while wielding power behind the scenes and making a killing selling insurance on the side. This Soul has his hands in his own business, is influential with others, and uses the media to promote his own programs while also running the local bar, dance club, or casino (with a live tiger in a cage to attract customers). These people are here to tell you, and sell you, a thing or two—in their own self-interest.

Intermediate Souls are often charismatic, successful people who are largely in service to themselves, getting ahead at the expense of others. These Souls have figured out that there is a game being played here on Earth, and they are intent on winning it. They can see that there are a lot of people in the world who live in fear, and they are perfectly willing to exploit these fears if it will line their own pockets. Thus they devise ways to manipulate others. This may be through religion (fear of the devil), the health industry (fear of getting sick), the fitness industry (fear of getting fat), or by selling seaside property in Arizona (fear of Earth changes). Discovering these fears and exploiting them is the modus operandi of the intermediate Soul, who is out to make a profit.

Intermediate Souls are rarely fair-minded. These Souls are always asking "What's in it for me?" These folks have realized that there are winners and losers in the game of life, and they are committed to being winners at any cost. They are more concerned with getting caught than in doing what's right. They are not altruists, unless it is for their public image. Often highly intelligent, they have strong egos and the ability to think outside the box. Consequently, they are driven to rise to leadership positions through sheer ambition because they are looking out for number one. They can be quite enterprising and are often involved with overt or covert criminal activities. If they have chosen the path of gaining power through criminal activities it may be through drug trafficking, gambling, extortion, racketeering, illegal contraband, or the sex trade. These are the petty tyrants of the world who are not above using war, deceit, blackmail, extortion, or libel to meet their objectives. Because their primary mission is the acquisition of power and money, these people are often headlines-grabbing politicians, banksters, the richest CEOs, and million-dollar televangelists. Their grab for power can be expressed in the arenas of religion, politics, business, real estate, and legal services. They can be common criminals, loan sharks, gamblers and swindlers, bail bondsman, and bounty hunters, and they are especially prevalent in the military and the police. This group is all about action and not opposed to using violence.

The main lesson for the intermediate Soul is the right use of power. While these Souls are also driven by fear, they manage it by going for the acquisition of power. They believe that power will keep them safe—even if they have to take it from others. Thus they are stuck in a win-lose scenario that can take the form of manipulating others for pleasure or profit. Either way, this one-upmanship game runs this Soul's life, and the higher Self has taken a backseat. Their modus operandi is figuring out how to get power and use it. Intermediate Souls are masters at knowing the law and using loopholes to get their way, so many legal and financial types fall under this umbrella, either at the high end or the low end.

Metaphorically speaking, the intermediate Soul may be out to convince the masses that everyone needs tiger insurance so that he can profit from the fear people have of encountering a tiger. In the name of being a watchdog for the people, he creates games in which he profits from every transaction. These are the people who finance the coliseum games in which people are torn apart by wild animals—that way fear is kept alive in the populace, and it's good for business. While intermediate Souls may appear to be the guardians of our public safety, they are often the ones who are trying to take away our freedoms by orchestrating social unrest. That way we will hand over our freedoms without resistance. In truth, they are selling us the "solution," because they are the ones manufacturing the "problem," and they plan to profit on both ends.

Of late, many bankers and Wall Street types fall under this umbrella. This group also likes to have control of the media. In the name of education and entertainment they create fear-based TV shows teaching us to fear aliens, plagues, sickness, and death, all to manipulate us for their own agendas. This group is usually only drawn to religion as a social affiliation to legitimatize their public personas, using it to endorse their campaigns. Ironically, this group is often in charge of organized religion, politics, insurance, the pharmaceutical industry, genetically modified foods, and of course, the monetary system. Let me be clear: this is not to say that there are not some good, well-intentioned people in these professions. Many pharmacists, for example, are people who are genuinely interested in helping others, but they are stuck in the trap of working for large corporate interests that are far more interested in making a profit from the sick than in truly curing cancer.

At a personal level the intermediate Soul is often jealous, controlling, possessive, and abusive, and thinks of his family as his personal property. Territorial and controlling, the intermediate Soul wants the best the world has to offer and will often do anything to get it. Status symbols express their sense of superiority, and they put great value on possessions. This Soul gives little credence to anything he can't touch, see, hear, or smell, since spiritual "nonsense" will not help him achieve his goals. These people are quite judgmental of others but are rarely self-examining. Today, it is the intermediate Souls who are ruling this crazy, mixed-up world. Hopefully this will change as we strive to create a more balanced and enlightened society.

The intermediate Soul is steeped in the lessons of power and often creates a lot of negative karma along the way. These Souls will ultimately learn that when we play the PVR game—Persecutor-Victim-Rescuer (discussed in detail in chapter 17 on page 360)—we go back and forth between being a petty tyrant and a victim of abuse. This negative cycle is one that many Souls are caught up in here on planet Earth, and it is a chain that we must break if we are to create a better world.

Intermediate Souls have a lot to learn about win-win dynamics, inner values, and that most important of qualities, love. Like all of us, the intermediate Soul must learn the lesson of true, altruistic kindness, sharing with others, and finally self-sacrifice. He must learn integrity and trust and how to treat others as he wishes to be treated. The abuse of power is always destined to bring us down from high places to a place of hardship and suffering, and for most of us, stubborn as we are, this is the only way that we will finally learn the lesson of compassion. Many Souls stay stuck in the intermediate stage of evolution for hundreds of lifetimes. Finally, these Souls will realize that all the power in the world will not advance us one iota without love. So, like Ebenezer Scrooge, with this great realization, the intermediate Soul can finally move forward to its next phase of development.

TABLE 15.4. FOR THE INTERMEDIATE SOUL— 4 TO 5.5 BILLION YEARS OLD

Greatest Strengths	Greatest Obstacles	Lessons
This Soul is usually intelligent, ambitious, materialistic, and driven. Often they are courageous risk-takers working to get ahead, either through legal or illegal means. Usually excellent in the materialistic world, they are often charismatic, focused manifesters.	Highly self-centered, these Souls are often materialistic, controlling, and territorial, and it is easy for them to get caught up in the passions of greed, lust, vanity, and ego. Usually these Souls only believe in what they can see and are not in touch with the realm of Spirit. These are the self-serving wealthy elites of the world, as well as the criminals. They are committed to win-lose dynamics.	Intermediate Souls need to develop love and a generosity of spirit toward others; to let go of control and the dominating use of power; to learn how to think beyond the confines of the ego and to embrace a win-win dynamic. They need to cultivate humility, kindness, selflessness, love, and service to humankind.

The Advanced Soul

Image: The image of the advanced Soul is that of the Peace Corps worker, the diplomat, the doctor, the nurse, the teacher, the healer, the conscious business leader or statesman who is able to interface with many people and cultures and work for the betterment of all.

Advanced Souls have graduated to a win-win dynamic, where they have finally learned that we must live according to the Golden Rule: Do unto others as you would have them do unto you. They have figured out that how we treat others returns to us in spades, and thus they are committed to doing good in the world and giving back to others in a meaningful way.

The advanced Soul is also trying to balance heart and mind to be successful in the world while still making a difference. These are usually heart-based, intelligent, capable people who are looking further afield than their own creature comforts, even though they may enjoy a good life on the physical plane. These Souls have come through many stages of learning already and have discovered how to balance the rules of society with their own individual thoughts so that they are able to live in harmony with others, yet they strive to follow the beat of their own drum. They have learned how to manifest jobs, relationships, and success in this dimension. Since they may have had many worldly possessions during their time as an intermediate Soul, they are not driven by greed. They no longer care so much about having the big house or the expensive car, yet they want to make a good living. They have finally realized that having too many things can actually be a burden; thus they may decide on a simpler kind of existence that does not enslave them to the material game.

The advanced Soul is not immune to selfishness, but does strive for fairness most of the time. In the beginning this Soul may decide to have a family and fit into society's rules. But as this Soul matures she is often driven by the desire to want to make a positive difference in other people's lives, and that becomes her focus. These folks are often accomplished in more than one career, having gained lifetimes of experience along the way. Often creative, they may work in the fields of music, healing, teaching, writing, or artistry. They may help others through counseling, nursing, healing, diplomacy, volunteer work, or becoming a doctor, fireman, teacher, or Red Cross worker. They may work within traditional charities or religions, or become advocates for the suffering of children, animals, landmine victims, refugees, the Earth herself, or the oceans. Some advanced Souls create their own organizations for human or animal rights, working outside of traditional support systems since they know how to think outside the box.

Advanced Souls can also be missionaries, rabbis, psychologists, or ministers who are dedicated to doing good in the world. However, the challenge they face is having to work within a more limited framework, with people often less evolved or tolerant than they are. Advanced Souls are in the beginning stages of seeing past all the dogma, illusion, and control systems, and right to the heart in all beings. They have let go of the judgmental thinking that binds their younger cousins. Often this Soul is the "bridge person" between traditional systems, helping others to find a more authentic path to spiritual connection. This role also allows this Soul to practice forbearance, patience, and forgiveness of those who are less evolved than they are. Learning to trust one's own guidance system then becomes the test of this higher truth. If the advanced Soul can connect with her higher Self and learn to trust that guidance, then she will graduate to the master Soul stage of evolution.

TABLE 15.5. FOR THE ADVANCED SOUL— 5.5 TO 7 BILLION YEARS OLD

Greatest Strengths	Greatest Obstacles	Lessons
The master Soul has an innate turning toward God, a higher morality, and the understanding of the emotional dangers of blame, guilt, and human suffering. It has gained a win-win attitude that includes fairness to others. This stage marks the beginning of the opening to the Soul's higher gifts as it strengthens and learns to trust the intelligence of its connection to Spirit.	The greatest obstacle for a master Soul is to release the wounds of the past, let go of the situations they have outgrown, and believe in the wisdom of their own inner guidance. They must overcome the fear of standing out and have the courage to step forward and act on their convictions. They must realize that they are here to be in service to their families, friends, and communities. These Souls must remember to connect their head and their heart, and they can truly connect with Spirit and fulfill their mission.	This Soul needs to learn patience with others, forgiveness for itself and others, and to embrace the imperfections of its own Shadow self and love it into wholeness. It needs to learn to align its life consciously with Spirit and step into empowerment, manifesting its spiritual and material goals. These Souls are on the path of spiritual service, and the more they can walk this path, the faster they will grow.

The Master Soul

Image: The master Soul is a mature person who thinks and feels deeply. The person at this level may be a visionary, a humanitarian, or a thinker-philosopher who writes books, starts visionary projects, or works for the healing of the whole. This kind of spiritual service can take many forms, from the dedicated entrepreneur or businessperson, to the psychologist, altruist, or naturopathic healer. The core motivation of this Soul is the discovery of truth and the betterment of humanity. Examples include Plato, Socrates, Rudolph Steiner, Emmanuel Swedenborg, Pythagoras, Madame Blavatsky, Nelson Mandela, Albert Einstein, and Mahatma Gandhi.

The master Soul has gone to the mountain and come back many times. She has loved and lost, hoped and suffered, and seen many phases of life. At the core of her being she knows the beautiful and the ugly, the sublime and the unforgivable, and has taken it all into herself and made it her own. These are the people who are deeply connected with their higher Self and have returned to Earth to help their brothers and sisters. Although they are not without blemish, they have largely incorporated their Shadow into their being and healed those parts with love. They understand that all Souls are reflections of the Divine, and they continually strive for patience and forgiveness.

The master Soul endeavors to live without judgment, knowing that "you" are simply another "me" who is merely experiencing another place on the wheel of life. These Souls have gained a direct experience of the cosmos as an intelligent, beneficent being who has created every shade of experience for the evolution of the Soul, and they have come to the realization that we are all one. The master Soul sees through the illusions of social customs, material wealth, sexual avarice, and the five passions of the mind. She is not owned by lust, greed, vanity, or fame, for she knows that she is here to bring light to others. This person's mission is not to create co-dependent students, but to empower others by reminding them of the divinity within. The master Soul has been a student of the Mysteries many times before. Through trial and error, she has found the answers that allow her to acquire equanimity, strength, patience, and love. She is attuned to her own inner male and female aspects and works to keep these in balance. Despite what life may have handed her, she returns to a place of unconditional love as her guiding star.

As a master Soul evolves, she may begin to exhibit some of the various siddhis, or spiritual powers, such as telepathy, clairvoyance, clairaudience, or claircognition. She may have spiritual healing abilities, either consciously or through the transmission of her peaceful presence. The challenge for this Soul is to remain humble and to remember that despite her considerable wisdom, pride and vanity are the last things to go. While these Souls may have largely mastered the little ego, it is through consciously aligning the personal will to the Angelic Twin that they can become true servants of the Creator's will. This deliberate alignment and surrender will then allow them to attain their next step of evolution.

TABLE 15.6. FOR THE MASTER SOUL— 7 TO 9 BILLION YEARS OLD

Greatest Strengths	Greatest Obstacles	Lessons
Their greatest strength is knowledge of the One in the many, the many in the One. Unconditional love, nonjudgment, personal empowerment, the ability to move in tune with the synchronicity of the universe, and the continuation and evolution of the gifts of the Spirit are their primary qualities.	Trying to take on too much and overreaching in their desire to help others can cause advanced Souls to fall into the co-dependent traps of the emotional world. They can tend to take themselves too seriously and not remember to hold their power in a light way.	Advanced Souls need to develop balance and discipline between the demands of the physical world and the inner ones, the emotional and social aspects of life and service to humanity. They must learn discernment in creating priorities both personally and in the world, as well as balance between detachment and compassion.

The Bodhisattva Soul

Image: The best way to paint an image of a true bodhisattva, one who has chosen to return to the world for the sole purpose of bringing enlightenment to others, is to contemplate the lives of the great avatars: Jesus, Buddha, Sai Baba, Babaji, Pythagoras, St. Germaine, St. Francis of Assisi, Kuan Yin, Amachi, Yogananda, Mother Meera, Kuthumi, Isis, Osiris, Horus, Mother Mary, and the masters and gurus of the East.

A bodhisattva is one who has completely freed herself from the Wheel of Karma and has chosen to return to Earth to assist humankind. These Souls have gone to the mountaintop and returned, so they are no longer seduced by fame, fortune, or worldly things. They have attained the jewel of perfection within the Self. They know that the lover and the beloved are one. Having reached a state of such compassion, they have put off their own journey into the higher realms to return to the physical world to help their younger brothers and sisters. These are the avatars who have accomplished the Great Work and have returned to share it with the world.

Because many people living on Earth today are intermediate Souls, these avatars have their work cut out for them. When they become too public they are often made a target by the power- and fear-based establishment. This was the case with Jesus, who taught spiritual liberation, which was a threat to the establishment. Once the bodhisattva avatars are martyred, the intermediate, power-based Souls raise statues to these masters or create nonprofit foundations in their name, and then they start religious wars using corrupted versions of the master's teachings to enact their own agenda. In the process, the intermediate Souls will enslave others through fear-mongering, and then do exactly what they have wanted to do all along, all the while exploiting the sage's teachings for personal gain. Thus, those who seek to discover a higher path here on Earth must look behind the curtain of traditional religions to discover what the sage or avatar was really saying before his teachings were corrupted, suppressed, or edited by the intermediate forces.

TABLE 15.7. FOR THE BODHISATTVA SOULS— 9 BILLION YEARS OLD AND UP

Greatest Strengths	Greatest Obstacles	Lessons
Oneness with God and unconditional love is the bodhisattva's greatest strength. Their very presence creates an emanation that raises other people's frequencies through its direct transmission. These Souls are wise, heart-based and spiritually attuned, and embody the highest frequencies of the God-man or God-woman in human form.	In the development of the siddhis, or spiritual powers, it is easy to let pride creep in. These Souls must remember to remain humble and avoid falling into any of the traps of the five passions of the mind: these are anger, lust, vanity, greed, and undue attachment to anyone or anything. Because their kundalini energy is so highly developed, they must also watch out for the misuse of the sexual force. Many of these Masters have become ascetics, although some of them have married. However, since it is difficult to find an equal partner, they must guard against promiscuity or inappropriate sexual encounters with others.	These Souls are already profoundly awakened. They must continue to stay in the heart, remain humble, and have patience with the many Souls around them who are nowhere near their evolutionary level. One of their main challenges is loneliness, because although they are constantly practicing the presence of the Divine, they are still in human form. Human bodies long to be held and nurtured in a very human way. Thus these Souls must balance their human needs with their missions. They must continue to remember that all experiences are perfect in the Eyes of God, that the entire circle is who we are, and that to incarnate as human is to be human and flawed, as well as Divine and perfect.

Through the centuries, the key points of wisdom of the bodhisattvas have been distorted to promote the personal agendas of those who have carried on in their names. Yet history shows us that true enlightenment or peace does not lie in the falsehoods of war and oppression. It also does not lie in the centuries of Souls who have argued, fought, and killed in the name of religion. It does not lie in suicide bombers, religious hangings, inquisitions, or seditious judgments, and it does not lie in the rants of fundamentalist preachers, racial bigotry, gender prejudice, jihad, violent massacres, or political assassinations. Truth lies in a personal relationship with the Creator that opens our hearts, brings us into alignment with Oneness, and brings us harmony and peace. It lies in the balance between the male and female aspects of all of us, and the path of union that treats all beings with kindness.

Any religion that teaches the superiority of one gender, race, country, or religion over another has gotten out of balance. Any religion that teaches the divine right of rulership over others is skewing the bodhisattva's original message and changing it for social, political, or financial reasons. Religions that legitimize the oppression, murder, torture, sacrifice, or annihilation of animals, humans, or even extraterrestrial beings visiting this planet from elsewhere (who also are a part of the Divine) have in essence lost their purity and their way.

∽

As you flip back through these tables you may recognize many people in your life and others on the public stage who fit easily into these categories. Hopefully, by understanding these various stages of the Soul's journey, you can begin to see why you resonate so well with some people and are so challenged by others. Yet every phase of evolution has its own opportunities for growth and understanding. Knowing where you are in this journey, as well as where others may be, can help you develop patience and forgiveness for all people. After all, each of us is on the same spiritual journey, just at a different point along the way. By reminding yourself that we are all works in progress, we can gain the patience and wisdom to walk our path with humor and grace.

PART 4

THE COURSE CURRICULUM OF THE SOUL

*Every newborn being indeed comes fresh and blithe
into the new existence, and enjoys it as a free gift.
. . . Its fresh existence is paid for by the old age
and death of a worn-out existence which
has perished, but which contained the
indestructible seed out of which the
new existence has arisen:
they are one being.*

ARTHUR SCHOPENHAUER

16

Dismantling the Illusion of Separation

As we live through thousands of dreams in our present life, so is our present life only one of many thousands of such lives which we enter from the other more real life and then return after death. Our life is but one of the dreams of that more real life, and so it is endlessly, until the very last one, the very real, the life of God.

LEO TOLSTOY

So now that we have reviewed the six stages of the Soul's journey, let us consider how we might use this knowledge to accelerate our evolution. What are the things that keep us from living in a state of love, and how are these dysfunctional patterns played out in the world today? Since the nature of the Soul is unity with Source, how could we forget our primary, original nature? How is it possible for us to know anything other than perpetual unity and bliss? What is the mechanism that causes us to have temporary amnesia?

This brings us to the mechanism of Adi-karma. Adi-karma is the instrument by which the Soul experiences an illusory separation from God, giving each of us the opportunity to experience contrast and to exercise free will through choice. Adi-karma is "karma not earned by the individual Soul. It is established by the Lords of Karma in the beginning of the Soul's journey in the lower worlds; [it is] also called Primal Karma; [an] action of the creative force."[1] While inflicting such a state of illusionary separation on any Soul may at first seem cruel or unkind, it is part of the rules that the Soul agrees to play by when it comes into this world. Why would anyone ever make such a choice, one might ask. After all, an eternity of bliss and union with God sounds great, doesn't it? But is it possible that you might get bored? That's like saying that a hot fudge sundae is your favorite food, yet after billions of years of eating hot fudge sundaes you might yearn for something else. You might want a squash soufflé, a green salad, or a T-bone steak. So, the Soul makes a different set of choices. It chooses to learn through the experience of yearning, separation, pain, and struggle, and in this way the Soul gets to explore and grow. This is how it entertains itself and evolves throughout eternity.

Because we are small expressions of the Divine One, the nature of the Divine is very similar to our own human nature—inquisitive, loving, adventurous, explorative, and eager to share its thoughts with others. So, of course, the Creator, through us, wishes to explore. Just take a moment to consider any healthy adolescent who wants to push his boundaries, try new things, and hopefully fall in love. But since the Divine exists in a state of perpetual unity, how can it experience separation from itself? God is simultaneously the lover and the beloved, the teenager and the one he falls in love with. So in this knowledge of absolute Oneness, nothing new can be learned. So it is only through experiencing separation and reunion that we create an array of choices. Through the *absence* of love, we come to appreciate its *presence*. Having loved and lost, and loved again, we can then truly know how sweet it is to return to union once again.

Thus, just like our Angelic Twin who remains in a state of perpetual light and bliss, the larger part of God remains in the higher realms. Yet another part is eminent or present in all of nature, and yet another part courageously travels through the realm of duality. And God is experiencing this through each one of us, through the lives and experiences of trillions of creatures, not only on this world, but in other systems as well. This is the immensity of the Creator. And at a personal level, this process allows the Soul to also have millions of experiences as it travels through the creational worlds, forgetting and remembering through the process of separation and yearning, until the day when it awakens to its true nature.

The Creation of the Ego

In Eastern spiritual traditions much is said about dissolving the ego, but the ego actually serves a very useful function in the lower worlds. We can compare it to a car, a vehicle that gets us from place to place; it's a necessity if we want to drive in the fast lane, which in this case is planet Earth. Like a car, the ego holds a portion of our spirit, but only for a limited amount of time. There comes a time when we dissolve the ego because the Soul has discovered that its natural state is to fly. At that moment the car has done its job. It has allowed our Souls to have a vehicle for experiencing the contrasts of life until we evolve to the point that we no longer need it. Then the ego melds with the higher Self, creating a perfect synthesis of the human being and the Angelic Self.

So the ego is the device by which the Soul develops its individuality in lifetime after lifetime. This egoic self develops over many lifetimes, being created anew in each life through the acquisition of a new set of subtle-energy bodies. These are the mental, emotional, astral and physical bodies. Each of these new aspects is created from the seeds of our past learning, personality traits, interests, and spiritual merits, so that the progress we make in our various lifetimes is cumulative. Nothing is really lost. While some part of us may believe that we have forgotten who we are, the affinities we have developed in each life remain in the causal body and can be reactivated. Once we begin a new life, we still must teach our new fingers to play the piano, to paint, or to throw a football. However the skills that we have developed in earlier lifetimes will return quickly if we choose to go down that path.

I remember years ago picking up a sword at a Renaissance Fair. I deftly began to fence, driving back my six foot two boyfriend, quickly cornering him against a wall. Everyone was stunned at my natural ability, which I also had with archery, jumping horses, and running. However in this life, that athletic temperament has been rechanneled into spiritual pursuits. So in every life we must deal with the temperament of the body we have chosen, the direction of our talents and interests, and the limitations of our genetic makeup. Sometimes our genes will give us musical, writing, or creative talent, perhaps chosen by the Soul to follow those creative interests. Other genetics give us a propensity for beauty, physical appearance, or diseases. Sometimes we choose a fiery body or one that is sluggish, stocky, muscular, or fat. Adjusting to these changes can take some effort, but when we can befriend our body, then we do not have to be mastered by it. Thus the mind, emotions, and physical body are vehicles that we use on the playing field of life. However we must also contend with the ego, and that brings us back to the subject of Adi-karma.

Adi-karma is the original karma that was given to us when we first descended into the physical world. We did not earn it, rather it was given to us so that we could play the game of life. Through thousands of Soul readings I have discovered that each one of us has one of the three lies of Adi-karma embedded within the ego. These lies are: (1) "I'm not worthy of God's love; (2) "I've been abandoned or betrayed by God"; and (3) "I'm alone down here." These false beliefs allow the Soul to experience the illusion that we are separate from God. In other words, as a result of the veil of separation or illusion, we have an opportunity to exercise our free will and to take all the time we need to make choices that allow us to learn, grow, and make mistakes. While each Soul is only assigned one of the three lies of Adi-karma at the start of our incarnational journey, over the course of many trials and tribulations we may inadvertently acquire the other two false beliefs, thus deepening the veils of illusion and separation. These false beliefs then become a part of the structure of the ego, or little self, until such time as we can see past them. This is one of the reasons why emotional clearing work is so vital to our happiness. These three lies are aspects of the Shadow that binds us in sadness, fear, and anger in the lower worlds. However once we make a connection with our higher Self and attain self-realization, this illusion of separation is broken and the Shadow becomes integrated into the whole. Then we are free to continue our journey home, back to Source.

Identifying the core wound that you carry can greatly assist you in seeing through the veils of separation. While many people feel a lack of self-worth, alienation, or even a fear of rejection, they may be afraid to face it. By understanding that this is not just *your* wounding pattern, but that of millions of other people, we can stand back, heave a sigh of relief, and know we are in good company. Then we can begin the work of emotional clearing. The subconscious programs of Adi-karma are part of the game of life, and the sooner we identify them, the better off we will be.

"I'm not worthy of God's love."

This belief creates a lack of self-worth and the resulting emotion of sadness. People who have this belief are often big givers, many times giving way too much to others and not enough to themselves. These folks may also have a hard time receiving love and may spend their lives constantly trying to prove that they are smart enough, good enough, and lovable enough to be worthy of approval or love. This desire to be loved and acknowledged, or seen and appreciated, can cause that person to become the unwitting victim of other people eager to exploit their generosity.

The antidote to the belief in one's unworthiness is to affirm that you are worthy of God's love; otherwise you would not exist! Clearly, God found you worthy, so who are you to argue, especially when the Divine has a much larger perspective? So start your affirmations today; affirm that you are healthy, wealthy, and wise; that you are worthy, loved, and abundant; that you are blessed, beautiful, and successful. And tell your inner critic to go sit on the couch and take a powder!

"I've been abandoned/betrayed by God."

This belief creates an undercurrent of anger. People who hold this belief may come from homes where they were abandoned or betrayed by their families or the circumstances of early life. They feel like victims, and then, when they grow up, they become victimizers as a result of their own unconscious beliefs. These are the people who walk around with a chip on their shoulder and have huge control issues with spouses, friends, and associates. These control dramas are just an unconscious way that the Soul tries to protect itself from experiencing abandonment once again. Unfortunately, these anger and control issues can be so oppressive to others that it creates the very thing that this person most fears: spouses, friends, and children eventually leave them because no one wants to be the target of their anger.

The antidote to this lie is to examine the facts. You haven't really been abandoned by God, although I'm sure it feels that way. In reality you volunteered for this job. You are the kamikaze diver who insisted on coming down here. And now that you've arrived, your little self wants to blame your departure from the higher realms on everyone else. Get a grip! God has never abandoned or betrayed you, because you have the God spark within you. God lives inside of everything around us. So it's not like someone is having a great party that you weren't invited to. You are *in the middle of the party,* so it's about time you start acting grateful for all of the many blessings in your life. After all, there were about a billion other Souls who wanted your slot, and you, you lucky dog, got to come here after all!

"I'm alone down here."

This belief engenders fear. People who have embraced the belief that they are alone and always will be alone are often afraid to be alone. Consequently, they may surround themselves with people while still feeling unfulfilled and lonely. Sometimes this need is so strong that the person is desperate to get married and as a result she chooses someone who is not capable of meeting her at a deeper emotional level, thus creating that sense of loneliness again. Or she may unconsciously cut herself off from receiving the love of others, convinced that she is alone and will always be alone. So she becomes reclusive. She may never commit to a lasting relationship like a marriage, and instead becomes afraid to take chances, afraid of new experiences, afraid to let others in, and fearful that no matter what she does she will still wind up alone. For this person, fear is at the foundation of life. This belief is isolating, whether in the work environment, in social interactions, and even in friendships.

So what is the antidote to this false belief? Let's take a closer look at the simple fact that you couldn't be alone if you tried! As we have seen, God is everywhere and in everything, so the only thing you have to do is to begin to practice that Divine presence. Let the blinders fall from your eyes. Go talk to your dog, your cat, your car, your flower garden, the sky, the moon, the sun, the wind, and practice the presence of your higher Self that has been with you all along, patiently tapping its fingers and wondering when you're going to wake up!

Four Defense Mechanisms That Keep Us in the Illusion of Separation

In addition to the lies of Adi-karma, over the course of thousands of sessions I have discovered four basic mechanisms by which people defend the little ego self and keep themselves in bondage to the illusion of separation. While these defense mechanisms may appear to work in the short term, they prevent us from examining the false beliefs that run our lives, thereby sabotaging our connection with the light of our true Self. These defense mechanisms give power to the Shadow. Let's take a look at them one by one and see how they mostly don't serve us.

Denial
Denial is the belief that "there is nothing wrong with me" and "I don't have a problem, and in fact, you do!" Denial is used by those who are afraid to look at themselves because if they did they'd have to address

their own fundamental problems, and this would mean admitting that they are wrong. Often a person who uses denial becomes an expert at deflecting the criticism of others by being critical or judgmental of them, thus projecting their own issues, fears, and faults onto the other person. Denial may also take the form of the person who puts her head in the sand because it is just too painful to look at the truth. If she was willing to acknowledge what is right in front of her, then she might have to drastically alter her life and her image of herself. Denial can take a thousand forms:

"No, I don't have a drinking problem. I can handle my own life."

"Nonsense, my husband is just working late for the thousandth time. He's too tired to have sex anyway."

"I had a perfect childhood! How dare you think that I'm to blame!"

"My little girl is depressed, but that's normal, isn't it?"

"I'm open-minded. I just think that all Commies [Jews, 'Spics, Muslims, niggers, etc.] are going to Hell."

"I'm a sensitive ladies' man, as long as they just give me what I want."

The root of denial is fear—the fear of being wrong; the fear of being a bad parent; the fear of being a bad boss; the fear of having to admit the compromises you've made; the fear of not being good enough, smart enough, or having to change your life as a result of what you've discovered about yourself. After all, if people knew who you really were, then you would not be lovable—something you were probably conditioned to believe by a dysfunctional family, religion, and society in general.

The antidote for these fears begins with honest self-examination, a complete suspension of all blame, accepting responsibility, and genuine forgiveness, beginning with oneself and extending to all others. This is, in fact, the core of the Twelve Step Program. All of us make mistakes. We are imperfect beings in an imperfect human world, and that's okay. After all, we are still on the Wheel of Becoming, so it's okay not to have arrived yet. Knowing that you are loved no matter how wounded you are is the first step. You are loved by God. You are loved by your spiritual guides. And you are loved no matter what you might need to change about your present thoughts, actions, or attitudes. Who needs to work on loving you more is you yourself, and that is okay too. Knowing that you are loved, forever and ever, will give you the strength to look at yourself honestly, figure out how you can do better, and have the courage to stop denying your Shadow, for it is only by identifying and loving your Shadow into wholeness that you can really step into the light.

Rebellion

Most of us are familiar with the defense mechanism of rebellion because it is an important part of growing up. When children become teenagers it is natural for them to pull away from the constraints of their parents and try to define their own values so that they can begin to establish their own way of being in the world. So rebellion is part of the natural order of self-discovery. However, as we move into adulthood, if we succumb to a reactive form of rebellion that is fueled by a deep underlying, unchecked anger, then rebellion becomes a mechanism of self sabotage. Rebellion can be expressed in angry, reactive actions or in more passive-aggressive ways. It can take the form of dressing sloppy, blowing off appointments, constantly being late, "forgetting" to follow through, breaking agreements, or refusing to work with others in a harmonious way. When the source of rebellion or anger is left unhealed, it can ruin a career, relationships, and opportunities for happiness. Let's take a look at a couple examples:

- Steve was controlled by his father and mother when he was young, and he is still angry about it. Once he entered adulthood he projected his anger and resentment onto any authority figure. First it was his teachers in college, so he cut classes, was perpetually late, and found a way to discount any teacher who seemed too authoritarian. Then, when he entered the workforce, these same bad attitudes made him late for work, talk behind his boss's back, and "forget" to call in to work when he was sick. Eventually this got him fired, sabotaging any promotions and earning him a reputation as a difficult employee. This anger also spilled out into his romantic relationships, making him shoot for the stars with his girlfriend Sally, as he dreamed big, promised big, and then failed to deliver. All of this only caused his resentment and anger to grow, looping him in a continuous cycle of self-blame and blame of others.

- Dirk grew up in poverty, convinced that his ancestors were victims of the upper and middle classes. Consequently, Dirk judged those with money, convinced that they were his oppressors. Angry and resentful of others' success, Dirk sought money so that he could feel more empowered, but money seemed to elude him. Even when he had it, he quickly lost it through misunderstandings and betrayals. Dirk did not realize that his resentment of those who did have money and success had created a block to his own financial success. His resentment and rebellion sabotaged his prospects at every turn. Ultimately, this rebounded on him in such a way that Dirk became the one who was judged by others— usually around issues of money and trust.

Most rebellion is fueled by anger. This may be the anger of early abandonment, abuse, betrayal, or an upbringing that was negligent or too controlling. Whenever these issues are left unhealed, rebellion can set in. This negative cycle of reaction can be so self-sabotaging that it's like cutting off your nose to spite your face. While in the moment you may have won the battle of wills with your boss, your spouse, or your friends, you have actually lost the war because you have pitted your energies against those who could have been your allies. Through your own contentious attitudes you may have made your point, but it is you who are damaged the most because you have refused to work in harmony with others. Rebellion reveals a serious lack of gratitude for the opportunities you have been given. Thus the person who has adopted rebellion as a defense mechanism becomes the one who can never listen, never apologize, and never learn the lessons that life presents, because his energy is still locked in an endless war that he is fighting with his original sparring partner—his parents.

The antidote to this defense mechanism is to discover who it is that you are still angry at and resolve this core entanglement. This may mean learning something you didn't know about that person—why he was abusive, why he left you at a critical moment in time, why he was so overprotective or over-controlling. By revising your understanding of your own history and his, then the person who has wronged you can be seen as the person he actually was, not the person he was to you. That individual may have been struggling with his own emotional problems that were too complex to explain to a child. His own checkered history may have caused him to act in unloving or unreliable ways, resulting in your wounding and disappointment. He may have been unable to give you what you most needed, either because it was not in his character to do so or because of his own past history.

Over and over I have seen that once this defense mechanism is acknowledged, it opens a way for healing to begin. Then you can find a way to express your disappointment, anger, and sadness, whether through writing a letter to the person who hurt you (even if he is no longer alive), working with a therapist, or simply talking to that person. Then you can decide whether you have it in you to forgive him. Forgiveness is a crucial part of the Soul's journey, especially if someone has done you wrong. Then you must ask yourself if you can find a higher meaning behind these difficult life lessons. How has this negative experience been of service to your spirit? Did it give you any tools or strengths that you otherwise would not have had? Is there anything there that you can use as fuel to help you achieve your life's goals? Can this deeper understanding assist you now in attaining your life's purpose?

Once you have answered these questions, it's time to decide what you want to do with your life now that you are coming from a place of true balance and understanding. Defining your priorities and knowing that you can achieve your goals by treating others with the same kind of respect that you want to be treated with is critical to this process. Along the way you may have to make amends for some of your earlier behavior. But when the seeds of our wounding become the tools of our empowerment, then we can finally see its higher purpose in our life. "I will bend like a reed" is a good mantra for this stage of consciousness, once the pain of the past has been jettisoned. Then you can transcend these patterns and focus on an attitude of gratitude and the positive manifestation of your own hopes and dreams.

Self-Righteousness

Self-righteousness is the belief that "I am right and others are wrong," end of story. Self-righteousness is pretty easy to spot from the outside, but it is difficult to identify for anyone who is in the midst of it. Of course, self-righteousness can always be justified by a million excuses, and it is often transmitted to us through the prejudices of previous generations. Self-righteousness is also a big part of our religions, which seem to be so good at pointing fingers. Fundamentalists the world over are entrenched in this particular defense mechanism, whether they be Moslem, Christian, or Jewish. But in the end it all comes down to having to be right. For these people it's "my way, or the highway."

Self-righteous people are rarely open people, even if they appear to be that way in an effort to win you over. Yet they are not really open to considering any way of thinking other than their own. Their need to be right stems from ignorance and arrogance. Ironically, arrogance is the flip side of insecurity, two sides of the same coin. The more pompous a person acts, the more insecure they really are. If they were truly in touch with the spirit of love they would not have to push their beliefs onto others. Then it would not matter whether you believed them or not. They could allow others to have their opinions without making anyone wrong.

The cure for self-righteousness is surrendering your own opinions about a person or situation to the higher wisdom of Creator. After all, no matter how smart you think you are, God is smarter. The Divine has a plan for everyone, even if it's not *your* plan. It may actually be a much bigger plan than we would ever have thought of with our limited human viewpoint. God's timing is not the timing of the world; rather, it is the perfect timing for the unfolding of that particular Soul. Each person is on his own amazing journey; before you criticize a man (or a woman), walk a mile in his shoes. The person we judge is an immortal being just like us, who will ultimately find his own way into the arms of God. Sometimes the real test of our character is whether we can love someone unconditionally, just as they are, and let Spirit do the rest.

What we do know is that we do not have to be in charge of anyone else's life. No matter what our opinions may be, we must remember to "let go and let God," knowing that sometimes our self-righteous judgment actually impedes the other person's spiritual progress, depriving him of the very thing they most need: unconditional love. Remember, fear and judgment constrict, while love and compassion expand, so it is love that will ultimately set us free.

Withdrawal

Of all the defense mechanisms that we might employ in times of danger, withdrawal may be the healthiest. Yet even this defense mechanism can go too far. Certainly there are times when we simply need to reflect on our own feelings, avoid an argument, or replenish our own energies. In such cases withdrawal is not a negative choice. However, as a communication strategy it is not very effective. Sometimes learning to speak your truth is exactly what you need to do, and when withdrawal is used as a mechanism for not engaging in your own life, distancing yourself from loved ones, or not participating in a love relationship you've signed up for, then it doesn't serve you. In this way it can sabotage you just as surely as any of the other defense mechanisms.

What lies at the heart of withdrawal? The fear of being hurt, of course. This is the fear that what we say or think or who we are will be rejected by others, that by emotionally showing up for the events of life, things will become harder instead of easier. So while withdrawal can sometimes be a good thing, when taken to extremes it can amount to withholding one's love and emotional distancing. This can then be used as a way of stealing another person's energy rather than simply regathering your own.

Withdrawal as a defense mechanism usually has its origins in families where the children did not feel safe to express their feelings. These are environments where anything that rocked the boat was unsafe. This mechanism is often adopted by adult children of alcoholics who experienced early life as unpredictable, random, and frightening, never knowing whether the environment of the home was a dangerous place to be. Like small woodland animals who sense when a dangerous predator is close by, withdrawal becomes the instinct for survival.

Once we are adults, however, and can create safety in our own home, then it is time to examine whether this learned behavior still serves us. Have we learned to use words to communicate our feelings? Has our partner learned how to hear us so that we feel safe? Are we emotionally available to ourselves and to others? How can we use our adult skills to speak up without becoming the victim? How can we respond to danger or conflict instead of reacting to it, thus withdrawing into the pain of our childhood again? These lessons can most easily be learned by healing your own inner child. This means that if you did not have a safe environment growing up, you must become the parent to your frightened inner child. There are a number of ways to do this, including "firing" your old parents and creating a new set of parents through alchemical hypnotherapy. These new, loving parents are then built into the foundation of your psyche. In this way you can create the safe, nurturing environment you need to transform the unconscious patterns of childhood trauma into unconditional support.

Today there are excellent techniques available to assist us in changing old patterns that have been passed down to us through countless generations. For the first time in ages we know how to work with the subconscious mind to delete these old tapes and replace them with new ones. The most powerful of these techniques allow us to access the alpha, theta, and delta brainwave states, where our subconscious programs are stored. Through a variety of methods, including hypnotherapy, holographic repatterning, voice dialogue, eye movement desensitization and reprocessing (EMDR),* holotropic breath work,

---

*EMDR, or eye movement desensitization and reprocessing, is a breakthrough therapy for overcoming anxiety, stress, and trauma in a remarkably short period of time. When its results were first published in 1997, it was hailed as the most important method to emerge in psychotherapy in decades. Applicable to survivors of trauma, PTSD, as well as people suffering from phobias and other experience-based disorders, in the past twenty years EMDR therapy has successfully treated psychological problems for millions of sufferers worldwide.

emotional freedom technique, theta healing, inner child work, and many others, we now have many ways to transform these unproductive places where we may have gotten stuck along the way. Realizing that our generation is actively working to change these inherited dysfunctional patterns, we can all remember that this is the alchemical work of each and every one of us.

17

Energy-Stealing Styles and Techniques for Better Communication

What we achieve inwardly will change outer reality.

PLUTARCH

*N*ow let us take a closer look at the energy-stealing styles that people adopt in dysfunctional relationships. These no-win strategies are all about taking energy from others and losing touch with the true source of our personal power, and they are being played out in the world by about 80 percent of people today (especially in politics). No doubt in the course of your life you have found yourself involved in this kind relationship dynamic and not known how to extricate yourself. The three interconnected styles of energy-stealing are the persecutor, the rescuer, and the victim. This PRV triangle not only prevents psychological equality in relationships, but it is a training ground for bullies. It is also perfect for promoting the negative life scripts that many people carry with them from childhood on, perpetuating the illusion of separation found in Adi-karma.

Let's see if any of these statements sound familiar:

I've been shafted. How dare they do that to me!

Why do these things keep happening to me?

Everyone else is better than me. I'll never get that promotion!

I'm not pretty enough to attract a guy! If only I could lose some weight, then I'd get his attention!

Why does everyone else have it easier than I do?

I hardly have time for myself because I just keep giving, giving, giving, but there's no one else to do it but me! No matter how much I do, it's never enough!

If only [fill in the blank] would get his life together, then I'd have time to [write that book, take that vacation, go back to school, nurture myself, etc.].

These statements all reflect some aspect of the PRV triangle.

While many of you may be the natural helpers or healers of others and do not identify with being the victim or the rescuer, the insidious thing is that as long as you play *any* of these positions, then you are still caught up in the PRV drama. The nature of this game is that while many of us have a default position in this cycle, when anyone in the triangle changes roles, the other two positions will change as well. In fact, the game will go on only as long as someone is willing to be the victim. So let's take a quick look at each of these interconnected positions and see if you can recognize yourself or any of the people you know.

The Three Roles of the PVR Triangle

The persecutor blames or criticizes others, convinced that whatever happened to him is someone else's fault. He keeps his victims oppressed, is mobilized by his own anger, and often plays the role of the critical, overbearing parent. This person usually acts in an authoritarian, controlling way and sets strict rules or limits that are not necessary.

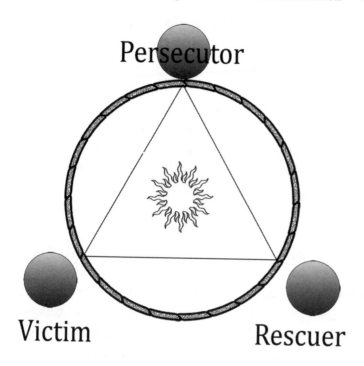

Figure 17.1. The PVR Triangle

The victim is the "poor me" person. She feels shamed, oppressed, or victimized, and powerless to change her situation. This leaves her feeling hopelessly blocked from making any empowering decisions or solving the real problem at hand.

The rescuer believes that it is her job to "save" others. This person may have the best intentions in mind, but in trying to help others she often oversteps her boundaries. Without meaning to, she reminds the person whom she is trying to help (the victim) that he is powerless, which makes him angry. So he lashes out against the rescuer, who then becomes the new victim, while the original victim has transformed into a persecutor.

Most of us are familiar with the persecutor personality because it has been an archetypal figure in movies for generations. In fact, the persecutor has a huge place in history, in famous despots like Hitler, Stalin, Mussolini, Nero, and Caligula. Yet there are many subtle ways in which a small-scale persecutor, a petty tyrant, can show up in your life, as his pattern is less visible to the world at large. A petty tyrant could be your boss, father, mother, brother, or even a friend whose charm can suddenly turn ugly when his or her energy needs are not being met. But these are the obvious examples, as in truth any of us can become a temporary persecutor of those around us simply because we had a bad day. We lash out at those we love, saying things we don't mean, becoming abusive, and causing pain to others. Of course, later we feel terrible about it, but in those moments we have become the petty tyrant who has taken out our frustration on someone else in a very unconstructive way.

Many times when you lash out there's a good reason for why you feel angry, but it rarely has anything to do with what's going on in the present. The anger of the persecutor usually stems from a childhood in which you felt taken advantage of, unappreciated, overextended, or wronged in some way. So this long-simmering anger gets triggered by some stressful event in the present and you explode, and anyone who gets in your way becomes your next target. This creates a chain reaction, such that the person you hurt then lashes out at others, continuing the cycle of reactivity. Let's now take a closer look at the dynamics of these three positions.

PVR Dynamics

Let's call him Ed. Ed is facing a tough day at work because he didn't get enough sleep last night, he's overbudget on a project, his foreman just quit, and he's worried that someone else will get that promotion that he's spent a year working for. So Ed is already feeling like the angry, frustrated victim. He storms into his office, takes a dozen phone calls about the crisis on the job, and then yells at his new assistant. Ed has just become the persecutor. Then his wife, Tracey, calls him, and he yells at her over the phone. He hangs up and immediately feels bad. His new assistant is just trying to learn her job, and Tracey was trying to be romantic. Guilt sets in. After all, he's been a horse's ass, and he knows that yelling is unprofessional. Plus he needs their support to get through the crisis at work. So Ed decides to apologize by bringing his wife flowers when he comes home. He has swung from being the victim to being the persecutor and is now about to play rescuer in an effort to make amends to his wife.

But when Ed gets home that evening, he finds that Tracey is still hurt. She is busy playing the part of the victim. She rebuffs Ed's flowers and a huge argument ensues. Tracey has now become the angry persecutor, and Ed has returned to his role as victim. Angry at being in the victim role again, Ed storms out of the house, slamming the door behind him. He decides to call his buddy Frank for consolation. Maybe he can stay overnight at Frank's pad. Frank is now about to be drawn into the PVR loop.

Frank had a date planned with Jill, a hot redhead he's been trying to woo for months. Meeting Ed means that Frank will have to cut short his plans with Jill. Even though Frank explains the situation to Jill, Jill lets him know that she's miffed, so by the time Ed shows up at his pal's apartment Frank is thoroughly put out. After all, it had taken him two long months to get Jill to even go out with him, and now he's blown it. He may never get another chance. But when Frank sees Ed's downtrodden look he realizes that he is supposed to play the part of the rescuer. Suppressing his anger, Frank lets Ed in. Grateful, Ed follows his buddy inside. Frank throws him some blankets and then goes off to bed in silence, afraid that he'll blow up. Now alone on Frank's couch, Ed feels more like the victim than ever. Not only has he hurt his wife and insulted his assistant, his best friend is now evidently mad at him too.

The next morning Ed apologizes for ruining Frank's date. This stirs Frank up. He is caught between feeling like the rescuer, the victim of Jill's rebuff, and the angry persecutor. After all, this isn't the first time he's had to bail Ed out. Before he realizes it, Frank is reading Ed the riot act. "Grow up, bro! You and Tracey are always arguing. You've got a temper like a steam engine, and you can't expect the whole world to revolve around you!" Of course, later on Frank feels terrible for laying into Ed like this. He calls him at the office and, returning to the role of rescuer, proposes that they get a drink after work. Ed, still in victim mode, shifts into the rescuer as he realizes that he should do something nice for Frank. After all, he did come to his aid. Over beers Ed gives Frank the tickets to the basketball game that he's been saving to share with Tracey. Later he'll feel bad when he returns home because he meant to share those tickets with his wife. Ed then reflects on the fact that everything was his fault to begin with. Once again, he screwed up . . . and feels like he can't do anything right. This is the beginning of another terrible day.

This story is but one of a thousand scenarios that reveal how once we start playing the PVR game we create pain not only for ourselves, but for everyone around us. These various positions are exacerbated by the underlying belief that we are alone, unworthy, or betrayed—reflecting the three lies of Adi-karma discussed in the last chapter. For most of us, the belief in unworthiness lies at the bottom of our patterns, and this belief is held by millions of people everywhere. This is the aspect of the Shadow that whispers to us that if we admit we've made a mistake it will confirm our deepest fears: that there really *is* something wrong with us, that we really *are* unlovable. But these are only the murmurings of the little self.

Of course, as we have already discovered, we are each a spark of God having a human experience in the physical world. And at the heart of this experience is the opportunity to learn a whole series of huge life lessons about love, patience, forgiveness, and compassion— beginning with ourselves and extending to others. While our true Self may be perfect, our human ego self will never be perfect because we live in a world of duality. That is not to say that we cannot strive to do better, to be more conscious, more loving, and more aware; but we cannot beat ourselves up about being human and making mistakes. Perhaps we should say that we are perfect in our imperfection, for that is the way Spirit designed it. Knowing that everyone else is also grappling with these same issues, we can then roll up our sleeves, develop a sense of humor about life, and begin to clear out the blocks to self-awareness.

Four Ways People Steal Each Other's Power

Here I want to address some of the most dysfunctional patterns to be found on our planet. These are four immensely negative communication styles that are basically subsets of the PVR dynamic. These four styles are so toxic, so lethal to true intimacy, that they rob us of energy and true power and fail to give us the very things we most desire—validation, intimacy, and connection. These communication styles are all driven by a lack of love. Those who engage in them learned long ago to substitute getting power for getting love, so their relationships with others have evolved into a game of one-upmanship. This leaves the other person feeling exhausted and drained, while the one who perpetuates any of these roles feels like a happy vampire after a satisfying meal.

The four toxic emotional energy-stealing roles are:

- The intimidator
- The martyr
- The withholder
- The interrogator

Let's take them one at a time.

The Intimidator

The intimidator, or tyrant, is a subset of the persecutor and a familiar figure in the world of politics, found in such characters as Saddam Hussein, Adolf Hitler, and Joseph Stalin. Yet the intimidator, like the persecutor, doesn't have to amass great armies to do his bidding. He can live right there at home with you, as your overbearing father, your dominating husband or wife, the neighborhood bully, or your cruel, obnoxious boss. As an archetype he is a wielder of threats, intimidation, fear, and control. His threats are both obvious and clichéd, like the Mafia don who threatens to exterminate his rivals. He can also function at a more clandestine level, appearing charming and charismatic, yet able to turn on a dime and browbeat his victims into doing as he wishes.

As a personality type the intimidator is often a natural leader who misuses his leadership skills. He is certain that he is right and others are wrong; therefore he views life as black and white, believing that the world is full of either allies or enemies. Those closest to him, including his spouse, children, and employees, must bow before his authority or expect retribution. Since this personality type is not capable of true intimacy because he equates it with vulnerability, the people around him become resources to support his own agenda. They are objects to be controlled, punished, or expelled, either literally or emotionally. When taken to extremes, the intimidator's blind self-righteousness can border on narcissism.

Of all of our four energy-stealing types, the intimidator is the most obvious for he engenders fear in those he targets. Control is his major objective, but beneath his proud, victimizing exterior lies an angry, frightened child whose needs for nurturing, approval, and love were never met. Often raised by perfectionist, disapproving, judgmental, or absent parents who did not have the capacity for unconditional love, the intimidator tries to control the possibilities of ever experiencing such pain again. So he has hardened his heart and lets no one in, always afraid of betrayal. Feeling small, he must compensate by playing big. He must have the best house, the prettiest woman, the most money, or whatever will give him a sense of importance. But since he has never been emotionally supported by those who should have loved and nurtured him, his bravado is only an outlet for his unprocessed rage.

Over time, as the heart closes down, this sense of hurt and impotence is replaced by the rush of power and control, and the awareness of the original hurt becomes sublimated. In his daily life he learns to control his environment with words, bullying threats, and even physical muscle if necessary to ensure that he remains in charge.

The Martyr

The martyr is less easy to spot than the intimidator but is nonetheless a masterful manipulator of other people's energies, using guilt as her primary weapon. In the PVR triangle the martyr occupies the victim position, but with a complicated twist: she has learned that the helplessness of victimization can be used to manipulate and steal other peoples' energy, time, and attention, thus creating dysfunctional relationships built on duty, shame, blame, and resentment rather than on the flow of joyful love. Like the intimidator, the martyr has probably never received the kind of love or attention that she needed as a child, so she is constantly trying to fill up her emotional cup from the energies of others. What she lacks is self-love, although on the surface she may actually appear to be selfish. What she thinks she needs is the attention of others, but because she must guilt-trip those around her into giving it to her, in the end she still feels empty and hollow. Like the archetypal nagging Jewish mother, she captures her victims in a double bind. Her need for attention is couched in such a forlorn, hopeless, guilt-producing way that the unwitting victims usually give in rather than endure the verbal reprisals that will assail them should they resist.

"Norman, why do you never call your mother? I think you've forgotten that I gave you birth, that I wiped your tookus, that I made your lunches every day for that goddamn pissant school . . . So Norman, when you get home from that cushy job where you make more in a month than your father and I ever saw in a year, do me a favor—pick up the phone and call your poor mother before she croaks. Then it will be too late!"

For the martyr the glass is always half-empty, not half-full, so she lives in resentment instead of gratitude. Martyrs are great at telling you about all the many problems in the world, the predicaments with the neighbors, and the many difficulties in their own lives, yet no matter how many problems you might help them solve there are always others arising. No matter what good news is being shared at a party, a holiday gathering, or an anniversary, the martyr is there to remind you of all the people who got sick, the ones who have died, and the bad honeymoon that the neighbor's children went on. They believe that the world is a dangerous place, that no place is safe, and they will gladly bend your ear to share all the many things that are about to go wrong.

At a deeper level, this person feels that she has never been loved. The martyr is convinced that she has given far more than her fair share and has shouldered the burdens of others. She feels that she has not gotten her due, whether it is from her husband, her children, or the world in general. Now it is her turn to receive, even if she has to bleed her friends and relatives dry to do it. Yet because the energy that she captures from others is given grudgingly, and no amount of outside attention is enough to fill that inner void, the martyr will continue to remain emotionally hungry and unfulfilled until she can learn how to reconnect with the true source of love, which is the Divine and her own higher Self.

The Withholder

The withholder wields a far more passive form of energy-stealing than either of the other two types. He is the master of minimalism since he chooses not to communicate his real feelings to others, but would rather use the power of emotional withholding to get what he wants. This is how the withholder's game works: He gets triggered, feeling the shock of hurt, anger, and loss of control registering deep within him. Immediately this trips the defense mechanism of judgment toward the person he believes has wounded him. This real or imagined slight goes all the way back to those secret issues from childhood that made him feel unloved, unnoticed, and out of control. This activates his worry, lack of self-esteem, and the unhealed wounds that made him feel unheard, reminding him of all of his past rejections. These wounds are so deep and personal that he doesn't want anyone to know about them. Often they have to do with shame, disapproval, or humiliation, all of which he will pass on to his unsuspecting victim as this game unfolds.

At this point, the withholder's internal "protector personality" emerges; he battens down the emotional hatches and projects an aura of disapproval to the one who has offended him. Then he waits to see how much energy his victim will give him as that person tries to discover what the heck he has done to trigger such an extreme shutdown. Let's consider an example:

Don and Mary have been married for years, and they are on a road trip together, perhaps a vacation. Don is driving, as usual, because Don likes to be in control. They have just pulled away from a truck stop, where Mary spent money on a new purse. She gets in the car excitedly, showing him her trophy.

"How much did it cost?" Don asks glumly in a carefully modulated voice.

Mary's smile falters a bit since she recognizes "that" tone of voice. "Well, not too much. But look how beautiful it is. Besides, we're on vacation, and I thought I'd splurge a little. It's not only pretty, it's functional too!"

Don makes a small attempt to actually tell her how he feels. "But you already have a purse, Mary. Just because we're on vacation doesn't give you the license to go spending my goddamn money!"

Now Mary is sweating. She knows where this is going. After all, she's been down this road before. She shrinks down in her seat, all of her earlier excitement now gone. "But it didn't cost that much, Don . . ." she trails off. "Only thirty dollars."

Don gives her a stern look of disapproval and then silently turns back to the road. The wall between them goes up. Mary can almost feel the temperature dropping in the car. She realizes that she has overstepped an invisible, unspoken boundary. She has made Don angry, and he's not going to tell her why her buying the purse was such a crime. She felt so innocent and free and now she feels like a criminal. Through the silence her mind begins churning furiously, and she returns to that powerless place of her childhood. Her mind goes into overdrive trying to figure out what she has done wrong. *He earns the money*, she thinks, *so he gets to decide how it will be spent. I have no real authority here. I'm not really his equal. I'm not allowed to make my own decisions . . .* She is back to feeling like a child, trying to get her father's approval. "Honey . . . don't be mad," she finally whispers.

"I'm not mad," he lies, then stares silently at the road for the next ten minutes.

Mary can feel the freeze-out. This was supposed to be a vacation, something fun, but now she wants to disappear. She makes one last effort, scooting a little closer to him in the car. "I got something for you at the truck stop, too," she offers. Don doesn't speak. "Do you want to see it?" He shrugs, never taking his eyes off the road. She pulls out some bubblegum. "It's your favorite kind. Do you want some?"

"No," he says with a trace of disappointment.

"You don't even want to try it?" He shakes his head silently. Their stalemate goes on. After a few minutes, Mary turns on the radio. *Maybe music will break his silence. After all, we were having such a nice time . . .* Don reaches over and turns the music off, plunging them back into the same exhausting silence. He throws Mary another disapproving look. It is clear that he is punishing her.

You can see how this situation only goes from bad to worse, because now Don has to defend his bad mood. In truth this was just a small hiccup, but he has made a molehill into a mountain, and he must now justify his extreme reaction. As the morning goes on, Don becomes increasingly stressed out, cursing at drivers who pull out in front of him, complaining about the price of gasoline, and angry that the air conditioning is not working as well as it could be. This is a no-win situation for both parties. Mary, whose joy and zest for life flew out the window, is now completely miserable. The best she can hope for is to make it to the motel, be as invisible as possible, and let Don sleep off his bad mood with the help of a couple of beers. Then perhaps she can sneak out of the room, go to the swimming pool alone, and have a few minutes of peace by herself. Some vacation, right?

Millions of people live like this all over the world, using a combination of emotional withholding, anger, and passive-aggressive punishment to steal each others' power. In each of these relationship styles you will notice that the person who perpetrates the problem has convinced himself that he is the victim, and he uses this identification with victimhood to justify his emotional bad behavior. In truth, while he may have originally been the victim of a difficult upbringing or emotionally abusive parents, now he is the one perpetuating the dysfunctional patterns that have become engrained since childhood.

The Interrogator

The interrogator is the most subtle and insidious of all the energy stealers, for his methods are initially concealed under a cloak of charm. The interrogator has learned to play a game of bait and switch, luring his unsuspecting victim into a trap that is not only difficult to spot on the front end, but is equally difficult to address afterward in a straightforward manner because of the interrogator's ability to twist the meaning of virtually any conversation. This approach is especially suited to highly intelligent people, and sociopaths can usually play with the skill of a chess master.

Here's how it goes: In an attitude of sharing, the interrogator asks his prospective victim to open up emotionally. This sharing can be about any subject, from a hiccup in the workplace to some deeper emotional wound from the past. This sharing is done with a feeling of genuine sympathy and interest and a series of seemingly well-intentioned questions. This creates an atmosphere of trust and confidentiality. During this exchange, the interrogator appears to be the new "best friend" or confidant, yet is, in reality, gathering information about the other person's actions, feelings, and motivations. Then, at some point, whether it is during the first, second, or even third exchange, the interrogator switches tactics after gaining his target's trust. This emotional shift can be subtle or obvious. The unsuspecting person, who up until this point believes that there is trust forming between two like-minded friends, is taken completely off-guard, not seeing this turnaround coming until it's too late. Then he feels like he's just been socked in the stomach. Surely he cannot have heard the interrogator correctly! Did his new best friend mean to call him a coward, a jerk, an idiot? Did those words really come out of the interrogator's mouth? When this happens, the unwitting victim may not even be able to respond. Suddenly, trust is gone, and this new person to whom he has just confided the most important details of his life has just become his enemy. Furthermore, now this adversary has knowledge of the target's most vulnerable doubts, fears, and behaviors. This has all the hallmarks of a surprise attack. If the stunned target can even gather his wits enough to respond, the interrogator is still several steps ahead, using the element of surprise, criticism, manipulation, and superiority to establish control. There is a brilliant arrogance to this type of energy-stealing, for it clearly establishes the interrogator as being "right" and the target as being "wrong." Let's look at an example:

Tom is a brilliant manager of a newly formed institute of professional trainers. He has used his charisma to convince his superiors that he is the man for the job. Yet since his position is maintained by a series of political favors to upper-level colleagues, his priorities are already divided. To succeed as the institute manager he must get his staff to do the institute's work, but to advance politically he must continue to curry favor with his superiors. So he decides to do favors for his superiors by lending out members of his staff from time to time (after all, they are *his* resources!). In this way Tom hopes to ensure that his superiors will stay indebted to him so he can parlay this into future leverage.

At the institute, however, Tom has an interrogator style. This means that when he opens his weekly staff meetings and presents problems for feedback, he doesn't really want to hear what's wrong; all he wants to hear is that things are running smoothly with the timetable he has already set, a timetable based entirely on his own goals and desire to impress his bosses rather than on the actual amount of time it takes for the staff to do the tasks at hand. So when his staff gives him feedback about their time constraints and compromised resources, Tom is displeased. After all, his staff is only a stepping-stone to his true objectives: money, power, and looking good in the eyes of his superiors. Tom believes their feedback is evidence of a conspiracy against him. He is convinced that he is not being supported, so he begins to mentally target certain staff members who speak up at the meetings. If someone is not onboard with his objectives, then she is "the enemy." As his demands become more and more unrealistic, any staff member who voices concern is plotting against him. They are saboteurs who must be talking behind his back. Now Tom must find a way to get rid of them so he can come out looking like the good guy. Thus his objective now becomes how to use his considerable mental powers to draw his staff members out emotionally, trap them in wrongdoings, and then fire them. If Tom cannot succeed in this, then he must make them so miserable that they will want to quit. He can do this by intimidating them in front of others, casting dispersions on their character, or demoting them to menial tasks. If any of these things are directly addressed by the staff, then Tom will simply resort to his initial statement about timetables and failing to live up to the job they were hired for.

This is a no-win situation for everyone, since there is no actual listening going on here. One person's unprocessed emotional issues have gotten in the way of the rest of the group's functioning because Tom's real agenda has nothing to do with the goals of the institute, but rather the promotion of his own personal ambition.

Let's look at another example. Paul and June met on an online dating site. Her online profile and picture were clear, but while Paul's profile sounded great to June, his picture was blurry. Paul's requests for more photographs of June had her e-mailing a few more shots of herself, which Paul warmly responded to. Based on this, he began getting more suggestive in their conversations on the phone at night. June started to get concerned about this since they still hadn't met. She asked Paul for better photographs of himself, hoping to get clear as to whether she was even attracted to him, but Paul cited various technical difficulties. The only photos he sent were badly taken or shot at a distance. When June asked him again for pictures, Paul accused her of being vain and superficial.

"Fine," she said, "forget the pictures. Let's meet in person instead."

At first Paul seemed pleased, but when the logistics of planning the meeting had to be worked out, Paul ended the conversation by saying that June was not making time for him and was choosing her work over her personal relationships. "If you're too shallow to know a good thing when you see it," he told her, "I won't bother calling you again."

After Paul hangs up on her, June is devastated. After all, she had spent the last three months of her life talking to this guy on the phone thinking he was a good prospect. What just happened? What had she done wrong?

This exchange illustrates the interrogator style: because of Paul's underlying insecurity he couldn't respond to June's request or her concerns in a balanced adult way. His fear of rejection was projected onto her with the belief that if she met him, she would not want him. If instead Paul had actually heard that she was really saying "I'm trusting my heart to you, and I need to be reassured," and responded appropriately, then June would have felt supported by feeling like he had heard her. Instead, Paul lashed out, using all the emotional leverage he had accumulated with her thus far to punish her by withdrawing his affection and approval.

This is the classic intimidator at work in a bait-and-switch drama.

The relationship died before it even got off the ground. This kind of "blame" dynamic is prevalent in all kinds of relationships. This kind of verbal assault can cause even the most trusting person to back away from any further involvement because it delivers the message that it is not safe to be spontaneously trusting or authentically yourself around the intimidator.

There are energy thieves who have learned to play the game in two, three, or even four negative relationship styles. This means that the person might start out as an interrogator, then switch to becoming the enraged intimidator, then later become the withdrawn martyr. This is crazy-making at its worst. Changing styles like this can happen when the targeted person becomes wise to a particular pattern and calls the manipulator on it. The energy vampire will then change the game in midstream, throwing his target off-balance again. This is so exhausting that after a while any rational person begins to feel slightly insane. If you are caught up in this kind of situation you are always walking on eggshells, not knowing how or why that tender, trusting moment between you and the other person will suddenly vanish, to be replaced by something ugly and emotionally toxic.

Recognizing the Core Wound

The central issue in all of these negative defense mechanisms is always related to the original wound the person still carries. This core wound stems from early childhood, from a lack of love, self-esteem, forgiveness, and acceptance from the person's family of origin. This may have happened because of an unstable or unavailable parent, an abusive household, or growing up in a judgmental, perfectionist family where approval was a substitute for love. Suffice it to say that we usually don't come up with these negative relationship styles on our own; they are almost always learned behaviors.

Breaking old patterns and creating new, healthy ones is always a challenge but is far better than remaining stuck in old wounds that seem to repeat again and again in life. While it may be impossible to directly address an energy manipulator about his patterns or point out how he is contributing to his own misery, self-awareness is always a good first step. Most of us have not been taught that our thoughts, actions, and feelings are what create the circumstances of our lives, or that what we most fear will often manifest in order for us to heal it. This means that until we change our core beliefs, we will continually draw to us the things that we most fear: abandonment, disapproval, and the lack of true intimacy, friendship, or love. So if you or anyone you know finds themselves falling into these old, tired patterns, you might need the help of a professional to uncover how they first developed, how to heal these childhood wounds, and how to create relationships in which you get the love that we each so richly deserve. In a marriage or long-term relationship sometimes two people must separate in order to break the cycle of an unhealthy dynamic, especially if it has been in place for a while. This allows both parties enough space to get some perspective, reevaluate personal needs, and do the needed inner work.

So once we are aware that we are caught up in a negative relationship dynamic, how do we break out of it? There are four steps: awareness, assessment, acknowledgement, and change. First, we must become aware that we have fallen into a negative pattern, realizing that it is just one of the many ego traps that plague us in the third dimension. The little self is always caught up in duality, swinging back and forth between feeling less-than someone else, or greater-than someone else. *Am I smart enough? Pretty enough? Strong enough? Fast enough?* These programs are constantly running in the background, so it is easy to be sucked into these relationship dramas.

Next, we must assess where this pattern has come from and how it is affecting our life today. This means to recognize that in all situations we are all learning about the right use of will. Understanding that the lack of love and connection with Source leads to the wrong use of power, we now have a *choice* as to how we act in any situation. Power is never a worthy substitute for love, for it will never make us happy. Assessing your actions and reactions with this kind of objectivity will help you see the negative relationship dynamics for what they really are, so that you can then choose to break those unproductive dynamics.

The third step is acknowledgement—to yourself and to the other people involved—of what is really going on in your life. Many times we fail to let people know what we are really feeling because we fear it makes us vulnerable. But acknowledging the truth to a trustworthy friend or therapist, or to the people you wronged, is the first step in healing your relationship dynamics.

Finally the last step is change. This means a change in your thinking, beliefs, and actions that will allow you to receive the love you most desire. While awareness, assessment, and acknowledgment come first, now you must put your realizations into action. This means changing the old belief systems of your original programming. Such change is not easy, but it is possible. This is where emotional healing comes in. By choosing a healer, therapist, or outside support system that can help you to heal and reframe these original beliefs, you can create a powerful change in your life.

As you go through this process, take time to notice which of these negative patterns you fall into. This way when the ego begins to pull you back into these patterns, your higher Self can catch you. Self-awareness and taking personal responsibility are the only ways to change these scenarios. By taking responsibility for our own part in the drama, being willing to apologize when we mess up, and really listening to the other person, we can then choose to act instead of react. We can also discover our own "hot buttons" and heal them so that we no longer feel so triggered. Finally, by releasing these old patterns, we will cease to attract the kind of people who want to play these games, freeing ourselves from these kinds of no-win situations.

In brief, here are three quick remedies that can help for each of the PVR positions:

The remedy for the persecutor is to define and clear the structural agreements between you and the other person so that it's clear what everyone's responsibilities are in the relationship, whether it is work-related or personal. That way there is no reason for blame. This can help redefine relationships between friends, workmates, parents, lovers, spouses, or children, allowing each person to be treated with respect and feel valued.

Some healthy boundaries and rules must be set and agreed to. This way each person takes responsibility for what he has consented to, and the persecutor is released from having to be the critical parent or watchdog.

The remedy for the victim is to stop feeling sorry for yourself and powerless, and get on with solving the problem at hand. Everyone has moments of uncertainty and fear, but mobilizing yourself into constructive, logical steps of action will empower you to realize that you can take control of your own life and feel good about your choices. Try to give yourself credit for the little victories, for this builds confidence and self-esteem. Refuse to let anyone take this from you, and remember that action and self-respect build character and strength.

The remedy for the rescuer is to choose to engage only in healthy, clear nurturing of those you love and always remember not to overstep your boundaries and thereby disempower the very person you are trying to help. Check in. See what *she* wants to do. Make a plan together and let *her* do the part of it that will build her own self-confidence. This kind of healthy support will really be appreciated by the other person. When you can assist someone in figuring out the best course of action for her to take, then she will not need to be rescued nearly as often, and you will not wind up feeling like you have overextended yourself.

Six Steps That Heal the PVR Cycle*

1. Identify the PVR pattern and your role in it.
2. Decide to break the cycle and do something different.
3. Make sure that both parties are actually hearing each other's thoughts and feelings.
4. Hire a professional therapist trained in identifying the underlying patterns of emotional disconnection from the original source of love (i.e., mother, father, etc.). These are your

---

*There are several great sources for information on the PVR triangle, including *Scripts People Live By*, by Claude Steiner; *Born to Win*, by Muriel James; and *Talking to My Selves: Getting to Know Your Voices in Your Head*, by Debbie Unterman.

wounding patterns that were created in childhood, which you have unconsciously dragged into your adult life. Just realize that there is nothing shameful about getting help. Everyone needs help sometime in their life. Some people just don't know it or they don't have the courage to ask for it. Choose a therapist trained in understanding the dynamics of the PVR triangle, and the many subpersonalities that lie at the base of our lives.

5. Know that while you can work on yourself, you cannot do the inner work for someone else. Ultimately we must all do our own healing work.

6. Be willing to consciously reshape your responses to old triggers. This means learning what the positive emotional response is and replacing the negative response with a new one.

Healing the Inner Family

If you notice that you continue to attract PVR patterns in your life, it may be that you were programmed from an early age with this dynamic. These patterns often stem from negative dynamics we experienced in early childhood, when we were the victim of one of our parents, while the other parent ran to the rescue. Classically the father is the persecutor, while the mother is the rescuer. However I have worked with clients where these roles were completely reversed. The secret to breaking this cycle of programming lies in changing the subconscious script that you have been imprinted with. This repeating pattern lies in a deeper level of the mind, usually stored in the alpha and theta memory sections. So in order to change this subconscious programming, we must enter into a deeper state of consciousness through hypnosis and rewrite it. During this profound process we transform our old dysfunctional family script by establishing an Inner Family that loves, supports, and nurtures us.

In some cases this means actually "firing" your original parents, who may have done the best they could at the time, but who will never be able to give you the understanding that you need in life. While we continue to love our parents, and even interact with them, by establishing a deep powerful base of secure nurturance and well-being, we can completely transform our inner landscape, heal our past, and ultimately change our future. Then the persecutor becomes the protector; the rescuer transforms into the nurturer, and the wounded child has the safe, magical haven that he or she was always meant to have.[1] This is alchemical mastery at the deepest level.

Three Techniques for Better Communication

While it is clear that none of us want to be burdened by negative dynamics in relationships, even the best people experience communication challenges from time to time. The following three communication techniques build intimacy, self-awareness, and flow. Each technique focuses on better listening between partners, which in turn creates intimacy and understanding. I have personally used all three of these processes in my own relationships and also with clients, and they really work!

The Container Process

First, two people should agree that there is a problem. Then decide that you and your partner will set aside time to discuss it. Issues between people can often escalate into arguments because one or both parties do not feel they are completely heard. So make sure that you have at least an hour or more to talk without any interruptions. Agree on the rules of listening and talking before you even begin.

Next you are going to create a "container" for one of the two of you to get a chance to express yourself without interruptions. A container is a space that one person holds so that the other person can speak without being interrupted. The person holding the container merely needs to be present—to listen and most of all, *not react*. The other person will do *all the talking*. Then the two of you will switch places. First, decide who wants to speak first. Usually this is the person who has the most emotional charge. Begin by asking your partner how much time he thinks he will need. Maybe he will think he only needs ten or fifteen minutes, but often, it will be twenty or even thirty minutes, depending on how charged the issue is. If you have not stayed clear with your issues in the past, you may need more time. If what your partner really needs is twenty minutes, that's okay, but when the agreed-on fifteen-minute time limit is up you can hold up a sign or gently stop her and say, "Okay, that's fifteen minutes. Do you need another five or ten minutes to finish up?" Then she can say yes or no.

While there are some simple but important rules to this process, remember that nothing is set in stone and that the time is flexible. If your partner really needs more time, that's fine, but that means you will have an equal amount of time once you switch places. It is very important in this process that both parties *really* listen to each other. Part of resolving an issue comes from each person knowing that he or she is fully heard, even if you and your partner have to go back and forth several times. You will discover that after the first go-round, the rounds become shorter, but again, decide on the length of time before you start, so that stopping is not an arbitrary choice.

Then, after your partner has spoken, you will switch places. Now the first person holds the energetic container as the listener for his or her partner. In this way there is a specific amount of time when there are no interruptions. Try to speak from a nonaccusatory place if at all possible, using "I think" or "I feel" statements. For example, "I feel that our love life is in the toilet." "I feel undesirable because you never want to have sex anymore." "I feel overwhelmed at work, confused about where we are going in this relationship, or uncertain what you want from me." You get the picture.

By going back and forth like this, the stress levels will go down, and often by the third round the real issue will begin to surface. Many times it takes this kind of verbal stream of consciousness for us to discover the real issues that are bothering us behind what we *think* we are upset about.

The Question Process

This technique is like the container process except that person A decides on a question that she wants person B to ask her. For example:

"Why are you feeling so angry?" or "What is it that you really want?" or "Why aren't you happy?" Then, with an attitude of total receptivity, person B will ask person A the question she has chosen, allowing her to answer it without interruption. This way they can answer spontaneously. When person A gets to a stopping point or a pause, person B can simply say, "Thank you for sharing." Then she repeats the question again, each time allowing person A to go deeper and deeper into her feelings.

Let's take an example: Teresa tells Bob that she wants him to ask her, "Why are you so upset?" Sitting opposite her, Bob asks, "Teresa, why are you so upset?" Don't try to paraphrase; ask the question exactly as she wants it asked. Teresa immediately launches into explaining why she has had such a terrible day. For the next five minutes she rambles on about missing an appointment, her frustration with her computer, and how she had a flat tire coming home from work. Finally, she comes to a pause.

Now Bob's job is not to analyze, fix, or give any opinions. His only job is to hold the container for her to express herself. Once more he asks, "Teresa, why are you so upset?" Teresa gives a big sigh. After all, it felt really good to just vent. "Well . . ." she begins. This time she talks about why she doesn't like her job, how she feels creatively stifled, and how the entire company has changed management teams and is not really being run correctly.

When she pauses again, Bob says, "Thank you for sharing." Then, once again he asks, "So Teresa, why are you so upset?" This time she sits back, digging deeper. Tears catch in her throat. She begins to explain that she really feels like she is at a dead end, that the job she is doing is making her miserable, that what she really wanted to be was an artist, and that she realizes she became an accountant because her parents wanted her to. Now she wishes she could go back in time and change things. As we can see, we are finally getting to the root of the problem.

Bob nods sympathetically, taking her hands. "Hmm . . . I really hear you. Thanks for sharing." After a long pause, once again he asks even more sympathetically than before, because he realizes that this is the real reason she has been so irritable for the past six months, "So, Honey, what's really making you feel so upset at this moment?"

Teresa can barely say it. "I think I want to quit my job. But I'm afraid that if I do we won't have enough money. I'm scared that if I tell you what I want, you'll just get mad that I want to go back to school and change professions." So now we can see that everything has come full circle. Bob realizes why Teresa has been taking her frustrations out on him, why their sex life has gone down the toilet, and why she is always bitching about the bills and her job. Teresa has also discovered the real reason why she has been so distant. In fact, until she said it, she hadn't realized that what she was lacking was creativity and having fun with her job. They have both connected the dots.

"Thank you for sharing, sweetheart." Bob gives a long pause while they look at each other, realizing how much they love each other. "Do you feel complete, or would you like me to ask you another question?"

At this point Teresa says, wiping her tears, "No, I feel complete. It's enough for now." Bob can now hug her and say, "Let's just think about this. Maybe we can figure out a way to make it work, but let's sit with it a day or two." So now, you've just completed the session, unless of course Bob would like to have a turn.

But maybe instead Teresa says, "I'd like you to ask me what I really want to be doing with my life." In which case, Bob can ask her that question, and they can both discover what happens. After all, this is a free association, like thinking out loud, and Teresa is just discovering what she really feels. Maybe she says, "I don't know what I want to do . . . something fun . . . something creative . . . something different."

Bob answers, "Thank you for sharing. Honey, what do you really want to be doing with your life?" This time Teresa is even more in touch with her feelings. "I don't know, but I do know that I want to be with you, whatever it is." As each one of these rounds progresses, notice that the frustration that Teresa had has dropped to nothing. She has moved from chaotic emotions, to cooler thinking, to deeper feeling, and finally to a place of self-connection. In the process she is able to move into a deeper love for Bob because he is really listening to her. Through conscious listening, he is helping her to figure out her own wants and needs.

The Reflective Listening Process

This technique is similar to the others in that a container is established for speaking and listening. However, in this method person A will only speak for a minute. Then person B will mirror back exactly what was said. This way person A knows that person B has actually heard him. If he did not hear person A correctly, then person A will have a chance to correct person B's misperception. Let's consider a hypothetical scenario:

Helen says to Josh, "I guess the reason why I'm feeling so angry is because you said you were going to take out the garbage, and sometimes I just feel like I am doing everything around here. I work, just like you do. I take care of the kids, just like you do. Plus I cook and clean, and now, when I ask the simplest thing, like taking out the garbage, you can't even do that!"

Josh nods, holding up his hand to indicate that's all he can hear from her and remember right now. Then he says, "What I hear you saying is that you are very frustrated with me. You feel like I should have taken out the garbage, and because I didn't, you're mad."

Helen nods. Maybe that's all Josh heard, since he is focused on hearing how she is being critical of him. "Go on," she encourages him.

Josh sighs. "You feel like you do more around the house than I do. I mean, we both work, we both take care of the kids, but you feel like you do all the cooking and cleaning, and so it's not fair. Is that right?"

Helen nods, feeling better. He *has* heard her. She sees that he didn't miss this essential point about fairness. "Yeah, can I go on?" Helen asks. Josh nods. "I just hate getting so angry with you. The truth is, I really look forward to seeing you at the end of the day. It's just that I feel overwhelmed with my new boss and my schedule, and I need some help around here."

Josh signals that he needs her to stop. "Okay, what I heard you saying is that you really do want to see me at night. You don't like being mad at me. But you're feeling . . . overwhelmed? I mean, you're saying that your new boss is being so demanding that you don't have time to do everything."

She gives him a little smile. "Yeah, and I need some help. I mean, it doesn't have to be you. We could hire a maid once a week, or twice a month. Even that would help."

Josh is getting it now. "Okay, you're saying that it's not so much me, but that you need some kind of help with the housework. Is that right?" Helen nods. "And if we could hire a maid once a week, that would take care of all this pressure, right?" Helen nods again. Her heart opens up. *He heard me!*

"I know that it's an added expense," Helen says. "Maybe we could just try having a maid for two months and see it if would work. If you can come up with a better solution, I'm open. I just think I need some extra help right now, and I'd rather spend my time going to the movies with you, or having dinner, or taking a bubble bath, rather than yelling at you about the stupid garbage."

Josh laughs. He likes that idea. In fact, he can think of some other fun things he'd like to do with Helen if he could get her in a better mood. "Okay, you're saying that if we hired this maid for a couple of months, you might be more inclined to go out and play, or to have some intimate time in bed with me. Is that right?"

Helen grins. "Exactly!"

You can see how this back-and-forth style of communication can quickly get to the root of a problem and help both people reach a solution, while making sure that there are no misunderstandings along the way. The key to this process is to not be defensive. Often the very thing we think we are upset about is really just concealing deeper issues that we ourselves may not be in touch with. Being willing to be vulnerable, to go a little deeper each time, means that you will get to the heart of a problem quicker. And to be vulnerable, you need to know that you can trust your partner to not blow up in your face or make you wrong for your feelings. By truly hearing what another person is feeling and not invalidating them, we gain genuine insights into what will make our own lives more harmonious and happy.

We hope that you will try some of these techniques in your own relationships, for these approaches are far healthier than the negative patterns that have only brought us pain, misunderstanding, and misery. These techniques take a little effort and some time, but they deliver a huge win in terms of the kind of true intimacy that is needed to have a healthy relationship.

18

Life Lessons
in the Course Curriculum

Every soul comes into this world strengthened by the victories and weakened by the defeats of its previous life.

ORIGEN

By now we have taken a look at the very nature of the Soul itself, the stages of its evolution, and some of the ways in which our little self gets trapped in the patterns of duality, taking us down a rabbit's hole that keeps us feeling separate from our intrinsic nature, which is the Divine. So let us now examine some of the lessons that the Soul must master over the course of its long journey. Each lifetime contains valuable lessons unique to the individual, yet in truth we must all ultimately master every one of the important lessons in life, whether in this lifetime or another. The question is always this: How can we best use the life that has been given to us?

Here are some of the most important life lessons that I have discovered over the course of thousands of readings. Take a look at table 18.1 on the facing page and see which themes seem to be playing out in your life today. Because self-realization is a constantly evolving process, all of us are somewhere on the continuum between "just beginning," "crisis," and "mastery." There are check boxes beside each virtue so that you can do an honest evaluation for yourself. Remember, there's no one judging you but yourself. In other words, this is between you and your higher Self. Also, try to bear in mind that whatever we resist learning in this life will persist, continuing to present itself as a lesson again and again, in this or future lifetimes, until we have found a way to embrace and make peace with it.

TABLE 18.1. DISCOVERING YOUR LIFE LESSONS

Place a check mark where you are on the scale for each value.

Quality	Just Beginning	In Process	Full Crisis	Continued Practice	Already Mastered
Truth					
Honor					
Kindness					
Patience					
Speaking up					
Listening					
Humility					
Selflessness					
Gratitude					
Generosity					
Allowing					
Sharing					
Creative self-expression					
Compassion					
Devotion					
Nonjudgment					
Honesty					
Leadership					
Discipline					
Responsibility					

Quality	Just Beginning	In Process	Full Crisis	Continued Practice	Already Mastered
Independence					
Interdependence					
Commitment					
Team-building					
Respect					
Endurance					
Right use of power					
Focus					
Communication					
Multitasking					
Giving					
Receiving					
Letting go					
Surrender					
Detachment					
Courage					
Faith					
Love					
Forgiveness					
Balance					
Healthy boundaries					
Strength					
Imagination					
Service					
Spiritual connection					
Inner peace					
Love of self					
Love of others					
Healing self					
Healing others					
Male-female integration					

Quality	Just Beginning	In Process	Full Crisis	Continued Practice	Already Mastered
Wisdom					
Connection with nature					
Awakening your spiritual gifts					

Soul Themes

When a person's life is considered as a whole, there are powerful themes that emerge. Some themes may be about learning to balance one's masculine and feminine energies, particularly because these aspects have been so out of balance in the world at large. Earlier generations of men were not taught that it was okay to express sensitivity and emotions, considered attributes of the (feminine) right side of the brain. Likewise, countless generations of women have been oppressed by this same patriarchy and prevented from creatively expressing their power (except in the household), creating a huge imbalance in the world today. As a result we have shut down many of our innate spiritual abilities and our connection with the heartbeat of the cosmos. So in our era, many people are still grappling with finding this balance within themselves, as well as in their personal relationships.

In addition, this authoritarian patriarchal mentality has played out in our approach to religion, in the workplace, in our disregard for the Earth, in our cruelty to animals, and in our dualistic system of medicine that does not see the body, mind, and spirit as a related whole. Another way this imbalance is seen is in the PVR triangle, discussed in the last chapter. The negative aspect of the female plays out as the victim, while the negative male aspect is seen as the persecutor, regardless of what gender body we are in. We can see these destructive dynamics expressed in personal and romantic relationships as people struggle to redefine how to rebalance their yin and yang energies. Yet things are getting better with each generation, not only because we are finally coming around to acknowledging that "women's rights are human rights," but because women are stepping more fully into their own creative power, and men are being encouraged to feel, examine, and express their emotions.

Soul themes run on autopilot in the background of our lives. Some themes appear small, while others are epic. Some lives seem to be about creating a family, fitting into a community, and the daily sacrifices required to raise an emotionally healthy child. While these lifetimes might seem unexceptional on the surface, they can be big in terms of long-term rewards. Through the experience of learning intimacy, communication, and doing for others, the Soul learns patience, humility, listening, compromise, forbearance, prioritizing goals, and unconditional love. Life is in the details. In our daily interactions we get to apply these spiritual principles at a practical level and test the limits of how these virtues have grown in us. So no life is average. Each lifetime is extraordinary, provided the Soul uses it in the proper way.

When we look around us, it is clear that some people's themes center around learning the lessons of faith, integrity, honesty, courage, or humility. These lifetimes are full of challenges designed to test how well each one of us can embody these spiritual values. There are also the great heroic lifetimes, like those of soldiers who risk their lives on the frontlines of danger. These themes are clearly about bravery, strength, camaraderie, and vigilance. Yet even these lifetimes have a million small lessons contained within them: patience, tolerance, interdependence, solitude, discipline, teamwork, and strategy.

Some people's lifetimes are more about learning how to express themselves creatively, either through painting, drawing, writing, singing, music, dance, or theater. These lives teach us to listen to the Divine, follow our dreams, hold a vision, and develop the single-mindedness of purpose to manifest that dream into form. And if that discipline turns into success, then to remember not to be carried away by fortune, fame, ego, or pride. Other themes are about overcoming generational patterns of bigotry, prejudice, ignorance, and fear that has plagued our world for millennia and is seen in discrimination based on race, nationality, gender, or sexual orientation. Such blind judgment is really based on an illusion, of course, since each one of us incarnates in many different forms over the course of our Soul's long evolutionary arc. But since these themes are also global, the transformation of intolerance is a personal issue that also has a major impact on our planet.

Choosing the New Life

Before we incarnate in every lifetime we meet with our own Council of Elders, beings who have overseen our spiritual development for many lifetimes. Along with our personal spirit guides, this group of advanced Souls, sometimes called the Lords of Karma or Council of Light, helps us to review our strengths and weaknesses and establish objectives for the upcoming life. Then we enter the Ring of Destiny and select the life we wish to live, based on the goals for that particular incarnation. We decide on the environment, the family, the body, the soul agreements with others, and the challenges we will face, all designed to build our character, overcome a past weakness, atone for unresolved karma, or carry out our greater mission. The masters tell us that in each new life we acquire a new mental and astral body that springs from the seeds of our past accomplishments and from the "germs" of our previous thoughts and emotions that carry over from lifetime to lifetime. Theosophist Alice Bailey explains this well:

> When the man . . . has thus clothed himself with a new body for his coming life on the lower mental levels, he proceeds, by vivifying the astral germs, to provide himself with an astral body for his life on the astral plane. This, again, exactly represents his desire-nature, faithfully reproducing the qualities he evolved in the past. . . . Thus the man stands, fully equipped for his next incarnation, the only memory of the events of his past being in the causal body, in his own enduring form, the one body that passes on from life to life . . .
>
> In past lives he [the Soul] had made ties with, contracted liabilities towards, other human beings, and some of these will partly determine his place of birth and his family. He has been a source of happiness or of unhappiness to others; this is a factor in determining the conditions of his coming life. His desire nature is well-disciplined, or unregulated and riotous; this will be taken into

account in the physical heredity of the new body. He had cultivated certain mental powers such at the artistic; this must be considered, as here again physical heredity is an important factor where delicacy of nervous organization and tactile sensibilities are required. And so on, in endless variety . . .

All this is done by certain mighty spiritual Intelligences, often spoke of as the Lords of Karma, because it is their function to superintend the working out of causes continually set going by thoughts, desires, and actions. They hold the threads of destiny which each man has woven, and guide the reincarnating man to the environment determined by his past, unconsciously self-chosen through his past life.

The race, the nation, the family, being thus determined, what may be called the mold of the physical body—suitable for the expression of the man's qualities, and for the working out of the causes he has set going—is given by these great Ones [the Lords of Karma], and the new etheric double [that surrounds the physical body], a copy of this is built within the mother's womb by the agency of an elemental, the thought of the Karmic Lords being its motive power.[1]

Thus we find that the choice of the body, mind, and emotional temperament we recieve in each new lifetime is based on the desires, thoughts, and accomplishments of past lifetimes, which helps to build a continuity between life lessons. This slow, gradual accumulation of experiences leads to wisdom, creating a powerful foundation for ultimate mastery. Likewise, the physical body that starts anew in every lifetime, but the talents, gifts, and affinities we have developed through time come with us. This allows the Soul to begin developing strong Soul themes that follow us from life to life. When we look around us we find people who are naturally gifted as mechanics, engineers, or builders; this is because they have acquired these practical abilities over lifetimes. Others are gifted musicians, singers, writers, teachers, or playwrights and show genius from an early age, like Mozart, the brilliant five-year-old prodigy who obviously spent many lifetimes developing his talent. This is also true of the subtle spiritual gifts of clairvoyance, clairsentience, clairaudience, telepathy, healing, and dream interpretation. While the propensity for a talent can certainly be inherited from one's family line, natural levels of talent really emerge as the result of lifetimes of collective experience in a given field. Thus we should never be jealous of another person's talent or success, for he has earned those abilities through many lifetimes of focused effort.

In the many thousands of Soul readings that I have done, I find that many Souls have spiritual themes that I would call their "strong suits." One person's themes may involve justice or freedom, leading her to choose lifetimes as a diplomat, journalist, political activist, statesman, or freedom fighter. Another person may develop skills in governance or warfare that can be used in this lifetime to become a fireman, policeman, National Guardsman, or city council member. Sometimes two or more of these themes can work together. For example, teaching and the arts, or teaching and healing are skill sets that work well in tandem. A person may be focused on upholding justice or peace, so she may have lifetimes as a diplomat, a therapist, a mediator, a judge, a lawyer, a psychologist, or a translator. A person who is interested in working with his hands may become a blacksmith, a farmer, an auto mechanic, a horse trainer, a cabinetmaker, a sculptor, a potter, a stonemason, a steelworker, a builder, or an engineer. A Soul that is focused on communication may incarnate as a writer, an editor, a publisher, a reporter, a spokesperson, a mediator, a translator, a public speaker, a radio host, a disc jockey, a scriptwriter, or a web designer. A Soul pursuing spirituality may incarnate as a preacher, a priest, a therapist, a healer, a teacher, a writer, a mediator, a nun, a Peace Corps worker, an inspirational singer, a philosopher, or a history professor. A Soul focused on healing may incarnate as a doctor, a nurse, an acupuncturist, a naturopath, a qigong teacher, a nutritionist, an organic farmer, the owner of a health-food store, a physical therapist, a gym owner, a bodybuilder, an athlete, a chiropractor, a Reiki practitioner, a hypnotherapist, or the developer of vitamins, cosmetics, or pharmaceuticals. You get the point.

For every theme there are a wide variety of ways to explore our interests. Many lives are lessons in courage, from the military hero who saves his buddies on the battlefield, to the single mother working two jobs just to feed her children. From our list of virtues we can see that there are many lessons to be learned no matter what your occupation. In one life we may be learning only one part of the lesson, while in another we learn the opposite.

For example, Karen's current lifetime may be about learning the nuances of love, relationship, and intimacy, while Donna's is about learning to stand on her own. Yet every lifetime has its pluses and minuses. Karen may feel overwhelmed with her family's needs and have no time to cultivate her own interests, while Donna loves her freedom and career but wonders why she never got married. Between these two extremes is Kayla, who has managed to figure out the lessons of both of these two extremes and is able to develop a rewarding career and have a healthy family at the same time—clearly a course in mastery! Woven among these circumstances are the spiritual lessons we are constantly learning: the themes of patience, kindness, commitment, and love, all set against the backdrop of friendships, family, war, and the conventions of the age in which we live. Sheesh, no wonder Earth is such an advanced program!

Gathering New Experiences

As well, there comes a point when a Soul is asked to do something new so it doesn't stagnate and can continue the dance of evolution. Thus the Council of Elders may encourage that Soul to step outside its comfort zone. For example, a Soul that has relied on fabulous good looks might decide to select a body with an average appearance to learn compassion or humility, or to focus on mental or spiritual development. A Soul that has been a warrior again and again may decide to sustain an injury so great that it cannot continue to go down that path and must begin to cultivate other talents. A Soul that has misused its own personal power repeatedly may choose to become the willing victim of abuse in the next life in order to learn about the pain and suffering caused by such an abuse of power.

Along these lines, one particular reading comes to mind. This was for a twenty-seven-year-old man who in his former life had died as a British fighter pilot in World War I. He immediately returned in another body as a British fighter pilot in World War II, where once again he died in war at an early age. Determined to continue fighting, this Soul quickly reincarnated, this time in America, where once again he enlisted in the army and subsequently died in the swamps of Vietnam. In his current life this young man's Soul has apparently decided that enough is enough! He became a conscientious objector, openly opposing the philosophy of war. Now he is a rehabilitation specialist focused on helping wounded veterans.

Each life is planned so that it can contribute to our Soul's evolution—if we let it. And while the mental and emotional abilities we achieved in past lifetimes have followed us into our current life, perhaps whispering to us to make a bigger difference in the world, sometimes that is not the path of our greatest evolution. In some lifetimes we are meant to develop the missing parts of ourselves that we have put to the side because we were dealing with larger issues. For this brave, courageous Soul, who had given so much to others at a larger leadership level, playing small is not always comfortable or easy. I have read for Souls that have incarnated as leaders in so many lifetimes to the exclusion of a personal life, that in this lifetime they have been told to take a vacation in order to address these neglected parts of themselves. They have pursued work and world service at the expense of personal intimacy, so their mission in this life may be to develop the bonds of familial love. Conversely, so many Souls have been steeped in the confines and responsibilities of a family life that in this lifetime they may have decided not to marry so that they can develop other parts of themselves. So while these Souls may be consciously pining after that "perfect" soulmate relationship, that is not their path in this life. It is always best to use the time that is given to us to find our greatest service and to step up in our own lives so that we can make a difference.

The Soul's reluctance to try something new can also apply to the choice of race or gender. For example, a Soul that has been male in many past lifetimes might be encouraged to choose a female body. Once she arrives on Earth, however, she doesn't feel like she fits into the female form so she becomes a lesbian or transgender person. She may even go so far as to undergo surgery, because she is so uncomfortable in the body of a gender with which she is unfamiliar. However, at a higher level this choice to change genders in midstream may actually be self-defeating since this was not the person's original life plan. Yet let me say that there are many reasons why a person may choose to undergo a life as a born homosexual or a transgender person, and one size *does not* fit all. For some, this may be the only way that the Soul can make the transition from one sex to another with ease. Another Soul may have chosen to be born as a gay person for other, more evolved reasons—perhaps they came to experience the lessons of courage, speaking up, nonjudgment, self-honoring, or forgiveness of others. Perhaps they came to teach that lesson to their families who are steeped in gender prejudice. Each situation is different, and each path unique. Yet the more we can embrace the lessons that are presented to us by our current circumstances, the better off we will be. By asking ourselves how the early circumstances of our life can catalyze us into our life purpose, we can find the silver lining behind these choices. When we do so, our life flows with greater ease.

Whatever our original Soul choices might have been, some of us are more stubborn than others. Yes, we agreed to make a change in this lifetime, but now we resist it. So events must occur to alter that Soul's path. Perhaps a Soul has been a warrior in so many lifetimes that the Soul agrees to sustain a physical injury so that its old path is now closed. Perhaps that same Soul is here to awaken the inner artist, inspire others, write inspirational books, or teach children. Now, with the old path closed to them, through what appears to be tragedy, the Soul can open to the new frontier before it. It is important at this juncture not to be afraid to ask for mentoring while stepping into this new endeavor. This lifetime is not about clinging to old patterns, but rather about embracing the new. Something great is in store for the person who takes this step, knowing that a rebirth will come from these outwardly difficult events.

Adversity is always a part of the path of mastery. For example, one Soul may take on a childhood illness that seems to be a tragedy. Yet we agree to such things before we ever arrive on Earth, and the reasons can be most insightful: to inspire others, to launch a life mission, to allow the parents to experience unconditional love, to balance karma. Perhaps this Soul is destined to become a great healer and having this infirmity is what is needed to catapult that person onto their path. From the ashes of our disasters rise the victories of our Souls. Many years ago I remember reading about a man who was wrongly convicted of murder. He used his time in prison to start a spiritual study group in the prison, uplifting his fellow inmates for many years until he was finally exonerated and released. So whatever our circumstances, however grim they may be, we must always ask ourselves what we could have intended when we agreed to these challenges.

Resolving Karmic Relationships

While career occupations may seem to be the central focus of some peoples' lives, other lives are primarily focused on resolving karmic relationships. This can be with our parents, our siblings, our children, our bosses, or our spouses. While some of these relationships may flow smoothly, other relationships seem to be a thorn in our side. However most people to whom we have strong emotional reactions and entanglements are those we have known in past lifetimes. These people may even be members of your Soul family who have incarnated to help all parties resolve past issues. While in some of our lifetimes we may have been supportive of one another, in others we might have experienced betrayal, abandonment, or abuse, and thus we return to this lifetime with these same Souls to resolve all those particular issues. In Heaven, these people may even be our friends; however in this life, we may have volunteered to play the role of the challenger so that both parties may grow. Once we incarnate, however, we don't remember these Soul agreements, and thus it is easy to fall into the pattern of blaming others for our problems. In some cases, these "old friends" may have been with us many times. While some lifetimes may have been supportive, others were not. Thus we have returned in this lifetime to resolve old resentments. By understanding that life is like a cosmic play where everyone has agreed to play their part, we can avoid falling back into creating negative patterns. To untangle these threads we must be ever vigilant and committed to a path of self-examination and forgiveness.

Over the course of thousands of readings, I have seen many dances take place between "friends" and "enemies." In some cases these two Souls are actually dealing with two sides of the same issue. One person may be too much of a taker, while the other is too much of a giver. Yet both people are dealing with the same core lessons: boundaries, energy, fairness, and self-love. One person falls into the role of victim, while the other one plays the persecutor, yet the lesson for both individuals is about the right use of power. In one relationship person A is too rigid or controlling, while person B is an irresponsible gambler. Yet both people are grappling with the same core issues of trust, lack, fear, and flow, just at opposite ends of the spectrum. Their issues arise from not feeling enough love, causing both people to look outside themselves to shore up their sense of insecurity.

The Wounded Healer

Whatever our karmic lessons, unless we make an effort to clear that issue, we will remain blocked in that area of life. Along these lines I want to relate the story of a wounded healer who could not seem to heal herself.

Years ago I read for a woman who had trained as a nurse, yet she could not bring herself to practice that profession. Upon inquiring I learned that she had taken a dozen classes on various forms of healing, some modern and some ancient, yet she could not bring herself to apply what she had learned. What was the reason for this? During the course of her reading I saw that she had been a doctor, a nurse, an herbalist, and a healer in about 60 percent of her lifetimes, so clearly this was an important Soul theme. However, in one of her more recent lifetimes she had been a British nurse on the front lines of World War I. When the war broke out, her father, brother, and fiancé all enlisted in the army, and during that conflict they died one by one. First, she learned that her father had been killed in action. Then news arrived that her brother had died. Finally, in the midst of her nursing triage, with bleeding men coming in from the frontlines, she received a telegram that her fiancé had died in battle. Then she herself perished when a mortar shell hit the triage tents. At the time of her death she carried with her all the anguish, despair, and hopelessness of her losses, believing that nothing she could ever do to help others would really matter. *After all, what is the point if everyone I loved perished?*

In her current life this young woman still carried this same unhealed belief, even though her Soul was trying to direct her back toward healing work. She needed to heal her past-life experiences so that she could reclaim her power. This is how past-life healing works, whether through hypnotherapy, time-line therapy, or holographic repatterning—all modalities that I have practiced for years. These memories, beliefs, and unconscious patterns are all held in the causal body and seep into our current life as mental and emotional blocks. Until we can discover and release the underlying cause behind these blocks and mend the traumas and wounds of the past, we are unable to move forward again with joy and ease.

In doing emotional healing work for over thirty years I have discovered that by resolving these hidden conflicts, our lives can change fundamentally. For many this means untangling the threads of personal relationships or resolving old feelings of powerlessness created by past-life tragedies. For others it means releasing a vow or negative belief from the past. For still others it's about dissolving the feeling that you have done something wrong, changing a core belief, or needing to find forgiveness for yourself or others. These powerful, misaligned emotions brought on by previous life experiences may have been festering in the present life at a deep subconscious level. Once they are dissolved, you can move on and are free to reclaim your power in the present and achieve your dreams.

The Power to Change Our Lives

Today I see these old patterns emerging particularly among the reincarnated priests, priestesses, healers, shamans, and medicine keepers of ancient times, all of whom are advanced or master Souls. These spiritually oriented human beings have returned at this time to assist in the evolution of planet Earth. They are here to bring about revolutions in the fields of science, medicine, ecology, government, the arts, communication, spirituality, healing, and education, and many of them are extraordinary individuals. In this lifetime their Soul themes may center around saving the animals, protecting the environment, educating children, ending domestic abuse, or creating new forms of holistic healing. But to accomplish these aims they must clear away the rubble of their past lifetimes, which contain tragedies in which they might have been hanged, shamed, stoned, imprisoned, or burned at the stake during the many centuries of religious oppression in the Middle Ages. Now, in this lifetime, before they can fully step into their missions, they must first heal their own past wounding patterns, in order to bring forth their healing gifts.

While it is true that we are given new astral and mental bodies before each new incarnation, the echoes of the past still live on inside of our subconscious personalities. While each of these past lifetimes will contain gifts and talents, some of them may also contain the imprint of unresolved fears and traumas that play out in the present. Imagine, for example, that you are someone who has been a priest, a monk, a hermit, or a nun in several lifetimes. If so, you might find it harder to access your sexuality in an intimate relationship or you may feel a low level of guilt about sexual expression. This is because you have taken vows of celibacy in the past, and now, no matter how much you might want to have a passionate, fulfilling love life, the residue of these past vows lives on inside of you.

Similarly, someone who has been a Quaker, a Puritan, or an Amish person might lean toward simplicity in this life. Such a person will have a natural love of nature, duty, and fundamentalism, carrying with her the inclinations of her past lives. Someone who was persecuted for speaking out for writing or for bringing forth new inventions may have a reluctance to be seen in public for these very same abilities. She may feel misunderstood, persecuted, or judged for her ideas. If she is still writing, she may find it hard to connect with a publisher or to get financial support for her discoveries, at least until such time as she clears the traumas surrounding these past life events. A healer who was killed in a previous lifetime for her healing skills may deliberately run away from cultivating such gifts today for fear of reprisal or judgments.

When we think about it, we are the survivors of at least 1,700 years of religious intolerance and persecution by the Roman Catholic Church. This includes at least six centuries of the Inquisition where men, women, and children were arrested, hanged, imprisoned, tortured, and burned at the stake for thinking outside the box and for cultivating those spiritual gifts that are natural to human beings. Our ancestors were witnesses to those atrocities, and thus many of us, even those who are advanced or master Souls, have inherited the cellular memories of the individuals who survived these holocausts. Thus such a Soul might side-step or avoid their natural healing gifts. This brings us to the concept of love and power, which is the classic core curriculum that each Soul must master.

19

Mastering the Lessons of Love and Power

At this time in history, we are to take nothing personally,
least of all ourselves. For the moment that we do,
our spiritual growth and journey comes to a halt.

HOPI PROPHECY

While we can clearly see that there are hundreds of combinations of life lessons and Soul themes being played out around us, at the heart of the Soul's Course Curriculum is the right use of power and love. These two qualities are the pure attributes of the Divine Father and Divine Mother. True power derives from truth, represented by the Divine Father. Love is the power of emanation and vibration that allows the universe to come into being, the Holy Spirit of the Divine Mother. When love and power are joined together, they create wisdom, which is the essence of God. When this divine union is in balance, it has the power to create the entire cosmos. But when these two aspects are out of balance or misused, they generate chaos, war, loneliness, oppression, heartache, and abuse.

Over the course of the last few chapters we have taken a serious look at a number of dysfunctional patterns being played out in the human world today. These dysfunctional dynamics are created when there is an imbalance between the forces of love and power, and oftentimes a lack of love of the self or others. They are also created when we abdicate or abuse our power. Let's take another look at how this plays out in terms of the PVR (persecutor-victim-rescuer) triangle, see table 19.1 below.

TABLE 19.1. LOVE AND POWER IN THE PVR TRIANGLE

PVR Triangle Positions	The Use of Love	The Use of Power
The persecutor	The persecutor has too little love or sensitivity for the feelings of others, and too much self-centeredness.	The persecutor abuses his power inappropriately, similar to using a grenade to swat a fly.
The victim	The victim has too little love for self, and thus too little self-esteem.	The victim has too little personal power and this paralyzes him into inaction.
The rescuer	The rescuer cares too much for others, and perhaps too little for herself. Her self-worth may depend on feeling like she is useful to others.	The rescuer overextends her power to help others, and as a result becomes co-dependent, thus making the person she is helping feel less powerful and competent.

Now let's take the four negative communication styles that we examined earlier, see table 19.2 on page 404.

The Lack of Self-Love

One of the biggest problems that we have in the world today among so many people is a genuine lack of self-love. This lack of love creates fear—the fear that we are unworthy, unloved, unsupported, and unimportant. Why do so many of us feel this way? In part it is because we are taught judgment at our parents' knees. This is an inherited belief system that has been placed on us by religious authorities over many

TABLE 19.2. LOVE AND POWER AND THE FOUR NEGATIVE COMMUNICATION STYLES

Negative Communication Styles	The Use of Love	The Use of Power
The intimidator	The intimidator clearly does not have enough love or consideration for others and appears to be completely self-absorbed, having too much love for self and little awareness of the feelings of others.	The intimidator overuses and misuses his power, leaving others feeling oppressed and disempowered. In this way he becomes the persecutor.
The interrogator	The interrogator, like the intimidator, has little respect or love for others. He is primarily interested in how he can manipulate or use other people to further his own position.	The interrogator, like the intimidator, misuses his power in a vicious way to gain control. He violates the primary trust of friendship as he baits his victims.
The withholder	The withholder believes that she is the victim who has been wronged. Thus she has little sympathy for the feelings of others since she is wrapped up in feeling unloved, unappreciated, and wounded. In truth, she has too little love for herself, and thus she treats others the same way.	Being convinced that she has been abused, the withholder uses her power in a passive-aggressive way to punish with silence. But in truth the withholder has no real confidence in herself or her position since she does not use her power directly or in a healthy way. If she did, then she would explain why her feelings have been hurt and would be able to resolve the matter directly.
The martyr	The martyr, like the withholder, suffers from a lack of self-love, yet she is constantly manipulating others to get the love, energy, and attention that was probably missing in her childhood or marriage. She is oftentimes run by her fears.	The martyr, like the withholder, uses a passive-aggressive form of power to get her own way. Rather than owning her true feelings, which stem from of a lack of self-love, she uses her power inappropriately to try to get that love from others.

centuries. When we believe that we are unworthy to be loved by God (or by others), then it is hard to claim our essential nature. Instead, we are motivated to seek the "cure" that many religions have historically put a claim to. In fact, some religions say they offer the "only cure." Some have even held that if we do not fall in line with their particular brand of religious dogma, our punishment will be so great that we will be doomed to Hell forever. Well now, we know that Hell is only one of the temporary levels of the lower astral plane, and a great deal of negativity is required to get there. So while these threats are not true, for millions of people across the world the idea of eternal damnation is very real. Such heavy-handed intimidator tactics on the part of religions are not only falsehoods, they represent a great abuse of power at a planetary level—all done in the name of God!

Yet the wisdom of Lord Jesus reminds us that we are all gods in the making—divine beings capable of living in the light of which we are a part. In John 10:33 Jesus says, "Is it not written in your laws, 'I said, You are gods?'" What laws is he talking about? An even older law taught by Moses tells us that the spark of God resides in each of us if we will but bring it forth. In the Gospel of Thomas (70:1–5) Jesus reminds us: "When you bring forth that which is within yourselves, this which is yours will save you; if you do not have that in yourselves, this which is not yours in you will kill you." Yet Moses's wisdom was derived from a still older teaching within the Mystery Schools that reminds us that each of us is a divine flame in the body of the Divine. Jesus goes on to remind us that "the Kingdom is in your center and is about all. When you know your Selves then you will be known; and you will be aware that you are the sons of the Living Father. But if you do not know yourselves, then you are in poverty, and *you are* the poverty" (Thomas 3:7–15). Thus each of us has a choice, every day of our lives, to either live in fear and lack or to fully embrace the eternal light within our very own being.

At a practical level, judgment creates enormous fear in the bodies, minds, and hearts of those who believe it. It engenders the belief that we are unworthy to be loved, one of the three false beliefs of Adi-karma. Consequently, many people do not feel capable of stepping into their own power or their own self-love. They may not even feel worthy of receiving the love that has been shown to them by others. These people are often successful givers with wonderful hearts who are unconsciously driven by a need to prove themselves worthy to be loved through their good deeds. In their deepest heart of hearts they hope that they will be seen and acknowledged by those they have helped, thereby soothing the wounds they still bear from the love and support they never got in childhood. Yet no matter how perfect we try to be or how much we give to others, nothing can ever substitute for the love we deny ourselves. The only remedy for this is to make a connection with the Divine, the Source of *all love*. God, Atum, or whatever we choose to call the One, loves each and every one of us utterly and completely, and that has nothing to do with our human imperfections.

Substituting Power for Love

If a person becomes a rescuer or abnegates her power totally and becomes a victim, then she may develop life strategies in which she seeks power as a substitute for the love she never got. Such a choice only places her further away from the love she really wants. We must always remember that fear and love are opposite forces. Though the Soul wants love, by misusing personal power a person creates fear in others, driving them away. Fear and judgment contract the energy field, while love and approval expand it. Thus the original wound, which was the withholding or absence of love, causes the person to attempt to feed that inner void in order to stop the pain. While some people might try to anesthetize these feelings with drugs or alcohol, others may try to expel their pain by becoming the bully, taking the attention of others as a substitute for the love they really want. Without meaning to, they then continue to perpetuate the same vicious cycle of judgment, control, and abuse that got them into this mess in the first place.

Complicated, isn't it? When we look at it like this, we can see how the dysfunctional patterns of our ancestors have been passed down to us from generation to generation. Those who have wounded us were themselves the recipients of the same negative patterns they inherited from their parents—and on and on back through the generations. In truth, any person who is steeped in the misuse of his own power, no matter how rich, charismatic, intelligent, or persuasive he may be, is there because he has not made a connection with his higher Self.

Fear and Violence versus Love

So what are the things that block us from love, that make us believe in bigotry, hate, and separation? When we look around us it seems that we are constantly being sold the poison pill of fear and violence at every turn. We absorb it from the nightly news, lap it up in television shows and movies, and imbibe it in the form of the rantings of religious figures who alternate between preaching love and telling us how we are sinners who will be judged and condemned. We pay millions to professional athletes to beat one another to a pulp, make blockbuster movies about psychopaths, and consume bestsellers about serial killers. Each night we are glued to the brutality of the nightly news and live vicariously through the soap opera jealousies, illicit affairs, and petty stories of celebrities. We destroy our oceans, torture and exploit our animals, and continue to expand our nuclear facilities, even in the face of deadly earthquakes that could annihilate everything on our planet. In truth, it seems like we are committed to the destruction of everything except ourselves, including Earth's ecosystem. The average person, burdened with credit cards and house payments, is often so exhausted from the day's run on the hamster wheel that he or she is hardly aware that we are being conditioned to believe that violence, fear, and conflict is a normal way of life. This debilitating negative agenda is designed to keep us so out of balance that we never really stop to ask the question: "Is there another way to live?"

Today, many scientists believe that society has hardwired our adrenal glands to continually dose us with a shot of adrenaline, cortisol, and other stress-related hormones. These hormones are pumped into the bloodstream and fire up the nervous system to create the fight-or-flight response that we have become so accustomed to. This is the survival mechanism that is connected to the reptilian brain, the most primitive of the three parts of the human brain. These three parts are the reptilian or survival brain, the limbic or emotional brain, and the cerebral or cognitive brain. The reptilian brain is focused on what I call the four *F*s: feeding, fighting, fleeing, and fornicating. This primitive brain is designed to help the human body survive in times of danger, but it is not meant to be activated on a daily basis. The fight-or-flight response stimulates the adrenal glands, creating premature aging and stress. Fear activates this response, quickening our heart rate, raising our blood pressure, and sharpening our senses, giving us those passionate, knee-jerk reactions that we have learned to associate with an emotional high. Fear causes us to react from a place of instinctual survival instead of rational thought and deeper reflection.

Imagine a caveman running from a dinosaur, or the energy it takes as we swerve through traffic in a speeding car, or a crowd full of movie-goers running from a psychopath chasing us with a chainsaw. Yes, we feel alive, because our adrenal glands have kicked into gear. When we don't die we feel the rush of victory and a false sense of empowerment. When the adrenaline wears off, our bodies are flooded with feel-good endorphins thanks to the parasympathetic nervous system, which calms us down, grounds us out, and soothes our anxiety. But after a while we get bored again. Then we sniff out other sources of drama and upheaval and we repeat this cycle all over again.

Can we break this cycle of conflict, fear, and false empowerment? How can we rewire our nervous system so that we can ease ourselves off of the chemical high that keeps us trapped in this continual loop? Is it possible to wean ourselves off of the violence, brutality, and conflict that seems endemic in the world and learn to seek excitement through healthier means?

In recent years researchers have found that the power of our beliefs, our emotions, and our thoughts has great bearing on the outcome of our life. In the early 1990s biologist Bruce Lipton became involved in the study of epigenetics, a new science focused on studying the effects of our environments at the cellular level. What he discovered is that cells respond to our environment in one of two ways; they either stay open, which promotes growth and the exchange of life producing nutrients in the body and brain, or they perceive danger and close down in a protective mode. We can liken this to the two forces of love and fear. One allows us to feel safe and open, while the other throws us into the fear-based survival of the reptilian brain. The choice of how the cells respond is controlled by the brain and what we see and feel about our lives, sending a series of signals to the body, which triggers a series of chemical and mechanical switches found in our genetics.[1]

This means that when we perceive our environment as safe, we naturally relax, allowing growth and stability. However if we perceive our environment to be dangerous, stressful, or unsafe, then the cells close down to protect themselves. Lipton explains the science behind this discovery, which has profound implications for understanding the effect of environmental stress and negative programming on a person's health.

> Our new understanding of the universe's mechanics shows how the physical body can be affected by the immaterial mind. Thoughts, the mind's energy directly influence how the physical brain controls the body's physiology. Thought 'energy' can activate or inhibit the cell's function—producing proteins via the mechanics of constructive and destructive interference . . . that is why . . . I actively monitored where I was expending my brain's energy. I had to examine the consequence of energy I invested in my thoughts as closely as I examined the expenditures of energy I used to power my physical body.[2]

Lipton goes on to talk about how our positive and negative beliefs not only impact our bodies, but every aspect of our life.

> My point is that you can choose what to see. You can filter your life with rose-colored beliefs that will help your body grow or you can use a dark filter that turns everything black and makes your body/mind more susceptible to disease. You can live a life of fear or live a life of love. You have the choice! But I can tell you that if you choose to see a world full of love, your body will respond by growing in health. If you choose to believe that you live in a dark world full of

fear, your body's health will be compromised as you physiologically close yourself down in a protection response.

Learning how to harness your mind to promote growth is the secret of life, which is why I called this book *The Biology of Belief.* Of course the secret of life is not a secret at all. Teachers like Buddha and Jesus have been telling us the same story for millennia. Now science is pointing in the same direction. It is not our genes, but our beliefs that control our lives.[3]

In a similar vein, the HeartMath Institute has discovered that the positive and negative emotions that we think and feel can actually program our DNA. In other words, our feelings activate genetic codes stored within human amino acids. There are sixty-four possible combinations of these amino acids, but only twenty of them are ever activated at any one time. Fear is a long-wave pattern that contracts the DNA strands, giving us little access to our genetic potential or spiritual gifts. Love, on the other hand, is a short-wave pattern that relaxes the DNA, producing a high-vibrating frequency that allows us to activate more of our godlike potential. Thus the emotion of fear that society seems bathed in actually blocks our spiritual potential, dumbing us down and making us easier to control.[4]

In recent years there have been a handful of Russian scientists who have also been studying the connection between our consciousness, the quantum field, and its effect on our DNA. Russian biophysicist and molecular biologist Pjotr Garjajev and his colleagues do not believe that our DNA is ninety percent "junk," but instead is a quantum mechanical bio wave computer. Their research explains how such phenomena as clairvoyance, intuition, remote healing, positive affirmations, and the power of the mind to influence weather-patterns can exist. They have discovered that our human DNA creates wormhole patterns that can allow information to be transmitted outside of time and space! These tiny wormholes are the microscopic equivalents of the Einstein-Rosen bridge known in astronomy, also called a black hole. Their research shows that our DNA attracts bits of information from the universe and passes them on to our consciousness. They have also found evidence to explain the phenomena of auras sometimes seen around spiritual masters like Jesus or Buddha.[5]

Along this same line is the DNA research of Russian scientist Vladimir Poponin. Poponin placed human tissue into a vacuum tube and beamed a photonic laser light through it. Once the human DNA was inside the tube, he found that the light realigned itself along the axis of the DNA, revealing that our DNA has the power to "entrain" the light of the universe. Oddly enough, when scientists removed the human tissue from the vacuum tube, the photons of laser light continued spiraling on their own, and remained in this same helical pattern for twenty-four hours! He called this the "Phantom DNA Effect."[6] What this reveals is that the light of the universe entrains along the structure of our DNA, charging it with the energy of the universe. In practical terms this means that through the power of our words, beliefs, thoughts, and feelings we can create our own reality.

Since the entire cosmos is made up of light stemming from the billions of suns that glitter against the night sky, the presence of light is everywhere. Dr. Popanov's study reveals how the thoughts and emotions we store in our DNA can actually change our world. By understanding that the vibration of love has the power to open us up to growth and to activate our genetic potential, then we know that it is love and not fear that will allow us to create a long-lasting peace within and without.

Love and Power

At the heart of our very human lessons is our need to learn to embody both love and power in a positive, life-affirming way. We can call this the path of compassion and forgiveness, the path of truth and manifestation, for this is what they are: forgiveness of self and others. Yet this forgiveness is only possible when we realize who we are behind the illusions and inconsistencies in the play of light and shadows we see all around us. We are divine, eternal light beings having a mortal experience in the classroom of planet Earth school. We are here to meet our challenges, learn our lessons, discover our creativity, and make a difference, not only for ourselves, but for the world.

These twin pillars of love and power are not only the foundational energies of the Divine Father and Divine Mother, but two of the flames of the Sacred Heart that live within us. The third flame is the golden path of unity that we must walk if we are to claim our role as children of God. And it is the positive use of and merging with these seeming opposites that will ultimately bring us to mastery.

20

The Path of the Heart

Humankind has not woven the web of life.
We are but one thread within it.
Whatever we do to the web, we do to ourselves.
All things are bound together.
All things connect.

CHIEF SEATTLE

Whatever we give our attention to in life is what we cultivate in the garden of ourselves, not only in this life, but in the next. Are your thoughts mainly focused on the material world or are they centered on the path of service, truth, love, and light? Are you living with an attitude of gratitude or caught up in anger, fear, and resentment? Are you visualizing the positive life you want to create or are you locked up in the worry of negative dramas? How much violent television do you watch? The answer may surprise you, for the forces of duality are relentlessly programming us to believe that conflict is our natural state. Watching late-night television shows featuring conflict, horror, and violence will pollute your dreams and block your access to the higher realms. This keeps you in constant stress, directing your subconscious mind down to the lower levels of the astral plane. So it is important to take an honest inventory of what you are feeding yourself in terms of your daily thoughts. How many times do you tell yourself that you can't, or won't, or aren't even capable of creating a more positive life? How many friends engage you in gossip or in judging others? What activities do you engage in that support your personal empowerment?

As part of this moral inventory you should also ask which thoughts or feelings you refuse to let go of, because the mind is like a record player—the words you repeat to yourself and to others can magnify either the good or the bad in your life. Are the ways in which you have been conditioned to respond serving your highest good today? Are you still holding on to grudges about events that happened twenty years ago? Do you still blame parents, siblings, ex-spouses, or former best friends? If so, then the person you are really hurting is yourself. *The lessons that we resist will persist,* spilling over into the current events of our life, replaying all the negative dynamics until we are willing to resolve them. The law of Ma'at is a constant; it always tries to bring us back into balance, giving us chance after chance to resolve what is unhealed in our psyche.

As we have discovered, the heart-mind connection that is fundamental to our personality also plays a pivotal role in determining a great deal about our life in the here and now. It also plays a big part in determining where we will go when we die. People who are stuck in the lower astral level are bound by the negative mindset they carried in life. By healing these old beliefs and wounds of the past, we break the chains that bind us and gain the power to create a better life. Then we can step back and ask: "What was I hoping to learn that I have chosen the circumstances of this life?"

Imagine for a moment that you are an Angel who has decided to come to Earth, and you made a plan. What kind of mission could you have intended such that you used the events in this life to prompt you in a particular direction? What did you intend to teach yourself? How can these lessons be applied to fulfill a higher purpose? After all, you could have been born anywhere, to any family, on any continent, in any economic circumstance. While today our little self might want to shout "I will be born beautiful, rich, and famous," our higher Self might decide on something completely different. After all, your higher Self understands the big picture. The reason you were born into this life has nothing to do with fame, glory, or money, but rather the evolutionary purpose of your Soul. Could it be that the challenges you have faced in this lifetime were all part of a bigger design intended to help you reclaim your true identity? In truth, each one of our lifetimes is created from a set of absolutely impeccable yet invisible laws, and it is our job to discover what we intended when we agreed to human birth, so that we can fulfill the deeper mission of our Soul.

The Karmic-Dharmic Arc

In the Ring of Destiny we agree to the big events of each coming lifetime, events such as accidents, mental illness, handicaps, and disease, knowing that succeeding in facing these challenges will put us on the fast track of spiritual learning. This means that if we use these situations as opportunities for growth, our problems will catapult us toward our life purpose. I call this the *karmic-dharmic arc*. This is the Soul that uses the difficulties that it encounters to propel it toward a higher mission. Let's take a moment to review how this works.

We already know about the law of karma, the law that reminds us that what we reap is the result of what we sow, either in this life or another. So karma is the cause and effect mechanism that allows us to walk a mile in another's shoes. Thus those steeped in bigotry will incarnate as a member of the very group they have judged in a former life. Those who were slave masters will become the slaves. Those who oppress women will become oppressed women in a future life. So it is possible that whatever karmic difficulties a person has may have arisen from their past actions. This teaches us the importance of practicing compassion for all. We are all on the Wheel of Becoming, and so with every turn of the wheel the person that you are judging may be another you. This is why Jesus taught "Judge not, lest ye be judged" (Matthew 7:1). In truth, there but for the grace of God go any of us.

However, it is also possible that the difficulties of your childhood, your upbringing, your family, your body, your finances, or your environment may have been selected for a far deeper reason. Obstacles in any of these areas may have been chosen to catalyze you in a particular direction, to motivate you along a particular path. Perhaps they were meant to stir up questions about fairness, suffering, governance, forgiveness, sacrifice, or even God. Perhaps they were there to teach you to stand on your own, develop discipline, strive for excellence, learn compassion, or find a connection with patience, love, and gratitude. When you look at life like this rather than playing the part of the victim, you can ask yourself what your problems are here to teach you. This is true for each and every one of us.

This brings us to *dharma,* a Sanskrit word that means our purpose in any given lifetime, our life's work. This is the reason why you were born. If you succeed in learning your lessons, then you will have the strength to nurture others, inspire those around you, and touch the hearts of others with the beauty of your spirit. This is where life's challenges lead if we will rise to meet them. And like the alchemist who turns lead into gold, our challenges are the fire we need to spur us forward to become that shining light for others.

Let's take a look at a few examples of the karmic-dharmic arc that come from some of my readings:

- Steven was a young boy when his father died in Vietnam. As the oldest son he grew up protecting his two younger siblings. Moved by the difference he made in their lives, he later became the phys-ed coach at a local grammar school, inspiring boys to believe in themselves. Then later he became a part of the Big Brother movement, touching the lives of dozens of teenagers who were growing up without a father. He anchored a strong, positive male role model within their psyches, and thus the wound of his childhood loss became his motivation and the source of his greatest strength.
- Dorothy was a teenage girl who had watched her mother fight a slow, losing battle with cancer. After her mother's death she later became a naturopath, determined to find new ways to solve the cancer problem. In the process she taught people about better

nutrition, vitamins, alternative therapies, and the link between unresolved emotions, stress, and cancer. Today Dorothy has helped more than two hundred people overcome the deadly disease that took her mother's life.

• Paul was close to his grandparents when he was growing up. In fact, each summer Paul went to stay with them on their farm in the country. Then, when their health took a turn for the worse, Paul took a year off from college to help them die at home, with dignity. This connection of love motivated him to later change his major in college. He became a physical therapist working with the elderly, giving hope back to older people in the last years of their lives. But Paul could just have easily chosen to become a doctor, a nurse, a paramedic, or an activities coordinator in a senior-care facility. Thus it was through his experience of loss that he found his true calling.

The Overlighting Daimon of Our Destiny

Psychologist James Hillman writes about the idea of the overlighting daimon that steers our life from behind the scenes in *The Soul's Code: In Search of Character and Calling:* "Each life is formed by a unique image, an image that is the essence of that life and calls it to a destiny. As the force of fate, this image acts as a personal *daimon,* an accompanying guide who remembers your calling."[1] This *daimon,* spirit guide, or Angelic Twin acts to protect us, steer us, or call us to our purpose. It may cause an accident, send a dream, motivate us to read a book or take a class, or whisper to us in the wee hours of the night, urging us down a certain path. It leads us, even when we feel out of step with the world, speaking to us through our deepest loves, pains, and desires. For many, this spiritual calling may seem out of step with the daily tasks of consensus reality, "out of step with time, finding all sorts of faults, gaps, and knots in the [normal] flow of life . . . [for] it has affinities with myth, since it is itself a mythical being and thinks in mythical patterns [being from the higher realms]."[2]

Hillman examines how the pain and struggle of our early years, which he likens to an acorn, transforms into the flowering of a powerful tree that is the pinnacle of our adult life. This pain and struggle, he believes, are the very catalysts that usher a child into a world that they otherwise would never have known. "The so-called traumatic experience is not an accident, but the opportunity for which the child has been patiently waiting—had it not occurred, it would have found another, equally trivial—in order to find a necessity and direction for its existence, in order that its life may become a serious matter."[3] He cites many examples of the adversities visited upon great men and women that in the end became the very catalysts that propelled them toward their destinies:

- Winston Churchill was known to have language problems as a child, yet it was his eloquence in speechmaking that rallied the Allied forces during World War II. Later, in 1953, Churchill was awarded the Nobel Prize in literature. He once wrote:

  What is the use of living, if it be not to strive for noble causes and to make this muddled world a better place for those who will live in it after we are gone? How else can we put ourselves in harmonious relation with the great verities and consolations of the infinite and the eternal? And I avow my faith that we are marching towards better days. Humanity will not be cast down. We are going on swinging bravely forward along the grand high road, and already behind the distant mountains is the promise of the sun.[4]

- Henri Matisse, the French painter, first started painting in 1889 during a period when he was convalescing from appendicitis. Before that he worked as a court administrator. Matisse said that in painting he had discovered a "kind of paradise" that led him to become one of the foremost artists in the early years of the twentieth century, along with Pablo Picasso and Marcel Duchamp.
- In 1874, science fiction writer H. G. Wells broke his leg when he was only eight years old. His father brought him books from the library during the long, bedridden months. It was during that difficult recovery that Wells's imagination opened up, and he

soon was devoted to the discovery of other worlds. Although he took various jobs to support his family, it was this love of learning that drove him to secure a scholarship to the Royal Academy of Science at South Kensington. Ultimately, his passion for futuristic science propelled him to become the famous science fiction author of *War of the Worlds, The Time Machine, The Invisible Man,* and *The Island of Doctor Moreau.*

- Helen Keller was born in 1880 as a normal child, but at the age of nineteen months she suffered an illness that took away both her vision and her hearing. In the process of learning how to communicate with the outside world again she became a prolific writer, speaker, and suffragist. Yet she often spoke about the joy that life had given her and said that helping others was the only excuse for being alive in this world, and that this was the secret to lasting happiness.

- Oprah Winfrey was born in poverty to a single mother in rural Mississippi. She grew up in Milwaukee, where she was sexually abused and became pregnant at age fourteen, giving birth to a child who subsequently died. Despite her challenges, her honest, heart-centered approach to life and its problems went on to revolutionize daytime talk shows. As a world-renowned philanthropist and advocate for the downtrodden, Oprah awakened a television movement focused on self-improvement, literature, and spirituality. But it is her ability to focus on the positive and rise above the challenges of life that has made her such a powerful champion in the lives of millions. Through the example of her life, Oprah has demonstrated that the power of love is stronger than the power of hate. Thus hidden in the catastrophes of her childhood traumas she found clues that allowed her to fulfill her destiny.

Plato also expressed the idea that each person's daimon guides the Soul toward its fate, a destiny that was chosen by the Soul long before coming into this world. In *The Republic* he explains the Three Fates of Greek mythology who determine each person's destiny or "thread of fate." These are Lachesis, Clotho, and Atropos.

When all the souls had chosen their lives, they went before Lachesis. And she sent with each, as the guardian of his life and the fulfiller of his choice, the daimon that he had chosen, and this divinity led the soul first to Clotho, under her hand and her turning of the spindle to ratify the destiny of his lot and choice, and after contact with her, the daimon again led the soul to the spinning of Atropos to make the web of its destiny irreversible, and then without a backward look, it passed beneath the throne of Necessity.[5]

Plotinus, echoing Plato, would later write, "Coming into this particular body, and being born of these particular parents, and in such a place, and in general, what we call external circumstances; that all happenings form a unity and are spun together is signified by the Fates."[6]

This Life Is Yours

When we can stand back from the story of our life and ask what the purpose of our challenges has been, then we can unravel the mystery at the center of our life. I know that for me this was certainly true as I watched my strong, intelligent father go down a path of pain and misery with alcoholism, taking our entire family with him. But this suffering also motivated me to become a student of the Mysteries, a healer, a clairvoyant, and a hypnotherapist, intent on peeking behind the curtain of our life to find the underlying patterns that make us unhappy or unfulfilled, and to heal them. I wanted to know why suffering exists, and I have discovered those reasons. Much of our suffering is the result of false beliefs and wounding patterns that we can heal, and it is through the process of suffering and learning that we come through the alchemical fires to mastery. As a child I prayed for two things: to see the highest and the best in everyone I met, and to be able to fly. Some years ago I realized that my ability to read the Soul records of everyone I met, and to track them back to their radiant angelic origins, was the answer to this prayer. So while like many of us I have known the pain of a dysfunctional childhood, it was the very catalyst that drove me to ask the pivotal questions and gain the tools that would enrich my life. As a result, I have been able to use my gifts to help others break the chains that bind them.

You, too, can try your hand at discovering your own your karmic-dharmic arc. Simply write down the five most difficult things you have experienced in your life and the five most wonderful things. Then beside each one write down how these events affected, shaped, or motivated you. What did you come to believe from these events? How did they change you? What decisions did you make? By doing this exercise you can discover how your challenges have influenced your character and pointed you in a direction that could help you find your own divine purpose. Perhaps your list might look something like this:

Early-life situation	*What I learned as a result*
I had to move around a lot growing up so we had to change schools frequently.	As a result, I adapted. I became an extrovert. I learned how to make people like me quickly, and these are good skills I can use in life.
I grew up with racial or religious prejudice all around me.	I saw how it didn't make people happy, so I made a choice to practice tolerance. This makes me a fair person, a good diplomat, and an excellent mediator.
We didn't have much money, so I had to go to work at an early age.	I developed a strong work ethic, discipline, and self-reliance. Now I know I can succeed at anything I put my mind to.
I felt fat and unattractive. This made me feel like I didn't fit in.	I got determined to start exercising and focused on healthy eating habits. I developed my mind and talents instead of my body, and now I am great at "fill in the blank" instead.

Early-life situation	*What I learned as a result*
I got in with the wrong crowd and started drinking, smoking, and doing drugs just so the other kids would think I was cool.	Now I've figured out that peer pressure isn't important. All that popularity stuff is for the birds, especially if it pulls me off-course. Now I realize that I have the strength and clarity to set my own goals, even if other people don't understand me.
I flunked a grade in school and this definitely made me feel like a loser. I was now "the big kid" because I was a year older.	Being the big kid had its advantages. I found that I was better in sports. I already knew a lot of the class material, so everyone looked up to me like I was smart. And the girls definitely were more interested!
I was always metaphysical. In fact, I grew up in a religious family that didn't understand my spiritual views, and this made it hard to communicate with them.	Well, since there was no one to talk to, I did a lot of reading. I also got online a lot and made a bunch of friends. So I got real good at the computer. In time, this meant that I became a web designer and a blogger. I developed skills as a "bridge person" who is now able to be true to my own point of view but understand the point of view of others.

Every Life Has Its Challenges

You get the point: from our challenges comes our strengths. And when we stand back to look at the major themes of a life we can see that each life has a divine purpose, often expressed in small, as well as large ways. Finding this divine purpose is quite important, for it gives us perspective on the many challenges that we face. Some lives are about developing the attributes of courage or self-worth, while others are about humbling oneself in quiet service to those around them. Some Souls face the heady heights of fame, wealth, and success, while others live saintly, barely noticed lives, known only to those they help. Some lives are about standing up to be counted, even when it's dangerous or not popular, while others are about working invisibly behind the scenes for the highest good. Some lives are about rising above our emotional losses to claim our own worth as a human being, while others are about overcoming hate, injustice, or prejudice. Some lives appear to be focused on a global mission with little time for a personal life, while other lives are so full of family, friends, and children that they can barely find a moment for themselves. You get the point. Each of us has a higher purpose, if we can only get enough perspective to discover what it is.

Over the course of our Soul's long evolution we will play many roles. Whatever life you have chosen, claim it with both hands, for you may not have the same opportunities ever again. And no matter how old a Soul may be, it is always our choices that are the determining factors in our spiritual growth. We do have free will, even if we have forgotten it. When it comes to the karmic-dharmic arc, I often think of that song about the man who prayed for strength, and to build that strength he was given more burdens to shoulder; the woman who prayed for forgiveness who was given people to forgive; the youth who prayed for faith who lived a life on the edge, having only enough money to pay his bills each week; and the soldier who prayed for courage who overcame his fears as he went into battle. While these lessons may look easy from the heavenly realms, for them to become a part of the warp and weft of the Soul we must throw ourselves at our adversities, meeting these obstacles head-on. This is the philosopher's stone that transforms the lead of our little self into pure gold. Only then will we find mastery.

The Hero's Journey

There have been many brave people on this planet who have listened to the calling of the Soul to join the adventure here on planet Earth.

Here, in this land of light and shadows, they have met the most arduous lessons of their many lives, tasted hardship and love, sacrifice and bravery, and come face-to-face with the Shadow. Yet by looking behind the curtain we can see that the Shadow is only an illusion, a negation of the true Spirit of God that has breathed life into us and every particle of the universe.

In the course of our journey through this book we have pulled back the veil and glimpsed the hem of God's garments in the realms of the invisible. We have entered these misty realms of Heaven and heard the reports of the many brave Souls that have returned from the Summerland to report incredible cities of light, Temples of Golden Wisdom, and the great Akashic Library that tells us that not one thing is ever lost in all of the cosmos; that God sees, knows, and loves every sparrow, every blade of grass, and every person. We explored the Great Chain of Being and the One who becomes the many, the many who return to the One. Finally, we uncovered the illusionary lies of Adikarma that keep us trapped in duality, derail us from true happiness, and instigate the kind of human discord that can plague our earthly relationships. We discovered the many life lessons we must master, the Course Curriculum of the Soul, and the mechanism of free will that will liberate us from the Wheel of Karma.

This is the archetypal hero's journey, the story of the prodigal son or daughter who has left the heavenly kingdom and gone into the realm of shadows to learn something crucial. Along the way he or she discovers the power of choice, the ability to rise above all difficulties, and the will to find the higher path. This prodigal child, like all of us, has felt vulnerable, alone, abandoned, and betrayed. She has made mistakes, fallen, and had her heart broken along the way. But she has also learned courage, humility, gratitude, faith, and service, and is wiser as a result of her journey. Finally she has discovered something incredible about herself: that behind all the play of light and shadows she is an indelible spark of the Divine, an eternal being who is infinitely love. Her Soul resides in the heights of Heaven, eternally waiting, loving, and enduring all things for the greater good. When we can fully embrace this truth, then this glorious prodigal child will return to the heavenly realms, where a great celebration awaits.

English writer Aldous Huxley, author of such iconic works as *Brave New World* and *The Doors of Perception,* reminds us that "the spiritual journey does not consist of arriving at a new destination where a person gains what he did not have, or becomes what he is not. It consists in the dissipation of one's own ignorance concerning oneself and life, and the gradual growth of that understanding which begins the spiritual awakening."[7]

Good journeys to all of you. We know you will do well. We believe in you. And we look forward to seeing you back in Heaven!

Sattvic, Rajasic, and Tamasic Activities

*T*o determine which activities in your life fall into the categories of sattva, raja, or tamas energies (upward, horizontal, or downward energies respectively), take a look at the charts below. While I am sure you will think of other, related activities in these lists, be aware that some activities like yoga, exercise, the arts, and sexual activity can certainly be done in a tamas, raja, or a sattva state of mind; the choice is yours.

Sattva

Sattva activities uplift your spirit and realign you in a creative or inspirational way. They make you feel more centered, happy, creative, and closer to God.

Gardening	Attending inspirational seminars	Connecting with Nature	Keeping a personal or dream journal
Singing	Meditating	Camping or hiking	Massage
Dancing	Prayer	Tai chi	Reflexology
Painting	Healing of self	Qigong	Acupuncture

Drawing	Healing of others	Educational programs	Chiropractic
Pottery	Tithing	Learning	Making love
Poetry	Chanting	Inspirational books	Mystical pursuits
Writing	Attending church, temple, or mosque	Sweat lodge	Inspirational concerts
Carving	Weaving	Sacred ceremony	Inspirational plays
Sculpting	Music	Service to others	Inspirational movies
Jewelry-making	Composing	Unconditional love	Attitude of gratitude
Choreography	Teaching others	Nonjudgment	Loving your pets
Embroidery	Nature TV programs	Being a peacemaker	Helping animals
Decorating	Volunteering	Listening to others	Helping children
Cooking	Giving to charities	Creative play	Deep sharing

Raja

Raja activities support your physical, financial, or mental well-being. They primarily serve your physical survival in the world.

Eating and going out to eat	Exercising	Paying bills	Going to work
Shopping for necessities	Going to the doctor	Accounting	Cleaning house
Errands	Playing baseball	Business management	Getting your hair done

The post office	Playing football	Real estate	Putting on makeup
Shopping network	Playing basketball	Computer repair	Massage
Noncreative cooking	Playing soccer	Engineering	Pedicure
Physical sciences	Playing tennis	Mindless TV shows	Dressing
Most textiles	Bowling	"Wheel of Fortune"	Business communication
Machine work	Ping-pong	"Shark Tank"	Portfolio management
Car repair	Running	"Washington Journal"	Job-hunting
Most shopping	Free weights	"College Football"	Apartment-hunting
Daily chores	Going to the gym	"People's Court"	Taxes

Tamas

Tamas energies drag us down and pull us out of our center, numbing us out and creating fear, worry, guilt, stress, anger, false pride, jealousy, addiction, sabotage, or shame. They are ego-driven activities that disconnect us from our higher Self.

Lying	Lust	Negative self-talk	Hunting or killing for sport or money
Cheating	Sexual aberrations	Holding on to fear	Killing for greed
Infidelity	Addictions	Shame or blame	Torturing animals
Thievery	Pornography	Guilt	Spousal abuse

Greed	Violence and aggression	Hating self	Child abuse
False pride	Hate rallies	Hating others	Verbal abuse of others
Arrogance	Bigotry	Self-sabotage	Physical abuse
Cursing	Objectifying the opposite sex	Anger	Blackmail
Vanity	Character defamation	Victim consciousness	Victimizer consciousness
Egoic ambition	War	Gossip	Swindling
Using others	Physical addictions	Horror movies	Fraud
Jealousy and spite	Ignorance	Mental addictions	Emotional addictions

Sample Soul Readings

*O*n the next few pages I have included sample readings from my case files that reveal how the layering of the various elements can affect the personality choices the Soul makes once it comes into the human world. These highly condensed excerpts come from fuller readings, and the names have been changed. Each case originates from a different order of Angels, and each person differs as to the number of elements in its matrix and its Soul age. The longer a Soul spends in the higher dimensions, the better equipped it is to manifest its dreams in this world. And the longer a Soul spends in the fifth dimension, the more personality integration it will have achieved before descending to the earthly plane. Through these complex layerings various life themes are revealed.

Case #1: Aurora Smith, a Ninth-Order Angel

In this life Aurora is a thirty-three-year-old woman who is a nurse at a local hospital who has been suffering from overweight and fatigue. Kind-hearted and giving, she is trying to figure out a solution to her exhaustion as she continues serving others.

Age of Soul: 6.5 billion years old, a midlevel advanced Soul

Order of Angels: Ninth-order Angel with the powers of creativity, giving, and service to others

How many elements: She has only one element in her matrix, water, where she has spent 3.5 billion years, and as a result she is highly empathic; she is naturally clairsentient and clairaudient, but these abilities are in a largely dormant state.

Overview: This high concentration of water, without any other stabilizing element like earth, is responsible for her physical and emotional exhaustion. Without even trying to she continually takes on the problems of others as her energy field attempts to transmute or cleanse others' problems and illnesses through the use of her own empathic field.

Length of time in the fifth dimension: 6 million years, not long enough to attain much increased integration or mastery but long enough to open to a high level of creativity, especially working with nature, plants, and aromas while inhabiting a body with a female polarity.

Incarnated on only two planets in the fifth dimension

Any recognizable systems: This lovely, kind-hearted Soul entered through the Arcturian stargate reserved for high-vibrating, healing Angels of pure hearts.

Lived on how many planets in the fourth dimension: Only eight planets in three separate solar systems

Recognizable systems: Arcturus in the fourth, and Sirius B system in its expression in the fourth, not the third. Like its third-dimensional counterpart, Sirius B is primarily a water-based world.

Lived on how many planets in the third dimension: Four planets in three separate solar systems

Recognizable systems: Sirius B, a water/land-based world where she spent long centuries as an aquatic mermaid, increasing her empathic abilities, clairaudient and clairsentient gifts, and her connection to water and wind. This gives her a high sensitivity for sensing and transmuting other people's disharmonious energies. On another planet she took the form of a flying manta ray with strong devic properties. These large, loving beings can move through water or air and have a spongy material on their underside where they take in energies from the sun to recharge. These beings are all about transmuting disharmony. They create a soft, musical sound that attunes the vibrations of those around them. Finally, she took birth on two planets in the Pleiades, where she was fully human. This was in preparation for coming to Earth. She was there for forty thousand to fifty thousand years. Earth is the only third-dimensional planet she has lived on.

Earth history: She arrived on Earth 26,000 years ago, initially taking birth in Lemuria, which was a more gentle culture attuned to light, sound, crystals, and harmony. This gave her a gentle entry into our world. She served as a healer and priestess in that culture, becoming an ambassador to Atlantis during her last few centuries there. She feared the growing scientific advances of Atlantis and eventually began incarnating into the civilization of Atlantis to try to bring more harmony back to it.

Lifetimes in Atlantis: Eight important lives in Atlantis, most of which were spent as a healer, priestess, or oracle who could receive clairaudient messages from the spirit world. She intuitively felt that Atlantis was headed in the wrong direction, but she felt powerless to change it. She died during the devastation of the Flood. This is an old emotional wound that should be cleared; it has set up a subconscious belief that all of her efforts are futile and will ultimately end in disaster.

Ancient lives of importance

India: Returned to Earth as a monk in the region of India or Tibet, taking a time-out before reentering the conflict of the busy human world. Working in that culture with other high-vibrating people, she helped to preserve some of the records of ancient Lemuria and Atlantis in the caves of Tibet. After several lifetimes she found the courage to return to the mainstream world.

Egypt: Seven lifetimes in Egypt, primarily priestess lives, or simple lives as a housewife with children and family. Three lives were dedicated to healing in the temples of Hathor in Denderah. One life was as a teacher of children, trying to pass on the importance of harmony in one's life and the knowledge of sacred records.

Greece: Nine lifetimes, two as a priestess of Hestia, goddess of hearth and home, and one as a priestess of Aphrodite, goddess of love. One life was as a virginal Sibylline oracle dedicated to learning, teaching, and oracle work. As a woman she was married with children in three lifetimes. She had two male lives working in the creative arts, involved in writing, plays, dance, acting, and music.

Italy and France: A female Essene, she and her daughter were early followers of Jesus and then became part of the Christian Gnostic community after his death. In the first century she was one of the Christians rounded up by Roman officials and torn apart by wild animals in the Roman Coliseum, becoming an early Christian martyr. She went on to become a male and then a female healer in three lives in Italy and France, and then a nun in five separate lives (in Portugal, Spain, France, and Italy). While in Italy, this Soul achieved a high level of union with the spirit of Mother Mary, where she became virtually a saint. This strong, radiant, overlighting energy has stayed with her ever since and is a protective force that helps her in her healing work with others today. In the early 1200s in Southern France she became a Christian Cathar, trying to reform Catholicism and bring it back to its roots. She died before the Cathars were destroyed at Montsegur by the mercenaries hired by the Catholic Church. However, her gift of prophecy had already foretold that the Roman Church would persecute and destroy the Cathar community.

Major soul themes

Female in 61 percent of all lifetimes

A healer in 52 percent of all lives

Lifetimes involved with teaching: 20 percent

Lifetimes involved with the arts: 20 percent

Peasant lives: 30 percent

Spiritually dedicated lives: 58 percent

Creative lives with an emphasis on writing, teaching, and the transmission of knowledge: 20 percent

Soul Blocks: Five key lifetimes of trauma associated with being killed for doing her spiritual mission, plus the trauma of her death at the time of the sinking of Atlantis. Several negative core beliefs have formed as a result of these past traumas. All these need to be cleared for her to successfully do her mission today.

Summary: This soft, lovely soul is all about bringing harmony into the world and helping others return to a place of heart and balance. Naturally shy, she is not a frontrunner kind of healer, but works well with others in almost any circumstance, using her innate empathy and heart energy to help rebalance people and environments. She is highly attuned to Spirit through her beautiful heart and needs to actively align with the Divine Mother again. She also needs to begin to cleanse her field on a regular basis with showers, baths, Epsom salts, and lavender oil because her exhaustion comes from taking on the negative energies of others. Earth-grounding practices are also highly recommended for her, and she needs to spend regular time in a garden or in nature to recharge her batteries. Psychic protection processes are also recommended if she is going to continue working in a hospital, although we suggest that she consider working with children or the elderly on a one-on-one basis instead. This will bring her more joy and be less of a drain on her energy. It will also allow her to begin to reactivate her clairaudient gifts so that she can deliver the messages of Spirit to those around her from the Otherside if she so chooses.

Case #2: David Longfellow, a Power

In this life David is a twenty-seven-year-old construction worker looking to find a woman and get married.

Age of Soul: 5.75 billion years old—a young advanced Soul that is still focused on self and family

Order of Angels: A sixth-order Angel—a Power, a strong builder-class Angel

How many elements: Two elements in his matrix, water (1.5 billion years) and earth (2.5 billion years), totaling 4 billion years of his 5.75 billion years in the sixth and seventh dimensions; a builder Angel focused on making, building, and protecting with his hands in a practical way

Length of time in the fifth dimension: Only spent time in the Milky Way galaxy (6 million years)

Lived on how many planets in the fifth dimension: Two planets

Lived on how many planets in the fourth dimension: Eight to ten planets in three separate solar systems

Lived on how many planets in the third dimension: Four planets in two separate solar systems, Earth being his fifth third-dimensional planet

Recognizable systems: This Soul has a strong history in the Hercules system, where he was involved in agriculture, planting according to a very intricate lunar calendar on a planet that had five moons. He is naturally very attuned to the land and to the astrological energies of the cosmos as they relate to the growth cycles of the plant kingdom, stone structures, temples, and astronomical alignments. He has a great power in his hands—the power to grow things, to heal others, and to protect the land itself. He is an Earth-keeper and builder and will be able to easily detect geophysical changes in the land, including earthquakes and pole realignments. He has a gentle way with animals. He could be an animal whisperer or communicator because he is a strong clairsentient and a natural healer. He lived 130,000 years in this system, a very long time, so he cultivated qualities most of which are dormant today. He went on to incarnate in the Pleiades, which brought him closer to Earth's incarnational orbit. He took birth on two planets in this system over a course of forty thousand years. He eventually took up arms to protect his planet during the Orion Wars. He is a highly capable warrior or soldier, but truly longs for harmony, nature, plants, forests, a family to love, and abiding peace.

Earth history: He arrived on Earth some thirty thousand years ago, incarnating in a rural land outside of Atlantis, where he was content for several lifetimes, living close to the land and growing food. Eventually he made his way to the continent of Atlantis at a time when technology had not yet taken over. It was still a time of kings and queens, where the entire culture was seafaring, and he entered the navy.

Important lives

Atlantis: He became a sailor in five lifetimes, rising to officer level in three of them. In two other lives he became a hydraulics engineer working with the structure of damns, sluices, and waterways in the Atlantis empire. Eventually, when Atlantis had advanced its technology, he became an engineer and deep-sea diver who worked on submarines. In addition, he had two lives as a botanist, was a farmer in five, and in three lives was a healer working with herbal salves, which he produced by communicating with the devic spirits of the land. In one of these lifetimes he became a shaman. Also, he was a priest twice, primarily using his healing work and calm energy to help his villages.

Egypt: Seven lives, an architect in one, a stonemason who built temples in two, and a building engineer in two. On the spiritual side, he had one life as a priestess, charging water with his hands and distributing it through the temples to the populace to assist in healing.

Italy: Five lives, three as a Roman soldier, where he was killed in battle; attained the rank of sergeant or captain in two of these; one life as a sailor, with no wife, who sent back money to his mother and sister.

France: A stonemason in two lives, helping to build the great cathedrals of France in the 1100s, then a life as a village elder during the Middle Ages, helping to build the local church and adding stained-glass windows. He loved the stained glass and insisted on doing these himself. He also incorporated knowledge of Masonic symbols into the architecture. Another important French life was as a soldier in Napoleon's army, where he died in the snows of Russia as a result of a foot injury while the army retreated.

Celtic lands: A Druid in five lifetimes—two lives before Christ and three lives in our common era. (I usually give a lot more details here about the century, the person's rank, his interests or talents, and his location). In Britain he became a tribal leader who fought against the Roman Empire during their invasion in the first century BCE. In Scotland he was a clan leader, working with other clans to repel the invasion of the British in the 1700s or 1800s. He was a major protector of the people and the sacredness of the land in all of these lives.

Major life themes

Gender and family: Male in 67 percent of his lifetimes. He was married in 62 percent of his lives. Children and family are very important to him. Children are in 55 percent of his lives.

A builder/farmer/craftsman in 55 percent of all lifetimes: The strongest theme (I usually give a complete breakdown of the various skills here.)

Lifetimes involved in the military: 35 percent

Lifetimes involved in the creative arts: 5 percent (this does not include lives as an artisan or sculptor)

Positions in leadership: 17 percent of all lifetimes

Nobility: 8 percent

Peasant: 25 percent

Artisan/craftsman: 42 percent

Merchant: 12 percent

Military lives: 30 percent

Soul Blocks

Vows: 275

Curses: none

Bindings: Over 200 mostly from those he has promised to take care of and has had to leave behind. These cords should be cleared immediately since they are draining his energy and keeping him stuck.

Erroneous beliefs: About 70, all about limitation of life, money, jobs, love, and success

Summary: A practical manifester and builder with skill in his hands, this Soul is very gifted with plants, animals, foods, crops, and working with leather and wood. He still needs to develop his spiritual and mental natures, since his focus has been in mastering the physical world.

Because of his density from the earth element, he has a hard time awakening his mental and spiritual consciousness. He has multiple lifetimes of suppressing his softer feelings, denying his feminine side, and shouldering through, no matter what. He has twelve lifetimes of wounding patterns around these matters and needs to find a way to break through to make a connection with his higher Self. In this lifetime he has not awakened his spiritual abilities, thinking that he must first focus on practical security matters and establishing a family before reawakening his healing abilities or his ability to communicate with animals and the land. He would benefit from getting a large companion dog that can begin to awaken these gifts in him.

Case #3: Melanie Parker, a Virtue

In this lifetime Melanie is a thirty-seven-year-old violinist who is also a Reiki healer. Melanie is just beginning to open up to a new level of healing work and has become interested in color therapy and crystal layouts.

Age of Soul: 6.75 billion years old, a late-level advanced Soul moving toward master Soul

Order of Angels: Fifth order Angel—a Virtue working with light, sound, and color, and a weaver

How many elements: Three elements in her matrix: 2.5 billion years in water; 1.5 billion years in earth; and 1 billion years in air, making a total of 5 billion years in the higher dimensions of her 6.5 billion years

Overview: A beautiful, high-vibrating planetary Angel with strong clairaudient and clairsentient gifts and a talent in the arts, she is not only a natural healer, musician, and artist, but has great access to the inner planes of ideas since she is clairvoyant as well. This Soul has strong themes directing her to work with light, sound, music, dance, movement, and color, all to create peace and harmony.

Length of time in the fifth dimension: Only in the Milky Way galaxy, 7 million years

Lived on how many planets in the fifth dimension: Five planets

Recognizable systems: She entered through the Arcturian stargate and then spent time in the Orion system, working with the Galactic Councils to broker peace and committed to harmony in all dealings.

Lived on twelve planets in the fourth dimension: Five separate solar systems

Lived on five planets in the third dimension: Four separate solar systems

Recognizable star systems: The Pleiades. She had many lives on four separate planets in three solar systems in the Pleiades over the course of sixty thousand years. She has also taken life as a mermaid and as a terrestrial human being on Sirius B, attuning to higher sensitivities of sonar, sound, and energy perception through the water world. Earth is her sixth third-dimensional planet.

Earth history: This Soul arrived on Earth some 120,000 years ago at the time of Lemuria. She was here for 20,000 years, working as a priestess most of that time, attuning the crystalline land matrix with sound in the establishment of a peaceful civilization. As a high priestess she was actively in touch with ambassadors from the Sirius B system and local aspects of the Galactic Council who were interfacing with Lemuria using stargates. After 20,000 years she left Earth to spend time on other planets. She returned about 24,000 thousand years ago at the time of Atlantis, arriving as part of a diplomatic delegation. She stayed for 3,000 years, then left. She returned some 18,000 years ago and then remained on Earth to help that civilization prosper, becoming a part of a star empire.

Important pre-Flood lifetimes

Lemuria: Six important lifetimes in Lemuria, primarily as a priest, priestess, seer, and high priestess working with devic energies and leadership for the greater good; highly developed connection with crystals, grids, and sound harmonies

Atlantis: Nine important lifetimes in Atlantis; a healer twice, a priestess twice, and a council elder three times. She also became a female scientist working with crystals and sound during the technological centuries. She also experienced a life as a male doctor working with lasers, light therapy, crystals, and psychological counseling of patients undergoing surgery, primarily for skin with lesions, scales, or issues of appearance. These are the "Temples of Beauty" that Edgar Cayce spoke about.

Important ancient lifetimes

Egypt: Strong history in Egypt, with nine lifetimes, five as a priestess and two as a priest; dedicated to Hathor for healing, sound, and the use of music and crystals in three of them; also strong alignments with Isis, goddess of wisdom, and Nuit, goddess of the heavens

Sumeria or Chaldea: One life as a male priest astronomer dedicated to the moon god Nannar

India: Two lives as a male priest/astronomer who was a counselor to the Indian rajas, or kings

China: One life as a male priest/astronomer serving the emperor of China

Persia: One life time as a Persian magi/astronomer caught up in the political intrigues of the day and the struggles of the good and bad people around him who were vying for power; feels like three hundred years after Zoroaster brought his teachings forth

Britain: Two lives as a Druid healer, one male and one female; he studied astronomy in the male life

Greece: A priest of Poseidon in ancient Greece, living on an island and working with the sea, dolphins, healing, and sound

France, Italy, Germany: A Druid in France in two lives, and also a Druid in Italy and Germany. In all of these lives she was hunted and killed by the Church for her healing abilities and her influence as a wisdom elder in the community. She was put to death by the Church in 563 CE, 920 CE, and sometime in the mid-eleventh century. She became a Christian Cathar in the 1200s. In that life she was once again murdered by the Church for political reasons. After this she took a break, joining several monasteries in various lives as a monk, a priest, and a nun to ensure her own safety. She worked with medicinal plants in these monasteries and continued to heal the sick, staying safe from the rising persecution by the Inquisition. In the late 1400s she began to incarnate again, this time in the royal class, seeking to become a leader. She had to navigate the political intrigues of the French and Italian courts. She had five lifetimes there over the course of three centuries, trying to make a difference through the influence of her noble birth. She faced many challenges dealing with the power-hungry politics of intermediate Souls who sought power at any price. She was poisoned in one of these lives, yet managed to support humanitarian policies of fairness despite major opposition.

Major life themes

Healing: in 40 percent of all lifetimes, the strongest theme

Science: 5 percent

Astronomy/astrology: 15 percent

Teaching: 15 percent

The arts: 25 percent of all lifetimes, with an emphasis on color, sound, light, and music

Positions in leadership: 22 percent of all lifetimes

Nobility: 25 percent

Spiritually dedicated lives: 37 percent

Peasant: 5 percent

Artisan: 22 percent

Merchant: 5 percent

Military: 1 percent

Soul blocks

Vows: 230 vows, 12 still positive, but the rest should be cleared

Bindings: 21 bindings or cords that are sucking her energy, 11 of which need clearing

Erroneous beliefs: 32 erroneous beliefs formed in times of trauma; must be cleared

Major traumas: 5 lifetimes of wounding that still remain and should be dissolved, including 5 lifetimes killed for religious reasons

Summary: Melanie is a noble healer/leader who aims to transform consciousness. She can work one-on-one with people or with large groups, at the local, national, or planetary level. She is a natural healer interested in the underlying harmony of the universe. Truth-seeking and pure of spirit and intention. She has some emotional and karmic clearing to do because of the many lifetimes in which she was killed, in order to fully embody her destiny in this life and in future lifetimes.

Case #4: Pam Parsons, Principality

In this life Pam is a business analyst who consults for a living. She wants to write books and establish a national speaking platform focused on the importance of societal values, generational differences, and how various cultural groups can work together to change the world. Frustrated in love, she has been married five times and is ready to give up on love relationships.

Age of Soul: 6.75 billion years old, a late-level advanced Soul

Order of Angels: Seventh-order Angel—a Principality, or Archai, pioneers in ideas, discoveries, and innovations

How many elements: Three—water (2 billion years), air (1 billion years), and earth (1.5 billion years), totaling 4.5 billion years of her 6.75 billion years. This person thinks globally because she came to work on a planetary level in the angelic kingdom, thus her desire is to help the planet and reach millions for healing and global change.

Overview: This Soul has been male in 61 percent of her lifetimes. In this lifetime she is female and challenged to find a romantic partner as strong as she is. She has tried to fit into the traditional female model of marriage and children, but this is not her destiny. In this life she is attempting to bring her successful lives as a male over into her expression as a woman, thus merging her male and female aspects that have separated for centuries. She has important, significant work to do on this planet, and marriage and children are completely secondary.

Length of time in the fifth dimension: 7 million years

Only incarnated in the Milky Way galaxy

How many planets in the fifth dimension: She has lived on only three, but the most important is in the Orion system, where she became connected with the galactic councils. This is where she first became interested in governance, statesmanship, and the administrative policies or philosophies that help to encourage the growth of millions of people living on various planets.

She has lived on thirteen planets in the fourth dimension, in seven different solar systems, including the peaceful society of Arcturus and a system called Centauri.

She has lived on five planets in the third dimension; Earth is her sixth. Sirius B is the only one I recognize, giving her increased empathy, sensitivity, and clairsentient abilities.

Arrived on Earth: Visited Atlantis in a peace delegation about 25,000 years ago, then returned to settle here about 14,000 years ago.

Important lifetimes in Atlantis: Six important lives in Atlantis, five of which were male: one as a hydraulics engineer working on the sluices and water power plants of ancient Atlantis; two as an elder or council member helping to establish and administer policies for one of the provinces of Atlantis; one as a sea captain with considerable leadership and respect, linked to the governance of the Atlantean rulers; one as a professor at a university, where he was the head of his department, focused on what today we would call sociology, with an emphasis on governance and statesmanship.

Major life themes

 Gender: 61 percent male

 Family: Married in only 20 percent of her lifetimes, and children in only 12 percent, being more focused on work

 Healer: 20 percent

 Arts, engineering, and building crafts: 20 percent, including two lives as a stonemason and builder. In one life (as a man) she built a church and did all the stained glass.

Leadership: Nine lives, including eight as a statesman/elder in Atlantis, a councilman in Greece around 220 BCE, and a senator in ancient Rome in the first century after Christ

Historian: Three lives, as a writer/historian in ancient Rome around 106 BCE, and as a writer and believer in the rights of democracy in France in the 1700s prior to and following the French Revolution

Philosopher: In Germany, writing about freedom and fairness, from around the late 1300s to the early half of the 1400s; a deep thinker in that life who was also a research scholar considering the works of both the Church and also other hidden treatises on the nature of human-kind, the Soul, and Spirit

Noble-born: in 20 percent of her lives, including three as a duke, one as a baron, and one as an earl, in all cases trying to oversee her people fairly in governance

Knight fighting for principles: in nine lifetimes, including one in England, two in France, two in Germany, one in Austria, one in Portugal, one in Poland, and one in Scotland.

Warrior: 12 percent of lives, including the Knights Templar in the late 1200s, and one life spent as a general in Rome. All these lives were about fighting for a country, a cause, a principle, or a way of life that supported a better set of spiritual principles that could be applied to society.

Future: This person is here to write two important books grounded in the energies of all three elements she has experienced. These books are breakthrough ideas (air) of practical governance (earth) that teach compassion and empathy for other tribal groups (water) to bring greater harmony to the world. As an Archai, a pioneer on the leading edge of thought, her job is about bringing higher consciousness ideas into practical forms to inspire others to reshape our world into a more altruistic and positive society. The pursuit of marriage will only pull her off of her course now. If she follows her plan, these books will come out in 2018 and 2020.

Soul blocks

Vows: She has 320 vows, most of which are irrelevant to this life and need clearing.

Curses: No curses

Bindings: Only about thirty cords or bindings, only two of which don't work for her today. The rest are to positive people and relationships in her current life.

Erroneous belief systems formed in times of trauma: Only forty-nine negative beliefs, some of which are connected to the fear of shaping her message based on the repression of information from the early Church and stemming from past-life programming. Other beliefs have to do with self-worth issues around being a woman and confusion about role models in romantic relationship with men. Only three major lifetime traumas need clearing.

Summary: This Soul has chosen to come into a female form at this time in order to merge her own masculine and feminine natures. Yet this is a personal challenge for her, and she will have to return to eventually allow herself to learn how to develop her divine feminine nature and be successful in an intimate family dynamic. This is the first life where she has been able to bring her strong male themes into a female body. In doing so, she is challenged to find a romantic equal, but is also contributing to the rise of female wisdom and leadership in the twenty-first century.

Case # 5: Michael Stronghold, Archangel

Michael is a forty-seven-year ex–military intelligence officer who has been opening to Spirit in the past seven years. He is now an inspirational teacher who has begun to do healing work with others.

Age of Soul: 7 billion years old, an early master Soul

Order of Angels: Eighth-order Angel—an Archangel, connecting others for inspiration and protection

How many elements: This Soul has all four elements: water (2 billion years), air (1 billion years), earth (2 billion years), and fire (.5 billion years), making for 5.5 billion years of his 7 billion years, meaning that he is a very large, complex energy powerhouse.

Overview: This is a powerful, noble planetary Angel in service to truth and justice. He is a warrior for truth with many talents and access to all of the spiritual gifts. He is a natural leader with a brilliant mind who is willful, charismatic, intelligent, problem-solving, and highly committed to his purpose. He protects men, women, and children, as well as deeper spiritual principles as long as he can stay aligned with his higher Self.

Length of time in the fifth dimension: 8 million years. This Soul spent time in service as one of Michael's Archangels for around 1.5 million years; thus he is strong, loyal, purposeful, resilient, powerful, and noble. This is a Soul of high integrity who is absolute in his approach to life, which in the past has been very black and white. He is now making the change from life as a warrior to life as a healer and leader who can inspire and transform others.

Number of galaxies the Soul has been in: Because of his time in the fire kingdom, this Soul has traveled through three separate galaxies—Andromeda, Pegasus, and the Milky Way.

How many planets he has lived on in the fifth dimension: Six

Any recognizable systems: In this galaxy this Soul has long been centered on activities closer to the center of the galaxy, in Orion's Belt. This is the seat of the Galactic Council. He brings with him a powerful will to protect the good, and he is daunting in his resolution. Loyal to a fault, he is the consummate noble warrior who has allowed himself little or no time for personal exploration, romantic relationships, family, or the development of his own artistic talents.

He has lived on twenty-eight planets in the fourth dimension, in fourteen separate solar systems.

He has lived on seven planets in the third dimension, in five separate solar systems.

Recognizable systems: The Orion system, particularly the blue star Rigel, where a strong contingent of warriors live. This Soul is very old, and thus he has a powerful connection with the old galactic empire overseen by Horus, the god of truth.

In recent times: Canis Major for 180,000 years, Nibiru for 50,000 years, the Sirius A system for 20,000 years, and the Pleiadian system for 120,000 years. Earth is his eighth physical planet.

Arrived on Earth: 55,000 years ago, with a delegation of warriors. Then he left Earth. He returned 38,000 years ago and settled in Atlantis around 29,000 years ago. Initially part of the establishment of structural order helping to build Atlantis as a galactic capital, he and some of his Archangel brothers were warrior-protectors who were involved in setting up the infrastructure of this civilization, including their navy and the rulership of Atlantean colonies. He is very connected to the Earth's grid.

Important lifetimes in Atlantis: Twelve, including one life as a king, three as a prince, and three as a general or admiral; also became a magician-alchemist in two lives, working to master the laws of the universe. Deeply private, this person was focused on spiritual law, the discovery of magnetism, electromagnetic ley lines or the grid system, and the creation of energetic force fields that were used as protective walls between warring provinces. He has a strong interest in science and engineering, as well as spiritual service.

Major life themes

Gender: 73 percent male

Family: Married in only 12 percent of his lifetimes, with children in only 7 percent

Warrior: in 68 percent of all lives, with little time for a personal life or developing artistic abilities

Noble birth: in about 45 percent of all lives; a prince eleven times—in Britain twice, France once, Austria twice, Denmark once, Russia once, Egypt three times (including Old Kingdom once and Middle Kingdom twice); became a king five times, in Egypt, France, Spain, and

Denmark, as well as Atlantis; an earl, duke, or baron seven lifetimes; took birth as a Persian prince in two lifetimes, taking a look at the spiritual beliefs of Moslems from the other side

Peasant: in only 2 percent of all lives

Stonemason: seven lifetimes

Rosicrucian: twice; naturally drawn to the Mysteries and a deeper understanding of the universe; five lives served as a diplomat or ambassador for Egypt, Persia, France, and Israel

Knights Templar: in two lives, in one a knight who defended Jerusalem from the Moslems

Knight: in seven lives, fighting in three of the Crusades as a Christian, for Britain, France, and Germany

Soul blocks:

Vows: As an Archangel, this Soul has many vows that bind him today. He has some 470 vows today, only 23 of which are still working for him. The rest should be cleared immediately since they pull him in certain directions that are no longer valid for his personal evolution.

Curses: Michael has two curses that need lifting. These are energetic barriers to creating a life of love and happiness, as well as obstacles to achieving his full potential and power. These negative astral thought forms create constant roadblocks on his path to having the love he needs to heal the wounds of so much personal loss that keeps him in conflict so that he constantly feels like he must fight through everything in his life to win. Although he is strong, this is exhausting.

Bindings: In addition, he has 312 cords or bindings that need to be cleared. Most of these are not of a personal nature, but rather cords created by commitments to save others who are now long dead, distracting him when he comes in contact with the reincarnations of any of these people.

Erroneous belief systems formed in times of trauma: Fifty-seven, including some that block him from having a fulfilling and intimate personal life with a partner of the opposite sex because of his fear of losing that person and because of his commitment to duty first. These personal ties are thought of as a vulnerability that he cannot afford.

Most of his closest relationships have been with warrior companions on the battlefield. He needs to open up his feminine side and allow himself to love again in order to grow. He has six major lifetime traumas that need clearing, and seventeen lives killed in defense of a noble cause.

Summary: This highly intelligent, gifted Soul began to turn away from his lust for battle about three hundred years ago, for the first time asking himself if there wasn't a better way. In his current life he is meant to open up to his shamanic healing powers again and to use his focus to take a different path. He will find that he has great healing powers in his hands, and as he opens his heart he will also discover that his natural charisma and alchemical powers will give him the ability to facilitate spontaneous healings in others. Many of those who come to him will be his own past-life warrior companions who need healing. He will also attract old enemies, giving him a chance to rebalance the karma created by centuries of battle. He is destined to become a charismatic leader, speaker, and healer of others, teaching them the path of diplomacy, forgiveness, and peace, but first he must find this in himself.

Case #6: Sarah Lawrence, Cherubim

In this life Sarah works with the blind, helping them to sense and feel colors and awakening their hearing and other senses to have a richer, more fulfilling life.

Age of Soul: 7.5 billion years old, a midlevel master Soul

Order of Angels: Third-order Angel—a Cherubim, using sound and light to transform others

How many elements: This Soul has three elements: water (3 billion years), air (.75 billion years), and earth (1.75 billion years). A planetary Angel, this Soul is focused on harmony and love at the global level. She spent 5.5 billion years in the sixth and seventh dimensions before ever arriving in the fifth dimension. Because of the long amount of time spend in the water kingdom she is naturally attuned to the creative arts, contact with the elementals, and also to the healing arts.

Length of time in the fifth dimension: 7.5 million years, where she became a creative muse, inspiring the minds and hearts of others in the third and fourth dimensions

Number of galaxies: Only the Milky Way

Planets in the fourth dimension: twenty-two, five of which were primarily water worlds. Here she spent 50,000 years as a devic spirit inspiring others in the third dimension below. She spent 10,000 years as a fairy on both fourth- and third-dimensional planets.

Planets in the third dimension: Four; Earth is her fourth 3-D world

Arrived in Lemuria: 40,000 years ago as a devic spirit summoned by a priestess of Lemuria to help harmonize the grids. Then she returned to the Sirius B home worlds as an aquatic human. She lived on that planet for the better part of 20,000 years. Eventually she took birth as a mermaid on Earth, in the Pacific Ocean, for about 5,000 years. Eventually she became fully human around 6,300 years ago.

Major life themes:

Gender: 63 percent female in her lifetimes, developing the gifts of intuition, compassion, and wisdom

Family: Married in 29 percent of her lifetimes, with children in 18 percent of them, dying in childbirth in two of them

Religious or spiritual lifetimes: 41 percent of all her lives on Earth have been dedicated to spiritual service. This includes being a priestess in twelve separate lives (five of which were in Egypt), including two lives spent in the temples of Denderah (dedicated to Hathor) doing light and sound healing work; two lives spent in Greece (one dedicated to Aphrodite, and one to Athena); five lifetimes as a priest, three of which were spent in Greece in the temples of Apollo at Delphi and in the temples of Poseidon; and a life as a nun in Spain in the late 1500s. Strong spiritual gifts developed in all of these lifetimes, including gifts as an oracle as well as a dancer, poet, singer, and musician.

The arts: 53 percent of her lives spent in the arts. The breakdown of artistic talents includes five lives spent as a singer, fifteen as a dancer, twelve as a musician, nine as a painter, two as a sculptor, three as a craftsperson doing mosaic tiles, five as a weaver, five doing needlepoint, three involving some acting, one in the circus working with animals and riding bareback on circus horses, seven acting as a creative muse for others, and five lifetimes as a poet.

Healing: 60 percent of her lives have been spent developing her healing gifts. The breakdown includes nine lives as an herbalist; five working with crystals; nine working with the healing effects of light, sound, and music; three working with color therapy and the effects of color healing on the aura and physical body; nine learning to channel healing energy directly through the hands; and five lives as a Druid (three of these in the BC period of time, and two in the last two thousand years, one during which she lost her life).

Nobly born: In about 25 percent of all of her lifetimes in order to help others; 12 percent born into the artisan class.

In more recent times: This Soul has a strong history in the Nile in Egypt, as well as in Native American tribes and particularly in the island cultures of the Pacific. This is because of her love of water. She has incarnated on the Hawaiian Islands in a least eight lifetimes. In one of these she was a female matriarch and tribal leader, and in another she was revered as an incarnation of the Mother Goddess because of her ability to communicate with the spirits of the land, water, wind, and volcano. She has great wisdom and patience and a love of whales, dolphins, the ocean, and Earth. She considers all beings her children. These were lives in which she was completely in spiritual service to the Divine, inspiring and wisely guiding her people to connect with their inner selves.

Soul blocks

Vows: Only 140 vows. Originally this Soul made many vows and commitments during the course of her spiritual service to others, but as a master Soul she had dissolved many of them, and so today she is not bound in present time by many of those agreements. Twenty of these original vows still serve her, but the rest should be cleared immediately.

Curses: No curses

Bindings: 300 small tendrils connected to her third chakra, to those people she is still sworn to assist in past lives. It would be best to clear these since they are, collectively, a drain on her energy bodies.

Erroneous belief systems formed in times of trauma: Only 21, a very low number. These beliefs are primarily about not feeling totally safe inhabiting a physical body since she was reluctant to move from the worlds of fairies and mermaids into the full density of our Earth. To be more effective she needs to release these fears and reservations so that she can more fully inhabit her body.

Summary: This beautiful, highly advanced master Soul has come in again and again to bring wisdom, beauty, harmony, and balance to Earth. She did not have to return to this planet but came back because of a vow she made at the time of Lemuria, a vow to assist the human race in its spiritual evolution. Her deeper life themes involve helping to heal the people of planet Earth by raising them to a higher energetic frequency, where the conflict and stress of their daily lives falls away. She has done this in lifetimes in both the healing and creative arts. She has brought joy, love, laughter, and inspiration to others through the use of her many artistic and healing gifts.

Glossary

Adi-karma: A Sanskrit term meaning "first karma." This is the mechanism by which the Soul comes to believe that it is separated from God, allowing it to descend into the worlds of duality and experience free will. Through Adi-karma we come to believe that we are alone, abandoned, or unloved. To regain entrance into the realms of unity we must find a way through this false belief.

Akashic Records: The recording mechanism for all events that transpire in the lower worlds. We can think of them as the memory banks of God. *Akashic* comes from the Sanskrit word *akasa,* meaning "the cosmic ether." Hinduism explains that the *akasha* is formed when Brahman, the Supreme Creator, mixes with the illusionary veils, or *maya,* to create the lower worlds. From the *akasha* all elements are born, forming the foundations of the physical realms and the subtle regions of Heaven.

Ammit: A mythical Egyptian creature composed of the elements of a lion, a hippopotamus, and a crocodile, Ammit was known as the "Devourer of the Dead" or the "Eater of Hearts." Ammit sits beneath the scales of justice in the Halls of Amenti to remind the Soul that if your life has not been one of goodness, then your heart will be consumed. This reminds us that a selfish, wasted life contributes nothing to the growth of the Soul.

Angel: A pure expression of the radiance of the Source before it acquires the attributes of a human being. The name is derived from the Greek *angelos* and the Hebrew *mal'akh,* meaning "messenger."

Angelic Twin: The Soul's eternal essence that dwells in the causal plane and is the integrating aspect of ourselves that processes and learns from every lifetime. This higher part of us never leaves the heavenly realms, but extends a part of itself into the physical and astral realms to take birth in the worlds below.

Anubis: The son of Osiris and Nepthys who weighs the deceased person's heart against the feather of truth on the balance scales of Ma'at.

Apophis: The many-headed serpent in Egyptian cosmology that the Soul must battle as it crosses the Duat on the way to Heaven. He is a symbol of all the negative traits, emotions, and thought forms that we have not yet conquered, including lust, greed, addiction, fear, anger, vanity, self-judgment, shame, and guilt.

Ariadne: Ariadne is the spinner of the red thread of fate who was said to be married to the judge of the Underworld, Rhadamanthys. She was the daughter of King Minos of Crete and the princess who helped Theseus, the Greek hero, escape from the Minotaur in the underground labyrinth. These symbols all represent the escape of the Soul from the labyrinth that is the world of matter.

Armaiti: The Divine Mother. She is the plenum, the hidden principle of dark matter, the Black Madonna, and the Virgin of the World who gave birth to the universe before anything else existed. This is the divine being that I know as Odeona.

arupaloka: A Tibetan term that refers to the formless worlds that do not have the same kind of structures as we do on Earth. These worlds include the sixth and seventh dimensions, and are far more fluid than our realm. Arupa worlds also comprise the higher three levels of the mental plane.

Asphodel Meadows: The Asphodel Meadows are a magical borderland between Heaven and Earth in ancient Greek cosmology. The Greeks believed that the Soul journeyed here at the time of death, taking a path upward to the Elysian Fields, or downward to the realm of Hades. The Soul also returned to this meadow when it was ready to begin a new life. The Asphodel Meadows were named after a white six-petal flower that symbolized rebirth. Like the lily, this flower has six petals, reminding us of the Merkaba field used to travel into the higher realms.

astral plane: The fourth dimensional realm governed by twenty-four primary laws and separated into seven distinct levels, containing both the realms that we think of as Hell, as well as those we call Heaven. This is but an intermediate plane that is governed by feelings and thoughts. To achieve union with the higher Self, a Soul must reach the higher octaves of the mental plane.

Atman: The aspect of Creator or Source that slumbers within every Soul, like a cosmic seed waiting to be awakened. It is the living Spirit that animates our Souls. If Brahman is the Soul of All That Is, then Atman is the cosmic Soul that has been scattered throughout the universe, the One whose living fire indwells us all.

Atum: The Egyptian name for the first primordial drop of movement in the Cosmic Ocean that set everything in motion. Atum is the Creator, the primordial Word that moved across the waters of the deep, bringing the cosmos into being.

Auriel: The goddess of compassion and love and Creatrix from which all other aspects of the Divine Mother flow.

Avici or Avitci: In Tibetan Buddhism, the lowest level of the astral plane, where Souls are steeped in negative thought forms and self-created delusions, making it hard for the light of God to break through. Also known as the City of Shadows, or in Judaism, Sheol, this is a place where Restoration Masters seek to break through and help the Soul to remember its own divine essence.

Ba: The Egyptian name for the luminous spirit or Oversoul that remains in the higher realms of light, sending a portion of itself into the world in each new lifetime.

bardo: *Bar-do* means "between two" things, a reference to its role as an in-between or intermediate dimension between our earthly life and the other dimensions.

Bardo Thodol: The Tibetan Book of the Dead, also known as "Liberation through Hearing in the Intermediate State," a reference to the Soul's ability to tune in to the celestial sound current in order to transcend the cycle of rebirth.

Boat of a Million Years: In Egyptian cosmology, the boat in which the Soul journeys through the Duat to Heaven. The Soul is accompanied by several stellar gods on this journey: Ra, the sun god or god of light; Thoth, the god of wisdom; Isis, the goddess of love; Ma'at, the goddess of truth; and Set, the god of the personality or little self.

Book of Life: Another term for the Akashic Records. These records are linked to the causal body, which is referred to by the masters as our "storehouse of good." Once we attain mastery, this storehouse is then released to us by the divine I AM presence.

Brahmandas: In Hinduism, the universal guardians that are the overseeing consciousnesses that help to regulate the immensity of Creation in the various universes. These are direct emanations of the Supreme Creator.

chi: The animating life force, equivalent to *prana* or *qi* in Indian and Japanese traditions, and the Holy Spirit in Christian thought.

Chikhai bardo: This is the intermediate state where the Soul goes between its mortal life and its time in the astral planes. The Chikhai bardo is described as a place of gray mists, similar to the Fields of Asphodel or the Halls of Amenti, which are thought of as the antechamber of Heaven. This is the place reported by near-death experiencers where the Soul receives its life review before going into whichever realm of Heaven is closest to its consciousness.

City of Light: Often described by those who have passed to the Otherside and returned, this luminous Crystal City has seven gates. It is described as a place of perpetual beauty, where light seems to radiate from everything, as if all things were lit from within.

City of Shadows: The lowest level of the astral plane, called Avici, where Souls who have participated in hideous crimes are kept. Here they are in healing with Restoration Masters who try to help them transform before they are ever allowed to return to Earth.

Cosmic Egg: Sometimes called the "world egg," the primordial egg or drop in which the Divine Mother and Divine Father reside.

Council of Elders: The overseeing group of sages assigned to each individual Soul. Since they reside in the higher levels of the fifth dimension, they appear as beings of pure white light, thus they are sometimes called the Council of Light. Others have referred to them as the Lords of Karma, because they oversee the spiritual and karmic evolution of every individual Soul. Each person has his or her own group of sages, or Council, which may consist of as few as three or as many as twelve enlightened teachers, depending on the maturity and complexity of your development.

Course Curriculum: This is the group of lessons that each Soul who comes into the lower realms must learn and master. While there are many traits, qualities, and attributes that we must experience and balance, the core of this program is the correct use of love and power.

daimon: A Greek term used by Socrates to refer to a spirit guide, overlighting spirit, or inner teacher. One's daimon is said to guide the unfolding of one's destiny here on Earth.

Demeter and Persephone: Two Greek goddesses who represent the Divine Mother and Daughter, just as in Christianity we have the Divine Father and Son. Persephone is the innocent, unevolved Soul, the cosmic seed that has fallen from the Tree of Life. Demeter is Mother Nature, the "measure of all things."

deva: *Deva* is synonymous with *Angel* but is also used to describe various elemental spirits that work in harmony with nature. *Deva* is derived from the word *div,* meaning "to shine."

Devachan: A theosophical term that means the "Land of the Shining Gods." In Tibetan Buddhism the similar *Dewachen* means "blissful land." This is a specially guarded part of the inner realms where the great masters oversee our spiritual evolution, excluding all sorrow and pain from our experience. It is equivalent to the higher levels of Heaven in the mental plane. Ancient wisdom tells us that the amount of time that a Soul spends in Devachan between lifetimes depends on the amount of wisdom, knowledge, and goodness that the Soul has achieved during the course of its earthly life.

dharma: A person's life work or mission.

Dharmakaya: A Tibetan term meaning "Truth Body," also referred to as the "Clear Light." This brilliant light seen at the moment of death is actually a reflection of the person's own Angelic Twin that has come to greet her. It is located at the top of the fifth dimension in the causal plane. This truth body is the pure white fire being that meets us after death and who has come to review what we have learned in each lifetime, flooding us with unconditional love and wisdom.

Dhyani-Chohans: Supreme masters, planetary spirits, or even the archangelic beings of light who help to administer the cosmos.

Duat: In Egyptian cosmology, the plane of transition between Heaven and Earth that the Soul must travel after death. Some believed it to be the starry skies; others to be a misty, veiled sea, but it is clearly a bardo or in-between territory between the physical and the astral dimensions.

elementals: These subtle-energy beings act as guardian spirits to the plant, animal, and mineral kingdoms and are young, benevolent agents of the angelic kingdom.

Eleusinian Mysteries: Perhaps the foremost Mystery School in ancient Greece, the Eleusinian Mysteries were created by the priestesses of Isis, who established their main center at Ephesus. Like the Orphic Mysteries, the Eleusinian Mysteries taught initiates about the eternal nature of the Soul and its journey into the inner realms.

Elysian Fields: A vast paradisiacal land on the western margins of Earth. These are the immortal lands of bliss in Greek cosmology, where those who have lived lives of goodness are transported after death. This realm is synonymous with the Field of Reeds in Egyptian cosmology, and the Isles of the Blessed.

Emerald Tablets: One of few remaining books of Thoth, the god of wisdom from ancient Egypt. The Emerald Tablets chronicle his experiences as an initiate of traveling in the subtle dimensions, giving us insight into what he found there.

etheric double: The energetic sheath closest to the physical body that acts as an interface between spirit and matter. While we are living, it extends about an inch from the body, mimicking its shape and appearance. It detaches from the body during the first thirty-six hours after death, and if the body is cremated, then it breaks up quickly, having lost its center of attraction. When a person is buried, this etheric double may float above the grave until it slowly disintegrates.

evolution: The inward-flowing wave of life that leads us back to Source, awakens us to consciousness, and brings us back to union with our highest Self. It is feminine in nature.

Field of Reeds: The Egyptian name for Heaven, or the higher astral plane that we go to after death. This is a paradise of shady trees, magical forests, and pastoral gardens, all blooming in a perpetual season of spring. Here Souls can experience friendship, joy, peace, and love without the heartache, pain, and struggle that we know in the physical world.

five rivers of Hades: In Greek cosmology these five rivers represent the five negative emotions that can bind the Soul to the lower astral realms. They are: Phlegethon, the river of fire, for those caught in the heat of their own unbridled passions; Cocytus, the river of lamentation and regret; Lethe, the river of unconsciousness or oblivion; Styx, the river of hate; and Acheron, the river of sorrow into which all the other rivers empty.

Galactic Council: An overseeing body of masters that resides at the higher levels of the mental plane and who overlight the development of beings living in the physical worlds. This council also includes physical beings who are part of the Galactic Federation. In the third, fourth, and fifth dimensions, this Federation is made up of over a hundred member worlds whose job it is to oversee younger planets until they reach a certain stage of maturity. Then these worlds are contacted directly and asked to join as fully participating members.

genesis matrix: The angelic place of origin that each of us comes from.

Great Central Sun: The vibrational center of the universe, understood to be a place of great enlightenment, ruled over by the vibration of the Christ energies. It is the central governing site for the higher light that descends into the lower realms of creation.

Great Chain of Being: The mystical concept of the descent of Spirit into the worlds of form and back again. This Great Chain of Being recognizes the existence of higher and lower life-forms that are constantly in spiritual evolution.

Great Work: A term used in the Mystery Schools for the transformational process of making lead into gold; an analogy for the conversion of the little self into the gold of the divine Self.

gunas: The three fundamental waves of movement that we swim in: sattva, raja, and tamas, representing the upward-moving energies back to the Source, the outward-moving energies to the material planes, and the downward-moving energies into the demonic realms.

Hades: A Greek name for the lower regions of the Underworld ruled by the god Hades.

Halls of Amenti: The antechamber of Heaven in Egyptian cosmology.

Heaven: Known in many traditions as Paradise, the Far Country, or the Summerland. Theosophists call it Devachan. In Hindu teachings this heavenly realm is called *Svarga;* in Sanskrit it is called Sukhavati, and to Tibetan Buddhists it is Dewachen, the land of light from which we come.

Hell: The Underworld, also known as Hades, Hel, or Acheron in Greek cosmology. This realm has three levels: The lowest is the City of Shadows; next is the region of violent angry spirits; and last is pretaloka, the realm of pretas, or hungry ghosts, that overlays our own physical world. These hungry ghosts have unresolved business that prevents them from emotionally moving on and letting go.

Hermes Trismegistus: Thrice Great Hermes is another name for Thoth, the Egyptian god of wisdom, travel, communication, astronomy, architecture, healing, and writing.

Horus: The son of Osiris, an incarnation of one of the Four Kumaras, or direct aspects of God. Horus is the Lord of Light who leads the Soul before the throne of Osiris in the Halls of Amenti.

I AM Presence: The I AM Presence is the portion of God that is individualized for each person and cannot be destroyed. Theosophical teachings tell us that the Self begins with a permanent atom of being, which is a God particle. This God particle is the permanent atom of your being linked to the Father/Mother God, which then becomes the cause out of which the effect proceeds.

involution: The outward-flowing wave of life that takes the Soul out into the worlds of form to begin its evolutionary journey. It is masculine in nature.

Isles of the Blessed: Greek term for the heavenly worlds, synonymous with the Elysian Fields.

Isis: The goddess of wisdom and healing.

Issa: Another name for Jesus, beloved the world over as the great world savior in Christianity; also an incarnation of one of the Four Kumaras, or direct aspects of God.

Ka: Associated with a person's fate and also connected to the goodness of his heart, it is said to be a spiritual twin, that comes with us into each lifetime, similar to a daemon or spirit guide. This spirit is said to guide the person's fate, and in Egypt it was even depicted as a second person or "double." Egyptians believed that everything that exists has its double, including plants, animals, and objects, so this may be like an overlighting spirit or astral body.

Kabbalah: A mystical path of Hebrew wisdom focused on the Tree of Life. This wisdom seeks to describe the descent of Spirit as it comes down from the higher realms to create the various dimensional realms, finally arriving in the worlds of matter.

kamaloka: A Tibetan term for the astral plane, taken from the word *kama,* meaning "desire." The astral plane is divided into seven different vibrational levels, and where we go after death is determined by our state of consciousness. For many, these realms are filled with joy, learning, peace, and light, yet there are also lower levels where the Soul can be trapped by its own negative passions and desires until such time as it can release this negativity and move on.

karma: One of the primary spiritual laws through which the Divine allows the Soul to learn the consequences of its actions. This law teaches that what we think and do returns to us, creating our reality. Thus our actions have consequences, not only in the here and now, but over the course of many lifetimes. This is equivalent to the teachings of Jesus, who said that, "What we sow in this life, is what we shall reap in the next."

Krishna: Thought to be a direct expression of Vishnu the Preserver in

Hindu cosmology; an incarnation of one of the Four Kumaras, or direct aspects of God.

life review: The process of viewing our former life after death in intimate holographic detail. This life review happens before we are escorted into the dimension of Heaven that is reflective of our consciousness at the time of death.

Logos: The divine blueprint of Creation, equivalent to the Word. Jesus, Thoth, and Pythagoras were all said to be direct incarnations of the Logos because of their profound wisdom and alignment with the Creator.

loka: A Tibetan word for "plane" or "dimension."

lotus: A mystical symbol of the Soul's spiritual awakening in Hindu, Buddhist, and Egyptian traditions. The lotus rises from the murky depths to blossom into the thousand-petal lotus, a symbol of the crown chakra that connects us with our divine Self.

Ma'at: The Egyptian goddess of spiritual law. Ma'at represents divine order and truth, and the law of karma that is designed to bring us to a place of greater love, unity, and mastery.

Maha Purusha: In the Vedas, "the selfless Self that permeates the universe," or the indwelling Christ, the eternal witness that lives within the Soul.

maya: The world of illusion that God, the formless One, cloaks itself in to create the worlds of form.

Merkaba: The energetic vehicle of light used to travel in the inner worlds, developed through meditation. In Enochian literature it is known as the "chariot."

near-death experiencers: People who have physically died and returned to their bodies to report their experiences on the Otherside.

Nuri Sarup: A Sanskrit term referring to the sparkling light body known to adepts as the astral body, used to travel in during our dreaming state. We reside in this body once we enter the astral plane on the Otherside.

O Mitakuye Oyasin: A Lakota phrase that means "All My Relations," referring to the interconnected state between all living beings: plant, animal, human, and cosmic.

Orphic Mysteries: Begun by the Greek musician and master initiate Orpheus around 700 BCE, this profound Mystery School taught the principles of reincarnation, the landscapes of Heaven, and the knowledge of the eternal existence of the Soul.

Osiris: In Greek mythology, the god of the Afterlife and the Underworld who taught the principles of spiritual rebirth; an incarnation of one of the Four Kumaras. His temple was at Abydos. Osiris, like Jesus, met the Soul in the Halls of Amenti for its life review.

Otherside: One of the most common names for the place where Souls go after death. This land has many subdivisions so that each Soul is drawn to the dimension or area that matches their overall spiritual development.

ouroboros: The snake biting its tail, a symbol used to represent the cyclical passage of time.

preta: In Tibetan Buddhism, an earthbound spirit, also called a "hungry ghost," whose cravings and unmet carnal needs from earthly life keep them perpetually trapped in the lower astral plane.

    Some earthbound spirits can also be temporarily trapped because of a sudden death that leaves the Soul confused, or emotions associated with addiction. Most of these Souls move on quickly, but others need our prayers or our forgiveness to move into the light.

pretaloka: In Tibetan Buddhism, the land of the hungry ghosts or earthbound spirits. This is the highest of the three lower regions of the astral plane, where the spirits of the deceased are trapped by their own physical addictions or by guilt, sadness, regret, or sorrow for misdeeds performed in their earthly life. These Souls need our prayers and forgiveness to move on.

raja: One of the three gunas or energies that move the universe. This is a horizontal current of abundance and materialism in the physical world.

Rakshasas: Demonic spirits created by negative emotions and thought forms that may continue to plague the Soul in the lower levels of the astral plane, once it has passed to the Otherside. These are the Furies in Greek cosmology, the destructive emotions of bitterness, rage, resentment, regret, vengeance, judgment, violence, and self-righteousness that trap us in this world and the next.

reincarnation: Once called *transmigration* or *metempsychosis* in the ancient world, reincarnation is the mechanism by which the Soul perfects itself over millennia of time, being reborn over and over in order to master its lessons.

Rigel: The Divine Father energy that is the spiral of creation.

Ring of Destiny: Described as an enormous circular sphere, the Ring of Destiny in the astral plane acts as a holographic projection system for the Soul to review its possible life choices before each new lifetime. It is overseen by the Lords of Karma, who allow the Soul to preview its possible choices. These masters help to direct the practical working-out of an upcoming life based on the recommendations of the keepers of the Akashic Records, who understand more fully the various Soul themes that must be addressed.

ruah: A Hebrew word that means "wind," as in "the Spirit of God that moved upon the Waters." The waters are the premanifest space known in Greek as *Okeanos,* the "Mother Substance" or *Prima Materia,* or in Christianity the Holy Spirit.

rupaloka: A Tibetan term that refers to the worlds of form. These are the realms of the physical and astral planes, as well as the four lower levels of the mental plane. In these levels we have trees, landscapes, cities, and bodies—all of the same reference points that we do in our world, but these various objects are all vibrating at either higher or lower levels of energy.

Saguna Brahman: The Hindu name for the Supreme Creator of all gods and goddesses, dimensions and universes. He, She, or It is the Unknowable One, the one without equal, the Supreme Brahman who lies beyond the universe, hidden in all beings; the one breath of the whole universe; the lord whom the sages know as the immortal Source. Contained within its being are the functions of Brahma the Creator, Shiva the Transformer, and Vishnu the Preserver.

samsara: This is translated as "suffering." The Wheel of Samsara is the rounds of reincarnation in the mortal worlds where suffering takes place.

sattva: One of the three gunas or energy movements of the universe. *Sattva* means "golden" or "holy." The sattva energies are the upwardly moving current that links us to God.

Shadow: Also known as the "Great Adversary," the Shadow is the unprocessed aspects of ourselves that make it difficult for us to connect with the light.

Shade: In theosophical literature, an aspect of the astral body that can sometimes form from lower mental attachments. It appears as an exact duplicate of the physical person, complete with all its idiosyncrasies. It is not a hungry ghost, but rather a trapped portion of the etheric double, or subtle energy field that connects the Soul with the physical body.

Shekhinah: In the Kabbalah, the daughter principle or "Breath of God" on which the spirit travels, equivalent to the Holy Spirit in Christianity.

Sheol: The Hebrew name for a land of darkness and gloom in the astral plane. This place of negative self-delusion is where the Soul is so lost that the light from the higher realms cannot break through. This is because these Souls have imprisoned themselves through their own dark thought forms, having forgotten their true nature.

Soul: That unit of divine consciousness that resides within every living thing. The Soul is a part of the immensity of God.

sound current: Equivalent to *the Word* in Christian thought, the sound current is called by many names in ancient teachings: the Bani, the Vani, the Shabda, the Eck-Shar, the audible life stream, the Logos, and the Music of the Spheres.

Star of David: The sacred Hebrew symbol of the yin/yang polarities in balance with each other.

string theory: In modern physics, the idea that within the atom are constantly vibrating subatomic particles named *quarks, neutrinos, leptons,* and so forth, which create a symphony of celestial sounds, all oscillating at different frequencies. This is the background "noise" of the universe that transforms energy into matter.

Tibetan Book of the Dead: Also known as the Bardo Thodol or "Liberation through Hearing in the Intermediate State," this scripture was among the many treasures composed by Padmasambhava in the eighth century CE. He secreted it in Tibet, foretelling that these texts would be found and revealed at the appropriate time.

vesica piscis: Known in Christianity as the Ichthys, this is the portal through which Spirit enters the world of matter. It is formed by uniting our male and female natures, and is reflected in the shape of the third eye.

Weighing of the Heart ceremony: This ceremony is similar to the life review reported by near-death experiencers. Here the deceased's heart is weighed against the feather of Ma'at, revealing that when a Soul lives a life of selfishness or cruelty it is bound to the shadow worlds for a time. What matters most is the love we share with one another.

Wheel of Becoming: This is the cycle of rebirth, the journey of the Soul on its way to enlightenment. In Tibetan Buddhism it is known as samsara.

Yama: The Hindu lord of the dead, equivalent to the role that Osiris plays in Egyptian cosmology, and that Jesus plays in Christianity.

yin-yang: The female and male currents taught in Taoist philosophy. The yang is equated with the masculine or expanding current, while the yin is the feminine or contracting current.

Notes

Introduction to Our Angelic Origins

1. Twitchell, *Eckankar Dictionary*, 3.
2. Wordsworth, *Ode*, 426.
3. Lundahl and Widdison, *Eternal*, 247–48.
4. Head and Cranston, *Reincarnation*, 9.
5. Recounted in McCannon, *Dialogues*, 27–37.
6. Hall, *Sacred Magic*, 22.
7. Besant, *Ancient Wisdom*, 38–39.

1. The Eternal Flame

1. Eliade, *Myth*, 86–89.
2. Vaughan, *Shadows*, 118.
3. Vallyon, *Heavens*, 167.
4. Hall, *Sacred Magic*, 11.
5. Doreal, *Emerald Tablets*, 20–21.
6. Pseudo-Dionysius, *Celestial Hierarchy*, 6.
7. Ibid., 8.
8. Shvetashvataropanishad, iii. 7, 8, 21, quoted in Besant, *Ancient Wisdom*, 12–13.
9. Hermes quoted in Blavatsky, *The Secret Doctrine*, I, 285.
10. McCannon, *Return*, 191.
11. Besant, *Ancient Wisdom*, 22.
12. Alexander, *Proof*, 47.

13. Rumi quoted in Mishlove, *Roots,* 191.

14. Hall, *Death,* 31.

15. Miller, *Bhagavad-Gita,* 31–32.

16. Shearer and Russell, *Upanishads,* 36.

17. Jayaram, "Purusha," www.hinduwebsite.com/prakriti.asp.

18. Vaughan, *Shadows,* 122.

19. Ibid., 126.

20. Matt, *Essential Kabbalah,* 148.

2. Mysteries of the Hidden Wisdom

1. Herodotus, *Histories,* 116–17.

2. Alexander, *Map,* 6–7.

3. Epicurus quoted in MacLennan, *Wisdom,* 18.

4. Ibid., 18.

5. Plato quoted in MacLennan, *Wisdom,* 120.

6. Prophet, *Reincarnation,* 69.

7. Ibid., 46.

8. The Compagno tablets quoted in Prophet, *Reincarnation,* 72.

9. Ibid.

10. Zeller, *History,* 71–72.

11. Hall, *Death,* 30.

12. Prophet, *Reincarnation,* 66.

13. Hall, *Death,* 69.

14. Epicurus fragment quoted in MacLennan, *Wisdom,* 69.

15. Marcus Aurelius's *Meditations* IV–40 quoted in MacLennan, *Wisdom,* 107.

16. Hall, *Death,* 70.

17. Ibid.

18. Mylonas, *Eleusis,* 284–85.

3. Reincarnation and the Circle of Life

1. MacLennan, *Wisdom,* 27.

2. Hall, *Secret Teachings,* 191.

3. Ibid., 192.

4. Ibid.

5. Ibid.

6. MacLennan, *Wisdom*, 31.

7. Prophet, *Reincarnation*, 74.

8. Hall, *Secret Teachings*, 196.

9. MacLennan, *Wisdom*, 28.

10. Baldock, *Tibetan Book*, 9.

11. MacLennan, *Wisdom*, 32.

12. Empedocles quoted in Leonard, *Fragments*, 8.

13. Ibid., 9.

14. Head and Cranston, *Reincarnation: Phoenix*, 209.

15. Paracelsus quoted in Blavatsky, *The Secret Doctrine*, vol. I, 281.

16. Blavatsky, *The Secret Doctrine*, vol. I, 274, and 277.

17. From the Greek Mystery School quoted in Vallyon, *Heavens*, 169.

18. Pythagoras quoted in MacLennan, *Wisdom*, 107.

19. Hall, *Secret Teachings*, 198.

20. Hall, *Death*, 31.

21. Head and Cranston, *Reincarnation: Phoenix*, 204.

22. Hall, *Secret Teachings*, 198.

23. Hall, *Death*, 33.

24. Loew, *Myth*, 208.

25. Hall, *Secret Teachings*, 18.

26. Plato, *Dialogues*, 360–61.

27. Plato quoted in Head and Cranston, *Reincarnation: Phoenix*, 213.

28. Cicero quoted in Mead, *Orpheus*, 189.

29. Schorn, *Reincarnation*, 23–24.

30. Alger, *Critical History*, 475.

31. McCannon, *Return*, 296.

32. McMillian, *We*, 239.

33. Emerson, "Nominalist," 320.

34. Tolstoy quoted in Head and Cranston, *Reincarnation: Phoenix*, 337.

35. Benjamin Franklin quoted in Head and Cranston, *Reincarnation: Phoenix*, 271.

36. Louisa May Alcott quoted in Drury, *Reincarnation*, 26.

37. McCannon, *Return*, 296.

38. Whiston, trans., *The Works of Josephus, Jewish War*, book 3, chapter 8, no. 5, 656.

39. Zohar quoted in Semkiw, *Return,* 27.

40. Hall, *Secret Teachings,* 16–17.

41. Head and Cranston, *Reincarnation: Phoenix,* 229.

42. Ibid.

43. Russell quoted in Head and Cranston, *Reincarnation: Phoenix,* 203.

44. Plotinus quoted in Armstrong, *Plotinus' Enneads,* 220–22.

4. The Isles of the Blessed

1. Besant, *Ancient Wisdom,* 137.

2. Homer quoted in *Bartlett's Familiar Quotations,* 59.

3. Pindar quoted in Head and Cranston, *Reincarnation: Phoenix,* 208.

4. Baldock, *Tibetan,* 9.

5. Cole and Cosmopoulos, *Greek Mysteries,* 194.

6. Plato quoted on www.brainyquote.com/quotes/authors/p/plato_2 .html#2BSjVf5WW58A5hdM.99 (accessed May 14, 2017).

7. Hodge, *Illustrated Tibetan Book of the Dead,* 19.

8. Ibid.

9. Baldock, *Tibetan,* 102–4.

10. Powell, *The Astral Body,* 168–69.

5. The Book of Life and Death in the Halls of Amenti

1. Naydler, *Temples,* 244.

2. McCannon, *Jesus,* 298–306.

3. Naydler, *Temples,* 249.

4. Newton, *Journey,* 22–23.

5. Ibid., 43–44.

6. Freke and Gandy, *Hermetica,* 67.

7. Doreal, *Emerald,* 56–57.

8. Cota-Robles, *Who,* 71.

9. Swami Nikhilanda, *Upanishads,* 58.

10. Cota-Robles, *Who,* 36.

11. Naydler, *Temples,* 201.

6. Glimpses of the Afterlife

1. Plato quoted in Head and Cranston, *Reincarnation Phoenix,* 215–16.
2. Ibid.
3. Besant, *Ancient Wisdom,* 204.
4. Blavatsky, *The Secret Doctrine,* vol. I, 104.
5. Newton, *Journey,* 207–13.
6. Lundahl and Widdison, *Eternal,* 31.
7. Newton, *Journey,* 207–12.
8. Ibid., 212.
9. Ibid., 213.
10. Parnia, *What Happens,* 11.
11. Plato quoted in Head and Cranston, *Reincarnation: Phoenix,* 215–16.
12. Ibid.
13. Parnia, *What Happens,* 11.
14. Ibid., 10.
15. Heim quoted in Noyes and Kletti, "The Experience of Dying from Falls," 50.
16. Origen quoted in Head and Cranston, *Reincarnation, East West,* 36.
17. Blavatsky, *Secret Doctrine,* vol. 2.
18. Richie, *Return,* 47–48.
19. Ibid., 50–51.
20. Ibid., 52.
21. Baldock, *Tibetan,* 92.
22. Richie, *Return,* 64–65.
23. Ibid., 66.
24. Besant, *Ancient Wisdom,* 92.
25. Ibid., 88–89.
26. Heneig, "Science," 48.
27. Brinkley, *Saved,* 7.
28. Ibid., 19–20.
29. Ibid., 27–28.
30. Ibid., 30.
31. Ibid., 45.
32. Alexander, *Proof,* 38–39.
33. Ibid., 40–41.

34. Ibid., 45.

35. Ibid.

36. Ibid., 46.

37. Ibid., 47.

38. Mozart quoted on www.quoteland.com/author/Wolfgang-Amadeus
-Mozart-Quotes/2015 (accessed May 14, 2017).

7. The Seventeen Stages of the Near-Death Experience

1. Charbonier, *Seven Reasons,* 20–21.

2. Lundahl and Widdison, *Eternal,* 175–76.

3. Baldock, *Tibetan,* 10.

4. Atwater, *Beyond,* 153.

5. Brinkley, *Saved,* 8.

6. Moody, *Reflections,* 170.

7. Ibid., 50.

8. Parnia, *What Happens,* 60–61.

9. Charbonier, *Seven Reasons,* 82.

10. Moody, *Reflections,* 68.

11. Atwater, *Beyond,* 53.

12. Parnia, *What Happens,* 64.

13. Brinkley, *Saved,* 25–27.

14. Lundahl and Widdison, *Eternal,* 249.

15. Ibid., 175.

16. Atwater, *Beyond,* 49–50.

17. Baldock, *Tibetan,* 92.

18. Lundahl and Widdison, *Eternal,* 155–56.

19. Ibid., 155.

20. Ibid., 158.

21. Ibid., 159.

22. Ibid., 164.

23. Newton, *Destiny,* 161–62.

24. Lundahl and Widdison, *Eternal,* 161.

25. Newton, *Destiny,* 157–161.

26. Hall, *Death,* 15.

8. The Seven Heavens of the Astral Plane

1. Newton, *Destiny*, 93–109.
2. Ibid., 94.
3. Atwater, *Beyond*, 49–50.
4. Besant, *Ancient Wisdom*, 58–59.
5. Ibid., 59–60.

9. The Mental and Causal Heavens

1. Besant, *Ancient Wisdom*, 145–46.
2. Ibid., 153–54.

10. The Great Chain of Being

1. Dossey, "Angels the Missing Link," in Sardello, *Angels*, 85.
2. Tolle quoted in De Pape, *Power*, 11.
3. Proclus quoted in *Bartlett's Quotations*, 120.
4. Wilson, "Journeys," in Parisen, *Angels and Mortals*, 209.
5. Blavatsky, *Secret Doctrine*, vol. 1, 274.
6. Ibid.
7. Williams, "On Re-Imagining Angels," in Parisen, *Angels and Mortals*, 29.
8. Ibid., 28.
9. Planck quoted in Walla, "Harvard," *Oracle 20/20 Magazine*, April 2016, (Atlanta, Georgia: Inner Space), 16.
10. Walla, "Harvard," 16.
11. Jeans quoted in Walla, "Harvard," 16.
12. Dossey, "Angels the Missing Link," in Sardello, *Angels*, 82.
13. Ibid., 82–83.
14. Origen quoted in Grosso, "The Cult of the Guardian Angel," in Parisen, *Angels*, 129.

11. Divine Origins

1. *Tao Te Ching* quoted in Besant, *Ancient Wisdom*, 8–9.
2. Besant, *Ancient Wisdom*, 21.
3. McCannon, *Return*, 316–18.

4. Freke and Gandy, *Hermetica,* 53.

5. Mundakopanishad II, 1, 2, 9, and 11 quoted in Besant, *Ancient Wisdom,* 12.

6. Cowen, "The Dethronement of the Angels," in Sardello, *Angels,* 107.

7. Hall, *Sacred Magic,* 21.

8. Brihaddranyakopanishad IV, 20, 22 quoted in Besant, *Ancient Wisdom,* 13.

9. Hall, *Sacred Magic,* 24–25.

10. Besant, *Ancient Wisdom,* 44.

11. Kaku, *Parallel,* 17.

12. Ibid., 17–18.

13. Ibid., 17–18.

14. Purce, *Mystic,* 8.

15. Blavatsky, *Voice,* 5.

16. Westcott, *Chaldean Oracles,* 33–34.

17. Purce, *Mystic,* 8.

18. McCannon, *Return,* 364–65.

19. Freke and Gandy, *Hermetica,* 39.

20. Hall, *Sacred Magic,* 36.

21. Freke and Gandy, *Hermetica,* 39.

22. Ibid., 61.

23. Jung quoted in Trammel, "Angels: a Way of Working," in Sardello, *Angels,* 133–34.

12. Angels, Devas, and Mortals

1. Godwin, *Angels,* 7.

2. Miller, "The Shining Ones in the Vedas," in Parisen, *Angels and Mortals,* 70.

3. Ibid., 72–73.

4. Ibid., 73.

5. Hodson, "The Greater Gods," in Parisen, *Angels and Mortals,* 229.

6. Swedenborg quoted in Stanley, "Angelic Nature," in Parisen, *Angels and Mortals,* 221–22.

7. Hodson, "The Greater Gods," in Parisen, *Angels and Mortals,* 226.

8. Farthing, "Humanity and the Cosmic Hierarchy," in Parisen, *Angels and Mortals,* 143.

9. Godwin, *Angels,* 19.

10. Miller, "The Shining Ones in the Vedas," in Parisen, *Angels and Mortals,* 73.

11. Szekely, *Essene,* 36.

12. Martin and Moraitis, *Communing,* 12.

13. Blavatsky, *Secret Doctrine,* vol. 1, 288.

14. Martin and Moraitis, *Communing,* 13–14.

15. The Southern Centre of Theosophy, *Devas and Men: A Compilation of Theosophical Studies on the Angelic Kingdom,* vii.

16. Ibid., xi.

17. Cannon, *Legacy,* 229–30.

18. Ibid., 231.

19. Algeo, "Dark Angels," in Parisen, *Angels and Mortals,* 149.

20. Blavatsky, *Secret Doctrine,* vol. 1, 277.

21. The Southern Centre of Theosophy, *Devas and Men,* viii.

22. Hodson, "Greater," 232.

23. Miller, "The Shining Ones of the Vedas," in Parisen, *Angels and Mortals,* 84.

24. Ibid.

25. Blavatsky, *Secret Doctrine,* vol. 2, 181.

26. Miller, "The Shining Ones of the Vedas," in Parisen, *Angels and Mortals,* 86.

27. Blavatsky, *Secret Doctrine,* vol. 1, 294.

13. Meeting Our Angelic Twin

1. Budge, *Egyptian,* 324, 332, 335.

2. Hoeller, "Angels Holy and Unholy," in Parisen, *Angels and Mortals,* 100.

3. Ibid., 102–3.

4. Barnstone, *The Gospel of Philip,* 100.

5. Ibid., 99.

6. Ibid., 90.

7. Clement quoted in Hoeller "Angels Holy and Unholy," in Parisen, *Angels and Mortals,* 103.

14. The Nine Orders of Angels

1. Dante quoted in Wilson, "Journeys," in Parisen, *Angels and Mortals,* 211.
2. Ibid.
3. Steiner quoted in Hines, "The Hierarchies," in Parisen, *Angels and Mortals,* 108.
4. Hines, "The Hierarchies," in Parisen, *Angels and Mortals,* 108.
5. Freke and Gandy, *Hermetica,* 38.
6. Zohar quoted in Sardello, *Angels,* 197.
7. Hines, "The Hierarchies," in Parisen, *Angels and Mortals,* 109.
8. Steiner quoted in Ibid., 118.
9. Sardello, *Angels,* 50.

16. Dismantling the Illusion of Separation

1. Twitchell, *Eckankar Dictionary,* 2.

17. Energy-Stealing Styles and Techniques for Better Communication

1. Unterman, *Talking to My Selves,* 147–57.

18. Life Lessons in the Course Curriculum

1. Besant, *Ancient Wisdom,* 203–5.

19. Mastering the Lessons of Love and Power

1. Lipton, *Biology of Belief,* xxvii–xxviii.
2. Ibid., 95.
3. Ibid., 113.
4. HeartMath Institute, "You Can Change Your DNA," July 14, 2011, www.heartmath.org/articles-of-the-heart/personal-development/you-can-change-your-dna/ (last accessed May 12, 2017).
5. Peter Gariaev and Vladimir Poponin, "DNA BioComputer Reprogramming," www.rexresearch.com/gajarev/gajarev.htm (last accessed May 12, 2017).
6. Ibid.

20. The Path of the Heart

1. Hillman, *Soul's Code*, 39.

2. Ibid., xi.

3. Ibid., xi.

4. Churchill quoted Ibid., 107.

5. Plato quoted in Ibid., 45.

6. Plotinus quoted in Ibid., ix.

7. Huxley quoted on www.azquotes.com/quote/535461 (last accessed May 15, 2017).

Bibliography

Alexander, Eben. *The Map of Heaven: How Science, Religion, and Ordinary People Are Proving the Afterlife.* New York: Simon and Schuster, 2014.

———. *Proof of Heaven: A Neurosurgeon's Journey into the Afterlife.* New York: Simon and Schuster, 2012.

Alger, William R. *A Critical History of the Doctrine of a Future Life.* Boston: Roberts Brothers, 1886.

Armstrong, A. H. *Plotinus' Enneads.* Cambridge, Ma.: Harvard University Press, 1969.

Atwater, P. M. H. *Beyond the Light: What Isn't Being Said about the Near-Death Experience.* New York: Carol Publishing Group, 1994.

Baldock, John, ed. *The Tibetan Book of the Dead.* New York: Chartwell Books, 2013.

Barnstone, Willis. *The Gospel of Philip.* New York: Harper San Francisco, 1984.

Bartlett, John. *Bartlett's Familar Quotations.* Boston: Little Brown and Company, 1980.

Besant, Annie. *The Ancient Wisdom: An Outline of Theosophical Teachings.* Glastonbury, England: Theosophical Publishing Society, 1879.

Besteman, Marvin J., with Lorilee Craker. *My Journey to Heaven: What I Saw and How It Changed My Life.* Grand Rapids, Mich.: Revell Books, 2012.

Blavatsky, Helena P. *The Secret Doctrine,* vol. 1. Pasadena, Calif.: Theosophical University Press, 1988.

———. *The Secret Doctrine,* vol. 2. Pasadena, Calif.: Theosophical University Press, 1988.

———. *The Voice of the Silence: Chosen Fragments from the Book of the Golden Precepts.* Pasadena, Calif.: Theosophical University Press, 1992.

Bodine, Echo. *What Happens When We Die: A Psychic's Exploration of Death, Heaven, and the Soul's Journey After Death.* Novato, Calif.: New World Library, 2013.

Brinkley, Dannion, with Paul Perry. *Saved by the Light: The True Story of a Man Who Died Twice and the Profound Revelations He Received.* New York: HarperCollins, 2008.

Budge, E. A. Wallis. *The Egyptian Book of the Dead: The Papyrus of Ani in the British Museum.* New York: Dover Publications, 1967.

Cannon, Dolores. *Conversations with a Spirit Between Death and Life.* Huntsville, Ark.: Ozark Mountain Publishing, 1993.

———. *The Convoluted Universe: Book One.* Huntsville, Ark.: Ozark Mountain Publishing, 2003.

———. *Legacy from the Stars.* Huntsville, Ark.: Ozark Mountain Publishing, 2014.

Charbonier, Jean Jacques. *Seven Reasons to Believe in the Afterlife: A Doctor Reviews the Case of Consciousness after Death.* Rochester, Vt.: Inner Traditions, 2012.

Cole, Susan, and Michael B. Cosmopoulos, eds. *Greek Mysteries: The Archaeology and Ritual of Ancient Greek Secret Cults.* New York: Routledge, 2003.

Collier, Robert. *The Amazing Secrets of the Masters of the Far East.* Tarrytown, N.Y.: Robert Collier Publications, 1956.

Cota-Robles, Patricia Diane. *Who Am I? Why Am I Here?* Tucson, Az.: New Age Study of Humanity's Purpose, 2010.

De Pape, Baptist. *The Power of the Heart: Finding Your True Purpose in Life.* New York: Atria Books, 2014.

Doreal. *The Emerald Tablets of Thoth the Atlantean.* Nashville, Tenn.: Source Books, 1995.

Drury, Nevill. *Reincarnation: Exploring the Concept of Reincarnation in Religion, Philosophy and Traditional Cultures.* New York: Barnes and Noble Books, 2002.

Eliade, Mircea. *The Myth of the Eternal Return*. New York: Pantheon Books, 1954.

Emerson, Ralph Waldo. "Nominalist and Realist," in *The Journals of Ralph Waldo Emerson*, vol. 1. Boston: Houghton Mifflin, 1909.

Freke, Timothy, and Peter Gandy. *The Hermetica: The Lost Wisdom of the Pharaohs*. London: Piatkus Publishing, 1997.

Godwin, Malcolm. *Angels: An Endangered Species*. New York: Simon and Schuster, 1990.

Hall, Manly P. *Death to Rebirth: Five Essays by Manly P. Hall*. Los Angeles: Philosophical Research Society, 1979.

———. *Sacred Magic of the Qabbalah: The Science of the Divine Names*. Los Angeles: Philosophical Research Society, 1996.

———. *The Secret Teachings of All Ages*. New York: Jeremy P. Tarcher/Penguin, 2003.

Head, Joseph, and Sylvia Cranston. *Reincarnation: Phoenix Fire Mystery*. San Diego, Calif.: Point Loma Publications, 1977.

———. *Reincarnation, an East West Anthology*. Pasadena, Calif.: The Theosophical Publishing House, 1961.

Heneig, Robin Marantz. "The Science of Death: Coming Back from the Beyond." *National Geographic,* April 2016.

Herodotus, *The Histories, Book II*. Trans. Aubrey de Selincourt. New York: Penguin Classics, 2003.

Hillman, James. *The Soul's Code: In Search of Character and Calling*. New York: Random House, 1996.

Hodge, Stephen, with Martin Boord. *The Illustrated Tibetan Book of the Dead*. London: HarperCollins, 1999.

Jayaram, V. "Purusha, the Universal Cosmic Male and Prakriti, the Mother Nature." Hindu Website, www.hinduwebsite.com/prakriti.asp (accessed May 10, 2017).

Josephus, Flavius. *The Jewish War*. Ed. Betty Radice and E. Mary Smallwood, trans. G. A. Williamson. London: Penguin, 1970.

Kaku, Michio. *Parallel Worlds: A Journey through Creation, Higher Dimensions, and the Future of the Cosmos*. New York: Random House, 2005.

Labaree, Leonard W., ed. *The Papers of Benjamin Franklin,* vol 1. New Haven, Conn.: Yale University Press, 1959.

Leclere, Alexandra. *Seeing the Dead, Talking with Spirits: Shamanic Healing through Contact with the Spirit World.* Rochester, Vt.: Destiny Books, 2005.

Leonard, William Ellery, trans. *The Fragments of Empedocles.* Chicago, Ill.: Open Court Publishing, 1908.

Lipton, Bruce H. *The Biology of Belief: Uleashing the Power of Consciousness, Matter, and Miracles.* Carlsbad, Calif.: Hay House, 2004.

Loew, Cornelius. *Myth, Sacred History, and Philosophy.* New York: Harcourt, 1967.

Lundahl, Craig R., and Harold A. Widdison. *The Eternal Journey: How Near-Death Experiences Illuminate Our Earthly Lives.* New York: Warner Books, 1997.

MacLennan, Bruce J. *The Wisdom of Hypatia: Ancient Spiritual Practices for a More Meaningful Life.* Woodbury, Minn.: Llewellyn Publications, 2013.

Martin, Barbara Y., and Dimitri Moraitis. *Communing with the Divine: A Clairvoyant's Guide to Angels, Archangels, and the Spiritual Hierarchy.* New York: Jeremy P. Tarcher/Penguin, 2014.

Matt, Daniel C. *The Essential Kabbalah: The Heart of Jewish Mysticism.* New York: Quality Paperback Club, 1995.

McCannon, Tricia. *Dialogues with the Angels.* Atlanta, Ga.: Horizons Unlimited, 1996.

———. *Jesus: The Explosive Story of the 30 Lost Years and the Ancient Mystery Religions,* Charlottesville, Va.: Hampton Roads, 2010.

———. *Return of the Divine Sophia: Healing the Earth through the Lost Wisdom Teachings of Jesus, Isis, and Mary Magdalene.* Rochester, Vt.: Bear and Company, 2015.

McMillian, Ronald. *We Are Forever Voyagers of Space.* Nashville, Tenn.: Scythe Publications, 1995.

Mead, G. R. S. *Orpheus.* London: Kessinger Publishing, 1995.

Miller, Barbara Stoler, trans. *The Bhagavad-Gita: Krishna's Counsel in Time of War.* New York: Bantam, 1986.

Mishlove, Jeffrey. *Roots of Consciousness.* Tulsa, Okla.: Council Oak Books, 1993.

Moody, Raymond. *Reflections on Life After Life.* Carmel, N.Y.: Guidepost Publishing, 1977.

Mylonas, George E. *Eleusis and the Eleusinian Mysteries.* Princeton, N.J.: Princeton University Press, 1961.

Naydler, Jeremy. *Temples of the Cosmos: The Ancient Egyptian Experience of the Sacred.* Rochester, Vt.: Inner Traditions, 1996.

Newton, Michael. *Destiny of Souls: New Case Studies of Life Between Lives.* St. Paul, Minn.: Llewellyn Publishing, 2002.

———. *Journey of Souls: Case Studies of Life Between Lives.* St. Paul, Minn.: Llewellyn Publications, 1995.

———. *Memories of the Afterlife: Life Between Lives, Stories of Personal Transformation.* Woodbury, Minn.: Llewellyn Publishing, 2014.

Noyes, Russell, and R. Roy Kletti. "The Experience of Dying from Falls." *Omega* 2 (1972): 45–52.

Pagels, Elaine. *The Gnostic Gospels.* New York: Vintage Books, 1979.

Parisen, Maria. *Angels and Mortals: Their Co-Creative Power.* Wheaton, Ill.: Theosophical Publishing House, 1990.

Parnia, Sam. *What Happens When We Die: A Groundbreaking Study into the Nature of Life and Death.* Carlsbad, Ca.: Hay House, 2006.

Plato. *The Dialogues of Plato,* vol. 1. New York: Random House, 1937.

Powell, A. E. *The Astral Body.* Wheaton, Ill.: Quest Books, 1996.

Prophet, Elizabeth Clare. *Reincarnation: The Missing Link in Christianity.* Gardiner, Mont.: Summit University Press, 1997.

Pseudo-Dionysius, the Areopagite. *The Celestial Hierarchy.* London: Kessinger Publishing, 2010.

Purce, Jill. *The Mystic Spiral: Journey of the Soul.* London: Thames and Hudson, 1974.

Richie, George. *Return from Tomorrow.* Grand Rapids, Mich.: Fleming H. Revel, 1978.

Ross, Hugh McGregor. *The Gospel of Thomas.* London: Watkins Publishing, 2002.

Russell, Bertrand. *History of Western Philosophical Thought.* New York: Simon and Schuster, 1972.

Salaman, Clement, Dorine Van Ovin, William D. Wharton, and Jean Pierre Mahe, trans. *The Way of Hermes: New Translations of the Corpus Hermeticum and The Definitions of Hermes Trismegistus to Asclepius.* Rochester, Vt.: Inner Traditions, 2004.

Sardello, Robert, ed. *The Angels*. New York: Continuum Publishing, 1995.

Schorn, M. Don. *Reincarnation: Stepping Stones of Life*. Huntsville, Ark.: Ozark Mountain Press, 2006.

Semkiw, Walter. *Return of the Revolutionaries: The Case for Reincarnation and Soul Groups Reunited*. Charlottesville, Va.: Hampton Roads, 2003.

Shearer, Alistair, and Peter Russell, trans. *The Upanishads*. London: Unwin Hyman, Ltd., 1989.

Shrestha, Romeo. *Celestial Gallery*. San Rafael, Calif.: Mandala Publishing, 2007.

Sigmund, Richard. *My Time in Heaven: A True Story of Dying and Coming Back*. New Kensington, Pa.: Whitaker House, 2010.

Southern Centre of Theosophy. *Devas and Men: A Compilation of Theosophical Studies on the Angelic Kingdom*. Wheaton, Ill.: Theosophical Publishing House, 1994.

Swami Nikhilanda. *The Upanishads*, vol. 1. New York: Harper and Brothers, 1949.

Szekely, Edmond Bordeaux. *The Essene Gospel of Peace II*. Los Angeles: International Biogenic Society, 1981.

Twitchell, Paul. *Eckankar Dictionary*. Las Vegas: Illuminated Way Press, 1973.

Unterman, Debbie. *Talking to My Selves: Learning to Love Your Voices in Your Head*. Charleston, S.C.: Booksurge, 2009.

Vallyon, Imre. *Heavens and Hells of the Mind, Vol. 1: Knowledge*. Hamilton, New Zealand: Sounding Light Publishing, 2007.

Vaughan, Frances. *Shadows of the Sacred: Seeing through Spiritual Illusions*. Wheaton, Ill.: Quest Books, 1995.

Walla, Arjun. "Harvard Visits the Himalayas." *Oracle 20/20 Magazine*, April 2016.

Westcott, W. Wynn. *The Chaldean Oracles of Zoroaster*. Wellingborough, England: The Aquarian Press, 1983.

Whiston, William, trans. *The Works of Josephus*. Peabody, Ma.: Hendrickson Publishers, 1988.

Zeller, Eduard. *History of Greek Philosophy*. London: Longmans, Green, 1880.

Index

Note: Page numbers in *italics* indicate illustrations.